Integrative Development of Brain and Behavior in the Dog

Integrative Development of Brain and Behavior in the Dog

Michael W. Fox

The University of Chicago Press

Chicago and London

International Standard Book Number: 0-226-25950-1
Library of Congress Catalog Card Number: 70-141887

THE UNIVERSITY OF CHICAGO PRESS, CHICAGO 60637
The University of Chicago Press, Ltd., London

To my cubs, Wylie and Camilla,
and to "Queenie" and hers

Contents

Preface

The main intention of this book is to bring together recent research findings and theories pertaining to the development of the brain and behavior. In the divergent evolution of such disciplines the application of different methodologies, interpretive analyses (although actually converging on almost identical research problems), and semantic differences in terminology can eventually result in the formation of conceptual barriers between disciplines and often prevents constructive interdisciplinary studies and exchange of pertinent information. Some attempt, therefore, will be made to synthesize converging deductions from both methodologically and semantically diverging disciplines. In reviewing the development of behavior and of the nervous system, the classical Pavlovian approach will be considered; in certain respects, the neo-Pavlovian school is primarily neurophysiologically oriented, and therefore enables some direct interdisciplinary correlations with classical neurophysiological, biochemical, neuroanatomical, and neurological (i.e., Coghillian) studies of developing organisms. Within the framework of ethology and comparative psychology (beyond the timeworn controversial dichotomies, such as how much is "instinctual" versus how much is "learned" and "nature" versus "nurture") some common areas of interest have emerged, notably the effects of "early experience," sensitive and critical periods, imprinting, socialization, and early learning. Where possible, underlying changes in the developing nervous system will be related to the ontogenetic processes that have been revealed in these behavioral studies. Genetic factors contributing to the organization, development, and acquisition of behavioral capacities have only recently attracted more intensive study, and reveal the constant genotype-environment interaction which occurs throughout the life of the individual and of the species as a whole. The geneticist's approach to behavioral development impinges upon the embryologist's field of research, and at the farthest pole in this interdisciplinary schema are the sociologist and the ecologist. This book will attempt to break down the conceptual *Umwelts* of these diverse disciplines and to consider the development of behavior and of the nervous system as a conceptually and ontogenetically integrated process.

Essentially this book describes in detail several experiments on various aspects of brain and behavioral development in the dog. These data provide a multidisciplinary basis for the comparative evaluation of the development of behavior and

ix

the integrative development of the nervous system. The postnatal development of reflexes and behavior in the dog will be correlated with electrophysiological and anatomical development of certain parts of the central nervous system. Such indexes of normal development in the dog will then be compared with other phylogenetically diverse species and common trends in development will be established to provide a basis for the analysis of behavioral development. There are many advantages in using the dog for multidiscipline studies of behavior and development, notably the ease of handling and management and relatively large litters which mature slowly, thus facilitating postnatal evaluation of development. Also, the dog is a highly evolved species, and has a rich repertoire of behavior.

According to the degree of maturity at birth, mammals may be divided broadly into the precocial, which are relatively mature at birth, and the nonprecocial, which are less mature and require considerable maternal attention. These nonprecocial animals are more dependent upon maternal care and have a longer postnatal period, during which the nervous system develops and adultlike behavior patterns are organized. The postnatal period of development will be described along the various parameters already mentioned until the dog reaches relative maturity at around 16 wk of age. Later development, notably the onset of sexual and maternal activities and underlying neuroendocrine changes which modulate adult behavior, will not be considered in detail.

The influences of environmental and experiential variables on behavioral development in early postnatal life are critical, and can greatly modify later organization of behavior. The influence of these "early experience variables" on postnatal development of the dog will be evaluated in terms of behavioral change in this study; biochemical, anatomical, and electrophysiological development in this species remain to be evaluated through manipulation of the dam during gestation or by embryonic transfer between behaviorally different strains; some research has been undertaken on genetic variables in this species by other workers (Scott and Fuller 1965), but they have not been investigated in the present study.

Studies on the development of behavior in the dog reviewed by Scott and Fuller (1965) and the work from their laboratory on critical periods (Scott 1962; Scott and Marston 1950; Freedman, King, and Elliot 1961) prompted this investigation and provide a useful baseline for more detailed studies of developmental processes in this species. A systematic attempt has been made to provide anatomical and physiological data related to changes in overt behavior, and additional studies on the development of learning abilities and of the effects of early experience in the dog have been undertaken and are detailed in this report.

These findings, and also the survey and discussion of pertinent literature, will be divided, for convenience, into different sections dealing respectively with postnatal development of reflexes and organization of behavior patterns; aspects of brain development, notably of the neocortex, and development of myelin in both neocortical and subcortical structures; neurophysiological development (electroencephalogram and evoked potentials); olfactory responses in the neonate, development of delayed response capability, conditioned avoidance, visual discrimination and development of exploratory behavior; effects of "handling," restricted socialization and partial social and sensory deprivation on postnatal development. These multidisciplinary studies will be brought together in discussion and compared with the development of the behavior and nervous systems of other species, including man.

Acknowledgments

I am especially grateful to Professor J. P. Scott, who provided me with the opportunity to initiate these studies in the Division of Behavior Studies at the Jackson Laboratory, Bar Harbor, Maine, while I was under tenure of National Institutes of Health grant CRT-5013. Both Professor Scott and Dr. J. L. Fuller gave me invaluable advice and encouragement during my fellowship at this laboratory (1962–64). Thanks also are due to Dr. R. L. Sidman and Professor P. I. Yakovlev, of the departments of Cellular Neuropathology and Neuropathology, Harvard Medical School, for providing me with laboratory space and facilities for histological work and to Mr. A. Zalkalns for assistance in preparation of the developing dog brain series, in part supported by National Science Foundation grant GB 3703.

A special acknowledgment is due to Dr. Williamina A. Himwich for her advice and encouragement in furthering the multidisciplinary research on the developing brain and behavior during my tenure as medical research associate at the Thudichum Psychiatric Research Laboratory, Galesburg State Research Hospital, Galesburg, Illinois (1964–67).

The guidance of Professor J. Myslivecek, visiting scientist from the Department of Pathophysiology, Charles University, Pilsen, Czechoslovakia, is greatly appreciated.

I also wish to thank Dr. Otillie Inman for her assistance in supervising the preparation of much histological material from some of these studies, and Dr. G. Pscheidt, Dr. H. C. Agrawal, and Mr. S. Glisson for undertaking adrenal gland analysis and brain amino acids, noradrenaline, and dopamine estimations, respectively.

Thanks are due to Messrs. J. Spencer, D. Stelzner, D. Callison, H. Spurgeon, and G. Stanton, research assistants, for their able help in many of the behavioral and neurophysiological studies and surgical procedures. The valuable comments of Dr. J. L. Fuller and Dr. Guenther Rose, for which I am extremely grateful, have done much to improve this monograph.

Without the skills of Mr. L. Tenneson and Mrs. E. Smith in preparing much of the illustrative material, and the patience of Mrs. M. Goff, who typed several rough drafts and the final manuscript, the preparation of this text would have been greatly encumbered.

xi

Some of the data included in this text have been presented earlier in a doctoral dissertation, University of London, and published in the following journals: *American Journal of Veterinary Research, Animal Behaviour, Behaviour* (Leiden), *Brain Research, British Journal of Small Animal Practice, Developmental Psychobiology, Electroencephalography and Clinical Neurophysiology, Journal of Comparative Neurology* and *Journal of Physiology and Behavior.*

1

Introductory Review: Neuro-ontogeny and Behavioral Development

A seed gives rise to a deed;
A deed impregnates a seed:
These three factors—
Are at once both cause and effect!

J. Takakusu, *The Essentials of Buddhist Philosophy*

This chapter is intended to introduce the reader to a number of issues pertaining to the development of the brain and behavior, which will be dealt with in depth in subsequent chapters. It is necessary to become familiar with various disciplinary concepts related to brain and behavior at this point, in order to set the stage for the multidisciplinary approach attempted in this text. Various aspects of neuroembryology, structurofunctional development of the nervous system, neurological and behavioral development, and the effects of environment or early experience on development will be reviewed in this chapter. A number of developmental concepts will also be alluded to, and will be discussed in greater detail in subsequent chapters.

The hypothesis of the critical period of socialization as originally presented by Scott and Marston (1950) was reviewed and extended by Scott (1962) in describing the behavioral development of nonprecocial mammals, which are born relatively immature. In this way, the term *critical period,* originally used in embryology, was applied to ethology, the objective study of animal behavior (Verplank 1957).

For purposes of this literature survey, the mouse, dog, and cat are considered as examples of the nonprecocial group and correlations in other parameters of neurological development common to these species will be used to extend the critical period hypothesis. Other critical periods, dependent on neuroendocrine and environmental factors, are seen during later life, notably in the onset of sexual and maternal activities. These activities are themselves greatly influenced by the developmental processes underlying the establishment of primary social relationships during the critical period of socialization.

1

Development of Research Concepts

In much of the research on behavior undertaken by American psychologists at the turn of the century, theoretical conclusions were drawn from empirical observations restricted to one species observed in a synthetic laboratory environment. Indeed plasticity and adaptability of behavioral development were considered undesirable variables and animals not conforming to the rigid theoretical model were often discarded. At about the same time in Europe the students of ethology were, in contrast, developing a discipline for studying adaptive behavior within the natural environment. The work of Hebb (1949) and Lorenz (1935) subsequently provided the major impetus for research in behavioral development in America and Europe, especially in relation to the effects of early experience (handling) and socialization or imprinting.

With a fundamental knowledge of the processes underlying behavioral development we may formulate systematic criteria of development within a species and make comparisons between groups of species, for example, precocial and non-precocial birds or mammals. Recent reviews on imprinting (Hess 1959, 1964; Sluckin 1965; Bateson 1966; Salzen 1967), on the effects of early experience (Denenberg 1962a, 1968; Levine 1962b) and on environmental enrichment or deprivation (Bennett et al. 1964) emphasize how a number of variables may modify development. The approach/withdrawal theory of Schneirla (1965), which closely resembles similar observations on approach/avoidance (active and passive defensive reflexes) described by Krushinskii (1962), and Anokhin's (1964) theory of systemogenesis as a regulator of development and adaptation are major contributions to this field of research. These theories will be reviewed subsequently.

Embryogenesis and Development of Reflex Activity

Carmichael (1927) placed one group of salamander embryos in a solution containing Chloretone anesthetic, before the age at which swimming movements are observed. After controls had been swimming for 5 days, he placed these experimental subjects in water containing no anesthetic and found that after a short time they were swimming as well as controls. Thus there may be some independence of maturational changes from sensory stimulation or motor activity. In contrast to Carmichael's findings, Fromme (1941) obtained different results with *Rana pipiens* embryos; Chloretone-exposed subjects showed marked deficits, and excessively stimulated embryos (activated in a turbulent water bath) were not superior to controls. In 1941, Weiss claimed that complete deafferentation did not impair swimming in tadpoles. However, Nissen, Chow, and Semmes (1951) produced severe motor deficits in monkeys reared with their forelimbs restricted in cylinders. Therefore, there are not only ontogenetic variables to be considered in the time of onset of motor activity, and the degree of stimulus-dependency for maturation, but also the wide phylogenetic differences even among apparently closely related species, as in amphibia.

Klopfer and Hailman (1967) suggest that the failure of a stimulus to evoke a response could be due to the absence of sensory-motor connections alone and not to an absence of sensory input to the centrum. A feedback system in which input to the brain triggers developmental changes and in turn modifies the subsequent input may be postulated.

On the basis of earlier classical studies of Coghill (1929) and of Hooker (1952), Hamburger (1963) has presented new and stimulating observations on the embryogenesis of behavior. He recognized two components of motility, spontaneous and reflexive, the former being the primary component. Reflexogenic activity develops later, and because of the paucity of varied exteroceptive stimulation in utero, is less important in the prenatal organization of behavior. He regarded spontaneous motility as the major factor in organizing behavior during embryogenesis. This activity was characterized by rhythmicity, with short phases of activity followed by longer phases of inactivity. Although not organized or integrated in the embryo, it may be the embryonic antecedent of the spontaneous component in adult activity. The development of patterned integrated and adaptive behavior from the unintegrated generalized motility of the embryo is still poorly understood. But from the basic observations of Hamburger (1963) we may postulate that rhythmicity with widely varying phases of activity is a natural phenomenon of organisms and is of adaptive and survival value; spontaneous motor activity in utero or in the egg results in stimulation through afferent proprioceptive feedback, and, consequently, through exercise, sensorimotor integration develops prenatally. Hamburger et al. (1965), however, propose that reflex motility can contribute little to the molding of behavior before hatching; behavior remains "latent" because of the lack of adequate stimuli. Corner (1964), in a study of the rhythmicity in the swimming of anuran larvae, concludes that the immature CNS generates several excitatory and inhibitory rhythms which act on an efferent mechanism which is capable of generating pulses at a constant mean frequency. Corner believes that there is no myogenic phase of development, the earliest movements being neurogenic. Sensory stimulation briefly alters the net level of central excitation resulting from these endogenous rhythms.

In Hamburger's laboratory, Oppenheim (1966) has demonstrated that amnion contractions, yolk-sac movements, and exteroceptive stimuli are most probably not important sensory input variables in relation to the cyclic embryonic motility in the chick and that cyclic motility is generated principally in the motor system. The random uncoordinated and periodic motility of the chick embryo, and even of isolated parts of the embryo (segments caudal to the level of spinal cord transection), increases with age; Hamburger et al. (1965) have shown that the brain adds discharges to the motility generated by the spinal cord, for the overall activity of isolated parts is 10–20% lower than that of normal embryos. The brain influence was found to cause a lengthening of the duration of the activity phases and a shortening of the inactivity phases. It is of interest to note that Hamburger et al. did not observe any inhibitory effects at any age during the period of study (up to 17 days). This spontaneous cyclic motility is nonreflexive at least up to the 19th day of incubation (Hamburger 1963), and is the manifestation of self-generated periodic discharges of spinal motor neurons. In discussing their findings, Hamburger et al. (1965) point out that Barcroft and Barron (1939) found that in the sheep embryo there was no influence on spinal motor activity following brain transection or stimulation until the 43d day of gestation. From this time onward a pontine center sustaining brief movements of the limbs for longer periods was disclosed. Between 50 and 60 days, until the 70th day, the fetus became inactive, suggesting some inhibitory effect by higher CNS structures. Hamburger et al. (1965) postulate that the spontaneous embryonic motility may be of a transitory and purely embryonic type. It may, however, persist throughout life as a latent component of the motor action system, which in certain instances may become part of the behavioral repertoire. In contrast to the chick embryo, activity is first reflexively evoked in the rat fetus at approximately 14–15 days of gestation, and it is at this age that the first signs of spontaneous motility are also observed (personal observation).

The question whether self-stimulation during embryonic and fetal life is instrumental in the organization of behavior has been tested experimentally by Hamburger, Wenger, and Oppenheim (1966). There is considerable evidence to support the notion that self-stimulation is important in the organization of behavior patterns in several species and in certain sensory-motor systems. Such evidence is drawn mainly from postnatal observations. Hamburger, Wenger, and Oppenheim (1966) have shown that deafferentation of the spinal cord in the chick does not interfere with leg motility, because this motility results from autonomous discharges of the lateral motor or internuncial neurons of the spinal cord; thus sensory input is not necessary for the triggering, maintenance, or periodicity of embryonic leg motility in the chick. However, Hamburger, Wenger, and Oppenheim (1966) are careful to point out that sensory systems which are indispensable in posthatching behavior are not entirely absent during embryonic development. For example, exteroceptive reflexes can be elicited only from the 8th day onward by appropriate stimulation. They do contend that these components remain latent owing to the absence of adequate stimuli, except perhaps for occasional self-stimulated responses. Hamburger, Wenger, and Oppenheim (1966) propose that the spontaneous motility is "primarily the overt manifestation of a primitive behavior which is neither inhibited by higher centers nor directed by sensory input"; it may have a special adaptive function, for it has been found by Drachman and Coulombre (1962) that curarization in 7–15-day-old chick embryos for 24–48 hr results in ankylosis. Thus spontaneous motility may prevent ankylosis and muscle atrophy. It is of interest that in their experiment Hamburger, Wenger, and Oppenheim (1966) found a marked decrease in motility at 17 days of age (15 days after deafferentation) which was associated with transneuronal degeneration of motor neurons. They state that

> since sensory fibers connect directly or indirectly with motor neurons, the absence of the ganglia may contribute to the transneuronal depletion of the motor column. But this is strictly a trophic influence of the sensory cells. It is one thing to invoke their trophic role in maintaining the structural integrity of the motor cells, and an entirely different matter to make the transmission of impulses by sensory fibers responsible for the discharge of healthy motor neurons. In other words, transneuronal degeneration cannot be used as an argument for the role of sensory input in generating motility.

One may deduce from these findings that before 17 days of age, embryonic motility is spontaneously generated by the motor neurons; but by 15–17 days of age, an important ontogenetic period may exist. At this time it appears that a rapid integration of sensory and motor connections takes place. Lack of afferentation in this integrative process would account for degenerative changes in the motor neurons, which before this function independently. The decline in spontaneous motility in normal chick embryos between 15 and 17 days of age suggests that some dynamic integrative processes are occurring, such as increased inhibition by other spinal centers or the influence of proprioceptive reflexes.

Windle and Orr (1934) found that in the chicken embryo the motor components of the nervous system developed first, and the sensory components were organized approximately 4 days after the first spontaneous movements were seen.

At the time of birth or hatching, the sudden increase in afferent stimuli evoke activities which can be rapidly elaborated or modified from the innately organized spontaneous motility. As postnatal development progresses, cortical control of movement emerges and, although overtly overshadowing these earlier activities, is nonetheless dependent upon them for integration of function in both the immature and the adult organism. The ability of the duck embryo to show components of action patterns, for example, wing-beating in response to self-induced proprioceptive and tactile stimulation, led Gottlieb and Kuo (1965) to stress that self-stimulation may be an important process in prenatal behavioral development. Lorenz (1965) states that the organism can learn (or more correctly, organize) important elements of behavior before being hatched or born. Information in the genome may be double decoded, first by morphogenesis and subsequently by trial and error (or test and success) learning, making use of morphological structure. Vince (1964) has shown that in several species of game bird, contact with other eggs serves to synchronize hatching. This responsiveness to external stimulation (especially auditory and vibratory) in the avian embryo (Vince, 1966a, b), together with the findings of Gottlieb and Kuo (1965) that avian embryos are sensitive to the consequences of their own activities, is worth further evaluation of the type of feedback mechanism involved and the variable effects of stimuli of different modalities at certain ages.

"Plasticity" of the Developing Nervous System

In his classical studies on limb transplantations in the salamander embryo, Weiss (1950) concludes that motor patterns develop in the same predetermined way independent of sensory innervation, and that these patterns persist after spinal cord transection. Sperry (1958, 1963), in his studies of eye transplantation in the salamander, proposes that the orderly patterning of synaptic associations in the CNS is determined by biochemical affinities that are specific for each component part of the retina. This proposal is supported by the findings of several workers who have reported that orderly connections are reestablished following transection of a variety of nerves or nerve tracts. Some degree of early plasticity or nonspecificity of connections before cellular differentiation has been shown by Jacobson (1969). DeMyer (1967) found that corticospinal axons find their way in spite of environmental derangement adjacent to or in their path of growth, following prenatal surgical lesions in rat fetuses. Similarly Hibbard (1959, 1965) found central integration of nerve tracts from grafts of central and peripheral nerve tissues in amphibian embryos.

Recent studies on the selective action of drugs on different parts of the CNS and of the possible presence of specific neurohumoral systems (e.g., adrenergic, cholinergic, serotoninergic, and dopaminergic fiber systems) support Sperry's notion that the ontogeny of many component systems of the CNS depends upon specific chemical affinities between different classes of neurons. The regulation and direction of growth and of integration of component parts of the CNS are thus regulated in a necessarily more complex way than in the development of less elaborate organ systems where such processes as embryonic fields and induction (Waddington 1966) have been postulated. From this preliminary evidence, we may advance the possibility that during ontogenesis of component units comprising the various systems of the CNS, periods of integration occur. During these periods, the various neuronal unit components of a given system become specified or differentiated and integrated (Jacobson 1969), possibly with earlier developed units, and in turn form the substrate upon which further unit components of the particular system can be integrated. Some of the data reviewed by Levine and Mullins (1966) on the hormonal control of development of certain parts of the CNS, and of their subsequent effect on behavior following experimental manipulation during sensitive or critical periods in early life (when the process of integration of the neurohumoral systems is occurring), support this general concept.

Returning to the concept of ontogenetically predetermined integrative processes (which are presumably genetically regulated), further necessary information pertaining to these processes should be revealed by evaluating the extent of recovery of function and structural reorganization (i.e., "plasticity" of the developing brain) following specific lesions in various CNS systems at different ages during development. Periods of integration underlying sensitive or critical periods may be revealed as being present in different systems and at different "levels" of the CNS at various ages. Also the effects of external stimulation, enriched environment, etc. may be beneficial under certain conditions (Smith 1959) or at particular times only, and indirectly reveal the processes involved in the integrative development of the CNS. For example, Green (1967) found that ventromedial hypothalamic lesions made in rats after puberty caused an increase in emotionality and activity and disinhibition of passive avoidance; but these behavioral changes were not observed if these lesions were made in rats before puberty.

Tucker and Kling (1967) found that lesions of the frontal granular cortex of monkeys in early life had less effect on color discrimination and delayed response performance than if the lesions were made later in life. Their paper discusses these problems of CNS reorganization and functional compensation following lesions in early life and reviews a number of studies dealing with these problems (for references, see Tucker and Kling 1967); behaviors shown to be spared following lesions in early life include: maternal responses in the rat following partial decortication, affective-vegetative reactions in kittens after amygdalectomy, maze learning in rats following hemidecortication, somatomotor functions following lesions of motor and sensory cortex in monkeys, visual pattern and frequency discriminations following lesions of visual cortex, auditory duration discriminations following ablation of temporal cortex in kittens, roughness discriminations in kittens following ablation of the somatosensory cortex, and object discriminations after destruction of the posterior association cortex in the monkey. Kling and Green (1967) have also compared the effects of neonatal amygdalectomy in the maternally reared and the maternally deprived monkey. In their studies of recovery from lateral hypothalamic lesions in rats, Teitelbaum, Cheng, and Rozin (1969) have discovered an intriguing phenomenon that warrants further investigation. They state that "the sequence of stages of recovery in the adult brain-damaged animal is an exact parallel to the sequence of development in infancy." These authors go on to suggest that recovery from lateral hypothalamic lesions is essentially a process of reencephalization of function and their behavioral observations certainly seem to support this notion. Their conclusion that recovery recapitulates ontogeny should stimulate other studies and close evaluation of recovery from lesions in other subcortical regions.

Development of Reflexes and Coordinated Action Patterns

It has been pointed out by many observers that ontogeny does not follow a series of sharply defined developmental phases, but comprises a more gradual, sequential unfolding of neural units organized into more complex integrated patterns of activity. The concepts of Coghill (1929), supported by Weiss (1939), and the similar views of Anokhin (1964) embrace the notion that localized, specialized acts are secondary manifestations of the initial total pattern. This theory has been called the total pattern theory. Windle (1950) and Barcroft and Barron (1939), in contrast, maintained that reflex activity develops from simple to complex reactions (local pattern theory). Kuo (1963) concludes that even apparently simple movements are ontogenetically so complex that integration versus individuation is no longer a fundamental issue. Research in our laboratory on rat fetuses has shown that the first evoked responses (following stimulation of the face or forelimb with a blunt probe) are weak, variable, and localized to the area stimulated. Subsequently the local response becomes stronger in amplitude and vigor of movement, and at the same time a total body or "startle" response involving movements of other regions occurs. Toward the end of gestation, the startle response is clearly recognizable, and the local responses of the forelimbs closely resemble action patterns observed postnatally such as wiping, grasping, pushing, and withdrawal (Narayanan, Fox, and Hamburger, 1971).

Recently, Humphrey (1964) has reported some original observations and also reviewed earlier studies on the ontogeny of reflexes in the human fetus, correlated with the development of the nervous system. It is interesting to note (in contrast to Schneirla's observations, see later) that she found that reflexes in the avoidance or withdrawal category could be elicited earlier than approach or orientation toward the stimulus. Humphrey also compares her own conclusions with the earlier observations of Pavlov; namely, "the initial decomposition of the whole into its parts or units, and then the gradual reconstruction of the whole from these units or elements." In other words, reflexes are initially generalized "mass responses" which eventually become localized and finally are recombined into more complex responses composed of two or more reflex components (see also discussion on the findings of Sedlacek et al.).

Sedlacek et al. (1961) ascertained the effects of CNS transection at various levels on washing, licking, combing, and shaking reactions elicited by cutaneous stimulation at different ages in rats, guinea pigs, and dogs. Their results are comparable with those obtained in the dog at different ages after being subjected to spinal cord transection and decerebration (see chap. 3). Sedlacek and his colleagues (1961) support the conception of Volokhov (1961), which attributes the development of reflex activity to qualitative and quantitative evolution of the CNS. Their concept equates with the ethological interpretation of initial "units" of behavior being integrated into complex specialized acts. The development of "unit" systems (components of fixed action patterns) in the neural organization of behavior in nonprecocial mammals is an important step in the maturation of reflex responses.

Sarkisov (1966) has reviewed some of the classic ontogenetic findings of A. A. Volokhov, who concluded that the development of reflex reactions in ontogenesis is a complex process of excitation and inhibition or regulatory function. In the rabbit fetus, he showed a *first stage* of development that was manifest as primary motor reflexes, which were local movements of the head and forelimbs in response to cutaneous stimulation. At this stage, reflex arcs are connected through the trigeminal nerve centers in the medulla and through cervical enlargements of the spinal cord. This stage is followed by the *second stage* of primary generalization, characterized by fast general movements of the head, trunk, and limbs, after stimulation of any part of the skin; these movements are effected by reflex arcs connected through more extensive regions of the medulla and spinal cord. The *third stage* of secondary generalization in the form of tonic, slow movements of the head, trunk, and limbs following cutaneous stimulation is brought about by afferent exteroceptive and proprioceptive fibers connected at the level of the medulla and midbrain. The *fourth stage* of specialization involves formation of complex specialized reflexes (sucking, swallowing, washing, scratching, licking, limb withdrawal reflex, and righting, thus involving participation of afferent parts of the motor, cutaneous, and vestibular analyzers, spinal cord, brain stem, subcortex, and cerebrum). New complex reflex patterns also appear in later life associated with orienting, investigating, play, and sexual activities.

Sedlacek et al. (1961), on the basis of Volokhov's observations, divided the development of reflex activity into seven evolutionary phases which were closely associated with rostral progression of function in the developing nervous system. Their hypothesis can be correlated with the postnatal emergence of conditioned responses and the ontogenesis of unconditioned reflex responses (fig. 1.1). Tuge (1961) stated that negative conditioned reflexes in the ontogeny of internal inhibition show a pattern of development similar to unconditioned and conditioned reflex activities but occur at a much later age. These reactions are at first diffused and generalized and later acquire a localized and refined form. Sedlacek et al. (1961) divided the development of these seven phases into two stages: first, the development of unconditioned (spontaneous) reflex mechanisms progressing to the phase of specialization of reflex action, and, second, the development of conditioned reflex mechanisms starting with inhibition of specialized reflexes. Thus, unconditioned specialized reflexes occur in the fourth and fifth phases, and complex natural conditioned specialized reflexes in the sixth and seventh phases. It must be emphasized that the division of reflex development as described by Sedlacek et al. is not absolute, for components of one phase are evident in succeeding phases.

A study of the postnatal development of reflexes and neonatal responses in relation to behavior in mouse and cat has been described by Fox (1965*b*, 1970*b*) following the observations of overt behavior by Williams and Scott (1953) on the mouse, and the less complete observations of Rosenblatt and Schneirla (1962) on the cat. The changes in the nature of these reflex responses when chronologically charted suggest that discrete periods of neurologic development are present in both of these species, with similar patterns of neuro-ontogeny being evident. Fox (1964*d*)

has correlated neurologic development of the dog with the periods of overt behavioral development described in this species by Scott and Marston (1950).

Studies of the postnatal neurological development of the human infant have
shown that changes in the nature of some reflexes such as the disappearance (or
inhibition) of primitive reflexes, for example, Magnus reflex, and the emergence of
visual orientation and fixation not only indicate the level of neurologic maturity
attained, but also may be correlated with behavior (Dekeban 1959; White and
Castle 1964).

Piaget (1952) suggests that in early motor development in the human infant
there is a functional similarity and ontogenetic continuity between reflex and nonreflex behavioral sequences, and that more advanced cortically controlled behavior

SCHEMATIC RELATIONSHIPS OF REFLEX, CNS DEVELOPMENT & TIME OF BIRTH
(After Sedlacek et al. 1961)

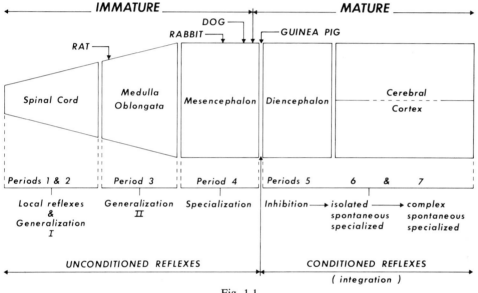

Fig. 1.1

is derived from primitive subcortically regulated reflexes and responses through
generalization, differential and reciprocal assimilation, and the later development
of a response schema (or possibly the ethologist's equivalent of a central neuronal
model or *Sollwert,* Hinde 1966). This concept is supported in part by the Pavlovian
interpretations of the ontogeny of reflex activities by Sedlacek et al. (1961).

In reviewing some of his earlier studies of the ontogenesis of infant behavior,
Gesell (1954) emphasizes that psychological growth, like somatic growth, is a
morphogenetic process, producing a progressive organization of behavior forms.
He defines several principles of development which have psychomorphological implications and which are concerned with the shaping of the action system and its
trends in oriented space and time. These principles include: *developmental direction,* in which the action system of the infant does not increase symmetrically but
is subject to anteroposterior (cephalocaudal) differentiation; *reciprocal interweav-*

ing (as for example in the development of the upright stance and locomotion), which implies the development of integrated functional relationships between paired and opposed motor organs; *function asymmetry,* a principle commonly seen in development, being exemplified in laterality, which Gesell emphasizes as being a dynamic form of asymmetry, as in the development of hand-preference; and the principle of *individuating maturation,* seen in the orderly specification of differentiation, in restricted spheres of total action systems during ontogenesis. Gesell recognizes one final principle, that of *regulatory fluctuation,* exemplified by the self-limiting of oscillations of the developing organism, which is in a state of unstable and shifting equilibrium; also of necessity the organism must restrict the modes and degrees of instability.

In the development of locomotor patterns in the human infant, Gesell demonstrates that there is a fluctuating dominance and progressive reintegration of component patterns, as a result of reciprocal interweaving. He states that

> none of the stages or patterns can be dismissed as being merely recapitulatory or vestigial. Each stage, however transient, appears to be a necessary feature of developmental mechanics, because of the numerous motor relationships which must be coordinated, that is, reciprocally interwoven. The organization of reciprocal relationships between the counteracting functions of neuromotor systems is ontogenetically manifested by somewhat periodic shifting of ascendance of the component functions or systems, with progressive modulation and integration of the resultant behavior patterns.

The tonic neck reflex provides a useful illustration of Gesell's third principle of functional asymmetry. It may play an important role in directing the eyes toward the extended hand, and thus in developing a conceptual "hand" schema and hand-eye (and subsequently hand-hand and hand-eye-mouth) coordination.[1] This reflex, Gesell insists, is not extinguished with increasing age, but becomes submerged by symmetric bilateral forearm patterns, which in turn are followed by a new unilateral pattern of one-hand reaching. Throughout early human development, therefore, there are several phases of periodic interweaving maturation, now of symmetric and then of asymmetric behavior form. The tonic neck reflex, according to Gesell, represents a "morphogenetic stage in which fundamental neurological coordinations are laid down to form the framework for later postural, manual, locomotor and psychomotor reactions. Indeed, the tonic neck reflex is part of the ground-plan of the organism pervasively identified with its unitary, total action systems." In this regard, the part played by neonatal reflexes and specific responses in the subsequent development of behavior patterns in the dog will be evaluated in this present study. Gesell (1954) concludes that the tonic neck reflex is elaborated and inflected and finally figures in innumerable adult acts of skill, aggression, and extrication. "Attitudinal asymmetry always remains in reflex reserve as well as subject to voluntary mobilization."

Gesell's principle of individuating maturation is very similar to Anokhin's heterochronous maturation theory. Gesell states that "environmental factors support, inflect and specify; but they do not engender the basic forms and sequences of ontogenesis."

Gesell's fifth principle, self-regulatory fluctuation, illustrates the plasticity and adaptability of the organism in establishing such patterns as feeding and sleep in

---

[1] See also Held and Bauer's (1967) study of development of visually guided reaching in infant monkeys following rearing with restricted opportunity to develop hand-eye coordination.

early life. Progressive fluctuations culminating in a more stable response are characteristic of all behavioral development, and are well illustrated in Gesell's studies of feeding behavior. He observes that these fluctuations, instead of being regarded as undesirable or as fortuitous irregularities, should be interpreted as effortful attempts on the part of the organism to accomplish increasingly mature adjustments.

Development of the Nervous System

Several aspects of the postnatal development of the cat and mouse have been reviewed from multidisciplinary studies and charted chronologically (figs. 1.2, 1.3).

NEURO-ONTOGENY OF THE MOUSE

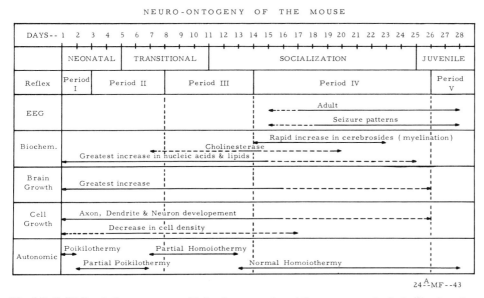

24 $\overset{A}{\_}$ MF--43

Fig. 1.2. Solid line indicates most rapid development, dotted lines more gradual. Arrow direction to left indicates first onset, arrow to the right indicates continuation of development beyond the age shown. Behavioral periods, Williams and Scott 1953; reflex periods, Fox 1965*b;* EEG, Kobayashi et al. 1963; biochemistry, Uzman and Rumley 1958, Gerebtzoff 1955; brain growth and axodendritic development, Kobayashi 1963, Kobayashi et al. 1963; cell density, Haddara 1956; and thermoregulation, Lagerspetz 1962.

In these species, the most dramatic alterations in CNS morphology in terms of cell density, axonal, and dendritic development occur during the neonatal and transitional periods. After this time, morphological changes are less easily detected and the changes that do occur are the more gradual processes of maturation as contrasted to the initially explosive developmental changes. Nutritional variables may severely interfere with normal development (Meyer et al. 1961), and should be carefully controlled in developmental studies.

    Considerable information is available on the development of conditioned reflexes in the dog. In this animal the responses at the higher levels of sensory organization are not stable until the end of the transitional period.

    Biochemical changes in the developing brain have only recently attracted intensive analytical investigation. Certain biochemical events appear to precede the appearance of electrophysiological and behavioral events (Dravid, Himwich, and Davis 1965).

Electrophysiological studies (Ellingson and Wilcott 1960; Kobayashi et al. 1963) have been well documented in the cat and mouse and indicate that direct correlates with behavioral development can be made in relation to the development of spontaneous EEG activity and evoked electrical brain potentials of various sensory modalities. From these various studies, the structural and functional development of the CNS may be correlated with periods of behavioral development. Changes in behavior must be considered on a physiological basis and are consequential to structural and biochemical changes (figs. 1.2, 1.3).

NEURO-ONTOGENY OF THE CAT

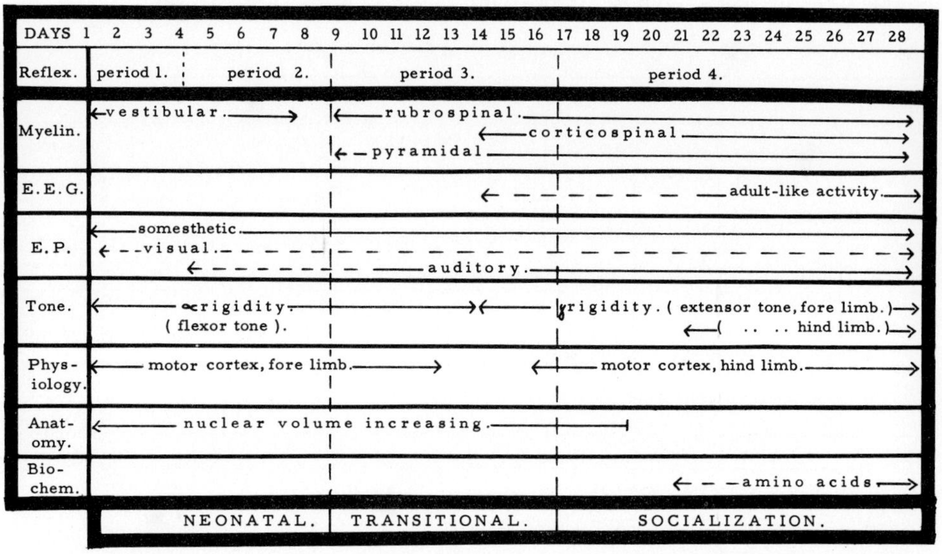

DAYS	1	2	3	4	5	6	7	8	9	10	11	12	13	14	15	16	17	18	19	20	21	22	23	24	25	26	27	28
Reflex.	period 1.			period 2.				period 3.									period 4.										
Myelin.	←vestibular.———→								←———rubrospinal.——┤ ←———corticospinal————→ ←—pyramidal————┤																	
E.E.G.											← — — ┤— — — — — ———adult-like activity.——→																
E.P.	←———somesthetic.———————————————————————————→ ←--visual.— — — — —┤— — — — — — — — ┴— — — — — — — — — —→ ←— — — — — —┤— ———auditory.——┤																										
Tone.	←———∝rigidity┬——┤ (flexor tone).								→←——┆rigidity. (extensor tone, fore limb.)——→ ←——(.. .. hind limb.)——→																	
Physiology.	←——— motor cortex, fore limb.———→								←—┆——— motor cortex, hind limb.———→																	
Anatomy.	←——— nuclear volume increasing.———┤———┤																										
Biochem.																		← — —amino acids┌——→									
	NEONATAL.					TRANSITIONAL.			SOCIALIZATION.																			

Fig. 1.3. Solid line indicates most rapid development, dotted line more gradual. Arrow direction to left indicates first onset, arrow to the right indicates continuation of development beyond the age shown. Myelination and physiology, Langworthy 1927, 1929; EEG, Grossman 1955, Marley and Key 1963, Petersen, DiPerri, and Himwich 1964, Scheibel 1962; EP (evoked potential), Ellingson and Wilcott 1960, Valatx, Jouvet, and Jouvet 1964; changes in muscle tone, Skoglund 1960*a, b;* biochemistry, Berl and Purpura 1963; reflex periods, Fox 1970*b,* Tilney and Kubie 1931; and anatomy, Brizze and Jacobs 1959.

Hormonal Influences on CNS and Behavioral Development

Young, Goy, and Phoenix (1964) have shown that sex hormones direct differentiation of the organism—not only of its reproductive organs, but also of its sexual behavior capacity. During fetal development, the androgens direct the differentiation of the hypothalamus, and the male mating pattern is established; in later life, androgens then activate or arouse this specific pattern of sexual activity.

Levine and Mullins (1966) have reviewed certain aspects of hormonal influences on the developing brain. They propose that the presence of hormones (sex, thyroid, or adrenal) during critical periods of development exerts a direct action on the CNS (see Michael 1966), producing profound and permanent changes in the subsequent psychophysiological processes of the organism. The work of Harris and Levine (1965), Eayrs (1961), Denenberg (1968), and others has shown how these three types of hormones influence subsequent behavior, as a result of either drug-injection, organ ablation (castration), or handling stress in early infancy. Levine and Mullins conclude that the effects of variations of both the external and the internal environment are mediated through basic, but as yet undetermined, biochemical processes, and that the elucidation of these processes should bring us much closer to an understanding of the intimate relationships between physiology and behavior. During a period of integration early in life between the gonads and the nervous system, sex hormones may have an organizational or inductive effect during early development, and an activational or arousal effect at the time of puberty. In the rat, administration of estrogen or androgen, if given early in postnatal life, causes the sexually undifferentiated brain to be organized so that the acyclic male pattern of hormone release occurs in the adult. In the absence of gonadal hormones, as in castration, the cyclic female pattern of hormone release is established. Estrogen or progesterone administered to male rats castrated before 5 days of age evokes entirely female behavior in later life. Testosterone or estrogen given in large doses to females during the first 120 hr after birth renders them incapable of responding normally to sex hormones in adulthood. Some females given estrogen in infancy show male sexual response to testosterone in adulthood, whereas adults not given estrogen in infancy only show mounting behavior when given the same amount of testosterone. "Replacement" therapy with appropriate hormones in later life is ineffectual; this indicates that it is not caused by a lack of hormone but, as Levine and Mullins suggest, arises from an abnormal setting of a "hormonostat" or regulator, whereby the concentration of hormone being produced early in life "feeds back" and affects the hypothalamus, which in turn controls the rate of hormone production.[2]

Neonatal hypothyroidism causes more generalized effects, such as retarding gross development and myelination, but does not affect specific behaviors. Administration of thyroxin to the newborn causes similar changes, suggesting that a "hormonostat" regulator is deranged; many of these deficits can be overcome if replacement therapy is instigated before 15 days of age; treatment after this critical period is relatively ineffectual.

Handling early in postnatal life causes an elevation of corticosteroids; this increase may possibly modify the central hormonostat so that in later life stressful situations causing an elevation in corticosteroids do not result in such extreme reactions as in controls, because the sensitivity of the central structures is decreased, or their tolerance as a result of early manipulations is increased. Levine and Mullins postulate that the controlling set-point of the brain hormonostat following handling in early life elicits graded adrenal responses appropriate to the demands of the environment; nonhandled subjects do not show this gradation, but more of an "all or none" response. It must also be emphasized that manipulations affecting one system of behavior or hormonal action may affect other apparently unrelated systems in later life as, for example, handling advances the onset of puberty (Morton, Denenberg, and Zarrow 1963).[3] The age limitations observed, in that hormones will have the most marked effect only during the first few days postnatally in the rat, suggest that the nervous system is particularly sensitive to these hormonal influences at a particular time; this age-limited sensitization "sets" or integrates

[2] Kulin, Grumbach, and Kaplan (1969) have demonstrated that a gonadal-hypothalamic feedback mechanism operates in man, which changes in sensitivity at the time of puberty.

[3] And sexual maturation in female mice is accelerated by the odor of males (Vandenbergh 1969).

the CNS with the endocrine system. Before and after the period when this neural-endocrine relationship is established, endocrine changes have less dramatic effects. Similar findings have been made in the development of other systems, such as the visual system (chap. 6), and it would appear that this type of integration, of many different systems at chronologically different times during ontogeny, is a common phenomenon of the integrative development of the nervous system and behavior. The interrelationships between these systems and neural control mechanisms remain to be evaluated.

The Hypothesis of the Critical Period of Socialization

The precocial mammals (e.g., sheep, guinea pig), being neurologically mature at birth, are able to interact with their environment and with members of their own species immediately after birth and thus can establish primary social relationships (Scott 1962). This rapidly developing phenomenon is termed imprinting; because the organism is relatively mature at birth or hatching there may possibly be considerable prenatal organization of behavior. Grier, Counter, and Shearer (1967), for example, have shown that exposure to specific acoustic stimuli during the later stages of incubation can facilitate imprinting to that stimulus after hatching. This prenatal or prehatching mechanism, in precocial birds at least, may account for their preference for species-specific vocalizations, or more specifically, for the vocal calls of their mother. In contrast, the nonprecocial mammals develop more slowly postnatally and have a clearly defined neonatal period during which they are dependent on the mother for shelter and food. It is only after this period, when sensory and locomotor development has reached a certain point, that primary social relationships can be established. This later emergence of a phenomenon having the same outcome as imprinting but occurring over a longer period of time has been termed the "critical period of socialization" (Scott 1962). Essentially, the two phenomena, imprinting and socialization in the precocial and nonprecocial animals, are similar in that there is an initial period which allows emotional attachment to any object (normally to the mother), after which strong avoidance behavior to novel stimuli develops. Such avoidance behavior acts as a natural survival mechanism for the young animal. The early dominance of approach behavior (as exemplified by the following response) facilitates the establishment of primary social relationships (which has been compared with smiling in the infant and which Gray [1958] compared to imprinting. This view has recently been critically reviewed by Ambrose [1961, 1963] and Kagan [1967]).

Ambrose (1966) proposes that the main functions of the smiling response in the human infant are to establish a bond with the mother and to develop a capacity for social relations (as postulated by Scott in the term "primary" socialization). Ambrose notes that smiling is not mainly a response indicating satisfaction over needs already fulfilled, but is a response with a strongly appetitive element (like the tail-wagging response of the dog).

Socialization Variables

In accordance with the approach/withdrawal theory of Schneirla (1965, 1966), there is a gradual emergence of withdrawal or avoidance behavior and the development of fear/escape reactions. This theory of Schneirla's will be evaluated in the dog (chap. 5), using the human being as the "reward stimulus"; that is, inducing a socialization variable, in an attempt to show differences in fear and escape reactions and the possible existence of a "sensitive period" within the critical period of socialization. The adaptive and protective mechanisms of such an ambivalent behavior mechanism are obvious, ensuring early socialization with like species and protection against potential predators at a later age, until learned discriminations are established.

Schaffer (1966) investigated the incongruity hypothesis, which attributes fear of strangers to the development of a discrimination between unfamiliar and familiar individuals, in the human; he found that there were significant correlations between the age of onset of the fear response and the number of children in the family and number of people to whom the infants had been exposed. Both the fear response and contact reinforcement (and pain, Kovach and Hess 1963) have facilitatory effects in socialization and imprinting (Salzen 1967). Elliot and King (1960) found that underfed pups that had little human contact except at feeding were socialized more rapidly than similarly treated overfed pups. Thus arousal of hunger may facilitate socialization, although this point needs further confirmation (Salzen 1967).

There is some evidence that experiential deprivation may extend the critical period; Moltz and Stettner (1961) found that the critical period for imprinting was extended in chicks deprived of patterned light. However, social deprivation after the critical period, even in socialized pups, may result in their becoming "desocialized." This frequently occurs in large breeding kennels, where pups receive plenty of attention in early life and are later returned from the rearing quarters to the kennels "to mature," where subsequently they receive less human contact or exposure to the outside world. Some dogs develop "kennelosis" and show timidity and avoidance of strangers and of novel stimuli. It would appear that social and exploratory behavior are affected, and that frequent reinforcement of the social attachments established during the critical period is important in maintaining the social bond, especially in more innately timid breeds or individuals (as shown by Krushinskii 1962). Woolpy and Ginsburg (1967) similarly observe that subsequent confinement of socialized wolf cubs results in their regression or desocialization. However, nonsocialized wolves caught when adult, when eventually socialized, after approximately 6 mo of careful treatment, remain permanently attached. Thus the stability of learning and retention must be considered in evaluating the effects of early experience and the age limitations to the critical period of socialization.

Collias (1951) has divided the stage of socialization into five categories: (1) *Predisposition to respond to organisms of the same species*—for example, Gottlieb (1965) found that naive ducklings and chicks prefer the parental call of their own species; prehatching auditory stimulation during incubation may play some part in this phenomenon; (2) *autoreinforcement of initial responses*—the following response strengthens the probability of its maintenance; (3) *increasing social discrimination*—recognition of peers, and dominant and subordinate members of the group; (4) *socialization controlled by the group or family*—infant begins to learn the traditions of the family, its territorial limits and its intraspecific social signals; (5) *final period of social independence and later reintegration*—following weaning in many species, the younger members, during a juvenile period before the onset of sexual maturity, form a separate group, as in many ungulates. As sexual maturity is attained, the individual gradually reintegrates with the main group.

Other "Critical" or "Sensitive" Periods

Scott (1962), in his discussion on critical periods, emphasizes that there are periods other than the critical period of socialization which can be critical or sensitive for the effects of experience on behavioral organization. McGraw (1946) has shown that in the human infant there are certain critical periods for the optimal development of certain motor skills, and Forgays and Read (1962) find that in the rat experience in an enriched environment has its greatest effect at 20–30 days of age (see also Hymovitch 1952; Nyman 1967). Excessive stimulation to accelerate development of a particular activity may have no effect until the organism has attained sufficient maturity so that a response can be elaborated, or such stimulation may actually accelerate development and the activity may appear at an ontogenetically earlier time. However, excessive stimulation before the optimal period may result in the formation of "mechanical" or unskillful habits which actually interfere with the normal pattern. The complex interaction between different critical periods, each having dependent interrelationships, may in part account for these variable effects of early experience. Scott (1962) states that the critical period concept would be of little value if there were a critical period for each behavioral and physiological phenomenon; but some sort of order can be obtained by dealing with different classes or systems of behavioral phenomena, such as the process of socialization. There are, however, complex interactions between the different critical periods of particular classes of behavioral phenomena, as, for example, the later preference of sexual partner is in part influenced by earlier filial relationships (Guiton 1966; Klinghammer 1967) and the development of complex motor skills is to some extent governed by the previous experience and already organized abilities of the organism (Schiller 1957). Thus we must consider the molecular components of the systems of behavior, as emphasized by Riesen (1961b), in contributing to the molar units of behavior. The development of both CNS and behavior cannot be oversimplified along a conceptual framework of discrete and unrelated periods of development, but should be approached from the notion that there are ontogenetically determined critical periods of development which are closely interrelated. This interrelationship stresses the significance of a continuum of experience throughout development, variations in which might cause experiential increments or decrements that may modify the termination (or waxing and waning) of one critical period and the onset of another.

Klopfer and Hailman (1967) refer to a "critical period" in the goat's acceptance of her offspring; only 5 min contact immediately *post partum* is needed to establish the mother-infant bond, but if the infant is removed for 1 hr immediately after delivery, the mother will not accept it. They note that this critical period is not tied to a specific age of the animal, but rather to a specific point in the reproductive cycle, a point which occurs many times during the life of an individual.

Olfactory responses play an important role in the development of social relationships in some animals. Marr and Gardner (1965) and Mainardi, Marsan, and Pasquali (1965) have shown that early olfactory experience influences subsequent sexual preferences in the rat and mouse. A similar olfactory-gustatory mechanism may be operating in the development of food preferences in many young animals, especially wild species raised from early life in captivity. Burghardt and Hess (1966) postulate an imprintinglike process in the development of food preferences in the snapping turtle.

Thorpe (1961*a, b*) observes that there is a critical period in the development of song in male chaffinches. If socially isolated at 3–4 days of age, they will develop an incomplete song pattern; but if they are given exposure to the song of adults as fledglings, even before they are able to sing, they will, when mature, produce the species-characteristic song pattern. During the first few weeks of territorial singing they acquire the local "dialect"—the final embellishments—and apparently do not or are unable to modify their song in subsequent years. Thus, learning the complete pattern may interfere with or block further learning, and this final crystallization may represent the end of this critical period.

Thorpe (1961*b*) provides a detailed review on the sensitive or critical periods in learning in a variety of species, including man. In many animals, play has an important role in developing adult patterns of social behavior; possibly the decline in play with increasing age sets an upper limit for the critical period during which normal adult, species-characteristic behavior is developed. Kagen and Beach (1953) found that young male rats reared only with mature females failed to develop normal sexual responses in later life; they associated this with the fact that the young males developed a pattern of play activity with the females which in some way conditioned the young males so as to bar their recognition of females as sex-objects. Possibly the development of normal patterns of play and dominance-subordinate relationships (in which aggression in the male is important for later consummation of sexual behavior) were disrupted under these conditions of restricted socialization.

Although in the development of learning abilities, previous experience is often facilitatory (e.g., learning to learn), Scott (1962) suggests that negative learning, or learning not to learn, may act to bring about the termination of the critical period for the development of a particular ability. He presents a provisional hypothesis that "the critical period for any specific sort of learning is that time when maximum capacities—sensory, motor and motivational, as well as psychological ones—are first present." There clearly are critical stages of learning, and what has been learned earlier in life may be critical for whatever is learned in later life.

Early experience may modify the ability to perform certain tasks or the fear of such, depending on the environment in which the infant is raised. Emlen (1963) found that newly hatched herring-gull chicks withdraw from the edge of an artificial cliff. At a later age, however, those reared on an artificial cliff were content to sit right at the edge of the low cliff, and occasionally jumped down, whereas those reared on a flat surface reacted in the same manner as newborn chicks.

The data of Rosenblatt, Turkewitz, and Schneirla (1959) and Schneirla and Rosenblatt (1961) are not compatible with Scott's conceptualization of critical periods during which critical stages for learning may be evident. Instead, they emphasize the necessity of continuous interaction between the organism and the environment, which tends to change as development progresses. Early experience during critical periods may, however, influence this continuum of interaction between peers and between mother and infant, as in the initial attachments between goat and kid. As Scott (1962) stresses, the critical-period concept is of little value as a global concept, but should be applied to specific aspects or systems of behavior.

Scott (1962) observes that

> both growth and behavioral differentiation are based on organized processes. This suggests a general principle of organization: that once a system becomes organized, whether it is the cells of the embryo that are multiplying and differentiating, or the behavior patterns of a young animal that are becoming organized through learning,

it becomes progressively more difficult to reorganize the system. That is, organization inhibits reorganization. Further, organization can be strongly modified only when active processes of organization are going on, and this accounts for critical periods of development.

King (1968) has also emphasized this point and states that

> a critical period is that period in development during which the probability of a behavior pattern being emitted and the probability of it being reinforced by the environment are greatest. . . . Complexity is added by the fact that many responses develop simultaneously, interact and reinforce each other, and at the same time the environment provides a spectrum of stimuli and reinforcers. This complexity results in a population of probability curves for both the behavior and the reinforcers.

CNS Development and Critical Periods

It should be emphasized that the critical period is the time when neural organization is sufficiently developed to permit perceptual interaction and adaptation to the environment and the establishment of primary social relationships. The extension of this hypothesis leads to the idea that at specific periods during postnatal development the animal is particularly sensitive to changes that in turn affect behavior patterns in later life. Each period is dependent on the neural organization of behavior at that specific age. In her studies of the development of the song sparrow (which, like the pup, is a nonprecocial animal), Nice (1943) showed that development progresses through several stages which are rather comparable, as Scott (1962) has shown, to the development of the pup: such stages of development may be common to most nonprecocial species, with the exception of the human infant, in which motor development is more protracted (Scott 1968). McGraw (1946) has shown the existence of critical periods (or optimal times) for the learning of motor skills in the human infant; much of the work of Bowlby (1952) is also centered on the critical period concept, in terms of the development of socioemotional relationships in the human infant. The most important period, however, is the critical period of socialization when neural organization at the higher levels of behavior are integrated to permit the establishment of emotional (or affectional) bonds, learned responses, and more complete behavioral interaction with the environmental milieu (see fig. 1.4). In terms of animal behavior this period may be regarded as the time when the inherited characteristics of the organism facilitate adaptation to the environment, with concurrent learning or acquisition of additional adaptive modifications of behavior.

Although some of the "units" or component parts of the nervous system reach maturity before the onset of the critical period of socialization, they do not appear to become functional until other dependent structures reach maturity and can be organized with these more precocial units. Anokhin (1964) postulates that each phase of postnatal development is synchronized heterochronously; that is differential rates of neural maturation parallel specific behavioral maturation to promote maximal adaptation and survival of the organism at each phase of ontogeny. This heterochronous patterning means a selective maturation of receptor apparatuses in correspondence with ecological factors. In essence, this theory is similar to the views of Sackett (1963), where responsiveness to specific visual stimuli is attributed to differential rates of sensory maturation paralleling the maturation of certain behavior patterns. Consequently, the ability to perform a highly complex task is dependent upon neural development and experience; age differences in the ability to temporally delay a trained but spatially variable response are assessed in this investigation. Age-dependent differences in this test might, therefore, be related to other aspects of CNS and behavioral development (chap. 5). At this point we can trace the link with other theories based on information theory, filtering systems (perceptual abilities), and genetic coding of innate behavior reviewed by Thorpe (1964) and Lorenz (1965).

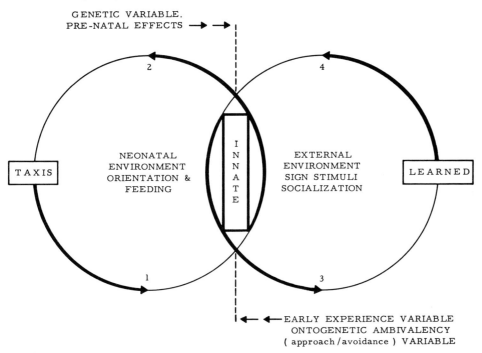

Fig. 1.4. Postnatal ontogenetic relationships of various levels of behavioral organization in a typical nonprecocial mammal. Taxes predominate in early life, followed by emergence of innate, species-specific behavior patterns and learned responses.

Phylogeny (Evolution) and Ontogeny of Behavior

Ethologists recognize that certain unit releasers act as specific key stimuli which unlock genetically determined unit behavior patterns, but Skinner (1966) emphasizes the importance of employing the change in frequency of a response as an important identifiable unit for behavioral analysis. The origins of variations in response frequency are based on ontogenetic and phylogenetic contingencies of reinforcement.[4] Ontogenetic contingencies remain ineffective until a response has occurred, and in phylogenetic contingencies, a similar limitation exists (see also Sackett 1966*b*). Skinner suggests that the entire repertoire of an organism must exist before ontogenetic or phylogenetic selection as "minimal" units, upon which ontogenetic and phylogenetic contingencies "shape" complex forms of behavior, being facilitated in those species having a broad and undifferentiated behavioral repertoire.

[4] See, for example, Hailman's study (1969) of the ontogeny of pecking in the gull chick, where contingencies of reinforcement influence an apparently "innate" response.

Skinner emphasizes that the principal difference between an instinct and a reflex is not in the complexity of the response but in the eliciting and releasing actions of the stimulus. Operant reinforcement strengthens a response and brings the response under stimulus control; thus the stimulus sets the occasion upon which the response is more likely to occur (i.e., the releaser sets the occasion, or puts the animal in a position to respond). Complex operant behavior can be programmed and the sequences of behavior may seem difficult to interpret in view of the complexity of the outcome; in evolution, in which the environment changes, Skinner suggests that a similar programming of phylogenetic contingencies occurs.

There is greater resistance to extinction of intermittently reinforced operants; thus certain phylogenetic and ontogenetic contingencies may be effective even though intermittent, so that the behavior survives without frequent reinforcement.

> To say that intelligence is inherited is not to say that specific forms of behavior are inherited. Phylogenetic contingencies conceivably responsible "for the selection of intelligence" do not specify responses. What has been selected appears to be a *susceptibility* to ontogenetic contingencies, leading particularly to a greater speed of conditioning and the *capacity* to maintain a larger repertoire without confusion [Skinner 1966].

Skinner theorizes that in imprinting what is inherited (or instinctive) is not necessarily the behavior of following but a susceptibility to reinforcement by proximity to the mother or mother surrogate. A distress call reduces the distance between mother and chick when the mother responds appropriately, and walking toward the mother has the same effect. Both behaviors may, therefore, be reinforced, but they appear before these ontogenetic contingencies come into play and are, therefore, at least in part phylogenetic.

In terms of adaptation, both phylogenetic and ontogenetic contingencies change the organism so that it adapts to the environment and behaves more effectively. According to Skinner (1966), phylogenetic contingencies are equivalent to natural selection, whereas ontogenetic contingencies are equivalent to operant conditioning. In both contingencies, effective responses are selected, but the selection processes are quite different. Many characteristics of behavior are common products of both ontogenetic and phylogenetic contingencies; for example, imitative behavior.

Skinner urges that we be careful in defining which behavior patterns are of phylogenetic or of ontogenetic origin. Phylogenetic contingencies are particularly insensitive to operant reinforcement (e.g., animal vocalizations), whereas vocal responses in the child are easily shaped by operant reinforcement (i.e., ontogenetic contingencies), and are not controlled by specific releasers. Thus, in the infant, the phylogenetic development of an undifferentiated vocal repertoire brought a new system of behavior within range of operant reinforcement through the mediation of other organisms.

These concepts of Skinner's, when regarded in terms of adaptation and the influence of inheritance and early learning on subsequent behavior, provide a valuable interpretation of the phylogeny and ontogeny of behavior and of stimulus-response relationships (see also discussion by Wickler [1965*a, b*, 1966] on certain aspects of the evolution of behavior and of morphological structures which act as sign stimuli or social releasers).

Additional components of learning which must be considered are the autonomic responses associated with overt behavioral reactions; these physiological reactions may act as reinforcing agents and may prolong the maintenance of behavior in the absence of primary reinforcements (Scott 1958*a*; Solomon and Wynne 1954). Ontogenetic development of the relationships between autonomic and overt behavioral reactions require further investigation in terms of learning and behavior in later life.

Environmental Deprivation Studies

Much valuable information pertinent to the critical period hypothesis is available from studies on the effects of environmental deprivation. Species-characteristic responses may not develop or may become modified or undergo spontaneous regression by interference of contrary learning processes (such as stimulus substitution or deprivation of normal stimuli or "releasers").

Konishi (1966) argues convincingly that the concept of instinct is valuable in considering certain motor patterns and sensory functions which develop without specific interactions between the animal and the environment. For example, Glickman and Van Laer (1964) observed that infant cats of the genus *Panthera* that were raised in incubators showed pouncing, swatting, biting, and carrying movements which were species-specific and which developed independent of maternal example. Several behavior patterns in the adult are composed of interdependent units, where innate responses are adaptively modified (or discarded) by learning processes and in turn may facilitate, modify, or restrict learning processes. This interdependency is demonstrated in isolation rearing, where innate responses, if not experientially reinforced, may undergo spontaneous remission. Essentially, the deprivation experiment underlines the information that is relayed by the genome, that is, "unlearned" behavior (Lorenz 1965).

In deprived animals, learning at a later age is difficult or impossible (Foley 1934; Padilla 1935), for it is especially during early life that the innate-learned associations most readily affect the adaptive organization of behavior. If the normal adaptive sequences of development are omitted, severe deficits may occur in later life (Freedman, King, and Elliot 1961; Harlow and Harlow 1962; Melzack and Scott 1957). An innate pattern when not expressed may be impossible to elicit once the critical period for its development and consolidation has passed. Conversely, if abnormal stimuli are given, abnormal behavior patterns may emerge, as in Padilla's (1935) chicks, which had great difficulty in pecking at and eating solid food after they had been raised on liquids fed by a dropper. Maladaptive pathological reactions develop, such as stereotypy and autistic reactions (Fox 1965*c*). Thompson and Schaefer (1961) have discussed these problems and conclude that primacy, plasticity, differentiation, and critical periods in development represent the most crucial characteristics of the young organism. The effects of early environmental influences are susceptible to analysis for the generality of change (number of functions affected), extent of change in a particular function, and the reversibility or permanence of the change in relation to the initial behavioral change.

A major problem in the deprivation experiment is the provision of an adequate stimulus situation. Lack of an adequate stimulus may lead to the incorrect conclusion that certain behavior patterns are defective, whereas the abnormality or absence of the pattern may actually be the result of information's being withheld from the animal. It may be surmised that although the mechanisms involved in postnatal development appear rigid and stereotyped, they are actually adaptive and are geared to promote survival. Adaptation may not be possible, however, if the environment is drastically altered or experience is denied, as occurs in social isolation or environmental deprivation. Such variables affect early experience by disrupting the normal sequences of ontogeny and may arrest or disrupt both structural and functional components of behavior (Wiesel and Hubel 1963a, b). Riesen (1961b), in his classical studies on the effects of light deprivation on retinal and neuronal degeneration in the lateral geniculate, observes that the rate of degeneration is negatively correlated with the age when the subject is first deprived; he concludes that the more complex the later behavior the more dependent it is on cumulative changes in earlier behavior. Riesen (1961b) recognized four categories of behavioral building blocks: innate response, perceptual learning (or sensory preconditioning), sensorimotor and motor-sensory integrations, and motor preconditioning or response-response learning, as in pure motor skills. Innate responses include stimulus generalization, discrimination, and innate emotional (fear) responses to novel stimuli. Held and Hein's (1963) work supports these concepts of sensorimotor and motor-sensory integrations, where several modalities (multiple afferent feedback) are required for visual learning. Thus early deprivation of one modality can affect many behavior patterns in later life as neurobehavioral organization is disrupted with consequent motivational, sensory, and perceptual manifestations of abnormality. Hubel and Wiesel (1963) and Wiesel and Hubel (1963a, b) have demonstrated in a series of neurophysiological studies in the kitten that if visual stimulation is denied, neuronal disorganization ensues—thus stimulation is essential for the maintenance, development, and maturation of neural systems.

In future research we must clearly define what constitutes a "normal" stimulus and elucidate the variables of innate responses and the afferent perceptual mechanism of the filtering systems involved (see also Lorenz 1965, critique of deprivation experiments).

Summary

In this chapter a number of issues relating to neuro-ontogeny and behavioral development are reviewed, notably the critical period hypothesis, the process of socialization, and the concepts of integration and of heterochronous systemogenesis. The patterns of brain and behavior development in the cat and mouse are charted to provide an interdisciplinary synthesis. Embryological studies of behavior (reflexive) development and various theories pertaining to embryogenetic processes are described. Hormonal, neuroendocrine influences on brain and behavior development are briefly reviewed, and the effects of various "early experiences" (handling, isolation) are introduced. Various aspects of the phylogeny and ontogeny of behavior are considered to emphasize the genotype-environment interaction, which occurs within the individual's lifetime and over successive generations in a given species. In subsequent chapters, more detailed interdisciplinary topics will be developed from this introduction.

2

Postnatal Development of Reflexes
and Organization of Behavior Patterns

In this chapter, attention will be focused on the development of a variety of reflexes and unconditioned responses in the neonate dog. These will be described in detail, and the integration of certain responses into more complex behavior patterns in later life will be discussed. Neurologic tests to elicit certain reflexes are used clinically to diagnose neurologic disorders. Similar tests instigated during development essentially constitute a regime of developmental neurologic diagnosis. Such tests will therefore provide useful information as to the degree of development of the nervous system, and some correlation will be made with what is known of the development of the canine nervous system. This will be elaborated further in chapter 4 when we consider various aspects of the structural development of the nervous system. The development of species-specific behavior patterns and also ritualization and emancipation of some of these patterns will be discussed in detail. Aspects of maternal and play behavior will be included and reactions to models eliciting social investigatory behavior described.

Development of Reflexes and Unconditioned Responses

Introduction

Thomas (1940) has studied the postnatal development of locomotor abilities in the dog, using postural, righting, and attitudinal responses as indicators of neuromotor maturation. The responsiveness of the superficial (exteroceptive, sensory) reflexes and reliability of elicitation have been investigated in the human neonate by Thomas, Chesni, and Dargassies (1961). Gessell (1945), Ingram (1959, 1962),

23

Dekeban (1959), Illingworth (1962), and McGraw (1943) provide detailed information on the normal neurologic development of the human infant, and Hines (1942) and Riesen and Kinder (1952) have studied the postnatal neurologic development of the Macaque monkey and the chimpanzee respectively. Paulson and Gottlieb (1968) have described the reappearance of certain primitive reflexes in senile human beings.

The present study was undertaken to investigate postnatal reflex development of the dog; in an earlier report (Fox 1963c), a series of reflexes were identified in this species and were classified according to the terminology of Thomas, Chesni, and Dargassies (1961), who have described in some detail the neurological development of the human infant. Correlations were made between a series of reflexes which were chosen as indicators that might determine how well the temporal changes in these reflex patterns compare with overt behavioral development of dogs as described by Scott and Marston (1950). The relationships between reflex components of behavior and the organization of behavior patterns might then be demonstrated, and might also give an indirect evaluation of the development of neural structures underlying behavioral development.

Langworthy has correlated reflex development with myelination of the spinal cord and CNS in the kitten (1929), opossum (1928), and human infant (1933), and Tilney (1933) and Windle, Fish, and O'Donnell (1934) have made similar correlations in the albino rat and the kitten respectively.

Materials and Methods

Forty-five pups from 11 litters of dogs were examined daily from birth to 4 wk of age and then at 3-day intervals for an additional 3 wk. All animals were reared under similar management and environmental conditions. Growth rates were recorded daily and any sick or physically inferior pups were not included in the experiment. These animals were all partially inbred (Jackson Laboratory strains), with low to moderately high coefficients of inbreeding as follows: sheltie, 11 pups from 3 litters (inbred to between 0.22 and 0.38); beagle, 13 pups from 3 litters (inbred to between 0.12 and 0.45); basenji, 12 pups from 3 litters (inbred to between 0.62 and 0.89); cocker spaniel, 9 pups from 2 litters (inbred to between 0.17 and 0.31).

A three-scale grading system was used to measure the ease of elicitation of certain reflexes during postnatal development in these dogs. Differences in these reflexes were roughly graded as strong and stereotyped, weak and variable, negative or adultlike.

The following reflexes were examined:

1. *Reflexes Associated with Locomotor Activities*

a) Crossed Extensor Reflex (animal in supine position). Pinching one hind foot causes a pain withdrawal flexion response in the same foot, while the opposite hind limb extends (Sherrington 1910).

b) Magnus Reflex (animal in supine position). Turning the head to one side causes extension of both fore- and hind limbs on the side toward which the head is turned; limbs on the opposite side are flexed (figs. 2.1, 2.3) (Magnus 1925).

c) Tonic Neck Reflex (animal standing on all fours or held suspended under chest). Forced upward extension of the head and neck causes increased tone in the forelimbs and decreased tone in the hind limbs; the forelimbs, therefore, extend, while the hind limbs are flexed (fig. 2.3) (Pollock and Davis 1927; Pacella and Barrera 1940; McCouch, Deering, and Ling 1951).

d) Extended Neck Response. Suspension of the animal held only at the mastoid region causes flexion of both hind and forelimbs and of the spinal column, or limb extension and opisthotonus at a later age (fig. 2.2).

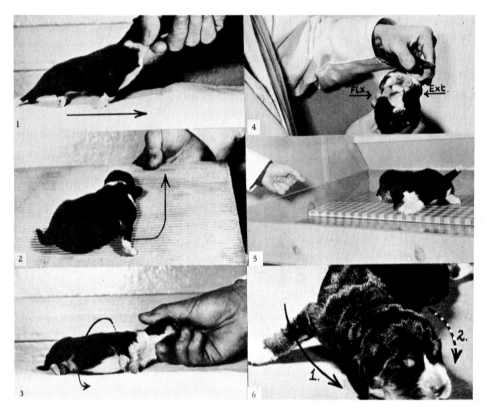

Fig. 2.1. Rooting reflex (1), negative geotaxis (2), and body-righting reflex (3) in 3-day-old pup. Magnus reflex in 5-day-old pup (4). Visual cliff test in 4-week-old pup (5). Head movements from side to side during locomotion in newborn pup (6).

e) Hind- and Forelimb Placing and Supporting Responses.[1] Lowering the blindfolded animal (or blind neonate), which is held securely by the forelimbs, onto a tabletop elicits reactions in the hind limbs; on contact with the tabletop, the limbs: (1) are positioned by the animal (placing response) and (2) are extended to bear the weight of the body (supporting response). These are the hind limb placing and supporting responses; forelimb responses are elicited by similarly lowering the blind-folded animal, suspended by the hind limbs onto a tabletop. Placing responses may also be demonstrated by holding the dorsum of the forefeet of the pup against the edge of a table, or by placing the chin on the edge of the table; one foot and then the other is raised and placed upon the tabletop (figs. 2.3, 2.4). Hopping responses,[2]

[1] First shown by Bard 1933 to be dependent upon neocortical function.
[2] Ibid.

which are essentially placing responses, may be elicited by holding the animal with only the hind or forefeet in contact with the ground and then twisting the body rapidly to one side; the limbs are then quickly replaced to maintain equal distribution of body weight (figs. 2.3, 2.4). The animal must be blindfolded to eliminate visual placing reactions.

f) Landau Reflex or Seal Posture (Bahrs 1927). With the animal held out horizontally by grasping it beneath the axillae, extension of the head, neck, spine, and hind limbs occurs with variable forelimb flexion; fixation of gaze occurs at a certain age (fig. 2.4).

g) Righting Response. If the animal is placed on its side in lateral recumbency, it will get up onto all fours (fig. 2.1).

h) Equilibratory Responses (Thomas 1940). The ability to balance when subjected to anteroposterior and and side-to-side tilting on a seesaw can be used to evaluate equilibratory responses (fig. 2.4).

i) Negative Geotactic Response (James 1956). The neonate will turn and crawl upward if placed head downward on an inclined plane (fig. 2.1).

In general, these reflexes maintain posture and control and coordinate locomotion.

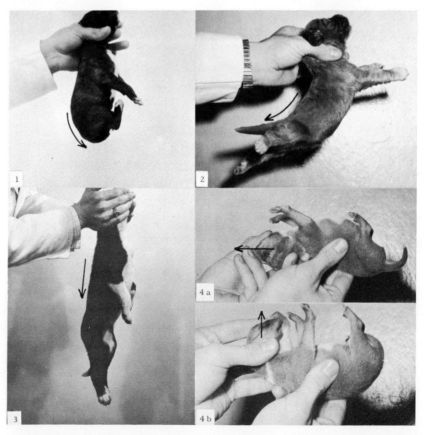

Fig. 2.2. Extended neck response at 2 (1), 12 (2), and 49 (3) days of age, showing periods of flexor and extensor dominance and normotonia. Note extreme opisthotonus in (2). 4a, b, influence of head position (labyrinthine effect) on distribution of fore- and hind limbs at 3 days of age (cf. similar effects in decerebrate adult cat, Pollock and Davis 1927).

2. Superficial Reflex Responses

Two important superficial reflexes, the panniculus and the abdominal, have been studied in the adult dog (Rijnberk and Ten Cate 1939; Ten Cate 1952; Fox 1963*a*). Superficial reflexes are those which may be elicited by stimulating certain parts of the skin and are, therefore, exteroceptive sensory responses; the function of some may be to promote survival and, under appropriate stimulation, to initiate innate behavioral mechanisms. Stroking the skin of the back elicits a unilateral or bilateral contraction of the panniculus carnosus muscle, and similar stimulation (or pinching) along the side of the body, in addition to the panniculus reflex, elicits flexion of the trunk (Galant's reflex). The abdominal reflex is seen as a brief contraction of the abdominal muscles following tactile stimulation of the abdomen.

a) Orofacial and Craniocephalic Responses

1. Palpebral Blink Reflex. Following tactile stimulation of the eyelids, the eyelids are closed, or if the eyelids have not yet separated, a marked palpebral contraction can be seen accompanied by narrowing of the palpebral fissure.

2. Labial Reflex. Movements of the lips are stimulated by stroking with a finger; a positive response was seen as a contraction of the angle of the mouth followed

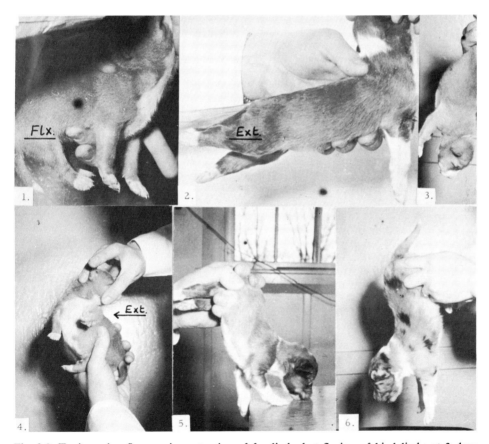

Fig. 2.3. Tonic neck reflex causing extension of forelimbs but flexion of hind limbs at 3 days (1) and extension at 12 days (2). Forelimb visual placing negative at 7 days (3) and positive at 28 days (6). Positive chin-contact placing reaction at 10 days (5). Magnus reflex causing extension of forelimb at 5 days of age (4).

by orientation of the head toward the side stimulated. The finger may be seized and sucked.[3]

3. Rooting Reflex. Bilateral stimulation of the head with the hand cupped around the muzzle stimulates the animal to crawl forward (fig. 2.1).

4. Auriculonasocephalic Reflex (Thomas, Chesni, and Dargassies 1961).— Stimulation by stroking one side of the face or behind the ear causes head-turning toward the side stimulated.

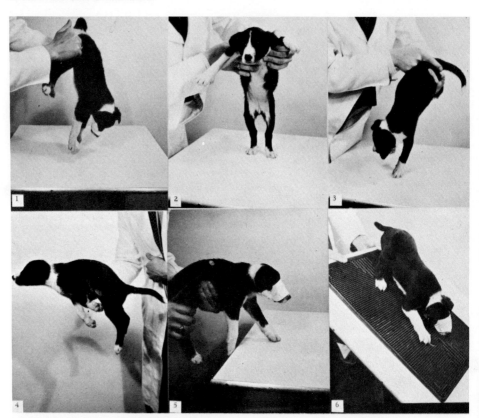

Fig. 2.4. Responses in 7-wk-old pup; note that subject is blindfolded to eliminate visual cues in some tests. Fore- and hind-limb placing and hopping (1), (2), and (3). Landau reflex (4), forelimb placing (5), and equilibratory response to anteroposterior tilting (6).

b) Cutaneous Body Responses

1. Galant's Reflex (Thomas, Chesni, and Dargassies 1961). Tickling the flank with a blunt probe results in flexion of the body at the site of stimulation and head-turning toward the side stimulated.

2. Panniculus or Cutaneous Muscle Reflex (Rijnberk and Ten Cate 1939). Stroking the skin of the back causes a brisk contraction of the integument.

3. Scratch Reflex. Tickling behind the ear causes scratching movements in the hind limb on the same side, with variable positioning and rotation of the head and lateral flexion of the spinal cord.

---

[3] A number of studies have been conducted to evaluate the effects of hunger and satiation on sucking behavior in pups, notably by Ross, Fisher, and King (1957), James (1957), and Stanley and Bacon (1963).

4. Abdominal Reflex (Rijnberk and Ten Cate 1939) (animal in prone position). Stroking the abdomen with a blunt instrument causes reflex contraction of the abdominal muscles.

5. Nociceptive Withdrawal Reflex. Pinching the digital web causes withdrawal of the limb, with variable distress vocalization and avoidance behavior.

c) Anogenital Responses

1. Superficial Anal Reflex. Tactile stimulation of the external anal sphincter with a stiff bristle causes contraction of this sphincter. Lowering of the tail over the anus (tail-drop reflex) frequently follows.

2. Reflex Urination. Stimulation by tickling the external genitalia produces reflex urination. Similarly, but less reliably, stimulation of the anus causes defecation.

These reflexes generally facilitate exploratory (contactual) behavior, feeding, and elimination, and also serve a protective (exteroceptive) sensory function, for example, pain withdrawal response and avoidance behavior.

3. Deep Reflexes

a) Patella Reflex (animal in supine position). Tapping the patellar tendon causes the knee-jerk response.

b) Abdominal Proprioceptive Reflex (Ten Cate 1952) (animal in supine position). Tapping the abdominal muscles near their tendons of insertion at the xiphoid region causes reflex contraction of these muscles.

4. Responses Involving Organs of Special Sense

a) Visual

1. Photomotor Reflex. Following sudden photic stimulation directed into one or both eyes, a palpebral blink reflex is elicited.

2. Pupillary Reflex. Sudden photic stimulation causes contraction of the pupil; an ophthalmoscope was used for both stimulation and evaluation of the response.

3. Visual Orientation. When the subject is placed in a darkened room and stimulated by a flashing light placed laterally in the visual field, the head is turned toward the source of stimulation.

4. Visual Cliff Reaction. A withdrawal response from a ledge simulating a cliff-drop (depth perception) is a positive (avoidance) reaction. The "drop" is covered by a sheet-glass tabletop (fig. 2.1) (Walk and Gibson 1961; Fox 1965*f*).

5. Visual Fixation and Following. The pup will look at and visually track the movement of small objects such as falling pieces of cotton, or the observer or littermates, if they are present within its field of vision.

6. Visual Placing Reaction. With the eyes uncovered, the pup is held by the hind limbs and lowered onto a tabletop; the head is raised and forelimbs extended to make contact with the solid surface (fig. 2.3).

b) Auditory

1. Startle Reflex. A sudden abduction of the limbs, flexion of the head, and blinking of the eyes is seen after the pup is startled by a loud noise (hand clap or Galton's dog whistle).

2. Auditory Orientation. Similar to visual orientation, the head is turned toward a sound stimulus originating from one side of the animal (Galton's dog whistle).

Results

Data are presented as average reflex responses and where pertinent, extreme variability in these responses will be discussed.

The neonate dog would frequently fall asleep during examination, and gentle shaking was necessary to wake it up so that the desired response could be tested. Random voluntary movements by the animal could easily mask the response; so several attempts might be needed to elicit a normal reflex. When they occurred, most responses of the neonate were strong and stereotyped. Inhibition due to fear reactions did not occur in the young puppy, for these higher emotional reactions are poorly developed in the neonate.

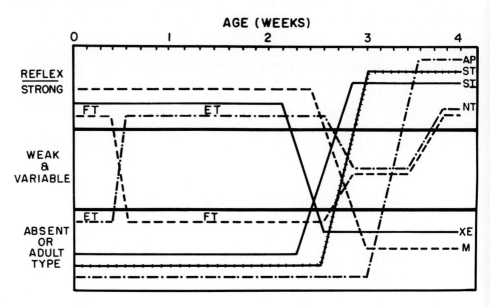

Fig. 2.5. Development of motor responses. *FT* = flexor tone. *ET* = extensor tone. *NT* = normal tone. *SI* = sitting upright. *ST* = standing upright. *XE* = crossed extensor reflex. *M* = Magnus reflex. *AP* = adult postures.

The developmental changes in the categories of reflexes will be described in relation to periods of neural development, and justification of them will be established as the results are presented.

1. *Motor Responses*

Period 1 (0–5 days) (fig. 2.5). The crossed extensor, Magnus, and tonic neck reflexes could be elicited immediately after birth and throughout this period. The righting response was present at birth, whereas the rooting reflex and negative geotactic responses were easier to demonstrate as locomotor ability improved, up to 4 days of age. Muscle tone was determined by manipulating the limbs and observing the posture assumed by the limbs and spinal column in the extended neck position. At birth muscle tone was flaccid, but as independent respiration was established, muscle tone increased rapidly, with dominance of the flexor muscles over the extensors. Consequently, reflex extension of the limbs during stimulation of the crossed extensor and Magnus reflexes was reduced, whereas flexion of the opposite limbs was increased; flexion of the hind limbs was marked during tonic neck stimulation. Hyperkinesis (random motor movements or twitches) was seen affecting the body and face during this period, and was associated with activated sleep (see chap. 3).

Forelimb contactual placing reactions were first seen as weak and variable responses from between 2 and 3 days onward. Lateral flexion of the trunk was marked when the animal was suspended by the hind limbs and tended to mask the forelimb placing response. When the dog was held under the axillae in the Landau or seal posture flexion of the hind limbs and spine occurred, with variable extension of the forelimbs.

Period 2 (5–18 days). The crossed extensor reflex could no longer be elicited at 18 days of age. The Magnus reflex ceased to affect the forelimbs after 14 days, but still affected the hind limbs at 18 days. Further changes in muscle tone occurred at the onset of this period. Extensor dominance causing hind-limb extension and opisthotonus (extension of the spine) persisted until 18 days of age. Caudal extension of the hind limbs was marked in the tonic neck position. Gross hyperextension with extreme hypertonia causing postural changes were seen in one litter of spaniels and two litters of shelties. Opisthotonus and pointing of the hind feet were marked. This was considered a normal variable of the period of extensor dominance.

Forelimb supporting reactions were first seen between 6 and 10 days, and hind-limb supporting reactions between 11 and 15 days as weak and variable responses, just after the emergence of hind-limb placing reactions at 8 days. When the dog was held by the hind limbs to elicit forelimb supporting, head raising and opisthotonus were observed. Hyperkinesis was restricted mainly to the face during this time.

Period 3 (18–28 days). The Magnus reflex ceased to affect the hind limbs by 21 days. Extensor muscle dominance in the hind limbs rapidly weakened from 18 days onward, giving rise to normal adultlike distribution of muscle tone between the flexor and extensor muscles. As reciprocal muscle tone became more evenly distributed, motor strength increased equally after the onset of normotonia. This was determined by passive flexion and extension of the hind limbs.

Limb positions in the extended and tonic neck positions were adultlike at 20 days, but it was not until 26 days that both flexor and extensor strengths (determined by passive flexion and extension of the hind limbs) were great enough to permit a more versatile range of locomotor activities.

Sitting upright on the forelimbs was seen at 20 days and preceded standing, which occurred at 21 days of age. Hind-limb tremor was marked at this time, indicating weakness in muscle tone and in reciprocal muscular coordination.

Maintenance of posture (equilibration) when subjected to seesaw tilting was initially poor, and the blindfolded animal could not maintain an upright posture when tilted enteroposteriorly (occipitofrontal) until between 25 and 28 days of age. The ability to remain upright when subjected to lateral (bitemporal) tilting was poorly developed throughout this period.

The Landau position elicited only weak response during this period.

When held upside down and dropped (blindfolded), the righting response in the air as determined by the animal's ability to land on all fours was seen as a weak and variable response at this time.

Facial hyperkinesis disappeared completely by 4 wk of age, indicating that the subjects remained alert and did not pass into activated sleep during observations.

Period 4 (28 days onward). This period was marked by the transition from variable locomotor responses to adultlike postural and equilibratory abilities. Not until 5–6 wk of age was it possible for the animal to maintain an upright posture when subjected to bitemporal tilting. The righting response became more efficient and these adult abilities improved during this final period of development. Similarly, the hopping reaction improved and all earlier motor responses were more rapidly elicited. In the Landau position the classical position of extension of the neck, spine, tail, and hind legs was seen, together with fixation of the gaze and variable flexion of the forelimbs.

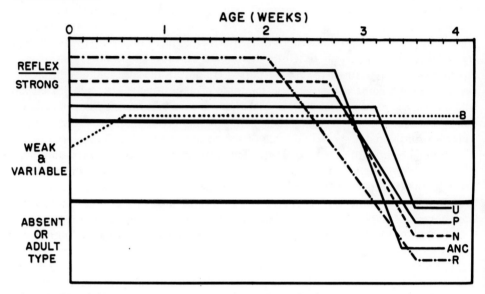

Fig. 2.6. Superficial (cutaneous) responses. U = reflex urination. P = panniculus reflex. N = nociceptive withdrawal reflex. ANC = auriculonasocephalic reflex. R = rooting reflex. B = palpebral blink reflex (tactile).

2. Superficial Responses

Period 1 (0–4 days) (fig. 2.6). The orofacial and craniocephalic responses to stimulating certain areas of the head were seen immediately after birth. The palpebral blink response to a light touch on the eyelids was present at birth, but the latency of response was much greater than in the adult, a slow palpebral contraction occurring some time after tactile stimulation.

Head turning was slow when the auriculonasocephalic reflex was tested. Toward the end of this period these reflexes were easier to evoke and the responses were stronger.

Constant stimulation of the head, eliciting the rooting reflex, resulted in forward progression, and one newborn pup covered a distance of over 50 yd on a turntable without any obvious fatigue or adverse effects.

The panniculus reflex was easily elicited and the response was seen as a generalized contraction of the cutaneous muscle.

At birth, the nociceptive withdrawal response to pinching a hind foot was slow and sustained; squirming, side-to-side flexion of the trunk, and prolonged distress vocalization were characteristic of the newborn dog.

Reflex urination was easily elicited by stroking the external genitalia; stimulation of respiration (increased rate and depth of ventilation) was also seen when this area was stimulated during this period.

Galant's reflex was strong during this time, stimulation of the flank causing considerable flexion of the body toward the side stimulated. The scratch reflex was easily demonstrated, although effector movements of the homolateral hind limb were very weak.

The abdominal reflex was difficult to elicit during this period because the dominance of flexor tone caused abdominal tension which tended to mask the response.

Period 2 (5–18 days). Few changes occurred in the superficial reflexes during this second period.

Reflex stimulation of respiration was no longer seen when the anogenital region was stimulated.

All craniocephalic and orofacial responses were more vigorous as locomotor ability improved during this time. Head turning and orientation toward the side stimulated were rapid, and during elicitation of the labial reflex the finger might be seized and sucked. Hind-limb movements when the scratch reflex was stimulated were stronger.

The rooting reflex was weaker and more variable from about 14 days of age onward; this was associated with opening of the eyes and development of the ability to crawl backward. Strong rooting responses were obtained if the animal was made fearful of the situation, for example, by pinching the tail or foot. This escape behavior was first seen during this period; nociceptive withdrawal responses after stimulating a hind foot caused less lateral flexion, and vocalization was less protracted. The animal would attempt to escape from the situation.

The abdominal reflex was easily demonstrated at this time, for increased extensor tone caused some relaxation of the abdominal muscles when the animal was held in the prone position.

Period 3 (18–28 days). The superficial reflexes during this period were often difficult to elicit; variable, strong, or weak responses were recorded on the same day in the same animal.

The labial reflex disappeared by 21 days, but in some undernourished pups (not included in the normal data records) it persisted until 5–6 wk of age, as did the auriculonasocephalic and rooting reflexes, which normally disappeared after 3 wk.

Galant's reflex disappeared by 3 wk of age.

The panniculus reflex was less generalized and negative results were seen if the animal was emotionally disturbed at this time.

Reflex urination after stimulating the external genitalia became weak and variable at 3 wk and by 4 wk could no longer be evoked.[4]

Avoidance behavior was marked when the pain withdrawal reflex was stimulated.

Period 4 (28 days onward). This period was characterized by the complete disappearance (or inhibition) of several superficial reflexes which were an integral part of neonatal behavior. The labial, rooting, auriculonasocephalic, and Galant's

[4] Bradley and Wright (1966) report that in the neonate rabbit, the urinary bladder is functionally isolated during the first 2 days of life, and only later becomes integrated into the lumbosacral spinal cord. By 2 wks of age the bladder is no longer capable of an organized reflex response if the central pathways are severed.

reflexes were no longer demonstrable. Other superficial reflexes, notably the nociceptive withdrawal, abdominal, and panniculus reflex responses, were less generalized and less stereotyped. Each response was adultlike in character, for both localization of response and variability due to emotional reactions were observed. The abdominal reflex was present in every dog at 7 wk of age, but was not found in the adult dog, confirming the observations of Ten Cate (1952). The exact time when this reflex disappeared was not determined in this investigation.

3. *Deep Reflexes*

Little change in the type of response was observed when the patellar or proprioceptive abdominal reflexes were stimulated.

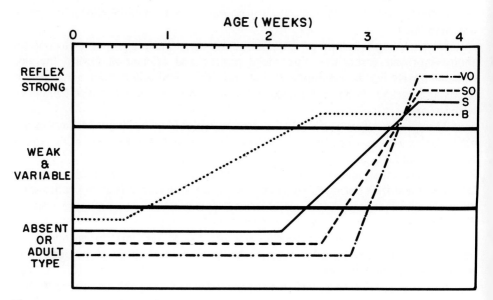

Fig. 2.7. Sensory organ responses. VO = visual orientation. SO = sound orientation. S = startle reflex to sound. B = blink reflex to light.

Weak or negative responses were seen at birth during the postpartum period of flaccidity. During the periods of flexor dominance (0–5 days) and extensor dominance (5–18 days) the excursion of the knee-jerk movement was restricted, owing to this disequilibrium of muscle tone. When weak normotonia was present (18–28 days) the knee-jerk was almost adultlike in character and was easily elicited. From around 28 days onward the reflex was similar to that of the adult animal. The proprioceptive abdominal reflex could not be reliably elicited until after the period of flexor dominance had subsided so that the animal could be placed on its back and the ventral surface exposed without undue pressure on the abdominal wall. No developmental changes were ascertained in this reflex.

4. *Organs of Special Sense (Visual and Auditory Responses)* (fig. 2.7)

Period 1 (0–5 days). No sensory responses of the audiovisual system could be elicited until 2–4 days of age, when the palpebral blink response to light (photomotor reflex) was first seen as a slow and easily fatigued response with a long latency.

Period 2 (5–18 days). Although the eyes began to open between 10 and 16 days, the photomotor reflex was not adultlike until 18 days of age. Weak auditory startle responses were seen at 18 days when the neonate was asleep, but were variable and absent when the animal was awake or feeding.

Period 3 (18–28 days). This period was marked by the emergence of positive orientation responses to visual and auditory stimuli which were strong at 25 days of age and adultlike thereafter.

Period 4 (28 days onward). Visual cliff reactions were first seen reliably at 26–28 days of age; visual and auditory recognition of littermates and observer occurred in association with the emergence of approach and avoidance behavior.

No significant differences in the above responses were found in the different breeds studied. Slight variations ($\pm$ 1 or 2 days) in the onset of the period of increased extensor tone, eye opening, positive visual cliff responses, and ability to assume an upright posture were seen among different breeds and different litters of the same strain. As these variations differed only slightly, the average figures presented in the results are considered a reliable index of normality (chart 2.1). Recent observations on locomotor development in Afghan hound puppies indicate that dogs of this breed (and possibly other breeds originating from the Mesopotamian greyhound type) attain greater motor coordination by 6 wk of age and are able to run, jump, and pivot on the hind limbs with greater ability than those breeds studied in this investigation.

To summarize these results the main reflex changes were recorded during the following periods: *Period 1* (0–5 days): disappearance of flexor dominance and reflex changes in respiration following cutaneous stimulation. *Period 2* (5–18 days): 5–13 days—appearance of adult type postural reflexes; 15–18 days—disappearance of crossed extensor and Magnus reflexes. *Period 3* (18–28 days): disappearance of rooting and reflex urination. Appearance of adult sensory (startle, visual cliff) reactions and motor activities.

Discussion and Conclusions

Changes in the nature of several reflexes in the dog are closely related to alterations in behavior patterns during development and are seen during four relatively discrete periods. During the first period, 0–5 days, there are changes in muscle tone especially, which may be related to a predominance of alpha (flexor) rigidity in the newborn, as shown in the kitten by Skoglund (1960). He found that the tonic stretch reflex (gamma rigidity or extensor tone) develops in a proximodistal direction in the limbs, in the forelimbs before the hind limbs, and thus in a craniocaudal direction. Buller, Eccles, and Eccles (1960) found that in the newborn kitten the slow and fast muscles of the hind limb are equally slow, but by 5 wk the fast muscles attain adult speeds of contraction and relaxation, whereas the slow muscles quicken more gradually over the first 5 wk, then progressively slow to the adult condition at 16–20 wk. They also observed that there is considerable development of skeletal muscles independent of differentiating influences from the spinal cord.

The effect of head turning on the forelimbs when eliciting the Magnus reflex disappears some time before the effect on the hind limbs disappears. Forelimb placing and supporting reactions (animal blindfolded) also appear before any hind-limb reactions are seen. Decerebration of the newborn cat (Windle 1950) and dog (see

Reflex response

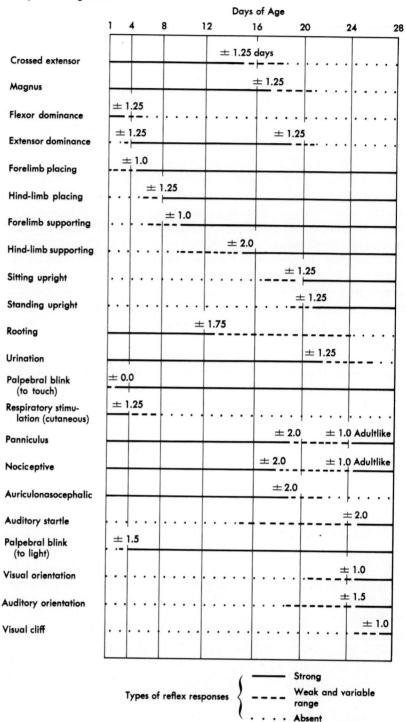

Chart 2.1. Developmental changes in reflexes shown as averaged range of variability (in ± days) of appearance or disappearance.

chap. 4) causes rigidity only in the forelimbs. These points imply that neural maturation of the forelimbs precedes that of the hind limbs. Sitting upright on the forelimbs
occurs just before standing, and progression at this time may be effected by walking
on the forelimbs and dragging the hind limbs. These observations may be correlated
with myelination of the spinal cord of the dog, which attains relative maturity between 5 and 6 wk of age (see chap. 4); the cervical region matures earlier than the
lumbar region, the corticospinal tracts being the last to myelinate, as in the kitten
(Langworthy 1929). Skoglund (1960a) reports that in the kitten the activity of
muscle-stretch receptors progresses from a phasic to a tonic response, and the lack of
gamma efferent stimuli in the neonate accounts for poor supporting reactions and
erratic and ataxic gait. By 17 days, a relatively mature tonic pattern is seen, at
which time reflex development in the cat (Fox 1968) corresponds closely to that
at 28 days in the pup, the onset of period 4. It would be of interest to determine
ontogenetically the onset of reciprocal innervation (Sherrington 1947), and of
Renshaw cell inhibition of tonus (which removes the resistance to phasic responses,
Eccles et al. 1961), and the development of presynaptic inhibition (Eccles 1964).

Alterations in muscle tone and posture with age have been described in the
human infant (Ingram 1959); primary and secondary flexor and extensor changes
were recognized, resembling similar phenomena here described in the dog. The
initial period of flexor dominance in the human is thought to be a residuum of postural behavior assumed in the intrauterine environment (Gessell 1945). Electro-
convulsively induced seizures in young mice at different ages (Coulombre 1950)
cause comparable postural changes in both fore-,and hind limbs; so similar periods
of extensor and flexor dominance may well exist in this species also. No significant
changes in reflexes occur during the second period, 5–18 days, except that changes
in respiration accompanying cutaneous stimulation disappear and feeding and orientation reflexes become stronger.

Slow reflex responses during periods 1 and 2 may be due to slow conductivity of
nerve impulses, for hypomyelination is a common feature of some pathways of the
peripheral nervous system of newborn animals. Other neural pathways may be well
developed where development coincides with functional activity at birth or shortly
thereafter. The facial nerve in man, for example, shows good myelination of the
labial branches concerned with ingestion, but the nerves controlling facial expression
are poorly myelinated (Golubova 1958).

During the period of variability of response to auditory stimuli, negative results
are seen, especially when the animals are feeding or awake and actively investigating
the nest. In the human, similar activities may cause inhibition of the auditory startle
reflex (MacKeith 1961).

The final period of neurologic development (from 28 days onward) is marked
by the emergence of adultlike sensory capacities and motor abilities; primitive
(neonatal) reflexes disappear as earlier behavior patterns are supplanted by more
complex patterns of behavior. Psychological changes also occur for inhibition of
reflexes, and fear responses are well developed by 4 wk of age. Adultlike electroencephalographic traces appear at this time (Charles and Fuller 1956; see also
chap. 3), together with very rapid development of the central nervous system, stability of conditioning (Cornwell and Fuller 1961), and visual and auditory orientation responses; and, according to Parry (1953), structurofunctional maturation
of the retina occurs between 5 and 6 wk of age.

The behavioral significance of these reflexes may be interpreted in relation to the needs and activities of the animal at a given age, modified by and adapted to a particular environment. The neonatal types of behavioral mechanisms may be linked with these reflexes where a continuum of reflexively evoked motor activity is concerned with orientation of the newborn toward the mother, location of the nipple, and ingestion (Ingram 1962).

When changes in the nature of sensory and motor reflexes occur, alterations and modifications of earlier neonatal behavior patterns also take place. Orofacial and craniocephalic responses are less stereotyped, and as feeding becomes more independent these responses weaken and eventually disappear. Tactile, thermal, and geotactic orienting responses weaken as audiovisual acuity improves and supersedes these more primitive mechanisms. Reflexes concerned, therefore, in orientating the animal and enabling it to find shelter and food are superseded by more advanced and maternally independent behavior patterns.

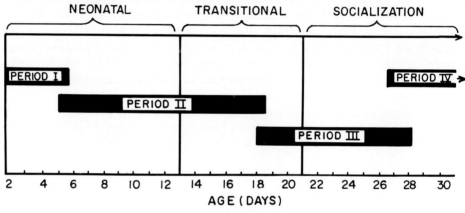

NEUROLOGICAL AND BEHAVIORAL PERIODS OF DEVELOPMENT IN THE DOG.

Fig. 2.8. Changes in periods of reflex development tend to precede changes in overt behavior observed by Scott and Marston (1950).

Scott (1958*b*), in describing the behavioral development of the dog, considers that development proceeds through fairly well defined periods of behavior, but that there is considerable overlap between the termination of one period of behavior and onset of another. These periods of development have been divided into neonatal (0–13 days), transitional (13–19 days), socialization (19 days to 12 wk), and juvenile (12 wk onward). Overt behavior is restricted by the organism's sensory and locomotor capacities; the emergence of new capacities allows the onset of new types of behavior. In the present study, the behaviorally determined periods of development, as described by Scott (1958*b*), were assessed neurologically. In general, the primary patterns of neurologic change also seem to form relatively discrete periods which slightly precede the appearance of Scott's (1958*b*) patterns of overt behavioral development (fig. 2.8).

During the neonatal period described by Scott, behavior is mainly concerned with neonatal nutrition and maintenance of body temperature. This postnatal phase of neurologic stability, here designated period 2, precedes the onset of the transitional period of behavior. The transitional period, according to Scott, commences with the opening of the eyes and terminates at approximately 3 wk of age when the startle reflex appears, marking the onset of the critical period of socialization, when a rapid development of motor, sensory, and psychological capacities occurs, so that primary social relationships may be established.

Neurologically, period 3 emerges before the onset of the socialization period, indicating that neurological maturation occurs before sensory capacities and motor abilities can be integrated and expressed behaviorally. Period 4, which commences at approximately 28 days of age, is the final neurologic period of development, where sensory and motor capacities reach relative maturity.

TABLE 2.1

RELATIONSHIP BETWEEN BEHAVIORAL PERIODS OF
DEVELOPMENT AND REFLEX DEVELOPMENT

Period[a]	Duration[a] (days)	Behavior[a]	Reflexes
I. Neonatal	0–14	Neonatal nutrition	Change from fetal to neonatal responses; flexion-extension of hind limbs; Magnus reflex; rooting reflex; crossed extensor reflex; reflex urination
II. Transitional	14–21	Unstable conditioning; eyes open (vision poor); no startle reflex to sound; transition to motor sensory and psychological capacities of adult	Neonatal reflexes predominate; slight variability due to central inhibition and fear responses
III. Socialization	21–84	Stable conditioning; startle reflex to sound; positive audiovisual orientation reflex and visual cliff response; formation of primary social relationships (notices observer, play and fear responses, etc.); weaning	Neonatal reflexes disappear; no reflex urination and rooting reflex weakens; Magnus and crossed extensor reflexes disappear, adult reflexes remain and fore- and hind-limb supporting reactions become stronger
IV. Juvenile	84 onward	Maturation of locomotor abilities and equilibratory responses; growth and development of motor skills	Adult reflexes and responses

[a] After Scott and Marston 1950.

Summary

Neurological Development. Changes occurred in a spectrum of reflexes employed in the investigation as indicators of neurological development. During certain phases of development it was found possible to group these changes into four arbitrary periods which preceded the behaviorally determined periods of development described by Scott and Marston (1950). These observations, which were correlated with earlier work concerning the emergence of adult EEG patterns, stable conditioning, morphological development of the cerebral cortex, and behaviorally determined periods of development, are summarized in table 2.1. These latter correlated points will be elaborated upon in subsequent chapters.

Reflex Components and Development of Behavior Patterns in the Dog

Introduction

Fuller and Fox (1968) and Fox (1971*a*) have provided a useful overview of several aspects of canine behavior, supplementing more specific texts by Scott and Fuller (1965), Fox (1965*a*), and Burns and Fraser (1966), dealing respectively with genetics (breed differences) and development of social behavior and behavioral and morphological abnormalities. Scott's earlier studies (1950) (see also Scott and Fuller 1965) comparing the social behavior patterns of dogs and wolves illustrate the usefulness of systematic comparative sociobiological studies in evaluating the influence of evolutionary (i.e., domestication) and phylogenetic factors. Matthew (1930), Zeuner (1963), Reed (1959), and Degerbol (1927) have discussed the phylogeny of the Canidae and the archeological evidence for the origins of the

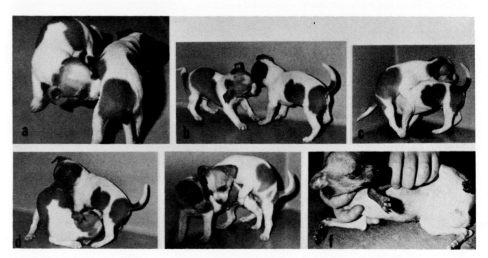

Fig. 2.9. Behavior patterns in 6-wk-old Chihuahua pups (*a–e*) and submissive hind-leg raising and urination in 12-wk-old pup (*f*). Genital-olfactory investigation, both pups submissive (*a*); lip-nuzzling approach (*b*); mounting, clasping, and pelvic movements as precocial sexual activities in (*c*) and (*e*); genital-olfactory investigation showing dominant-subordinate posturind.

domesticated dog. Vaulk (1953) has made some interesting observations on the reactions of different breeds to prey-stimuli, and concludes that domestication can dramatically modify certain instinctual reactions. As has been emphasized by Scott and Fuller (1965), Fox (1965*a*, 1971*a*), and Burns and Fraser (1966), domestication and selection have either enhanced or reduced various instinctual reactions and behavior patterns in the dog, such as aggression, herding, and tracking (trail-following) abilities, etc., in different breeds.

Kleiman (1966, 1967) and Fox (1969*a, b*, 1971*b*) have reported some preliminary studies on social behavior and scent marking in the Canidae.[5] Urinary

[5] Earlier studies of comparative interest include Schenkel's (1947), Murie's (1940), Crisler's (1956), Young and Goldman's (1944), and Rutter and Pimlott's (1968) wolf studies, Young and Jackson's (1951) coyote work, and Tembrock's (1957) studies of the fox. See Fox (1971*a*) for comparative ontogenetic studies.

pheromones and anal gland secretions are particularly important in the social life of Canidae; however, the complexity and elaboration of social gestures or expressions is determined to a great extent by the social organization of the species. More solitary Canidae have less elaborate social behavior patterns and rely more on communication by sound and smell, whereas those species that live in groups and have complex social relationships have more complicated visual signals or ritualized species-specific gestures.

ONTOGENY OF CANINE ETHOGRAM

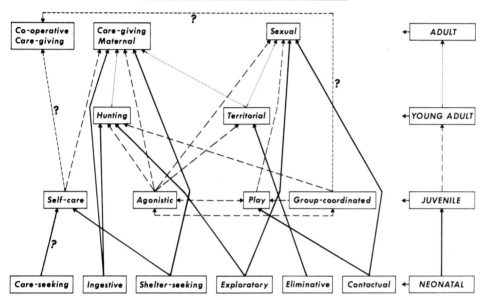

Fig. 2.10. Theoretical schema of interrelationships between behavior patterns during postnatal development. Neonatal behavior patterns composed of several reflexes (see table 2.2) form a basis upon which further behavior patterns are elaborated. For example, group-coordinated (allelomimetic) activities, as in play and play-fighting in the juvenile period of socialization, may facilitate the development of group activities such as hunting. Early eliminative behavior develops into territorial marking and lair-dwelling behavior (defecation in one specific area). Exploratory, agonistic, contactual, play, and territorial behavior are associated with later-developing sexual behavior. Agonistic patterns accompany later-developing hunting, territorial, sexual, and maternal (defense of young) behavior. (Solid and broken lines indicate approximate time of emergence and integration of behavior patterns.)

Vivid descriptions of agonistic reactions or expressions of dogs and wolves have been given by Lorenz (1952, 1954). These various expressive gestures involving the face, ears, tail, general body posture, and piloerection, especially over the base of the neck (hackles) and rump, are schematically represented (fig. 2.11) as an ongoing sequence and constitute a means of postural communication. Baring the teeth and "showing eye," are common aggressive expressions; the extent to which the jaws are opened may vary considerably (Fox 1969a, 1971a); an extreme gape may represent an agonistic display, and is particularly seen between two opposing dogs in adjacent cages (fig. 2.14). Similar "yawning" displays have been observed in the baboon by De Vore (1965).

Development of Behavior Patterns

The following observations are drawn from a detailed study of the development of behavior patterns in the dog under laboratory conditions. Subjects were observed from birth onward, being kept in nest boxes with runs, and were also observed outdoors in the "open-field" situation and in a behavior arena equipped with one-way windows.

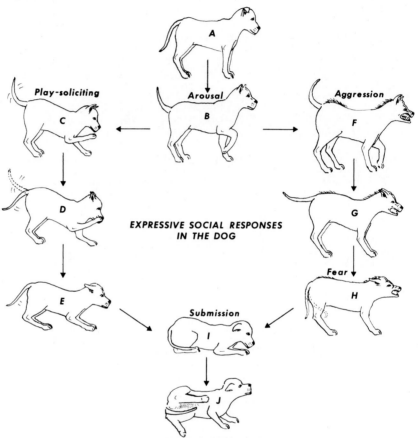

Fig. 2.11. Schema depicting gross body postures and expressions in the dog during various emotional states. A common "ambivalence" is seen when the dog is in a strange or novel environment; the behavior oscillates between *b* and *e* or *i,* in that the dog alternately "bobs" up and down. This transient "uncertain" reaction is subsequently followed by exploration or inhibition (even reactive sleep, see chap. 5, p. 219). Qualitative changes in behavior include: *a,* at rest; *b,* alert, may "point"; *c,* play-soliciting, tail erect and wagged, paw raising, may jump up and bark, movements are exaggerated; *d,* slightly more submissive, a common greeting posture to master or "pack leader." The wagging tail is semierect and neck may be extended and head lowered and moved from side to side as dog approaches. Also there may be some "inguinal presentation"; *e,* slightly more submissive, tail and ears lower and generally greater passivity; *f,* aggressive display, with erect ears and tail, fixed gaze and "show of eye," stiff-legged gait, lip curl, and snarl, with growling and occasional tail wagging; *g,* less confident aggressive expression, with weight distribution shifting to hind legs (contrasting with even distribution in *f* and predominance of weight in forelimbs in *c* and *d*), and lowering of ears and tail, may lick lips; *h,* increasing fearfulness, with less piloerection, flattening of ears and tail, and less display of eye and teeth; *i,* submissive posture (inhibition), which may be followed by lateral recumbency, inguinal presentation, submissive urination, and whining vocalization.

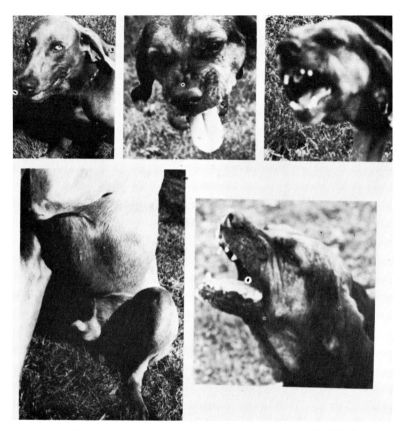

Fig. 2.12. Some social responses toward humans, showing various "smiling" expressions (in some cases closely resembling agonistic display of the teeth and wrinkling of the muzzle) and penile erection on being handled. Illustration at top left shows submissive grin.

TABLE 2.2

REFLEX UNIT COMPONENTS OF NEONATAL BEHAVIOR PATTERNS IN THE DOG

Behavior Pattern	Reflex or Unit Components
Care-seeking	Distress vocalization; pain; rooting
Ingestive	Labial; sucking; swallowing; gustatory; olfactory
Shelter-seeking	Rooting; +thermotaxis; +thigmotaxis
Exploratory	+Thermotaxis; +thigmotaxis; −geotaxis; olfactory; locomotor (placing, stepping, body-righting); proprioception; statokinesis
Eliminative	Urination, defecation
Contactual	Rooting; "perceptual homeostatis" (thermoregulation); +thermotaxis; +thigmotaxis

The pup is frequently born within its fetal membranes. The bitch will lick these off and ingest them and also sever the umbilical cord with the carnassial teeth (see also Bleicher 1962; Menzel and Menzel 1953; and Rheingold 1963, for further observations of maternal behavior in the dog). Attention is not focused specifically on the pup at this time, for the bitch will lick her vulva and also any fetal fluids that are on the ground. The moment of emergence of the fetus is accompanied by the bitch's orienting toward the vulva and licking the fetus, membranes, and fluids (see fig. 2.15). This immediate maternal response at the time of parturition is undoubtedly based upon previous experience of cleaning the anogenital region, that is, self-care. As soon as the pup is stimulated by the tongue of the bitch during removal of the fetal membranes, it responds violently by squirming from side to side, and will vocalize as soon as spontaneous respiration is established and excess fetal fluids escape from the upper respiratory tract. Before this initial stimulation

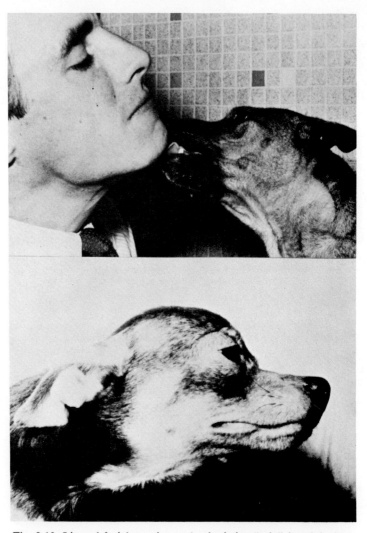

Fig. 2.13. Lingual-facial greeting and submissive "grin" in adult dogs

by the bitch, the pup will lie with little or no spontaneous movement, provided it is born with the fetal membranes intact. Tactile stimulation by the mother subsequently evokes a "mass response" and the pup will squirm, right itself, crawl (rooting reflex), and after a short period of irregular gasping respiration, commence to breathe regularly and to vocalize (mewing). The severed umbilical cord continues to exude blood for some time, and this area is licked intensively by the mother. Stimulation of this area reflexively stimulates respiration. Other parts of the body are licked also, and especially when the face and dorsum of the head are stimulated

Fig. 2.14. Agonistic expressions, including threat-growl with baring of front teeth and pupil dilatation; extreme agonistic gape to adversary in opposite cage; agonistic posture during initial attack by black dog and scent-post marking after a successful agonistic encounter.

the pup will crawl forward. Also, mere contact with the leg of the mother will stimulate rooting and, eventually, the pup will locate the mammary region (see fig. 2.16). Occasionally, some pups become "disoriented" and are found near the vulva of the bitch, having rooted between her tail and hind legs.

One aspect of the development of a young animal in its social milieu is the impact its presence has on the social organization of its conspecific milieu (both peer group and elders), and how social organization is affected as the animal matures. Such studies are possible in the field, especially in primates; Kuhme (1965) has reported some of his observations on the development of young Cape hunting dogs and the cooperative role played by nonparental pack members in the care of the young and eventual integration of the young into the pack. However, the onset of sexual maturity in many canid species heralds separation of the young from the parents, the former dispersing to establish new territories. In the domesticated dog, little information on these points is available, and it would be of interest to rear dogs under feral conditions and to observe the type of social development in different breeds—either pack formation or dispersal of the litter and pair formation. This may vary with breed differences in cooperative, group-coordinated behavior and in aggressiveness.

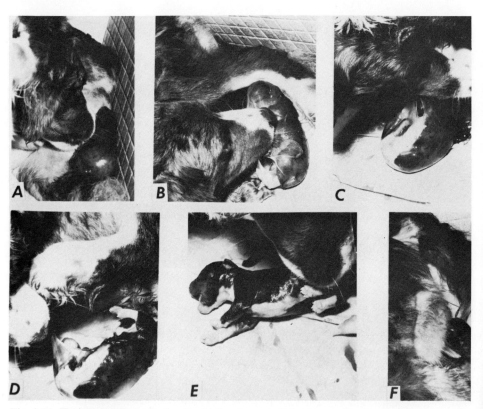

Fig. 2.15. Typical sequences during the birth of a pup, being born with the fetal sac intact (*a*) or already separated (*f*). The bitch removes the fetal membranes and severs the umbilical cord (*b, c,* and *d*) and licks the pup and oozing umbilical cord (*e*). At this stage (*e*), the pup commences to vocalize and to root.

Maternal Reactions

Preliminary observations, to establish differences in the reactions of female dogs of different ages to "stimuli," which were pups of different ages, disclosed some interesting findings. The "stimuli" were either 3–10 days of age ("neonate stimulus") or 4 wk of age ("infant stimulus") and were presented on successive days.

The "stimulus" was placed in an observation room and the reactions of the female subject were observed through a one-way window for 3 min, the duration of interaction (oriented toward or in contact) being recorded. Females aged 12 wk and 6 mo of age reacted significantly more with an "infant" stimulus than with a "neonate stimulus," implying that the former was more socially stimulating. Reactions included facial, inguinal, and anal approach and licking, pawing, and play. "Neonate stimuli" were given only a cursory facial or anal sniff and then ignored. In all instances, the "infant" stimuli would actively approach and follow the older dogs with tails wagging, and showed inguinal-oriented teat-seeking. All "neonate stimuli" vocalized distressfully on the cold arena floor. In two "experienced" females (both had successfully raised 3–4 litters) the "neonate stimulus" evoked a high interaction time; reactions included facial, inguinal, and anal licking, circling around the stimulus and then lying down in a nursing posture (recumbent inverted U) and allowing

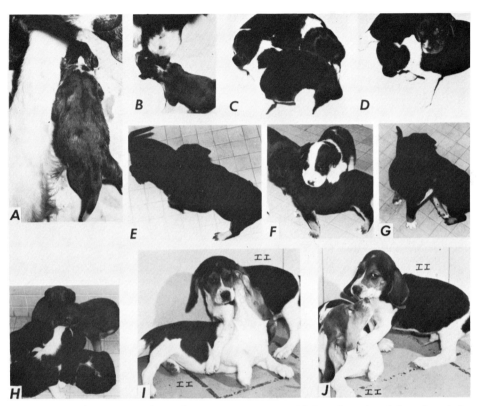

Fig. 2.16. Rooting responses in newborn pup on contact with leg of mother (*a*) and on being stimulated by the mother's licking its face (*b*). Contactual circling in 2-wk-old pups (*c* and *d*) can be recognized in older pups at 4 and 5 wk of age (*e, f,* and *g*), and was the predominant activity in hand-raised, dog-isolated pups (*i* and *j*, see chap. 6). Contact-seeking for warmth in 3-wk-old pups, forming a close "pile" (*h*).

the "stimulus" to root toward the mammary region; rooting was facilitated by the subject's licking the head and face of the "stimulus," thus providing thermotactile orientation. "Infant stimuli" were examined only briefly in comparison, even though the "stimulus" persistently followed the subject (see table 2.4).

Three females, which were experienced mothers but at the time of testing were nursing neonate pups aged from 3–10 days of age, were also tested. These subjects spent significantly longer with "neonate stimuli" than with "infant stimuli," but reacted consistently more when one of their own pups was placed in the arena. No nursing postures were assumed around a strange "neonate stimulus," but they were seen when the subjects were subsequently tested with one of their own neonate pups. One subject, after examining her pup, picked it up (not by the scruff or nape of the neck, but in the usual dog manner of gently grasping the pup around the chest and abdomen), carried it to the arena door, and remained there until the end of the observation period. The next day, when tested with "neonate stimulus," the same pattern occurred; but as soon as the bitch reached the door, it crushed the pup in its jaws. One can only speculate at the cause of such a reaction; possibly the alien olfactory and gustatory stimuli of the "neonate stimulus" broke the bite-inhibition. Difficulties in the past have often been experienced in attempting to cross-foster

TABLE 2.3

NEONATAL AND INFANTILE DERIVED ACTIVITIES IN ADULT CANIDS

Neonatal and Infantile Patterns	Adult Behavior
Contactual circling	Circling, leaning
Chin-resting	T posture
Successive paw-raising (nursing)	Playful approach and play-soliciting? (or merely exaggerated approach)
Side to side lateral head swinging—rooting to nurse	Social greeting, active submission
Vertical, upward head movements "butting," nose-stabbing—nursing	Social greeting, play-soliciting
Unilateral paw-raising, to reach up to teat, to paw mother's face	Play soliciting, as directed pawing or pawing intention
Face-mouth oriented licking to solicit food from mother	Social greeting, active submission
Licking intention before feeding: licking intention while approaching to lick face of mother	Social greeting, active submission and slower in passive submission
Passivity during anogenital stimulation by mother; passivity with inguinal contact during such stimulation	Passivity during social investigation. Submission, social greeting with inguinal presentation (C posture), submissive urination
Visually guided approach to inguinal area of mother to feed	Inguinal orientation and contact during social investigation
Distress vocalizations (whines and yelps) when cold or in pain	Passive submissive vocalizations, "cut-off"
Distress vocalizations (whines) when hungry (care-soliciting)	Care-soliciting vocalizations, active submission, social greeting
Nursing with tail down but arched away from anus	Eating or drinking, with tail down but arched away from anus
Eyes closed or partially closed during consummatory behaviors—eating, drinking, urinating, defecating, and scratching	Eyes closed or partially closed during consummatory behaviors—eating, drinking, urinating, defecating, scratching, and copulating
Squatting low on hind legs with tail out to urinate in male and female; female squats lower than male	Female and male show same urination patterns as in infancy but may raise one hind leg, more usual in male

pups of the same age; some good and experienced bitches will accept the pups, whereas others will kill them instantly.

These observations, in spite of being drawn from a small number of subjects, permit some conclusions. Previous maternal experience with a neonate pup facilitates the releasing value of a "neonate stimulus," notably the visual and auditory cues provided by a strange neonate pup. However, a bitch nursing her own neonate pup is similarly but only briefly attracted by the visual and auditory stimuli from a strange neonate pup. Additional cues, possibly olfactory and gustatory, sensitize (or imprint?) the bitch to her own pups. Olfactory-gustatory imprinting processes may occur in a wide variety of mammalian species, especially in ungulates. The importance of such a process is obvious when one considers what chaos would occur

TABLE 2.4

INTERACTION TIMES OF FEMALE DOGS AT DIFFERENT
AGES TO PUP "STIMULI"

SUBJECTS (females)	STIMULI (Mean interaction time in sec for 3-min observation)		
	Neonate (3–10 days)	Infant[a] (4 wk)	Own Pup (3–10 days)
2 at 12 wk of age.............	2.5	8.0	....
2 at 6 mo of age.............	2.0	8.0	....
2 adult "experienced" but not in whelp....................	74.0[b]	11.5	....
3 adult with pups aged 3–10 days	14.5	4.0	58.0[b]

[a] All these pups actively approached the subjects and showed inguinal-oriented teat-seeking.

[b] Lay down and allowed neonate to root into mammary region.

without it in a herd of ungulates, all giving birth at approximately the same time; visual, auditory, gustatory, and olfactory cues would be essential in maintaining the mother-infant bond and preventing indiscriminate attachments and even loss of offspring. However, the position of this type of imprinting in the dog remains an open question; how much domestication has influenced this process, and what natural selection pressures are exerted in the highly social and more solitary canid species, either to enhance or to reduce this process, is as yet unknown.

Reflexes and Behavior

During the immediate postnatal period, the following reflex components of the neonatal behavior patterns can be recognized: rooting reflex, negative geotaxis, positive thermotaxis, auriculonasocephalic reflex, positive thigmotaxis, righting reflex, reflex stimulation of respiration by umbilical-anogenital tactile stimulation, Galant's reflex, labial and sucking reflexes. These reflex components of neonatal behavior (together with olfactory-mediated responses, see chap. 5) can be recognized at birth, and are evoked by the mother and the "nest environment" or "situation structure" (i.e., warmth of nest, inverted U position of the mother, etc.). Throughout the first 2–3 wk, the bitch stimulates urination and also ingests feces from the pups. During this anogenital stimulation, the pup remains quiescent. By

3–3½ weeks, the pups are able to stand and to follow the mother. They still show the rooting response, and will reach up to the teats of the bitch while she is standing up, especially seeking the generally more productive and more pendulous inguinal teats (see fig. 2.17). Pups at this age will remain quite still while the bitch is licking the anogenital region (fig. 2.17).

Later Development of Social Behavior

Occasionally, the bitch will regurgitate food for the litter from 3–4 wk onward. This is not rare in the domesticated dog, and is elicited partly spontaneously and partly by the pups' licking the face and mouth of the bitch (see also Martins 1949; James 1960b).

After 4–5 wk of age, there is a change in the sleeping positions of the pups. Before this the pups form a "pile" or aggregated heap when the mother is out of the nest, undoubtedly a heat-conservation mechanism (fig. 2.15; see also Fredericson, Gurney, and Dubuis 1956; Fredericson 1952; Welker 1959a). When 2 or 3 pups are placed together on a cold surface, they "crawl around" and over each other (contactual circling), a pattern which is composed principally of positive thigmo-

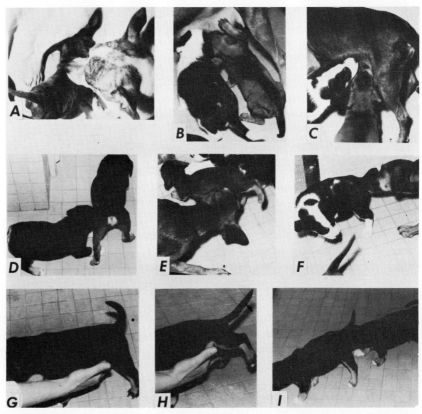

Fig. 2.17. Rooting and inguinal approach in nursing pups, *a–c.* Similar inguinal approach in older pups interacting together (*d,* see also fig. 2.9a, *d*). E and *f,* inguinal and anal approach by mother in cleaning pup; *g* and *h,* passive response and leg-raising following inguinal approach and contact in 6-wk-old pup; *i,* anal "investigation" in 6-wk-old pup, with the pup being investigated remaining passive.

taxis and thermotaxis, and the rooting, auriculonasocephalic and Galant's reflex (fig. 2.16). After 3 wk of age, thermoregulation is well developed (Jensen and Ederstorm 1955; Fox 1966*d*), and pups tend to sleep in rows and do not heap or pile, unless the whelping quarters are excessively cold.

From 3 to 3½ wk of age, the pups begin to interact playfully with each other; occasional chewing on the ears or licking the face of one pup by another elicits either avoidance and distress vocalization if the stimulation is too intense, or mutual chewing, licking, and mouthing (fig. 2.18). From this age onward, the pups learn through play how much pain they can inflict upon each other by chewing and biting. These early play responses become more variable as locomotor and perceptual abilities improve. Agonistic interactions, play-fighting, scruff-holding, and "prey-killing" head-shaking movements appear between 4 and 5 wk, together with pouncing, snapping, and aggressive vocalizations, such as growling and snarling with the teeth bared (fig. 2.18) (see also James 1955, 1961*a*). Submissive postures and care- and play-soliciting gestures appear also, including lateral recumbency, hind-leg raising,

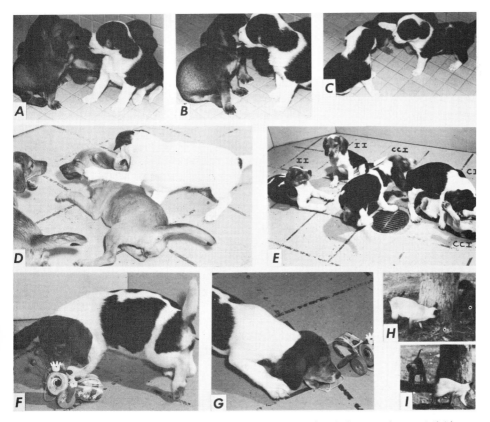

Fig. 2.18. Earliest playful social interactions in pups comprise facial chewing and licking, *a* and *b* and paw raising, *c*. Contactual circling and mounting also occur (fig. 2.16*e, f,* and *g*). Play later becomes more complex, including mock fighting, *d* (note scruff of neck attack) and wrestling, *e*). In *e,* hand-reared, dog-isolated pups do not interact (see chap. 7). Pups also become playfully aroused by inanimate objects, *f* and *g,* and will develop elaborate games often based on prey-hunting and chasing. The capacity to develop elaborate games between alien species (both wild and domesticated) is common to higher mammals, as seen in the chase and catch game between a young cat and dog, *h* and *i*.

and whining (as distinct from "distress") vocalization, licking, and foreleg raising (see fig. 2.9). It is of comparative interest that in the rhesus monkey (Harlow 1965*a*) infant males generally indulge in more vigorous rough-and-tumble wrestling and sham biting, and show more "precocious" sexual behavior than females do. This generalization also holds true for the pup, with the reservations of breed differences in aggressiveness (Fuller and Dubuis 1962).

Play behavior in animals has recently been discussed in an excellent review by Loizos (1967), and some of the more general aspects of play should be mentioned before we describe further ontogenetic aspects of canine behavior. As play activities develop, they become more *elaborate, exaggerated,* and *variable* (thus reducing ambiguity) and several *incomplete movements* associated with agonistic and sexual behavior in the adult are observed. They also become *stereotyped* and *ritualized* and characteristic *play-soliciting* gestures can be recognized (extending the forelegs with the hind quarters raised, with ears pricked, tail wagging, and vocalization). Some *inhibition* of movements and actions such as severe biting and shaking occurs; such actions may be *repeated frequently* and *rapidly* as either *intention* or *completion elements* within a sequence (Loizos 1967). Play appears to be *spontaneous* and *inventive* (especially with inanimate objects). Temporal sequences become highly variable, with reordering, omission, truncation, or insertion of apparently unrelated acts. Loizos (1967) observes that "in play the number of combinations or permutations of the available motor patterns is greater than in almost any other form of behaviour." Such spontaneous variability may be both self-rewarding and highly stimulating to conspecifics at the same or a similar stage of development.

Novel objects are first investigated, so that the animal plays only with that which is familiar to it. When the animal is hungry or in a fear- or anxiety-provoking situation, play behavior is inhibited. A lowering of threshold and increased readiness to play may occur after feeding, at certain times of the day, or at a particular place. Individual and sex differences can be recognized early in life in a litter of pups; females are generally less boisterous and indulge in little fragmentary sexual play compared with males, whereas physically superior individuals are usually more active and show more aggressive play. Play certainly appears to be important in socializing animals to each other, and in individuals' developing a "body schema" and recognition of each other. Domination and subordination experienced during play may result in social hierarchy formation within the group (although competition over food may contribute more to this process). Social play may broadly, therefore, result in social learning, adaptation, and acceptance. Play with inanimate objects may result in improved motor ability to manipulate or to perform particular acts (such as chasing, killing, or carrying a stick). Self-play may be a substitute for social play. Social play and play with inanimate objects may interact in socially cooperative species and facilitate the development of group-coordinated activities. Social play also occurs between mother and infants and could be a maternally directed activity oriented toward the establishment of group-coordinated activities.

It has been shown in Harlow's laboratory that play is important in establishing social relationships and that social isolation (and therefore denial of social play) interferes with later social, sexual, and maternal behavior. It may not be play-deprivation alone that produces such disturbances in later life, for the isolation-syndrome is complex (see chap. 6); nonetheless, play may contribute significantly to the organization of later patterns of behavior. Fear or arousal and curiosity, evoking either avoidance or intense investigation in an isolation-raised animal that is first presented with a member of its own species, may inhibit more appropriate reactions (such as sexual behavior if the two animals are physiologically sexually receptive).

To return now to the ontogeny of behavior patterns in the dog, the facial "expressiveness" of the pup at 5 wk contrasts with the masklike appearance of 3-wk-old pups. This is due especially to the later development of expressive ear movements, elongation of the muzzle, and possibly improved functioning of the facial muscles controlling elevation of the lips and display of the teeth. Also the repertoire of vocal patterns improves during this period from 3 to 5 wk. As early as 3–4 wk of age, pups show the "rooting approach" to the inguinal region of their littermates, who remain quite still during such contacts (see figs. 2.9, 2.17). This approach may be derived from the neonatal pattern of rooting and reaching toward the inguinal region of the mother (fig. 2.17), and the immobility of the pup evoking this response may be derived from its responses when the mother is stimulating and cleaning the anogenital region (fig. 2.17). From this age onward, this inguinal-approach persists as a highly stereotyped and ritualized pattern (Fox 1971*b*). Frequently, the immobile and passive pup that is being approached and contacted in this manner will raise its hind leg (fig. 2. 17). More submissive responses may follow, including lateral recumbency, raising of the uppermost hind leg, and urination. This posture is reminiscent of genital display patterns in certain species of primate. Ploog (1966) concludes that in the squirrel monkey this behavior represents a striving toward dominance and is also part of courtship; it has different meanings according to the rank and role of the animal and its age and sex. Infants display vigorously to their mother and to dominant males and the act is seen in subordinates avoiding a fight. This pattern also occurs in subordinate baboons, and is common in vervet monkeys (Struhsaker 1967; see also Wickler 1966 for further discussion on the evolutionary and social significance of these gestures).

At 4–5 wk of age, pups are frequently seen carrying small objects around in their mouths, and engaging in tugs-of-war. Rather rapidly after this, there emerges a defensive-protective agonistic pattern, in which the pup will covetously guard (prey-guarding?) a particular object or morsel of food. Several other pups may follow one littermate who is carrying something in its mouth; these are the first signs of group-coordinated activity, resembling group-coordinated tracking and hunting patterns in later life. At this age a sudden disturbing noise will frequently cause the entire litter to withdraw rapidly from the source of stimulation; again, this is a group-coordinated or allelomimetic response.

By 6 wk, most of the species-characteristic behavior patterns are present, notably the facial-lingual licking or greeting response (figs. 2.9, 2.13), inguinal approach, and anogenital investigations (fig. 2.9); also as a result of agonistic play-wrestling interaction, the bite is seen less as a chewing-licking, jaw-biting response than as a more specific grab-and-hold of the scruff of the opponent's neck (fig. 2.18). By 4 mo of age, relatively stable dominant-subordinate relations are established between littermates. The development of dominance, breed differences in dominance, and social organization among different breeds raised together have been described respectively by Scott and Marston (1948), Pawlowski and Scott (1956), and James (1951). Social facilitation causes a marked increase in food consumption in groups of dogs housed together (Ross and Ross 1949; James 1960*a*, 1961*b*), although competition over food reflects the dominant-subordinate relations

within the group (James 1949). Although the mature male hind-leg-raising urination pattern does not develop until around puberty,[6] fragments of sexual behavior
such as mounting, clasping, and pelvic thrusts are seen during play as early as 6 wk,
predominantly in male pups (fig. 2.9).

Pups aged 4–5 wk tend to crawl around each other in close contact (contactual
circling), in much the same pattern as seen in neonate pups in the nest (fig. 2.16).
With increasing age, this pattern is broken by anogenital investigation and inguinal-
oriented approach. In mature dogs, circling is seen especially during an agonistic

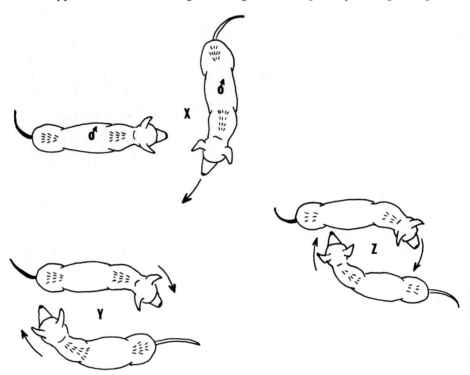

Fig. 2.19. Typical initial social reactions of two strange dogs of the same sex, meeting for the
first time. One usually stands its ground while the other approaches, *x,* and they begin to circle,
head to tail, *y,* but without physical contact. Eventually one, or both, approaches the inguinal
or tail area of the other, and mutual sniffing follows, *z.* These reactions, which may or may
not be accompanied by ritualized (no contact) or contact-fighting, or by submissive play-
soliciting behavior and actual play wrestling and chasing, are frequently followed by "ceremonial" urination.

confrontation, together with anogenital investigation and inguinal-oriented approach,
and may possibly have originated from the earlier contactual circling (fig. 2.19).
Also during agonistic interactions, urination (territorial or scent marking?), leg-
raising to urinate without urination, and erection of the tail, possibly to expose the
anal glands, occur. An agonistic interaction may intensify, and teeth are bared and
bite-threat movements are made, together with snarling. Actual attacks are in-
variably directed at the saddle area or scruff of the neck, although frequently the face
and mouth area are bitten as the bite-threat movements become overt attacks. More

[6] See also Berg (1944); however, the pattern of defecating and urinating in one particular
area develops earlier in life (Ross 1950), between 4 and 6 wk of age.

dominant dogs will turn their heads away from the opponent, although keeping a fixed gaze on the adversary, apparently "daring" an outright attack (Schenkel 1967). These gestures may be erroneously mistaken for submissive exposure of the vulnerable neck region: this does not occur in the dog. The submissive posture (passive submission) has been described earlier. Similar gestures (see table 2.3) are seen during active defense, but the dog tends to look away from its more dominant adversary (fig. 2.20).

The facial-lingual greeting, agonistic circling, inguinal approach and anogenital investigation, "scent-post" or territorial and ceremonial (agonistic) urination, and

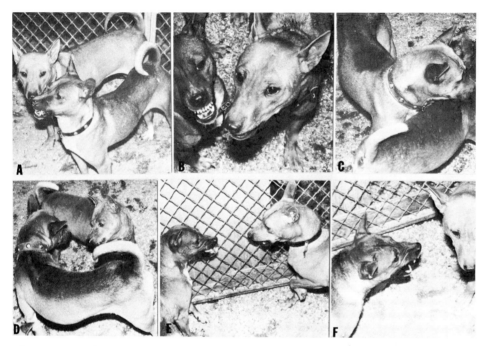

Fig. 2.20. Agonistic behavior in telomians (Malayan jungle dogs): *a,* Bitch (with collar) being incited by dominant bitch, active defense, while dominant bitch circles around; *b,* Head turning away from dominant bitch; active defense. *c,* ⊤ posture, dominant male standing over subordinate male. *d,* Agonistic circling by two males; note fixed gaze, erect ears and tail. *e* and *f,* Active defense, *e,* bitch on left being incited by dominant bitch (note curling of tongue in subordinate bitch, an "apprehensive" sign), followed by defensive attack, *f;* but dominant bitch is only threatened.

submissive posture and urination are species-specific, ritualized components of social behavior patterns in the mature dog. Their possible ontogenetic relationships with earlier components have been schematically depicted in chart 2.2 (see also fig. 2.10).

Responses to a "Social Releaser"

In order to determine what regions of the dog particularly evoke investigatory behavior in another dog during social interaction, a model of a dog in the form of a two-dimensional painting was made. This model was prepared with black and gray acrylic paint on a white background, with shading applied especially to the inguinal, elbow, and throat regions; the "expression" of the model was arbitrarily set in an "alert" posture. It was not anticipated that adult dogs would investigate such a crude stimulus, other than to orient toward it briefly. However, in pilot studies adult dogs not only oriented toward the model, but also approached and investigated it. A developmental study using this model was then undertaken in 4 groups of dogs aged 4 wk (2 male and 4 female); 8–10 wk (4 male and 4 female); and 20 wk (1 male and 2 female); and 8 adults, ranging in age from 3 to 6 yr (4 male and

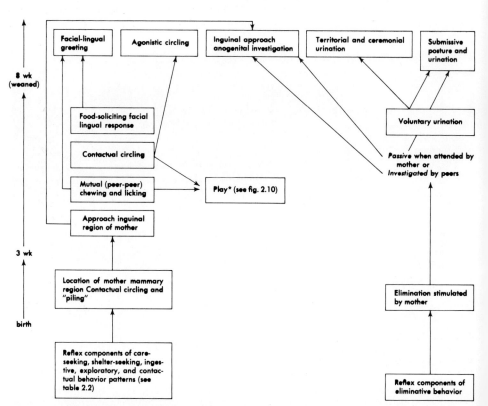

Chart 2.2. Ontogenesis of ritualized components of social behavior in the dog. Components marked by asterisk become organized through play integrated with agonistic, sexual, territorial, and maternal behavior patterns in later life.

4 female). Subjects were placed singly in an 8′ × 8′ arena, with one-way windows for observation, at first in total darkness. The arena lights were turned on after 15 sec, and reactions to the model were observed for a period of 3 min. The time each subject spent interacting with the model (oriented toward, approaching, sniffing, pawing, etc.) was recorded by one observer, and the area of the model that was investigated and the frequency of interaction was noted by a second observer (the area apparently being contacted by the nose of the subject). The model thus provided a visual stimulus which evoked orientation, arousal, and approach, and at close proximity evoked olfactory investigation (fig. 2.21; licking was also seen in some subjects). The model and the arena floor were carefully cleaned after each trial.

The results of these observations are summarized in figures 2.22 and 2.23.

Duration and total frequency of interaction was highest in the 8–10-wk-old pups, and this age represents a peak in the amount of time that an animal will repeatedly investigate novel stimuli. With increasing age, the model evoked less investigation, either because it was not sufficiently complex or "arousing" for older subjects, or else more mature subjects were more "efficient" in their speed of investigation and analysis of the stimulus.

The frequency of interaction with specific areas of the model revealed interesting differences across age. Four-wk-old pups approached the shoulder and inguinal regions more than any other parts of the model. The side-to-side head movements resembled rooting behavior, and it appeared that the young pups were seeking

Fig. 2.21. Approach and nose-contact with model in pups and adult dogs. F = facial approach; I = inguinal approach; A = anal approach.

contact with the mammary region—the most significant area in terms of their experience and needs at this age.[7] Pups aged 8–10 weeks similarly showed a strong predilection for these two areas, but also made frequent contact with the hind leg (thigh region), possibly associated with approach to the inguinal area. In older dogs, the inguinal approach was occasionally observed and, as proposed earlier, may be derived from inguinal approach to feed from the mother. The most frequent response at 8–10 wk was mouth-face contact (including licking, resembling the lingual-facial greeting, pawing the face of the model, and vocalization), and was considered identical to the food-soliciting response to the mother, especially at this age. It was postulated earlier that the lingual-facial greeting in adult dogs is a ritualized pattern emancipated from food-soliciting behavior. It is significant that at around 8–10 wk of age, weaning begins, and bitches are most likely to regurgitate food for pups

[7] Fox and Weisman (1970) have shown that hunger increases approach frequencies to this model at 6 and 8 wk, especially toward the inguinal region at 6 wk and the face at 8 wk.

at this age. The pattern persists subsequently, as shown in the relatively high frequency of mouth-face contacts in dogs aged 20 wk and in adults. Only in dogs aged 20 wk and older were specific contacts with the ear and anal (subcaudal) regions observed. These regions of the body may become significant only in older dogs as sources of information for social (olfactory) recognition. The ears produce considerable quantities of cerumen, a sebaceous, odoriferous substance, and similar

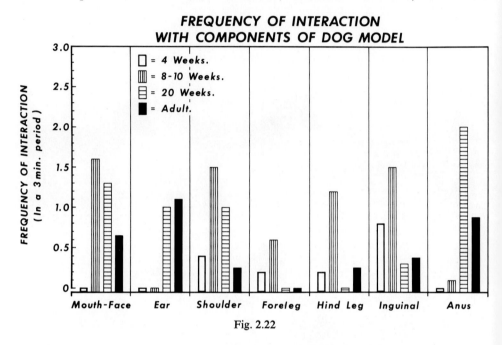

Fig. 2.22

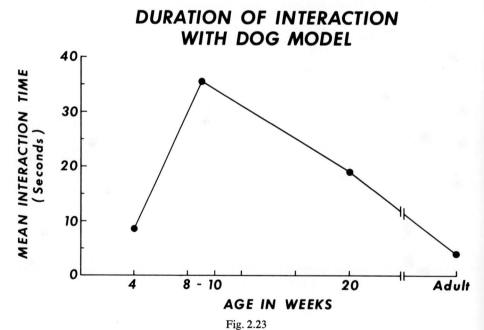

Fig. 2.23

secretions are produced by the perianal glands.[8] The high approach and investigation of the anal region may be due to this region's becoming particularly significant
to dogs aged 20 wk; at this age they are on the threshold of developing "territorial-
defensive" and sexual behavior patterns.

Frequent contact with the shoulder region of the model in older dogs may be
correlated with the rolling habits of Canidae. The shoulder regions are especially
rubbed against suitable objects or materials that evoke scent-marking behavior. In
the dog, this pattern frequently consists of first nosing and licking the material, such
as a particularly aged morsel of carrion, and then "diving" into it, so that the ventro-
lateral portion of the neck is impregnated. The "dive" then becomes a roll, as the

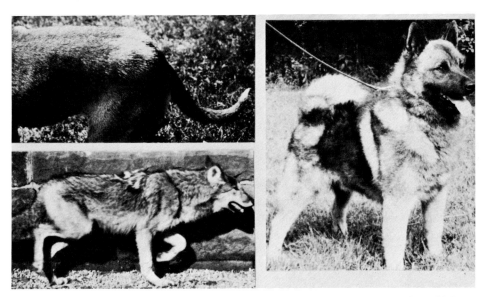

Fig. 2.24. Specific coat-marks in various Canidae; rump-bristles in male telomian (Malayan
jungle dog); white dorsal shoulder hackles in wolf; white shoulder-line and white ventral surface of curled tail in Norwegian elkhound. Also note black muzzle and lips which may enhance
teeth during agonistic display.

dog twists over onto its side (or back) and then proceeds to roll and writhe in the
material. Many breeds of dog (and mongrels) have a line of pale hair running dorsoventrally on each side behind the shoulder, which may serve to enhance this area
(see fig. 2.24). However, shoulder approach, including muzzling, chin-resting,[9] and
pawing is seen in young pups during play and in adults during precopulatory courtship. The neck-shoulder region is also specifically attacked during aggressive play
(see fig. 2.18) and in fighting, as in other Canidae, notably *Speothos* (Kleiman
1967).

This experiment has shown, to my surprise at least, that even adult dogs will
approach and investigate specific regions of a two-dimensional model of another

[8] Dr. Pickvance, of Birmingham University, recently suggested to the author, on the basis
of his own observations, that various regions of the dog's body can be classified into areas of
high "preference" for social investigation: ear, corner of mouth, side of shoulder, shoulder
hackles, and rump or rear hackles.

[9] Golani (1966) describes the T posture in the jackal *Canis aureus* during courtship, in
which the male stands perpendicular to the female and rests his neck across her shoulders.

dog. An attempt has been made to supply some of the reasons why certain regions of the model were investigated at different ages. It must be added that all dogs wagged their tails during approach (although the actual tail carriage varied from "submissive" to "dominant" or "confident"), and that no differences attributable to sex were found in the adults. On no occasion was the midthoracic region investigated. Future studies will be focused on the species-specificity or innateness of these regional preferences and response patterns, by hand-raising pups in social isolation from their own species and testing them with such a model.[10]

An interesting displacement activity or compromise movement (also observed in other test procedures with novel stimuli, see chap. 5) occurred in dogs of various ages in the presence of the model dog. This consisted of the subject's rapidly turning its head laterally (away from the model) and looking over its shoulder or toward its flank when first confronted by the model. This "flank-gazing," or looking to one side,[11] evoked by stimuli that arouse some conflict between approach-investigate and withdraw-escape, was seen in subjects aged 20 wk and older. This reaction resembles "flagging" in various species of seabirds, but may be more of a submissive "cut-off," redirecting the gaze from the stimulus. This side- or flank-gazing may be repeated several times, being interrupted as the dog directs its gaze forward for a moment to look at the stimulus. Flank-gazing may be followed by a cursory lick at the inguinal/genital area, or the animal may turn around and appear to be following or chasing its tail. Possibly an extreme example of this flank-gazing is attained in certain strains of Doberman pinschers that develop a habit, when excessively aroused by conflicting or anxiety-provoking circumstances, of seizing the flank in their jaws. Some dogs simply hold the flank-skin and salivate profusely, and others appear to chew and suck, often inflicting chronic traumatic lesions to this region.

Adult Patterns

There are several gestures in the dog that act as "sign stimuli" and that express the "internal state" of the animal. Facial expression and baring of the teeth, "balance" of the body (weight predominantly on fore- or hind limbs, or evenly distributed) position of ears, tail carriage, and extent of piloerection are important components of response patterns (see fig. 2.11). Other signs (and symptoms of emotional states) include "emotional" urination and defecation, penile erection, submissive urination, territorial and ceremonial (agonistic) urination, frequently accompanied by earth-marking scratching movements with the hind and forelegs.

The significance of the anal glands in the social organization and behavior of the dog have not been elucidated;[12] however, the arousal effect on male dogs of the urinary pheromones of the bitch in heat are well recognized. "Scent-post" or "territorial" marking in the male may have been greatly modified by the restrictions imposed through domestication.

---

[10] See Fox 1971*b* for further observations.

[11] This pattern has been observed in wolf cubs in simliar conflict situations and was also seen in a more exaggerated form during submissive approach and in play-soliciting (as distinct from "prey-killing" head-shake movements) in this species (Fox 1971*a*).

[12] However, Donovan (1967) has reported differences in the attractiveness and deterrence of anal-sac secretions during estrus and following voluntary expression of contents in frightened dogs.

The lateral position of the tail of a bitch in heat may be regarded as a specific sign stimulus (similar behavior is seen in the rhesus monkey soliciting the attention of a male; Harlow 1965a). Tail wagging develops after 3 wk of age as a specific social greeting response, the tail usually being held low and wagged rapidly from side to side in greeting the mother, submissively, the inguinal region may also be presented (see table 2.3). During social interactions with littermates, the tail is wagged but held higher. Similar wagging in the high position is seen in the confident friendly adult dog, and the submissive low position remains relatively unchanged as a submissive greeting. Tail wagging in the high position is also seen when young pups are excited by novel stimuli or are engaging in preliminary bouts of play. A very erect tail (exposing the anal region) and occasional sharp wags of the tip of the tail in the adult are characteristic reactions of a confident dog in the presence of a potential adversary.

Because of the heterogenicity of the domesticated dog, it is relatively impossible to recognize any specific body structures that have been modified through natural selection to enhance their effect as social releasers or "sign" stimuli. We may speculate that the white tail tip or pale coloration of the ventral surface of the tail (especially in curl-tailed spitz types) may enhance this structure when it is erect, and that black lips or muzzle-mask may enhance the teeth when they are bared. In some breeds, the hair at the base of the tail (rump hackles) and over the saddle (shoulder hackles) area is often slightly longer and of different color or texture than that in other areas of the body; this may enhance these regions during agonistic encounters (see fig. 2.24).

In many breeds of dog there is also a pale band of hair passing dorsoventrally just behind the shoulder. The possible significance of this has been discussed earlier. Also, many breeds show a break in the hairline, or a ring, whorl, or V of darker or longer and coarser hair approximately ⅓ down the tail on the dorsal surface. Pickvance (personal communication) has suggested that this may be associated with a supracaudal gland, which is functional in other Canidae. Dissection and histological examination of this region reveal that this gland is normally nonfunctional and indeed often absent in the domesticated dog (personal observations). In many dogs, emotional disturbances are accompanied by profuse sweating from the footpads. Such secretions may be deposited as the aroused animal investigates (and becomes familiar with) a new environment, or may be smelled by a conspecific during social/agonistic encounters. Territorial marking may have evolved from the animal's depositing certain body secretions such as urine, feces, or secretions from specialized glands such as the para-anal (potentiated by autonomic-emotional arousal), thus maintaining a "personal familiarity" with its environment.

In evaluating the reactions of dogs to a model (described earlier), genitalia were not incorporated in the model. It is conceivable that initial social investigation is not specifically oriented toward the genitalia (unless the male is sensitized shortly before by the odor of a bitch in heat), but that inguinal approach may lead to sniffing and licking of the penis, and caudal approach may lead to sniffing and licking of the vulva. In the bitch, enlargement and color change of the vulva during heat (deepening from a pale pink to a dark salmon pink color), often enhanced by pale-colored hair around the hindquarters, may act as a visual stimulus. In the basenji and possibly in other breeds, the hair of the tail becomes temporarily erect during the heat period, and the bushy tail may make receptive females more conspicuous.

Summary

Several species-specific components of social behavior patterns in the dog are described briefly. The development of these components is discussed; in several instances, these components can be recognized as parts of adult behavior patterns, having undergone varying degrees of emancipation and ritualization.

"Ritualization" and "Emancipation" of Behavior Patterns

Two important processes to be considered in the ontogenesis of behavioral systems are ritualization and emancipation, which have long been recognized by ethologists as important phenomena in the phylogenetic evolution of behavior. For example, threat movements in the greylag goose have been emancipated from their original motivation or direction, and in this species have evoked phylogenetically into a ritualized greeting or "triumph" ceremony, although young greylag goslings do display this behavior as a threat gesture in early life—thus some further ontogenetic modifications are involved (Lorenz 1966). In the dog, several behavior patterns from one behavioral system become emancipated ontogenetically (and are phylogenetically regulated, as the behavior patterns are species-specific, Fox 1971*b*), and form ritualized patterns of other behavior systems (table 2.3); licking and chewing the lips and muzzle, which in the young pup is a food-soliciting activity and may stimulate the bitch to regurgitate food, takes the form of a greeting gesture in later life (fig. 2.13). This food-soliciting response only rarely stimulates vomition in the bitch, and yet is commonly seen in wild canids such as the wolf and African hunting dog (Kuhme 1965). Possibly, therefore, the decreased responsiveness of the bitch and consequently the decreased motivation or direction of the food-soliciting behavior in the pup may indicate some degree of phylogenetic emancipation. It is not completely emancipated phylogenetically in the domesticated dog, for regurgitation is seen in some bitches following stimulation by the pups, and in wild canids it undergoes ontogenetic emancipation and ritualization. Thus the ontogenetic process possibly precedes the phylogenetic process in the emancipation of certain behavior patterns and their incorporation into different systems of behavior.

Anogenital stimulation of pups by the bitch evokes lateral recumbency, elevation of the uppermost hind limb and exposure of the anogenital area, followed by reflexive urination and defecation. The products of this stimulation are ingested by the bitch even when the pups are 4 wk of age and older—although at this age elimination is under voluntary control. Subsequently, this behavior pattern of lateral recumbency and anogenital exposure (and often urination, fig. 2.9) is seen as a submissive or appeasement gesture to older or more dominant dogs, and also to human beings (Fox 1962). (See table 2.3 for review of emancipated and ritualized behaviors "derived" from neonatal activities in canids.)

Some behavior patterns in the dog have undergone phylogenetic reduction or "atrophy" in that they are only seen as rudimentary or fragmentary intention movements. Skinner (1966) has discussed the possible role of domestication in causing reduction of certain behavior patterns, in terms of operant behavior and contingencies or reinforcement. The conditions of domestication have reduced the need for some behavior patterns which may be essential for survival in the wild state. Lair-treading behavior (circling and trampling the litter) is seen briefly as a rudimentary intention movement in many dogs before they lie down. Skinner observes that most domesticated cats carefully bury their feces, but the dog shows only fragmentary covering movements with the hind limbs; however, in the dog, these "fragmentary covering movements" are more likely to be movements employed to mark the ground around the scent post, both fore- and hind limbs being used to scratch and scrape the earth.

General Discussion of Organization of Behavior Patterns and Reflex Components in Postnatal Development

The purpose of this section is to discuss various aspects of behavioral development and to construct, on the basis of ethological terminology, a theoretical model of behavioral ontogeny. In the ethological appraisal of behavior, both genetic (innate or unlearned) and acquired (or learned) factors are involved in organization and expression of behavior in the adult organism (Lorenz 1965; Thorpe 1964). Depending upon the modality of stimulation and internal (neuroendocrine) factors which may interact with the environmental milieu (Lehrman 1958, 1963), behavior is expressed specifically in certain movements. These specific movements, some of which are highly ritualized (Tinbergen 1951), may be classified into systems of behavior (Scott and Fuller 1965), and on the basis of ethological analysis an ethogram of these systems and of their ontogeny will be constructed.

In the neonate dog, several specialized unconditioned reflexes can be identified, some of which may be related to specific systems of behavior (table 2.2). Some of the reflex components of neonatal behavior patterns undergo spontaneous remission (James 1952*a, b*). For example, tactile approach (rooting reflex) in the dog disappears at around 3 wk of age and is superseded by visual orientation and visually guided approach; other reflexes persist, such as those associated with ingestive behavior, although the labial and sucking reflexes disappear. Several reflexes, notably the Magnus reflex and reflex urination, disappear, for they are inhibited by higher, ontogenetically "younger," CNS structures as movements come under voluntary control. Generally the unconditioned reflexes present in the neonatal period ensure survival of the organism, in accordance with Anokhin's theory (1964), and may also be dependent upon and stimulate or solicit maternal, care-giving behavior.

Ausubel (1966) has recently criticized the observation of Piaget (1952) on the development of component elements of behavior. He observes that Piaget's theory does not account for the distinctions between reflexive and nonreflexive behavior, and that his descriptions of motor development, for example, obscure basic difference in rate, patterning, and regulation characteristic of these two forms of behavior. Ausubel considers motor development an outgrowth of nonreflex rather than reflex activity, and states that the wide, uncritical acceptance of Piaget's observations is surprising considering the well-established distinction made by American psychologists between reflex and nonreflex (voluntary instrumental) behavior and the Skinnerian distinction between respondent and operant behavior. Ausubel (1966) emphasizes that, except for a few reflexes that are suppressed by cortical inhibition, the neonate's vast repertoire of behavior remains intact throughout the life span. In this investigation, the importance of these reflex components for behavioral organization and adaptation in neonatal life has been shown, and the gradual regression of certain reflexes has been correlated with the emergence of new systems of behavior. Individuation of nonreflexive behavior continues until later life, both during the early "phylogenetic" phase when neural maturation occurs and in the later "ontogenetic" phase dominated by practice (Ausubel 1966). Ausubel stresses that reflexive behavior never acquires intentionality, whereas nonreflexive behavior in the neonate is a developmental precursor of intentional or voluntary behavior. But Piaget (1952) includes reflexive behavior in the development of sensori-motor coordination, as in the development of hand-eye coordination, and hypothesizes that there is a reciprocal assimilation of motor and sensory (prehensile and visual) schemata. (These "schemata" to which he refers may represent the "unit components" of behavioral systems alluded to in this discussion.) Both Piaget and Ausubel have demonstrated the importance of reflexive and nonreflexive components contributing to behavioral development; however, from the present investigation it is concluded that reflex components predominate in early life and play an important part in the organization of neonatal behavior, and also provide a basis for the elaboration of more mature behavior patterns in later life. These neonatal reflexes promote survival and also put the organism in a position in which it can elaborate more complex nonreflexive responses, and subsequently more mature and learned behavior patterns. For example, the rooting reflex enables the pup to locate and approach the mother, and at a later age it is replaced by visually guided, spatially oriented location and approach mechanisms. Therefore, reflexive behavior evoked by one stimulus modality in early life permits the establishment in later life of a similar response pattern, but now of predominantly nonreflexive components, the motivation and reward or reinforcement being similar in both instances. A process of association learning may therefore be involved, in addition to sensorimotor integration (Held and Hein 1963) and reciprocal assimilation (Piaget 1952).

Sears, Maccoby, and Levin (1957) alluded to an intriguing ontogenetic phenomenon in human infants; many children begin to wean themselves normally at around 24 mo of age, and at this time, the drive to suck begins to decrease quite independent of practice. They also report that there is little emotional disturbance if the child is weaned after this age. However, children that have been cup-fed from birth appear to lose their sucking reflex altogether by the time they are a few months old. Levy (1934) originally thought that there was an inborn drive to suck, an "oral tension" which under conditions of frustration was sublimated in displacement behavior such as thumb-sucking. Sears and Wise (1950), however, have shown how experience influences this behavior.

From these observations we may conclude that, in the organization of certain neonatal behavior patterns, contingencies of reinforcement are necessary, or else these patterns will disappear early in life if they have no adaptive, functional role to play. As the organism matures, some of these neonatal patterns disappear normally and are superseded by adultlike patterns (in this case, drinking and chewing supersede sucking); but if continued reinforcement is given, these neonatal patterns may persist. Meyer-Holzapfel (1968), for example, reported perseverance of the gape food-soliciting response in hand-raised starlings. The degree to which behavior is dependent upon the function of these primitive patterns may be correlated with the amount of appropriate reinforcement and with the degree of emotional disturbance when the infant is weaned later in life; the difficulties encountered in adaptively shifting to and utilizing a new behavior pattern (drinking) undoubtedly cause frustration and emotional distress, especially when the infant becomes more and more hungry and thus more specifically aroused to suck. It would be of interest to determine how later behavior is affected by early inhibition of certain neonatal behavior patterns; one would predict, for example, that infants that have been cup-fed from birth would encounter difficulties in sucking from a straw later in life. We may surmise that neonatal behavior patterns contribute to the behavioral repertoire in later life, but to what extent remains to be evaluated. Also, continued reinforcement and maintenance of particular behavior patterns beyond their modal period of duration under a specified rearing regimen may interfere with the normal ontogenetically regulated onset of the critical period of a subsequent behavior pattern.

In regard to the sucking response of human infants, Kessen, Leutzendorff, and Stoutsenberger (1967) have shown that sucking behavior is a prenatally or congenitally organized behavior pattern; Hippocrates (cited by Still 1931) observed that "if the child had not sucked *in utero,* he would not know how to suck the teats as he does directly when he is born."

Kovach and Kling (1967), in a study of sucking behavior in kittens, found that subjects which are socially isolated and are fed by stomach tube and not allowed to suck are unable to initiate sucking on the mother by 23 days of age. They correlated this postulated maturational disappearance of neonate reflex activities with the similar findings in chickens reported by Padilla (1935). Those kittens which were group-raised and fed by stomach tube were able to initiate sucking on the mother at 30 days because, as a result of their social interactions, mutual stimulation of neonate reflexes such as sucking and rooting occurred. Normally raised kittens showed a maturational improvement in their ability to learn to suck from a bottle, in two steps; the first at 1 wk of age, possibly associated with the emergence of vision, and the second at around 30 days of age, which paralleled the newly emerged response to solid food. Kovach and Kling went further in their study and ablated the olfactory bulbs (see also chap. 5). They found that the kittens were unable to initiate sucking from the mother, in that they appeared incapable of finding and responding to the mother's nipple; however, there was apparently no interference in learning to suck from the bottle. They discussed these intriguing findings with emphasis on the importance of neonatal reflex activities in the early establishment of persistent behavior patterns. They support the view of Rosenblatt, Turkewitz, and Schneirla (1959) that changes in behavior are attributable to both maturation processes and experience, and that every age is critical for the development of the sucking pattern. Kovach and Kling postulate an interlocked ontogenetic chain of maturational and experiential factors in the development of behavior, which, they say, should not and cannot be equated with epigenesis. They also state that the critical period hypothesis may be useful for identifying the separate maturational and experiential factors in the development of neonatal sucking behavior. The question of motivation or the effects of stimuli serving as contingencies of reinforcement and effecting organization of maturing reflex components of behavior were not discussed.

The authors give no reason why the ontogenetic chain cannot be equated with epigenesis, and yet their study emphasizes the genotype modulation of innate or species-specific reflex components of behavior and the environmental (experiential) modifications which can occur in these maturing behavioral components. It is surprising that in their studies both Rosenblatt, Turkewitz, and Schneirla (1959) and Kovach and Kling (1967) feel that their findings are at variance with Scott's critical period hypothesis, in view of the fact that they find an ontogenetic continuum in the organization of behavior, in which apparently "every age is critical for the development of a normal progressive sucking pattern." What they are showing, in fact, is that experience at a given age is critically dependent upon previous experience, and in turn is critical for the development of subsequent learning and normal patterning of development—a point which is clearly emphasized by Scott (1962). We cannot therefore refer to a single critical period of development, but should instead specify for what a given period is critical—for adaptation to the nipple, for socialization, for learning, and so on. Such critical periods are essentially equivalent to Piaget's developmental stages, at which times accommodation, assimilation, and equilibration occur. Experience is dependent upon contingencies of reinforcement, and the response pattern is a function of the capacity and degree of modification or elaboration (i.e., plasticity) of the repertoire of the developing organism. These are the critical factors involved in bringing about adaptation to the changed "structure" of the organism's experimentally modified environment and associated intrinsic contingencies of reinforcement.

Unlike the more gradual onset of the critical period of socialization, in establishing primary social relationships, the immediate postnatal critical period of adaptation, in establishing feeding patterns, is based on prenatally organized (genetically regulated and selected to fit with the presupposed situational structure of the extrauterine environment) units of ingestive behavior, of which sucking is one component. This behavior (and its components) is not rigidly fixed or stereotyped at birth, for it undergoes further development and elaboration, and because of early plasticity, can be adaptively modified. Ontogenetic patterning of development may be regulated by epigenetically selected processes, which bring into play (at a particular age, i.e., during a period of integration; see later) responses which are critical for adaptation or for subsequent development. Experimental manipulations of a specified rearing regimen may alter the normal ontogenetic patterning of development, because the organism has to adapt to these experimental effects. Consequently, the normal ontogenetic patterning of development (which is a function of genotype-environment interaction and is most probably not a fixed process independent of the "directing" influences of environmental stimulation) may be drastically modified, and normal developmental stages of integration, which underlie critical periods, may be altered. Therefore, as a result of adaptation to such extreme experiential effects during development, normal integrative and critical periods may be changed or their onset accelerated, delayed, or inhibited, making their recognition extremely difficult. Such experimental variations of rearing regimen are of value only when the sequences of ontogeny under natural conditions are known. It is only then that critical periods can be experimentally verified, and their duration and effects on subsequent development determined.

Both Piaget and Gessell have demonstrated an intriguing developmental phenomenon, namely ontogenetic limitation (or centration, according to Piaget). During a given period of development, training or experience to accelerate the acquisition and elaboration of new sensorimotor skills (which normally appear at a later age) has little or no effect. Training is effective, however, during the critical or integrative period when the organism has matured sufficiently and has the capacities to develop these new skills (decentration, according to Piaget).

Integration of Behavioral Systems and of Component Action Patterns

Most, if not all, systems of behavior seen in the neonate contribute to the organization of behavior patterns in later life. Tinbergen (1951) notes that lower units of the level of consummatory acts appear first in the life of a young bird, whereas appetitive behavior (much of which is learned) appears later; for example, precocial fragmentary nest building in infant cormorants (Kortlandt 1940).

Taxes and kineses predominate in the behavioral organization of lower organisms (Fraenkel and Gunn 1961), and these phenomena are also associated with orientation reactions in adult higher organisms, as in egg retrieving in the greylag goose (Lorenz and Tinbergen 1951) and in orientation reactions in the neonate mouse, cat, and dog (e.g., positive thigmotaxis, negative geotaxis [Fox 1964*d*]). Dethier and Stellar (1964) have discussed the phylogenetic changes which take place in the major modes of adaptive behavior; thus taxes and reflexes predominate in lower organisms (although more complex behavioral organization is possible [Jacobson 1964]), and more elaborate innate or instinctual patterns and learned activities are seen in higher organisms (see also chap. 7). Hinde (1966) has reviewed the development of movement patterns, and gives several examples of those which appear independent of postnatal learning; in the ethological sense these are the fixed-action patterns, which may, however, be influenced by intraegg or intrauterine experience. For example Prechtl (1965) has shown that the intrauterine proprioceptive input can influence postnatal posture and reflex patterns in the human infant. In both simple and complex movements, there may be a reafferentation feedback system for constant testing of the movement with a central "model" or Sollwerte (Hinde 1966). The recent studies by Held and Bauer (1967) on the development of visually guided reaching in primates clearly demonstrates that, although the reaching and grasping responses are present early in life, it is through exercise or experience that hand-eye and hand-eye-mouth coordination develops.

Kuo (1930) has shown that hunting and killing activities of the cat are made up of many components which are developed through play and mimicry (see also Wickler 1965*a, b*) and are influenced by previous experience. The development of the act of killing involves bringing together several part-processes into a functional pattern. Thus, with appropriate stimulation, the part-processes or elements of other behavior patterns are brought together, and this synthesis of new adaptive activities is dependent upon previous experience and the presence of behavior patterns that have been organized earlier in life. Eibl-Eibsfeldt (1956), in a study of prey-killing in the polecat, similarly concludes that there is intercalation or unit interweaving of learned and innate elements in behavioral development, as observed also in some canids (Fox 1969*c*). Welker (1964), in a study of the development of sniffing behavior in the rat, observes that as each type of movement appears with increasing age, it becomes synchronous with those already present. Intercalation and functional synchrony between component elements of not only behavioral systems, but also of central nervous systems, may occur during development (Anokhin 1964). Leyhausen (1965) studied predatory killing patterns in carnivores and concluded that there are many patterns (e.g., crouching and pouncing) which are performed independently, there being many possible ways in which these patterns can be integrated. Thus they differ from the long, stereotyped "chain reactions" in birds. He postulates that each act has its own instinct with its own "endogenous rhythm of accumulation and discharge of action-specific energy."

Scott (1967) notes that such neurophysiological interpretations, with only behavioral evidence, should be guarded and concludes that "the capacity for variation in behavior is an adaptive one and is as subject to natural selection as are fixed action patterns. The result should, therefore, be an equilibrium between processes which organize behavior previous to adaptive experience, and processes which keep it labile and unorganized."

The relationships of various systems of behavior, when schematized to show the possible relationships between these systems, follow a clearly defined ontogenetic pattern (fig. 2.10). Riesen (1961*b*) regards these earlier behavioral systems as "building blocks" for later developing systems. The development of behavior may be dependent upon the establishment of these ontogenetic relationships between various behavioral systems which are formed as a consequence of both maturation and experience. These ontogenetic relationships in the progressive organization of behavioral systems are speculative and deserve further analysis through deprivation and stimulus-substitution experiments. Hinde (1966) has reviewed the integration of discrete types of behavior into functional sequences and complex chain reactions sharing the same causal factors, as in courtship and mating, hunting and killing. There is considerable stimulus-response overlap, but through successive or antagonistic induction, goal directiveness and consummatory stimuli, the ongoing sequence of behavior can be directed or changed. It is conceivable that any disturbances in the ontogenetic relationships between the various systems of behavior, or inadequate development of certain systems at particular "critical periods" in life (e.g., at onset of sexual activity), would cause abnormalities or incompatibilities in the integration of functional sequences of discrete types of behavior. In addition, goal-directed behavior, or the specific drive, may be overridden by a conflicting motivation or drive such as fear. This is an important variable which may interfere with the normally predictable behavior of a naïve, isolation-reared animal and give the misleading impression of a disturbance in the ontogeny of a particular behavior sequence.

Although several neonatal behavior patterns "mature-out" of the animal's repertoire with increasing age, they may be elicited under particular circumstances. Food-soliciting behavior and infantile postures are seen in both adult avian and mammalian species, associated with courtship or submission during an agonistic encounter (Fox 1971*b*). These "neotenous" patterns may serve to appease (literally cut off agression) or remotivate the aggressor. With adequate reinforcement, a wide range of infantile behavior patterns may persist, as in the overindulged pet dog that is raised as a care-seeking "perpetual puppy" (Fox 1968). Under abnormal rearing conditions, immature food-soliciting responses may persist, as observed by Meyer-Holzapfel (1968) in hand-raised starlings. Similarly the rooting response persists beyond the normal ontogenetic limit in hand-raised (bottle-fed) dogs (see chap. 6).

Another intriguing developmental phenomenon concerns not the disappearance of immature patterns, but the *delayed* emergence of adult patterns occurring some time after the organism has received the stimulation (or information) necessary for the elaboration of these patterns. This phenomenon is exemplified by the development of song patterns in certain birds (reviewed by Marler and Hamilton 1966, and Nottebohm 1970). Exposure to conspecific song before these birds sing (and, therefore, have no period of practice and auditory-feedback control) and subsequent isolation does not disrupt the development of normal song. However, if such experience is denied, their song is deficient. One may postulate that in this phenomenon the song-template, based upon both innate and acquired information, is elaborated before maturation of the vocal system; thus the sensory (auditory) system must mature before the motor system. On the other hand, both sensory and motor systems may be sufficiently mature at the time of exposure learning, but the sensorimotor integrator has not yet matured or there is not adequate motivation (i.e., sexual maturity) to sing. The highly selective nature of auditory sensitivity to conspecific song and motor limitations as to the type of song that can be elaborated serve as additional sensitizing and limiting factors. Subsequent maturation and embellishment of the song pattern may or may not rely heavily on auditory feedback while the animal is singing, coupled with further modifications through learning the local dialect.

Andrew (1963) suggests that early experience organizes various behavior patterns into *motivational categories* through conditioning, because in normal development a particular behavior pattern can only be expressed in certain contexts where the correct eliciting stimuli are present and the correct reinforcing stimuli ensue. He comes to this important conclusion after observing the reactions of newly hatched domestic chicks to stationary objects of about their own size. A number of undifferentiated, unorganized, and unintegrated responses were observed, including body-pressing against the object, climbing on top of it, rapid pecking, approach, and exploratory pecking. Injection of testosterone altered these generalized responses; motor and vocal behavior associated with aggressive responses and copulatory attempts resembled adult responses, but were not given in the specific social contexts in which this behavior appears in the adult.

Hinde (1966) has presented a valuable review of developmental aspects of motivation and concludes from the few studies that have so far been undertaken that "the activities of young animals are often not related to the motivational factors associated with them in adulthood, and that the motivational bases of apparently simple activities often have a complex developmental history." Experiential variables in early life may severely modify subsequent motivation and behavior, as is shown in studies on the effects of handling, isolation rearing, and restricted feeding on subsequent hoarding and food consumption, and of hormonal influences on the premature organization of the CNS and subsequent behavior. For example, Rosenblatt and Aronson (1958) have shown that sexual behavior in male cats persists following castration only if they have had sexual experience before castration. Thus certain behavior patterns, once organized through the influence of hormones, may subsequently become partially or wholly independent of hormonal influences.

Although there is often a clear ontogenetic sequence in the emergence of action patterns, the concatenation of a sequence of behavior may be ordered because each component of the sequence has a different threshold which insures appropriate release of a given action pattern in accordance with the motivational state or shifting level of arousal. It has been emphasized earlier that in the young animal, action patterns (such as copulatory pelvic thrusts) may appear out of context or be released by inappropriate stimuli. Later such patterns are ordered into a more predictable temporal sequence or response hierarchy within a specific motivational (and stimulus) context. Scott (1968) has discussed the development and organization of motivation, and shows that the physiological sources of motivation develop at different rates and thus support Freud's theory of stages of emotional development (oral, anal, phallic), although we need much more physiological evidence. Scott concludes that there are multiple sources of motivation associated with different behavioral systems and that each of these sources has a different physiological basis and special characteristics. These sources develop at different rates and each of them can be modified by learning. The frustration or satiation of any particular source of motivation must have different effects at different ages. Scott proposes that frustration early in life should cause little immediate drastic effect because many of the motivational mechanisms are weaker in early development. He notes, however, that inhibitory training should be easier early in life when the motivational mechanism is weak, and that early negative training may have persistent and drastic consequences when the motivational mechanism is fully developed. The extent to which experiences in one motivational context (e.g., social experiences) early in life influence behavior in other motivational contexts (e.g., sexual) and subsequent motivation per se needs more rigorous investigation.

3

Development of EEG and Visually
and Auditorily Evoked Potentials

Introduction

The development of electrocortical (EEG or ECG) activity in the dog will be described in detail in this chapter. Qualitative changes in the EEG during various behavioral states, such as wakefulness and sleep, at different ages are followed and compared with ontogenetic changes in other species. Developmental changes in visually and auditorily evoked potentials are described, and the significance of these changes will be discussed and compared with other species. Qualitative changes in the duration of sleep and wakefulness will be described, and ontogenetic and phylogenetic variables will be considered in relation to activated sleep.

Some aspects of the development of electrocortical activity in the dog have been reported by Charles and Fuller (1956), Pampiglione (1963), Petersen, Di Perri, and Himwich (1964), and Gokhblit (1958, 1964). There is lack of concordance in these various reports, however, notably in the time of emergence or disappearance of certain EEG phenomena and their variations with age; these differences may be attributed in part to methods of recording, type of electrodes used, method of implantation, behavior state of the subject, and restraint or type of anesthesia used during recordings.

Valatx, Jouvet, and Jouvet (1964) have provided the most detailed account of EEG development in sleep and wakefulness in the cat, and it is from their paper that the terminology used in this investigation has been principally derived.[1]

[1] EEG development has been documented in other species:
Cat: Jouvet 1962; Grossman 1955; Marley and Key 1963; Scheibel 1962
Mouse: Kobayashi et al. 1963 [*Footnote continued on next page.*]

71

As the results of the present investigation are presented, the more pertinent aspects of these studies cited (see footnote 1, this chapter) will be compared with the developing EEG of the dog.

Postnatal development of evoked potentials recorded from specific regions of the neocortex (visual, auditory, and somesthetic and transcallosal) has been studied in a few mammalian species. Rose, Adrian, and Santibanez (1957), Rose (1965), Grafstein (1963), Scherrer and Oeconomos (1954), Hunt and Goldring (1951), Ellingson and Wilcott (1960), and Marty (1962) have reported developmental studies of evoked responses to visual and auditory stimulation in the cat and rabbit.[2] Evoked responses to visual stimuli have also been studied developmentally in the unanesthetized duckling (Paulson 1965). Dustman and Beck (1966) have shown that the amplitude of visually evoked potentials changes with age in the human, and, in this species also, Ellingson (1964) provides a detailed description of the postnatal development of visually evoked responses. Myslivecek (1965) has given a general survey on the maturation of evoked responses and more recently has investigated the effects of chronic starvation on the ontogeny of evoked potentials in the dog (Myslivecek, Fox, and Zahlava 1966).

As yet, few developmental studies employing intracranial stimulation have been reported; Kling and Coustan (1964) found that somatomotor responses could be elicited in neonate kittens following stimulation of amygdala and hypothalamus. Behavioral-autonomic responses were first seen at 2 wk of age with stimulation of the hypothalamus, but not until 3 wk accompanying amygdala stimulation. Vavilova (1967) observed head and trunk muscle contractions and licking, growling, and food-searching reactions with stimulation of hippocampus or amygdala in pups aged 3–4 days. After 14 days, the response latency markedly decreased, and in addition, sniffing, salivation, licking, and chewing reactions were seen. With food-conditioned reflexes, hippocampal stimulation was facilitatory between 2 and 3 mo of age, but inhibition occurred at 5–7 mo with higher stimulus intensity.

It is unfortunate that in many of these earlier EEG and evoked potential studies, subjects were anesthetized or curarized or both, and it is known that drugs, especially barbiturates, may have paradoxical effects on electrocortical activity at different ages (Fox 1964*b*). The present investigation was designed, therefore, to permit recordings of evoked potentials from normal, alert subjects on which no drugs had been used and no curarization employed to block motor responses to painful operative procedures. Frequent handling would accustom the animals to the gentle restraint necessary for good recordings, free of movement artifacts. Discomfort at having electrodes placed on the scalp was avoided by chronic implantation of electrodes; subjects were therefore relaxed during recording sessions. Some

---

Rat: Deza and Eidelberg 1967; Crain 1952
Rabbit: Bradley et al. 1960; Laget and Delhaye 1962; Verley and Mourek 1962; Schadé 1960
Guinea pig: Marley and Key 1963; Flexner, Tyler, and Gallant 1950
Chicken: Peters, Vonderahe, and Schmid 1965
Primates: Ramirez de Arellano 1961; Caveness 1961, 1962; Meier and Berger 1965
Pig: Pampiglione 1961
Sheep: Bernhard, Kaiser, and Kolmodin 1959; Kolmodin and Meyerson 1966; Meyerson 1968
Human: Parmelee et al. 1967; Ellingson 1964; Goldie and Van Velzer 1965; Walter 1953; Dreyfus-Brisac and Blanc 1956

[2] See also Huttenlocher's (1967) study of the development of electrical activity in neocortical neurons of the kitten.

discomfort was evident the first 1–2 days postoperatively, but after this time no problems were encountered. These points are emphasized in the introduction because the purpose of this investigation was to provide developmental data from normal dogs, which would permit more accurate correlation with what is known of other parameters of CNS and behavioral development in this species. Changes in behavioral state (attentiveness), either drug-induced or caused by pain and discomfort during recording sessions, may greatly modify electrocortical activity (Beyer and Sawyer 1964; Hernández-Péon, Scherrer, and Jouvet 1956) and with control of these variables, more reliable information from the normal, alert animal may be obtained.

Materials and Methods

A total of 20 pups and 3 adult dogs were studied; 5 pups were implanted with electrodes at 1–3 days of age and the remainder at weekly intervals to give both a cross-sectional and a longitudinal study of the group as a whole. The day before surgery, all subjects were given gamma globulin (mixed antiserum) subcutaneously and Chloromycetin intramuscularly, the latter being repeated the following day. Ether anesthesia was used in pups under 3 wk of age and surgery was performed with the subject resting on a heating pad to prevent hypothermia, to which pups are extremely susceptible (Fox 1966d). Older pups were given pentobarbital intravenously. In later studies, Innovar-Vet (Fentanyl and Droperidol, McNeil) was used in pups as young as 3 days, providing excellent analgesia and sedation. Under aseptic surgery, small holes (using a 23-gauge hypodermic needle, or a dental drill in older subjects) were made in the skull in the right frontal region,[3] for the indifferent electrode, and over the right and left gyrus ectosylvius medius (auditory analyzer) and right and left gyrus lateralis (visual analyzer). In 5 pups, additional electrodes were inserted in the gyrus precoronalis (motor region). Electrodes with stainless steel points were inserted through the skull openings so as to rest on the dura or in the superficial cell layers of the cortex. The depth of these electrodes was critical, for in pilot studies it was found that if they were inserted too deeply, evoked visual and auditory responses were extremely variable (see also discussion by Ochs 1965). Up to 2 wk of age, the electrodes were approximately 3 mm in length, for older pups they were 4–5 mm, and for adults 7 mm. The electrodes, which were insulated except for the tip, were connected with leads which ran subcutaneously and emerged at the scruff of the neck. After a small area of periosteum had been removed, the electrodes were secured to the skull using gelfoam soaked with physiological adhesive (methyl 2 cyanoacrylate monomer, Ethicon, Inc.). The incision was closed with monofilament nylon, a small opening being left in the skin at the base of the skull to allow exit of the electrode leads, which were of different colors to facilitate identification. Growth of the skull had surprisingly little influence on the recordings, although occasionally some electrodes became detached after 2–3 wk. In some pups

---

[3] In the cat, Rose (personal communication) finds that a large ERG component contaminates the visually evoked response when this reference is used. Using this reference in the dog, and comparing the visual EP with other recordings using a different reference placed caudal to the nuchial crest (cutaneous-scruff), no differences attributable to ERG contamination were found. This may be a species difference; dogs used in this study were relatively dolichocephalic compared with the brachycephalic cat.

operated on at 7 days, excellent recordings were obtained for 8 wk; the electrodes were found to have been grown over by the periosteum and to have become securely embedded in the skull.

When the EEG was recorded, the subject was held in the lap of an assistant (who was also grounded), with the pup's head resting on the palm of the hand; an indication of tonus in the neck muscles could therefore be obtained, thus permitting approximation of the degree of relaxation of the subject. Swaddling in a towel was necessary to reduce body movements during recordings of evoked potentials. Older dogs were held gently under the chin to reduce head movements; with frequent recording sessions, all subjects soon became accustomed to these procedures. Recordings were taken every second day. For greater precision and comparison of recordings, some subjects were recorded (bipolar and monopolar) on an 8-channel type R Offner dynograph as well as on a Grass 8-channel recorder. EMG and eye-movement recordings were also recorded on the Offner by using Michele wound-clip electrodes inserted over the neck and near the lateral canthus of each eye. During every recording session, which lasted for approximately 60 min, constant behavioral observations were made using a simple word-code which was noted on the continuous EEG recordings.

Evoked potentials were recorded from the chronic-electrode subjects on a Grass 6-channel recorder and monitored on an oscilloscope. Averaged evoked responses were recorded on a Computer of Average Transients (CAT 400 B). Stimulation was applied with the swaddled subject in a light- and soundproof box, in which was placed a flash lamp (Grass PS-1 Photic Stimulator, intensity setting "16," flash duration 10 μsec) and a loudspeaker giving a "click" of 5 msec duration. As a standard procedure, 10 stimuli were presented at each of the 3 frequencies employed (0.1, 0.4, and 1.0/sec). The evoked response was displayed on an oscilloscope, the application of the stimulus occurring 50 msec after the onset of the sweep. An average of the 10 stimuli was computed by the CAT and recorded on a Mosely X-Y plotter. Analysis times of 1,000 msec were used for both visual and auditory responses, and in addition an analysis time of 500 msec was used to permit more precise determinations of the shorter latency auditory responses. A criticism of this method of averaging evoked responses is that in younger animals rapid fatigue develops with repetitive stimulation. This, however, is offset by standardized procedures (same frequency and number of stimuli per session) and tends to accentuate age differences (i.e., comparing fatigue rate with age) in a developmental evaluation of the data. Responses to a single stimulus were also recorded at analysis times of 500 and 1,000 msec at different ages. Latencies of the first positive and negative waves were calculated, and also the more variable "onset" latency represented by a sudden change from the isoelectric point before the onset of the first wave.

Fifteen pups were studied at weekly intervals from birth until 5 wk of age in order to follow the development of sleep and wakefulness. For behavioral observations, they were removed from the mother and observed singly in a 1½-ft-square box lined with a heating pad (75° F) for 30 min. The observer was seated approximately 3 ft away from the pup and recorded the duration of the three behavioral states described below and the type of movement and activity, using a simple letter-code system. The following day, EMG (neck), EKG, and respiration recordings were taken, using a rubber-tubing plethysmograph and modified Michele wound clips attached to the electrode leads of a Grass 4-channel recorder. Recordings were terminated after representative periods of wakefulness, quiet, and activated sleep had been observed. These physiological recordings were made separately from the behavioral observations because the recording equipment and electrodes were disturbing to the subjects and disrupted their normal sleep-awake activity. The behavioral state and types of movement or activity were noted on the recordings using the same letter-code system as for behavioral observations.

The relative duration of various behavioral states associated with wakefulness and sleep in the dog at different postnatal ages was recorded using the behavioral criteria described in the kitten by Valatx, Jouvet, and Jouvet (1964).

Alert or Wakefulness. Attention to observer, maintenance of upright standing or sitting posture, or lying down but responsive to observer's moving hand; may attempt to escape from apparatus; in younger pups, crawling, rooting (directed movements) and constant vocalization.

Quiet Sleep and Drowsiness. Subject lying on stomach or side, often in characteristic curled sleeping posture with hind legs tucked up and head and neck turned caudolaterally; eyelids may or may not be closed; no vocalization, no directed movements, and subject not responsive to observer's waving hand; occasional stretching, yawning, polypnea, and infrequent body, leg, or neck jerks; may awaken briefly and return to drowsy state or quiet sleep.

Activated or Paradoxical Sleep. Subject in same posture as in quiet sleep, eyelids may or may not be closed; frequent vocalization, no directed movement, and subject not responsive to observer's movements; occasional polypnea, apnea, frequent vocalization, and rapid movements or jerks of the limbs and body, twitching of the panniculus carnosus, myoclonic neck and head movements, and rapid fibrillation or twitching of facial muscles and ears; rapid eye movements and fibrillary palpebral activity are commonly observed; limb movements may become tonic-clonic and the pup awakens suddenly after extremely violent activity.

Results of EEG Analysis

Birth—1 Wk. At birth and during the first week of life, electrocortical activity was predominantly of low amplitude (5–15 μv) and of variable frequency ranging from 6 to 8 cycles per sec interspersed with irregular bursts of spindlelike activity and periods of relative equipotentiality (fig. 3.1). Changes in behavioral state (e.g., sleep, alertness) were not accompanied by detectable changes in the EEG at 3 days of age, other than a slight increase in the frequency of occurrence of bursts of higher amplitude (50–150 μv) fast activity (16–18 c/sec), especially in the motor region during sleep. These bursts of activity, also occurring in the awake state, may be called "neonatal spindles" (fig. 3.1).[4] Sleep in the neonate, from birth to 7 days, consisted mainly of hyperkinesis (body jerks and twitches), coarse and and fine tremors affecting the face and body, occasional vocalization, sucking, crawling, and scratching movements; thus the behavioral state of the animal might be mistakenly described as alert. This type of sleep in the adult has been called activated or REM (rapid eye movement) sleep and was first described in the cat by Dement (1958).

[4] Similar phenomena have been described in fetal sheep by Kolmodin and Meyerson (1966).

The term "paradoxical" sleep is used by Valatx, Jouvet, and Jouvet (1964) instead of "activated" sleep; in neonatal kittens, where fast EEG activity is not yet developed in activated sleep, they use the term "sleep with jerks." In the neonate dog, however, quiet sleep was of extremely short duration and was not clearly recognizable until the 12th to 14th day, when slow wave activity was first seen. During quiet sleep, the amplitude and frequency of occurrence of neonatal spindles increase. Valatx, Jouvet, and Jouvet (1964) used the term "quiet sleep" to describe the neonatal phase of the same phenomenon in the adult cat, which they term "slow wave sleep."

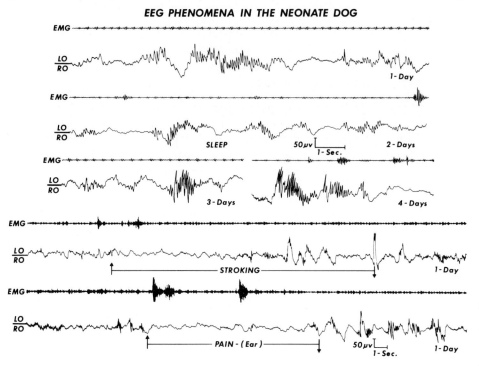

Fig. 3.1. Variations in neonatal spindle activity recorded from right and left occipital regions at different ages. Little EMG activity is present during these episodes of high-amplitude bursts of electrical activity. Stroking and painful stimulation (*bottom of figure*) cause flattening of EEG and reduction of spindle activity.

From birth to 7 days, an apparently alert and active pup showing slow orienting locomotor patterns might suddenly pass into activated sleep. A brief interval (5–15 sec) of cessation of body movements might be seen; this increased with age and might represent drowsiness or quiet sleep. Usually, however, the slow movements of the alert animal became rapid and irregular, nondirected (or nonoriented), and notably the facial and ear muscles began to contract, causing fine facial tremors and occasional movements of the neck, ears, lips, and jaws. The palpebral muscles showed fine tremors and when the eyelids had separated, rapid or slow vermiform eye movements were seen. Respiration was irregular. These were the signs of activated sleep, and during this state the frequency of occurrence and the amplitude of neonatal spindles increased, but might be absent or suppressed when body movements were intense (fig. 3.2). Tactile stimulation of the head, stroking the back, or painful stimulation by pinching the tail or digital web evoked an arousal reaction which could occasionally be detected in the neonatal EEG when not obscured by movement artifacts (fig. 3.1). A slight reduction in amplitude occurred (a general flattening or desynchronization of the EEG, indicative of arousal), and the neonatal spindles either disappeared or were greatly reduced in amplitude. Occasionally, immediately after the cessation of stimulation, an abrupt increase in amplitude and an increase in neonatal spindling occurred. Prolonged painful stimulation might occasionally elicit a hypersynchrony of the EEG pattern, characterized by regular slow waves (Ata-Muradova 1960); this phenomenon has been observed in 7-day-old pups but can be more readily recognized between 14 and 28 days (fig. 3.3).

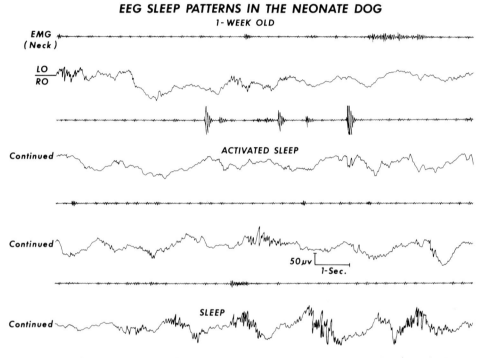

Fig. 3.2. Continuous recordings from left and right occipital regions during sleep in 7-day-old dog. Spindlelike activity reduced or absent during activated sleep, when EMG activity increases.

Because of movement artifacts, hypersynchronous recordings resulting from nociceptive stimulation are difficult to evaluate.

By 7 days of age, the electrical activity in the motor region, although still of low amplitude, had become regular in frequency, in contrast to the irregular, low amplitude (at times almost isoelectric) activity still evident in the less mature visual and auditory regions.

8–14 Days. During this period, definite changes in EEG activity occurred, the most dramatic phenomenon being the appearance of irregular slow waves 2–4 c/sec, generally of low amplitude, associated with quiet sleep at around 12–14 days of age, but occasionally attaining an amplitude of 60–100 μv (fig. 3.4). The interval between wakefulness and the onset of activated sleep increased markedly, and by 14 days a clearly defined sleep, devoid of rapid body movements, characterized by regular respiration and similar to the "quiet sleep" of the adult, was seen, which may indicate that functional integration of the thalamocortical pathways associated with quiet sleep occurs at this time. In the alert pup, by 14 days of age slow 2–4 c/sec activity of medium amplitude (25–50 μv) and faster 8–12 c/sec activity (amplitude 10–50 μv) could be distinguished. This fast activity occurred irregularly and might have been suppressed neonatal spindles. Occasional bursts of 6–8 c/sec activity of 25–35 μv amplitude were seen in the alert pup and also appeared during

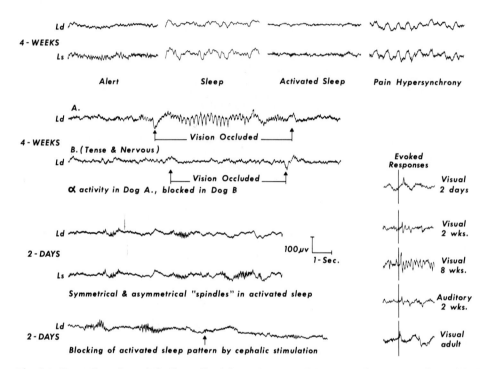

Fig. 3.3. Recordings from left (lateralis sinistra, *Ls*) and right (lateralis dextra, *Ld*) occipital regions, showing the following important phenomena: desynchronization of EEG in alert and activated sleep and synchronization in sleep and during painful stimulation: alphalike activity during occlusion of vision, and variations in neonatal spindle activity. Visual and auditory stimuli cause an evoked response to appear on the EEG (*right of figure*). Latencies (*marked by vertical line*) from the time of stimulation to the appearance of an evoked response rapidly decrease with age: auditorily evoked responses cannot be elicited until 2 wk of age.

activated sleep. Around 13–16 days very fast (18–20 c/sec) low amplitude (5–25 μv) activity was recorded during activated sleep. Neonatal spindles gradually lost their high amplitude (10–50 μv) but continued to occur in bursts of 3–6 waves at frequencies of 12–16 c/sec at irregular intervals during activated sleep and in the alert state. As in the kitten around 2 wk of age (Valatx, Jouvet, and Jouvet 1964), fast low voltage activity was evident throughout activated sleep; but in the alert state, this activity was not yet continuous. The motor cortex was the first to show continuous activity in some pups after 14 days of age. The EEG activity in the visual region early in this period was intermittent and by 14 days had become continuous, but fewer fast components were present than in the motor region (see fig. 3.5*a–d*).

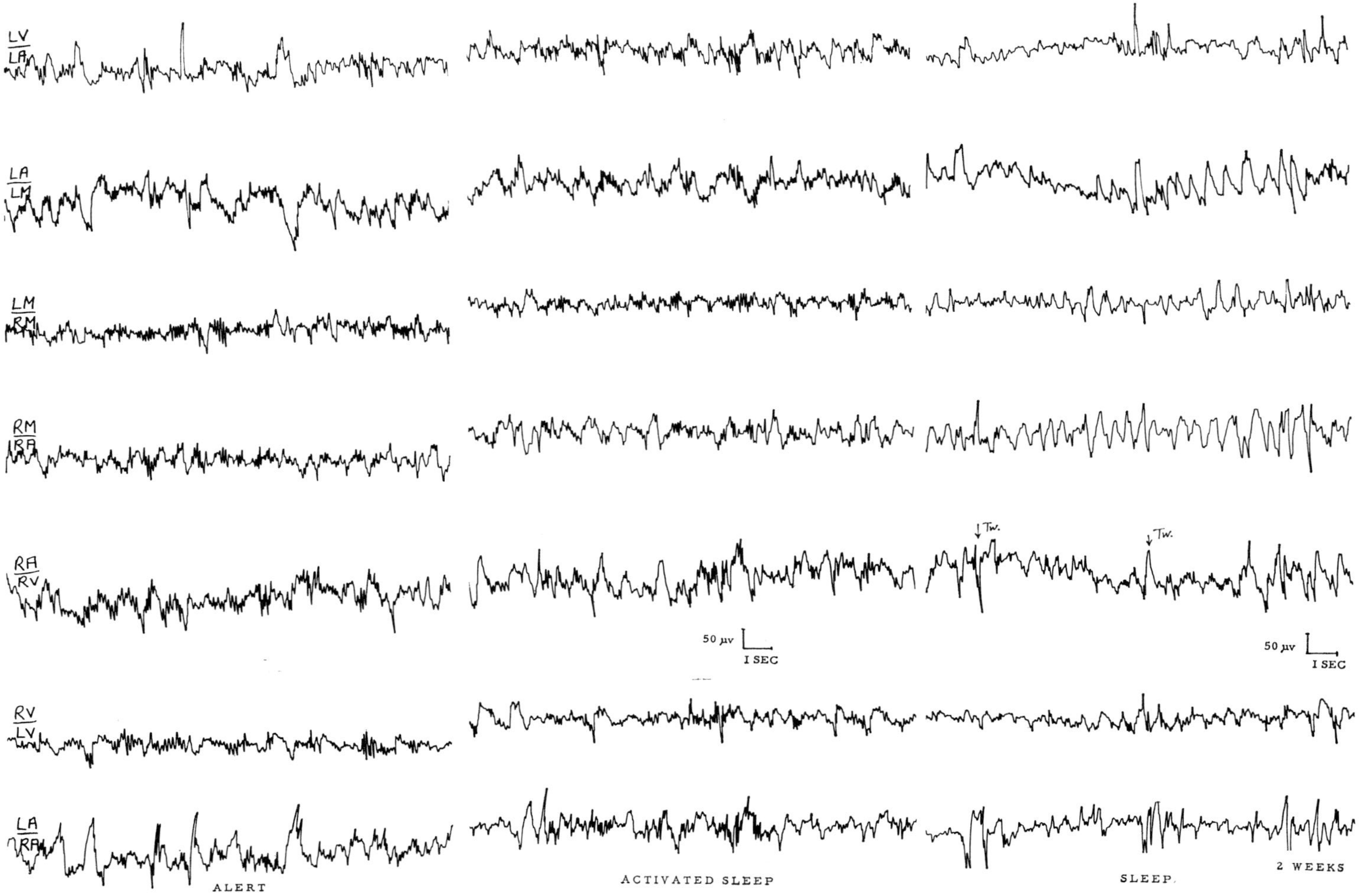

Fig. 3.4. Chronic electrode recordings (in cascade) from left and right visual, motor, and auditory regions in 2-wk-old dog. Top and center traces show bursts of spindle activity predominantly in motor and visual regions during alert and activated sleep periods. Trace at bottom shows slow wave activity characteristic of quiet sleep, with absence of spindling. (T_w = occasional body twitch seen during quiet sleep as contrasted to frequent rapid movements during activated sleep.)

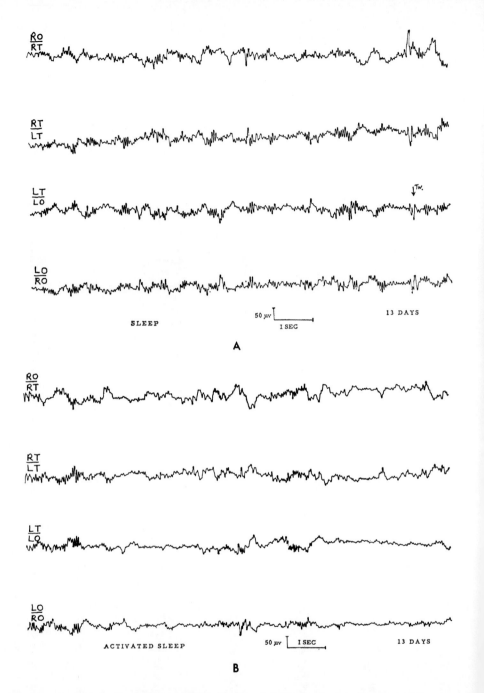

Fig. 3.5. (*a*) Chronic electrode recordings (in cascade) from left and right occipital and temporal (auditory) regions in 13-day-old dog. Frequent bursts of neonatal spindles during quiet sleep, with no episodes of relative flatness of EEG as seen in activated sleep.

(*b*) Recordings during activated sleep as in fig. 3.5*a*, showing periodic bursts of spindling between episodes of relative flatness of EEG (indicative of desynchronization).

80

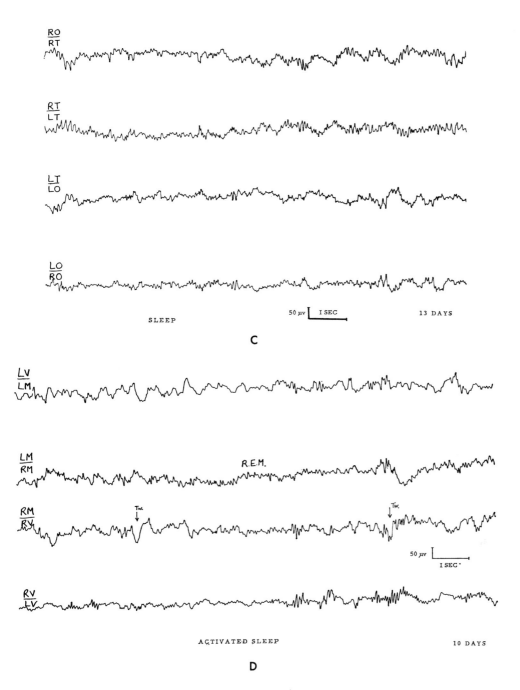

RO/RT

RT/LT

LT/LO

LO/RO

SLEEP   50 μν ⌐ I SEC   13 DAYS

C

LV/LM

LM/RM   R.E.M.

RM/RV   Tw.   Tw.   50 μν ⌐
               I SEC ·

RV/LV

ACTIVATED SLEEP   10 DAYS

D

Fig. 3.5. *Continued*

(*c*) Recordings as in fig. 3.5*a*, showing variation in quiet sleep: reduction in spindle bursts and predominance of low amplitude slow wave activity.

(*d*) EEG from 10-day-old dog during activated sleep. Left and right visual and motor cascade recordings. *REM* = period of rapid eye movement. *Tw* = body movement. Note continuous activity present in motor regions, whereas the less mature visual regions have lower amplitude. Occasional bursts of low amplitude neonatal spindles occur especially in visual regions.

81

15–21 Days. Slow wave activity associated with quiet sleep increased in duration and in amplitude and became more synchronous during this period, and in activated sleep and wakefulness, a regular low amplitude fast activity emerged. The appearance of the alert pattern and desynchronized low-amplitude arousal reaction in the rabbit has been correlated by Laget and Delhaye (1962) with the development of the theta hippocampal rhythm and functional integration of hippocampus and neocortex; a similar hippocampal-neocortical integration may be established in the dog during this period. Synchronous slow wave activity in drowsiness and quiet sleep was easily recognizable by 17 days. Neonatal spindles disappeared completely during this period; in the kitten also they disappear at 3 wk of age, according to Valatx, Jouvet, and Jouvet (1964), and may reappear at around 6 wk. A phenomenon resembling neonatal spindling could be demonstrated after nociceptive stimulation around 3 wk of age. This paroxysmal, synchronous 25–45 μv, medium amplitude 14–16 c/sec activity may be nonspecific thalamocortical activity. It was not normally seen in pups of this age, but a similar phenomenon was observed in 5-wk-old pups on emergence from 1 wk of isolation in a darkened room. These subjects were intensely aroused, and all isolation-reared subjects showed this paroxysmal fast frequency activity (see chap. 6). In the normal pup, it is possible that neonatal spindles are a manifestation of nonspecific thalamocortical activity, or they may originate from other subcortical structures (reticular formation?) to become submerged or masked by the later developing, predominantly slow wave activity of the more mature thalamocortical function related to quiet sleep. Occasional bursts of groups of 3–4 waves, 25–45 μv, and 14–16 c/sec were seen very rarely in normal pups aged between 3 and 4 wk; these may be "remnants" of the neonatal spindlelike activity.

In man, occlusion of vision causes the appearance of alpha activity, predominantly in the occipital region. Occlusion of vision had no detectable effect in pups at 14–15 days even though the eyelids had separated. Rhythmic 10 c/sec activity was not seen until after 16–18 days of age; by 3 wk the effect of visual occlusion was clearly demonstrated. The amplitude of these waves ranged from 25–65 μv up to 100 μv. In some older pups this rhythmic activity was not seen, especially in tense and highly aroused dogs (see chap. 6).

22–28 Days. With clear differentiation of high amplitude slow wave activity with superimposed low amplitude fast activity in quiet sleep at 3 wk of age and low amplitude fast activity characteristic of wakefulness and activated sleep, few major developmental changes take place during this period (fig. 3.6). The basic characteristics of the mature EEG are established during this period, with the exception of paroxysmal sleep activity and sleep spindles, which emerge later. By 25 days, the pup would only rarely pass directly from wakefulness into activated sleep. Activated sleep now followed a definite pattern, occurring most often after a longer period of quiet sleep and being greatly reduced in proportion to wakefulness and quiet sleep. Before the onset of synchronous, slow wave quiet sleep, a period of drowsiness was recognizable. In the drowsy state, the eyes were often open, respiration was irregular, and the pup might voluntarily shift its body position, scratch, and yawn; the alert EEG pattern was gradually modified by an increase in amplitude, but fast components were still present. Auditory or visual stimulation caused rapid desynchronization with a return to the low amplitude fast activity of the alert state. Some pups during this period would pass from drowsiness to quiet sleep (during which slow wave activity predominated), and then into activated sleep with the eyes remaining open. Sudden awakening from activated sleep often occurred after an abrupt body movement or almost convulsivelike seizure affecting the entire body. EEG changes were sometimes undetectable in the transition between activated sleep and wakefulness. Awakening from quiet sleep was always more gradual, slow wave synchronization often recurring at a slightly reduced amplitude (i.e., a state of drowsiness) between periods of relative wakefulness, during which low amplitude

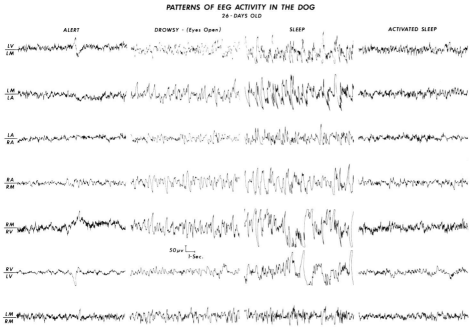

PATTERNS OF EEG ACTIVITY IN THE DOG
26 - DAYS OLD

Fig. 3.6. Chronic electrode, bipolar recordings from left and right visual, auditory, and motor regions of 26-day-old pup, showing the four major types of EEG activity: desynchronized, low amplitude alert and activated sleep, synchronized slow wave activity in drowsiness, increasing in amplitude in quiet sleep.

fast activity predominated. The pup might waken, move, and rest drowsily for some time or pass back into quiet sleep. Awakening from activated sleep was therefore abrupt; possibly reticular activation (Moruzzi and Magoun 1949) causing desynchronization in activated sleep may continue to function and the EEG shows little modification during the return of wakefulness.

29–40 Days. During this period activated sleep always followed quiet sleep, and its frequency of occurrence was greatly reduced compared with the 21–28-day age group. Decrease in frequency and increase in amplitude of slow wave activity continued during this period, and these waves often showed a notching, resembling the biparietal humps described in man during light sleep (Gibbs and Gibbs 1950). The induction of quiet sleep was preceded by an already recognizable phase of drowsiness, as synchronous slow wave activity appeared in the EEG traces. This activity might appear first in the visual or auditory leads, and then spread gradually to other cortical areas (fig. 3.7a–d). Arousal by auditory stimulation became in-

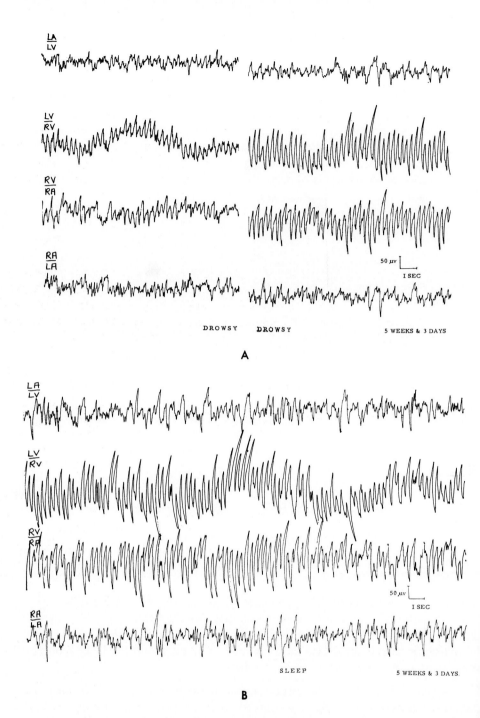

Fig. 3.7*a–d*. Chronic electrode, successive recordings from left and right visual and auditory regions in a pup 5 wk, 3 days old. In drowsiness (*a*), hypersynchronous waves develop predominantly in the right visual region, increasing gradually in amplitude (*right side*). There is a gradual increase in amplitude in the auditory regions as the animal enters sleep (*b*), which increases and becomes synchronous and widespread throughout all regions (*c*). In contrast, amplitude is reduced and the EEG becomes desynchronized in activated sleep (*d*).

84

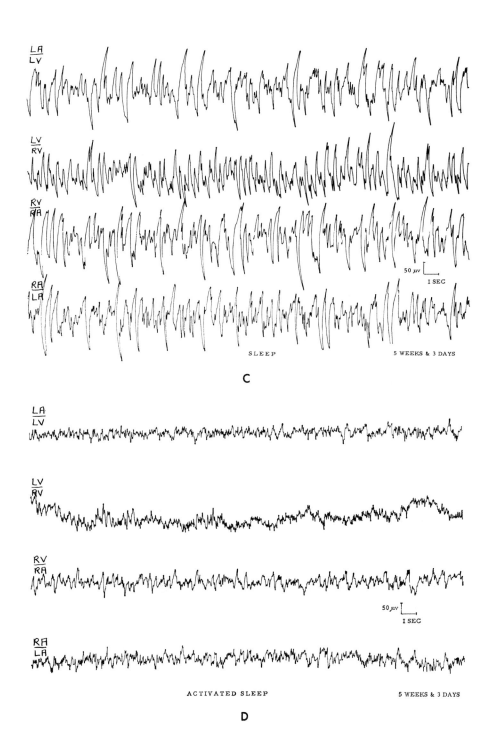

C

D

Fig. 3.7. *Continued*

85

creasingly more difficult as the amplitude and degree of slow wave synchrony in different cortical areas increased. This definitely suggests that there are "levels" or varying depths of quiet sleep.

The first evidence of paroxysmal sleep was seen toward 35 days of age, being identical to the phenomenon described in man (Gibbs and Gibbs 1950), and has been termed *somnus alternans* in the dog by Redding, Prynn, and Colwell (1964). Paroxysmal sleep was characterized by short bursts of high amplitude (100–200 μv) slow wave (4 c/sec) activity mixed with 25–40 μv, 6–10 c/sec activity and appeared predominantly in the visual region and to a lesser extent in the auditory region, ranging in duration from 2 to 6 sec and recurring at intervals of 5–20 sec.

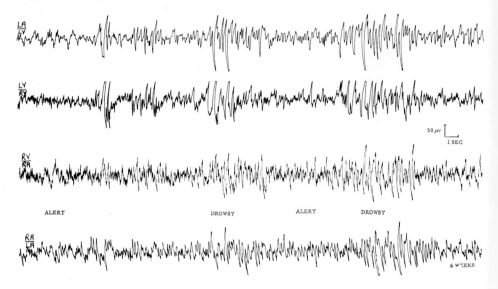

Fig. 3.8. Paroxysmal sleep (slow wave, high-amplitude activity interspersed with periods of alert, low-amplitude fast activity) in 8-wk-old dog; recordings from right and left auditory and visual regions.

Between these paroxysms, which might be mistaken for epileptiform discharges, there were periods of desynchronization, similar to the alert pattern, but occasionally of slightly higher amplitude; this activity consisted predominantly of 6–10 c/sec waves of 20–40 μv with occasional 4 c/sec waves of medium amplitude (30–60 μv). Paroxysmal sleep was seen from this age onward (fig. 3.8).

Adultlike spindle activity (14–16 c/sec) was first recorded around 5–6 wk of age, predominantly in the motor region, but also in visual and auditory areas during quiet sleep (fig. 3.9). These spindle bursts varied in duration from ¼ to ½ sec, and ranged from 100 to 175 μv in amplitude. They were usually superimposed on the high amplitude slow waves which were predominant during quiet sleep. Valatx, Jouvet, and Jouvet (1964) first observed adultlike spindles in the kitten at 6 wk of age. They correlated the development of slow wave activity, first seen around 4 wk, with the proliferation of basilar dendrites of the pyramidal neurones. They abolished slow waves after neocortical ablation; but with thalamic ablation only, slow waves persisted and spindles disappeared.

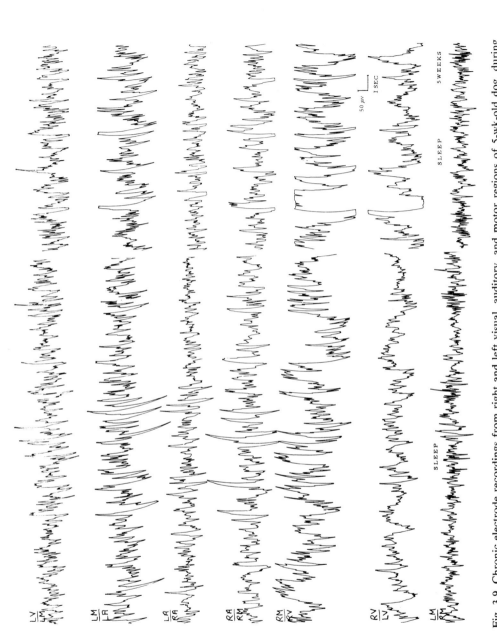

Fig. 3.9. Chronic electrode recordings from right and left visual, auditory, and motor regions of 5-wk-old dog, during quiet sleep. Note lesser amplitude of slow wave activity in motor regions where spindle activity predominates. This adultlike spindle activity occurring early in quiet sleep is first seen at this age.

40 Days Onward. The major changes in the EEG after 5 wk consisted of a further increase in frequency of the fast components and in the amplitude of the slow waves up to 10 wk of age (fig. 3.10). Between 12 and 16 wk, there was a diminution in the amplitude of the alert EEG, but the frequency continued to increase into adulthood (fig. 3.11). In the alert EEG, 4–6, 10–12, and 16–18 c/sec frequencies were seen after 5 wk of age, varying in amplitude from 25 to 30, 15 to 25, and 5 to 10 μv respectively, the faster activities predominating in the adult; in some pups over 3 mo of age, low amplitude fast activity ranging from 25 to 35 c/sec

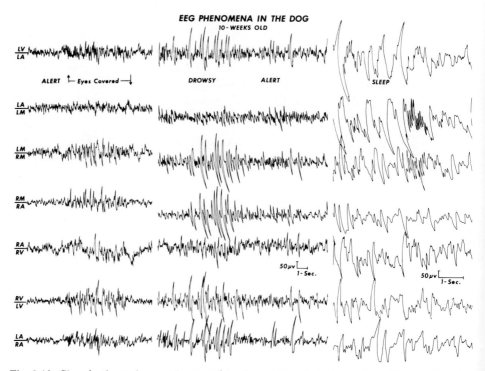

Fig. 3.10. Chronic electrode cascade recordings from left and right visual, auditory, and motor regions, showing increased amplitude during occlusion of vision, in transient drowsiness or paroxysmal sleep, and spindling in quiet sleep, predominantly in the motor regions.

was recorded. Similar frequencies were seen during activated sleep. From 5–7 wk onward, animals in the drowsy state showed predominantly hypersynchronous 3–4 c/sec 50–100 μv activity with some 6–8 c/sec 25–50 μv waves (fig. 3.10). In older dogs, bursts of 50–150 μv waves, varying in frequency from 10 to 12 c/sec, occurred during drowsiness (fig. 3.12*a, b*), resembling "slow spindles" in man (Gibbs and Gibbs 1950). In quiet sleep the predominant activity consisted of slow 2–4 c/sec waves varying in amplitude from 100 to 250 μv with superimposed 6–8 c/sec, 25–50 μv activity. Spindling in quiet sleep increased in frequency by 2–4 c/sec and occurred predominantly in the motor region (fig. 3.13). In more mature subjects, individual differences in alert EEG pattern could be correlated with behavior; the more tense, apprehensive dogs showed greater desynchronization, and low amplitude activity, often with muscle artifacts. (Additional EEG phenomena are shown in figs. 3.14–3.19.)

Results of Sleep-Wakefulness Study

The greatest irregularities in heart and respiration rates were recorded during activated sleep at all ages. These irregularities included cardiac arrhythmia, dropped beats, and short periods of polypnea or apnea (fig. 3.20). EMG activity was frequently seen during activated sleep, but only rarely in quiet sleep. Although the neck muscles are considered to be relaxed in activated sleep, EMG activity was frequently recorded because head and neck movements occur regularly throughout activated sleep and only rarely in quiet sleep. In the alert subject, EMG activity in the neck muscles is relatively constant. These data have been summarized in table 3.2. During activated sleep, independent of age, dropped beats were noted on the EKG, frequently accompanied by short periods of apnea. Similar phenomena were seen more rarely during drowsiness (fig. 3.20). Respiration and heart rate in quiet sleep were always slow and regular, but at the onset of quiet sleep (drowsiness), polypnea might be seen, which gradually gave rise to slower, more regular respiration accompanied by cessation of EMG activity.

ONTOGENY OF EEG IN THE OCCIPITAL REGION OF THE DOG

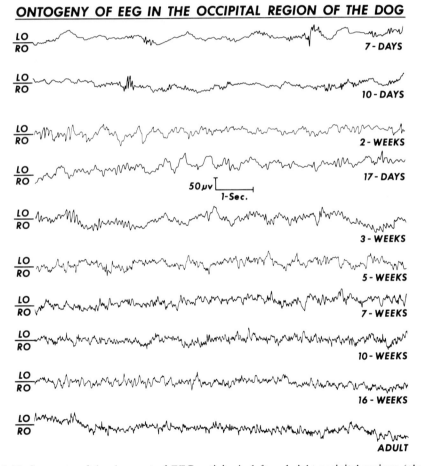

Fig. 3.11. Summary of development of EEG activity in left and right occipital regions (chronic electrodes) during wakefulness. Discontinuous activity, with bursts of spindlelike activity present until 14 days. From 14 days onward, there is a gradual reduction in amplitude of the alert EEG and increase in fast wave components.

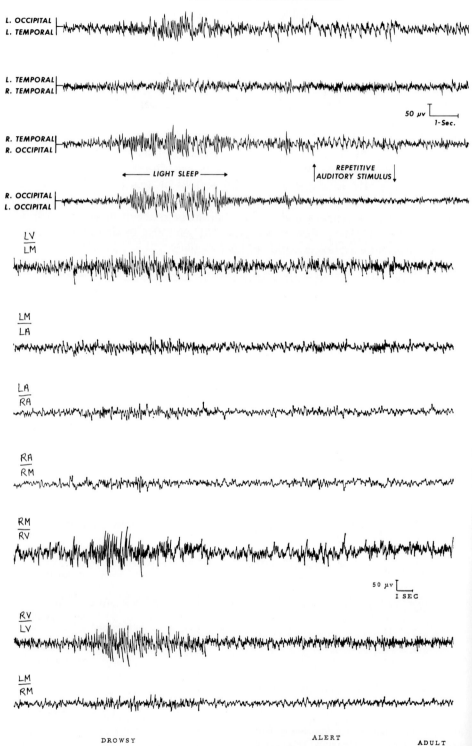

EEG RECORDINGS OF 5 WEEK OLD PUP
(SLEEP SPINDLES & AUDITORY DRIVING)

L. OCCIPITAL
L. TEMPORAL

L. TEMPORAL
R. TEMPORAL

50 µv
1-Sec.

R. TEMPORAL
R. OCCIPITAL

←— LIGHT SLEEP —→

↑ REPETITIVE
AUDITORY STIMULUS ↓

R. OCCIPITAL
L. OCCIPITAL

$\dfrac{LV}{LM}$

$\dfrac{LM}{LA}$

$\dfrac{LA}{RA}$

$\dfrac{RA}{RM}$

$\dfrac{RM}{RV}$

50 µv
I SEC

$\dfrac{RV}{LV}$

$\dfrac{LM}{RM}$

DROWSY   ALERT   ADULT

Fig. 3.12a, b. Burst of fast frequency high amplitude (spindling) activity during light sleep or drowsiness in 5-wk-old pup and adult dog (b) (predominantly in visual region in b), contrasting with the more usual high amplitude slow wave activity accompanying this behavior. Repetitive auditory stimulation in (a) causes arousal and "driving" of the EEG, in that slow waves appear and are in time with the frequency of stimulation.

TABLE 3.1

ONTOGENY OF EVOKED POTENTIALS IN THE DOG

AGE (in days)	NUMBER OF SUBJECTS	VISUALLY EP[a]		AUDITORILY EP[a]	
		+	−	+	−
1– 3	2	. . . .	275	. . . .	. . . .
7	5	. . . .	240	. . . .	. . . .
8–14	10	120	165	. . . .	. . . .
12–14	8	. . . .	. . . .	80	100
21–28	18	82.5	120	45	65
35–70	14	50	90	20	35
77–adult	9	40	85	15.5	30

[a] Averaged peak latencies of initial positive and negative components in msec.

TABLE 3.2

DURATION OF SLEEP AND WAKEFULNESS DURING 30-MIN OBSERVATION PERIODS

Age (in Days)	State	Number of Pups	Mean Time (sec)	Median Time (sec)	Percentage of 30 Min (1,800 sec)
1	Alert	10	64	35	3.55
	Activated sleep	10	1712	1765	95.11
	Quiet sleep	10	19	0	1.05
7	Alert	15	288	225	16.0
	Activated sleep	15	1498.73	1575	83.26
	Quiet sleep	15	10.6	0	0.58
14	Alert	13	270	160	15.0
	Activated sleep	13	1430	1565	79.44
	Quiet sleep	13	101.53	10	5.64
21	Alert	13	870.77	720	48.37
	Activated sleep	13	675.77	810.0	37.54
	Quiet sleep	13	271.92	230	15.10
28	Alert	15	1124	975	62.44
	Activated sleep	15	436.0	300.0	24.22
	Quiet sleep	15	240.0	80.0	13.33
35	Alert	12	1112.91	970.0	61.82
	Activated sleep	12	137.08	0	7.61
	Quiet sleep	12	551.66	640.0	30.64

Behavioral observations were run separately because the presence of electrodes and connecting leads was disturbing and only after prolonged periods would pups sleep during polygraph recordings. The pups were removed from their home pen and observed singly in the heated box. This change to a novel environment, and the presence of the observer, caused the majority of older subjects to remain awake throughout the 30-min observation period. The tendency to fall into activated sleep decreased with increasing age, showing an abrupt decline from birth to 2 wk. From this age onward, when slow wave quiet sleep is first noted in EEG (see earlier), there is a gradual increase in the preponderance of quiet sleep. Up to 3 wk of age, pups would frequently pass from activated sleep to wakefulness, the percentage duration of these two states being similar by 3 wk. At 4 wk of age, the

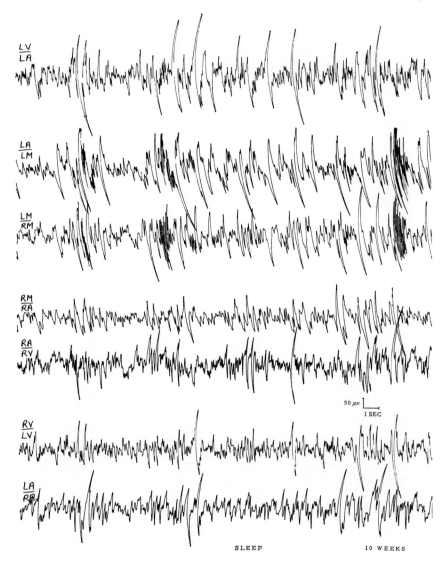

Fig. 3.13. More mature spindle activity in 10-wk-old dog (as contrasted with fig. 9), predominantly in the motor regions during quiet sleep.

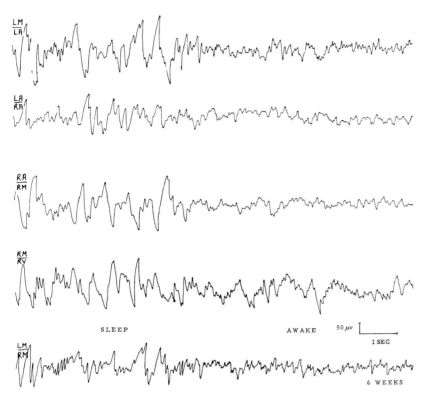

Fig. 3.14. Transition from drowsy or light sleep to wakefulness in 6-wk-old dog, showing marked change from high-amplitude slow wave to low-amplitude fast activity.

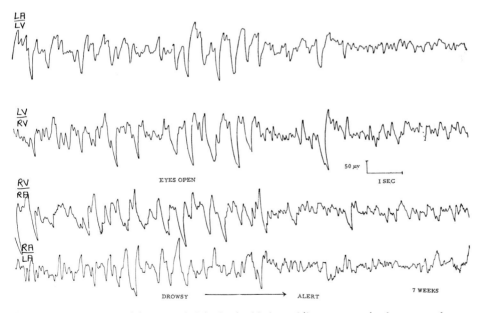

Fig. 3.15. Slow wave activity recorded in 7-wk-old dog while eyes remained open, a drowsy activity resembling daydreaming.

majority of subjects remained awake throughout the entire period of observation or passed into quiet sleep or "drowsiness" toward the end of the observation period. Young pups would frequently pass from wakefulness to activated sleep, but with increasing age, an increasingly longer period of quiet sleep became interposed between wakefulness and activated sleep. Activated sleep was rarely observed in pups at 5 wk of age (fig. 3.21).

Results of Evoked Potential Studies

These data are summarized in table 3.1. The following qualitative changes were observed:[5]

1–7 Days. No auditory evoked potentials were obtained during this period in

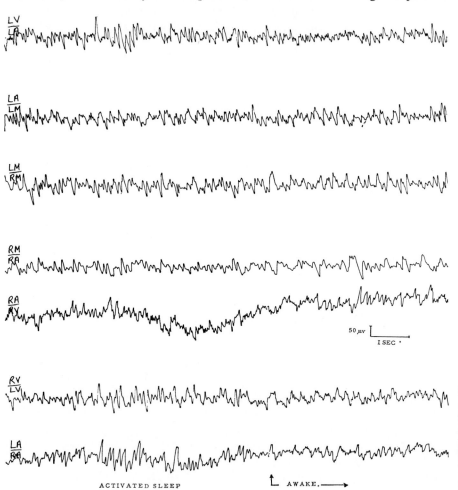

Fig. 3.16. Transition from activated sleep to wakefulness in 10-wk-old dog. Note little change in EEG, contrasted with marked change in behavioral state and return to consciousness.

[5] In all age groups, only the peak latencies of the positive and negative components of the primary evoked potentials are described.

all 10 animals, presumably because the external auditory meatus does not open until 12–14 days. Visually evoked responses were obtained in 2 pups at 1–3 days of age, but amplitude and latency of response were extremely variable and often asymmetrical (fig. 3.22). With increasing age, a positive component appeared in the visual response of 4 pups at 1 wk of age, which preceded the long latency negative component (fig. 3.22). In 2 dogs, a second positive component following the negative wave was recorded.

8–14 Days. In 8 of the 10 subjects, auditory responses were first evoked between 12 and 14 days of age, being relatively more mature than the earlier obtained visual responses (fig. 3.24). In the visually evoked response, in all subjects a double negative wave was recorded occasionally: this consisted of a negative peak of vari-

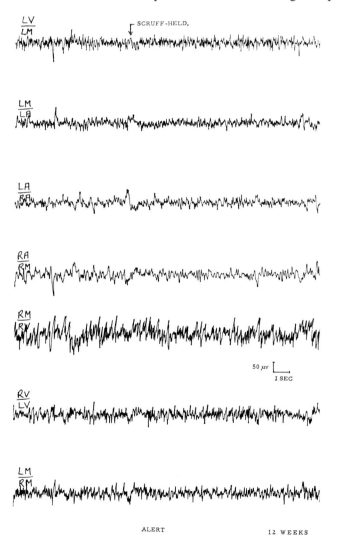

Fig. 3.17. Increased desynchronization with reduction in amplitude of slow wave components in 12-wk-old pup while held by scruff of neck. This indicates intense arousal (electrode *RV* shows some movement artifact).

able amplitude which preceded the initial negative component recorded at earlier ages, and which was separated from the second negative peak by a positive component of variable amplitude (figs. 3.23, 3.26).

15–28 Days. Auditorily evoked responses were obtained in all subjects (fig. 3.24). During the early half of this period, the double negativity of the visually evoked potential was pronounced, but between 24 and 28 days this phenomenon

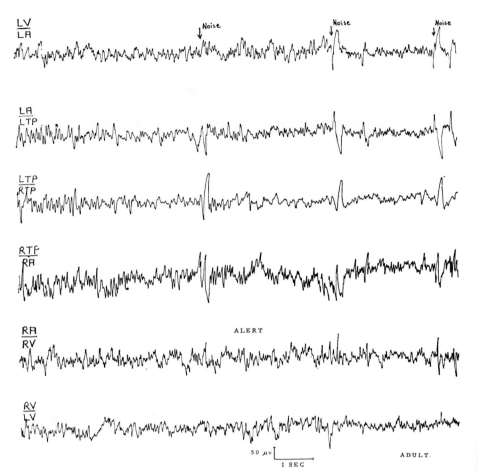

Fig. 3.18. Alert activity in a more relaxed adult, showing "K" complex evoked by extraneous noise, predominantly in the auditory regions (*RTP* and *LTP*).

disappeared: the two negative peaks coalesced (figs. 3.23, 3.26). During this time, the initial positive component greatly increased in amplitude. Between 15 and 28 days of age, the visually evoked response in all dogs was characteristically multicomplex; as many as 4 negative peaks were evident, the 2 additional peaks occurring as "afterdischarges" (figs. 3.23, 3.26).

5–10 Wk. Throughout this period, the visually evoked response gradually lost the multicomplex pattern observed earlier. The response comprised a high amplitude positive component, followed by a negative component which gradually decreased in amplitude with age (fig. 3.27*a*). Occasionally high amplitude polyphasic afterdischarges were recorded in all subjects, occurring when the subjects became drowsy. Auditorily evoked responses showed little qualitative ontogenetic changes during this period (figs. 3.24, 3.25).

11 Wk–Adult. After 10 wk of age, no further qualitative changes in either visually or auditorily evoked responses were observed. In 3 alert dogs, the initial positive wave of the auditorily evoked response varied from 5 to 20 msec during the same recording session. Variability in amplitude of component waves was associated with varying states of arousal; afterdischarges of high amplitude were recorded especially when the subject was relaxed.

Discussion: Development of EEG

Research findings on the development of EEG in the kitten by Jouvet (1962) and Valatx, Jouvet, and Jouvet (1964) are borne out in this study and support their observations that activated sleep develops before sleep with slow waves. Activated sleep is thought to arise from a bulbopontine sleep synchronizing center, and the

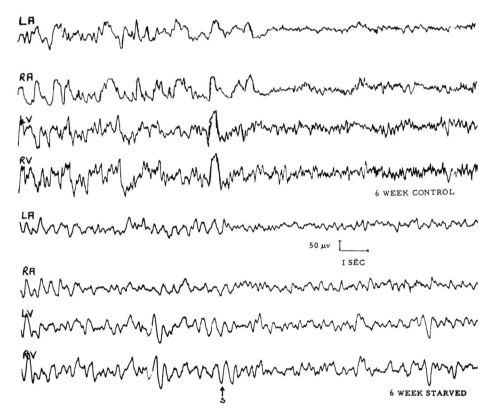

Fig. 3.19. Monopolar recordings (visual and auditory leads) from surface of cortex in control and chronically starved pups at 6 wk of age. Subjects under curare and light barbiturate anesthesia. Note relative paucity of low-amplitude fast components in starved pup and low amplitude of slow sleep waves. (*S* = nociceptive stimulation, causing desynchronization of EEG from synchronized, drug-induced sleep activity.)

later developing slow wave sleep from thalamocortical influences (also Walter 1956); that is, the ontogenetically "younger" thalamocortical sleep center develops later than the ontogenetically older bulbopontine center (Jouvet 1962). Strictly speaking, this is not a phenomenon of "phylogenetic recapitulation," but is more an ontogenetic phenomenon restricted to phylogenetically higher organisms. The rapid eye movements seen in activated sleep may be of vestibular origin (Pompeian

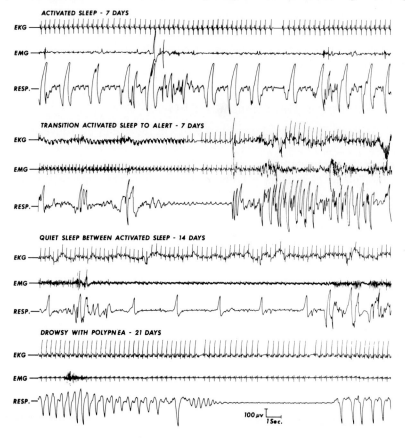

Fig. 3.20. Physiological changes during various phases of sleep and wakefulness in the dog at different ages. Irregular respiration and EMG activity during activated sleep, more regular during drowsiness and quiet sleep. Note frequent periods of apnea and dropped beats.

and Morrison 1966). Because of the preponderance of activated sleep in neonatal mammals, it may be essential for programming normal development and for organization of the CNS (Roffwarg, Muzio, and Dement 1966).

Morrison and Dempsey (1943) have demonstrated a synchronizing system in the thalamus; Magni et al. (1959) have also shown the presence of a synchronizing system in the lower pons and rostral medulla; and in addition to the reticular activating system described by Moruzzi and Magoun (1949), Nauta (1958) has demonstrated anatomically a possible limbic-midbrain arousal system (see reviews of Routtenberg 1968, and Jouvet 1962, 1967). On the basis of these findings, it is conceivable that during the early stages of EEG development the reticular activating system and synchronizing center in the lower pons and rostral medulla (in the nu-

PERCENTAGE DURATION OF SLEEP / ALERT PHASES IN DOG
(Averaged from 6.5 hours of observation for 13 pups per age group)

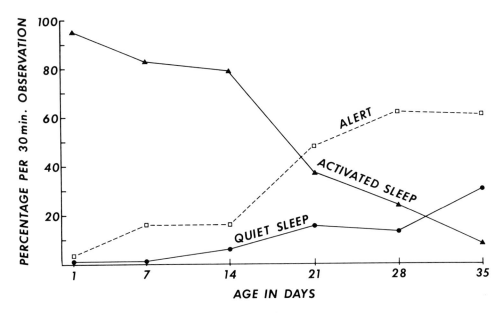

Fig. 3.21. Rapid decline in activated sleep between 2 and 3 wk of age and gradual emergence of quiet sleep: duration of alert increases between 2 and 4 wk and then remains constant.

DEVELOPMENT OF VISUALLY EVOKED POTENTIALS IN THE DOG
CHRONIC ELECTRODES - Ld Ls, FLASH FREQ. - 0.4 / Sec., DELAY - 50 ms., C.A.T. - 10 Stim.

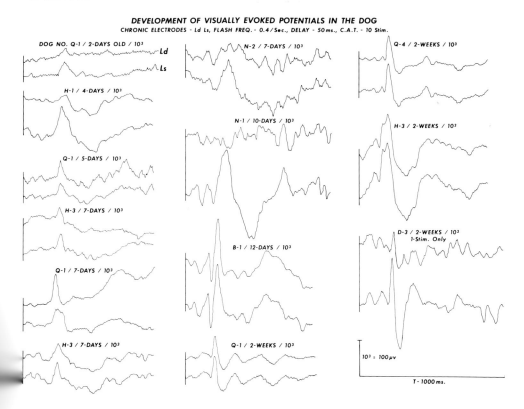

Fig. 3.22. (In figs. 3.22–3.27, code denotes subject's litter and number in that litter; *Ld* and *Ls* = gyrus marginalis dextra and sinistra; *ESMd* and *ESMs* = gyrus ectosylvius medius dextra and sinistra.) Responses early in life consist of a long latency negative wave; positive component well developed by 12 days. Marked difference in response to a single stimulus (*D–3 / 2* wk) as contrasted with summated response after 10 stimuli (fig. 3.23). Secondary positive afterdischarge well developed by 2 wk of age.

cleus tractus solitarius [Bonvallet and Allen 1963], which possibly inhibits the reticular activating center) first become functional. Subsequently, the cortical EEG develops high amplitude slow wave activity (synchronized) of quiet sleep and low amplitude fast activity of wakefulness and activated sleep, indicating a functional integration of thalamocortical and lower brainstem synchronizing systems. Before the development of these neural relationships, the lower brainstem synchronizing/ desynchronizing systems evoke only minor changes in behavioral state in terms of sleep, arousal, and wakefulness.

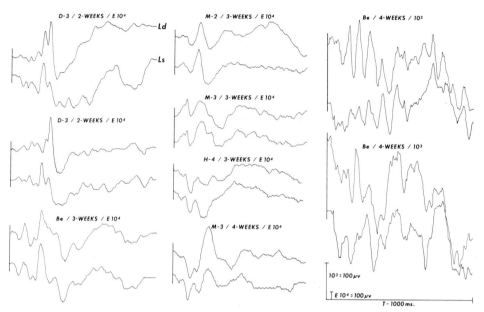

Fig. 3.23. Secondary positivity and negativity or afterdischarges develop in visually evoked potentials between 2 and 3 wk. Note marked variability in negative waves in successive recordings of *D*–3 / 2 wk. Several complex afterdischarges recorded after 3 wk of age (e.g., *Be*/4 wk).

Comparisons with Human Infant. Goldie and Van Velzer (1965) reported the presence of two sleep cycles in the newborn human. In one, the EEG shows low voltage, arrhythmic fast activity; respiration is irregular, and rapid eye movements and frequent body movements are seen, as in activated sleep. The other cycle is of shorter duration and is characterized by discontinuous EEG activity, slower EKG and respiration, no rapid eye movements, and only sudden infrequent body movements. This latter cycle they termed episodic sleep activity (ESA). It is typified by regular synchronous bursts of high amplitude EEG waves of mixed frequencies alternating with periods of relative flatness. A similar phenomenon has been described in the present investigation, occurring in pups around 10–14 days of age. Goldie and Van Velzer hypothesize that the synchronous bursts of activity may indicate an anatomical or physiological isolation of the cerebral cortex, which is normal and reversible in ESA.

Petre-Quadens (1966) describes four phases of sleep in the newborn human: Stage *A*, slight increase in amplitude of EEG compared to the alert EEG. Stage *B*, quiet sleep with occasional body twitches, no eye movements. During the latter stage, bursts of 6 c/sec spindlelike activity occur. Stage *C* (quiet sleep), runs of large slow waves appear with intermittent 12–13 c/sec spindles. Stage *D* (restless sleep), rapid low voltage EEG, rapid body and eye movements. Bursts of spindles may be observed at the onset of this stage. Stages *A, C,* and *D* can be recognized in the dog and in this report were described as drowsy, quiet, and activated sleep. Stage *B* is of considerable interest, as the recordings presented by Petre-Quadens are similar to the recordings obtained in this study from pups aged 10–14 days (except that in pups the bursts were of faster frequency) and may be comparable to the episodic sleep activity described in the human newborn by Goldie and Van Velzer (1965). The spindle bursts occurring in activated sleep observed by Petre-Quadens were also frequently seen in activated sleep in the young pup. The spindling phenomenon in the human infant may be related to the regular bursts of spindle-like activity recorded in pups, especially during the first week of life. As drowsiness and slow wave quiet sleep develop, the amplitude of these spindles diminishes, and at that time (around 10–14 days), the pup's EEG closely resembles that of the

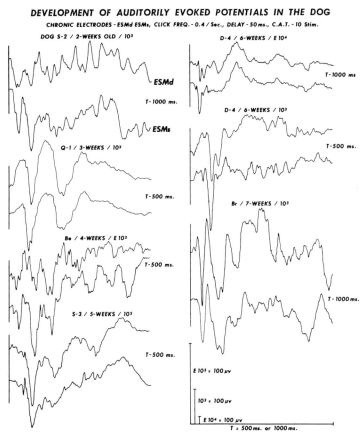

DEVELOPMENT OF AUDITORILY EVOKED POTENTIALS IN THE DOG

CHRONIC ELECTRODES - ESMd ESMs, CLICK FREQ. - 0.4 / Sec., DELAY - 50 ms., C.A.T. - 10 Stim.

Fig. 3.24. Earliest recorded auditory responses show well-developed positive and negative components, the positive component showing considerable variability in amplitude and latency (*Q*–1 / 3 wk and *D*–4 / 6 wk). Secondary positive and negative waves or afterdischarges are present at all ages, but are extremely variable. Complex afterdischarges appear after 3 wk of age.

newborn infant. The origin of this spindlelike activity is still an open question; Petre-Quadens sums up the problem with the following hypothesis: "The presence of spindles in the newborn in the second part of quiet sleep (Stage *C*) and at the beginning of restless sleep (Stage *D*) seems to indicate that the activity of the thalamus is earlier or contemporary with the establishment of an electrical circuit responsible for the EEG and behavioral appearances of Stage *D* of sleep." Thus, in

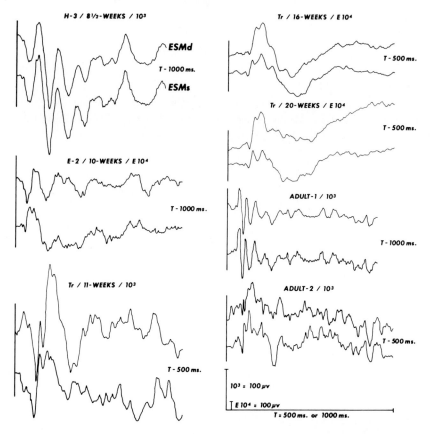

Fig. 3.25. Initial positive component of auditorily evoked potentials greatly reduced in amplitude (e.g., *H*–3 / 8½ wk at analysis time of 1,000 msec), but is more evident with a shorter analysis time of 500 msec (e.g., *Tr*/11 wk). Note marked consistency in character of auditory responses in *Tr* at 16 and 20 wk of age.

the newborn pup during activated sleep or sleep with jerks, spindlelike activity predominates, whereas fast low amplitude components (also present in the alert state) develop at a later age. Stage *B* in the pup is represented by a short and variable period of sleep with occasional jerks, in which bursts of spindlelike activity occur, especially around 2 wk of age. This stage may be a transitional phase between alert and activated sleep (i.e., episodic sleep activity) which disappears with increasing age as slow wave activity and associated drowsiness and quiet sleep predominate.

Discussion: Development of Sleep and Wakefulness

These findings illustrate the rapid decline in the percentage of activated sleep during early postnatal life, and the gradual development of the ability to maintain wakefulness (or attentiveness) in a novel environment, which is well developed by 4 wk of age. Three wk represents a transitional point when the relative durations of wakefulness and activated sleep are similar, and the duration of quiet sleep is increasing. Some differences between litters were noted; one litter remained alert throughout most of the observation period from 3 wk of age.

Many correlations can be made with the above findings; notably, the onset of relatively mature EEG occurs between 3 and 4 wk of age, which marks the onset of the critical period of socialization (Scott 1962), at which time the pup is neurologically mature. The ability to maintain wakefulness at 4 wk of age indirectly suggests that reticular activation attains adult functional integration with thalamocortical

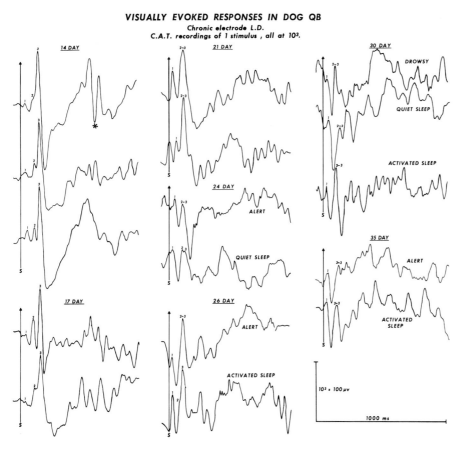

Fig. 3.26. Longitudinal study of visual EP in one dog, showing gradual merging of second negative peak (2) with ontogenetically older negative peak (3). The positive wave preceding 2 + 3 increases in amplitude with age, and the negative wave 2 + 3 decreases. Note secondary evoked potential at 14 days (*) and consistent negative wave onset phenomenon (1) recorded at all ages. Major qualitative change during quiet sleep is increased amplitude of afterdischarge; EP's similar during wakefulness and activated (REM) sleep.

structures at this time. It is known that the development of perceptual abilities (visual and auditory orientation reflexes) (see chap. 2) and of evoked visual and auditory responses are relatively mature by 1 mo. The animal is therefore more completely aware of its environment and consequently able to interact with its social milieu. The significance of the high percentage of activated or (REM) sleep in the neonate, to which Roffwarg, Muzio, and Dement (1966) attribute an organizing or programming function in modulating CNS development, is an open question. Valatx, Jouvet, and Jouvet (1964) observe that the predominance of activated sleep in young animals is due to a bulbopontine sleep-controlling center functioning in the absence of the slow-wave synchronizing thalamocortical sleep center, which is a phylogenetically more recent system and develops later in postnatal life. These sleep centers were originally investigated in the adult cat by Jouvet (1962). The rapid decline in activated sleep and gradual emergence of quiet sleep with increasing age in the dog tends to confirm this hypothesis. With increasing age, the frequency of occurrence of activated sleep and total circadian duration decreases, and begins to

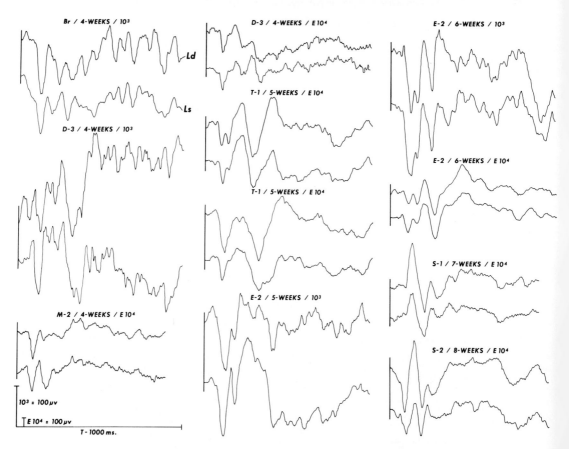

Fig. 3.27*a, b.* The complex afterdischarges in the visually evoked potentials become reduced in number after 4–6 wk of age in most subjects. The latencies of the primary positive and negative waves and positive-negative afterdischarge remain relatively stable after 5–6 wk, although their amplitude is more variable (e.g., *E*–2 / 6 wk and *T*–1 / 5 wk, consecutive recordings on same day). Subsequently there is a marked diminution in amplitude of positive and negative afterdischarges in visually evoked potentials with increasing age.

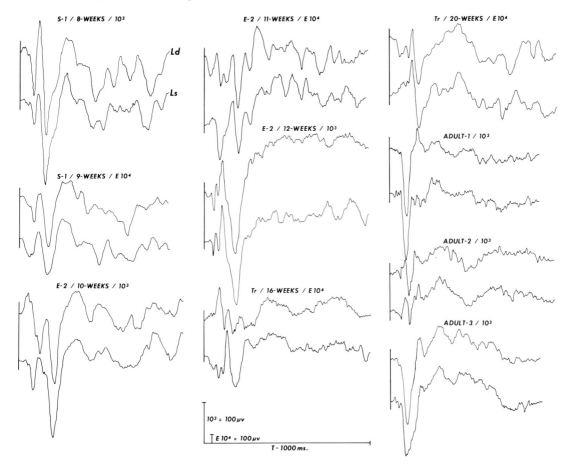

Fig. 3.27. *Continued*

fall into a predictable temporal sequence following quiet sleep, being of a fairly constant duration. Sleep deprivation in adult cats increases the percentage of activated sleep from the normal 25–30% to a maximum 60% by increasing the frequency of periods of activated sleep but not the duration of each period (Jouvet et al. 1964).

It should be noted that McGinty and Sterman (1968) have demonstrated the existence of a sleep center in the basal forebrain of the cat. Large bilateral lesions within the preoptic area resulted in a reduction of quiet sleep by 55–73%, and of activated sleep by 80–100%. They propose that these lesions must release a process which inhibits the brainstem mechanisms of activated sleep and speculate that the reduction in activated sleep during postnatal ontogeny may result from the maturation of forebrain neural structures that suppress primitive mechanisms organized in lower structures.

Snyder (1966) has discussed the evolutionary significance of activated sleep, which, contrary to Jouvet's (1962) phylogenetic hypothesis, occurs rarely in lower vertebrates. To resolve this argument to some extent we may quote Garstang (1922), who states that "ontogeny does not recapitulate phylogeny—it creates it."

As a postscript to this discussion, the work of Bernhard, Kolmodin, and Meyerson (1967) will be briefly reviewed. These authors list the following stages of responsiveness to electrical stimulation of the cortex in the fetal sheep, which provide a useful model for applying different neurophysiological techniques to evaluate brain development and function: 31–40 days (gestation age), appearance of steady potential; 41–50 days, appearance of positive wave of somesthetic evoked response and Metrazol activation; 51–60 days, spontaneous EEG, but activity discontinuous, waxing and waning (as observed in neonatal pups in the present investigation);

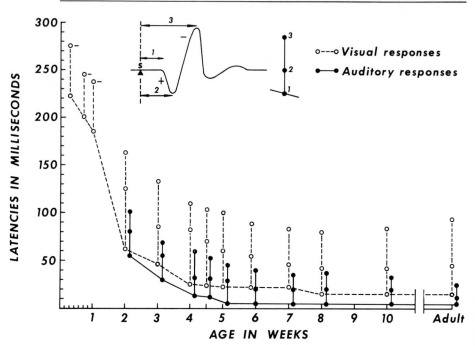

Fig. 3.28. Rapid reduction in latencies of visually and auditorily evoked potentials occurs during first 3 wk, which are relatively mature by 5 wk of age.

61–70 days, d.c. shift occurs on electrical stimulation of the somesthetic cortex; 65–70 days, the negative wave of the somesthetic EP appears, being preceded by the earlier positive wave; a transcallosal response can be elicited, decreasing in latency and threshold and increasing in stability with age; 71–80 days, spontaneous EEG activity becomes continuous; 85–90 days, the interhemispheric delayed response can be elicited; 91–100 days, poststimulation electrically evoked seizure discharges can be elicited.

Discussion: Development of Evoked Potentials

These data summarized in fig. 3.28 show that there is rapid development of both auditorily and visually evoked responses from birth to 3 wk of age. More gradual changes in latency occur between 4 and 6 wk of age. By 4–5 wk of age, it can be said that both auditorily and visually evoked responses have reached a point where rapid development is completed; more refined, qualitative changes occur thereafter. These findings on the development of auditorily evoked responses are confirmed in the study of Dmitriyeva et al. (1966), who report that relative maturity in the auditory cortex (in terms of threshold latency and amplitude of evoked response and myelination) is attained by 30 days of age. The most dramatic changes are the decrease in afterdischarges notable between 3 and 4 mo of age and the overall reduction in amplitude. This may be correlated with the EEG observations

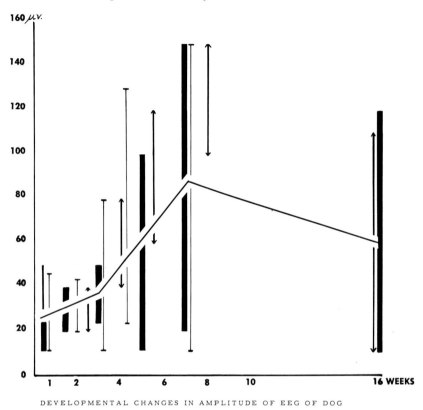

DEVELOPMENTAL CHANGES IN AMPLITUDE OF EEG OF DOG

Fig. 3.29. Averaged data from three studies using skin electrodes (Charles and Fuller 1956 I, Pampiglione 1963 ↕, Fox, present investigation I). Marked increase in overall amplitude occurs during 3–7 wk of age, and thereafter declines.

(Pampiglione 1963; Venturoli 1962; see also previous EEG data earlier), for around 4 mo there is a marked decrease in overall amplitude of the EEG, with an increase in frequency in the alert state (fig. 3.29). The sudden appearance of relatively mature and auditory responses at 2 wk of age may be correlated with the opening of the external auditory meatus, which occurs around this time. No similar abrupt changes in the visually evoked responses are seen when the eyelids open, between 10 and 16 days of age.

Myelination of the optic and auditory nerves is well advanced by 2 wk of age, although myelin is not histologically detectable in the auditory and visual cortices until 4 wk (see chap. 4) This immaturity of the peripheral nervous system may be reflected in the cortically evoked potentials obtained during the first 2 wk postnatally. Marty (1967) has shown that in the kitten there is rapid development of the cochlear and optic nerves (as shown by direct electrical stimulation), but a more gradual development of responsiveness to normal auditory and photic stimuli. To these differences he attributes a more protracted development of complex sensory receptors (retina and cochlea). Marty and Scherrer (1964) have also shown a hierarchy in the ontogeny of afferent cortical systems in the cat (by direct electrical stimulation); somesthetic responses mature earlier than cochlear, cochlear responses mature earlier than optic.

Dendritic development of neocortical neurons between birth and 2 wk of age is a gradual process, in which the deeper pyramidal neurons develop before those of the upper cell layers (see chap. 4). By 2 wk of age, the apical dendrites of the deep pyramidal cells are well developed, and a few basilar dendrites have been elaborated. At 4 wk the neocortical neuronal processes are well developed, and they undergo little further elaboration after 6 wk of age, although they continue to increase in thickness (Fox, Inman, and Himwich 1966). The initial slow negative wave recorded from the visual cortex during the 1st wk of life may be correlated with the immaturity of dendritic organization and paucity of neocortical synaptic connections. The appearance of positive and negative primary waves and positive afterdischarges after 10 days may indicate a greater functional (synaptic) integration of the various neuronal layers of the neocortex, with deeper subcortical structures influencing an increasingly larger neocortical receptor area. Secondary and tertiary afterdischarges may be attributed to the gradual elaboration and thickening of dendritic branches after 3 wk of age.

In summary of the qualitative changes observed in the visually evoked response (but not in the auditorily, because of the postnatal delay in opening of the external auditory meatus), the following component waves appeared with increasing age: (1) long latency negative wave; (2) long latency positive wave or afterdischarge following 1; (3) second negative wave with variable positive wave following it, on ascending segment of 1; i.e., double negative peak; (4) initial positive preceding 1; (5) occasional negative peak preceding 4 and one or two negative peaks following 2, and more rarely a secondary evoked response. Subsequently, 3 coalesces with 1, 2 becomes shortened in duration and simplified (i.e., afterdischarge negative waves disappear), and finally 4 increases in amplitude and 1 decreases in amplitude to resemble characteristically mature response (see fig. 3.26).

Rose and Lindsley (1965, 1968) postulate that in the kitten the initial long-latency, long-duration negative wave may be a nonspecific phenomenon, mediated via optic pathways to the tectum, and that the later emergence of the diphasic shorter latency positive-negative component is thought to be the specific component of the evoked response, mediated via optic pathways to the geniculostriate projections.

Laget and Delhaye (1962) hypothesize that the later development of the positive component in evoked responses from the somatosensory area of the rabbit may be correlated with neuronal development; but they emphasize that this is not a completely adequate explanation for the later appearance of the positive wave component.

Purpura, Carmichael, and Housepian (1960) and Purpura et al. (1964) postulate that the later maturation of deeper pyramidal neurons may account for the emergence of the positive component of the evoked response, whereas more precocial development of the superficial neuronal layers is associated with the initial long-latency negative response in young subjects. Purpura et al. (1964) propose that as the apical-axodendritic connections of the cortical pyramidal cells become more elaborate, the initial surface-negative response following pyramidal cell excitation gradually increases in amplitude and decreases in latency. Golgi type-II cells are elaborated in the kitten between 8 and 14 days of age, and axosomatic and dendritic connections associated with specific visual projections can be identified; it is also at this time that spines develop on the basilar dendrites and a short-latency positive-negative complex is seen following photic stimulation. The original negative wave becomes markedly reduced in amplitude and latency until it merges with the negative wave of the shorter latency component of the specific visual response. Rose and Lindsley (1968) propose that as the full complement of dendritic processes forms around the basilar region of the pyramidal cells, and as axosomatic contacts form, the deep negative surface-positive features of pyramidal cell responses are manifest. The gradual development of stellate cells in layers 2 and 4 may also be related to the gradual reduction in amplitude of the late nonspecific negative wave. Scheibel and Scheibel (1958) and Scheibel (1962) have also pointed out the importance of the elaboration of the neuropil in the fourth layer of the neocortex, composed of specific corticopetal "bushy" fibers and axonal plexuses of stellate cells. The development of this neuropil field coincides with the emergence of the surface-positive wave, and as the Scheibels have suggested, may contribute to this short-latency specific visually evoked response.

Anokhin (1964), in reviewing the work from his laboratory, concludes that the early negative wave of the evoked potential occurs in the plexiform layer of the cortex due to discharges arriving at the axodendritic synapses from slow conducting pathways of the nonspecific thalamus; the later-appearing faster positive wave originates from "specific" thalamic nuclei. Anokhin also relates that the "double negative" peaks occurring early during ontogenesis can be eliminated by increasing the intensity of stimulation to evoke a larger amplitude single peak negative wave. From these findings he concludes that the double negativity reflects a heterochronous maturation of subcortical synaptic connections; as more synaptic connections mature, confluence of the two negative potentials occurs. This argument closely agrees with the conclusions drawn from the present ontogenetic study in the dog.

Myslivecek (1968), in a detailed study of the ontogeny of visually evoked potentials in the dog, finds very similar phenomena at different ages, in terms of the presence of negative and positive waves in addition to the predominant positive-negative wave of the evoked potential, as revealed here. As Myslivecek has shown, the most predominant positive-negative component (i.e., greatest amplitude) may vary with age. As early as 10 days a double negative wave is seen, which is more easily recognized at 2 wk of age (by which time it may be preceded by an even earlier low amplitude negative wave). The first peak of this double wave may be followed by a positive wave; all these components vary greatly in amplitude at 2 wk, the earlier negative peak being greater or less in amplitude than the ontogenetically earlier-appearing second negative peak. Myslivecek reports that in his study, triple negative peaks first appear between 9 and 11 days, and that the number of negative peaks increases between 2 and 3 wk so that 4 and later 5 peaks appear, with 3 or 4 declinations toward positivity which vary greatly in amplitude. In the present study, this was most clearly evident between 3 and 4 wk of age. At 2 wk following 1 flash stimulus, a 2d evoked response appeared after the refractory or latent period following the final positive deflection of the first evoked response (see fig. 3.26). This phenomenon was seen occasionally (and more frequently as a "rebound" of 1 or 2 negative peaks), but was not evaluated ontogenetically. Similarly Myslivecek found an "expressive secondary" type response with a latency of approximately 700 msec at around this age.[6] Marked differences in the shape of the evoked response between 3 and 4 wk of age, also noted by Myslivecek, were due to the variable amplitude or dominance of different positive and negative components, although these waves had similar peak latencies in different subjects. The depth of the electrode is an important variable in this regard, but would not account for the extreme variability in the dominance of different components observed in the same subject during successive recordings; changing levels of wakefulness and sleep even in curarized subjects may account to some extent for this variability. After 6 wk of age, the "multipeak" complex oscillations of the visually evoked response become more simplified. Myslivecek emphasizes that the development of latency values is due to three somewhat contradictory processes, that is, growth and consequent lengthening of conduction pathways, change of synaptic transmission, and shortening of conduction rate, and that it cannot be concluded from his findings that the early long-latency negativity changes into an associative response of "extraprimary" character. In this regard Marty (1962) proposed that in the cat the early negative wave (wave A) has a wide distribution throughout the neocortex, and is of an "extraprimary" character and during subsequent development becomes an "associative" response. According to him, wave B (which appears later, and precedes wave A) develops into the primary response of the projection areas. These observations are not supported in the dog by Myslivecek or by the data in the present study. The complex oscillations and multiple peaks of the evoked response in the dog between 3 and 4 wk of age do not agree with the simple wave A/wave B hypothesis. Myslivecek hypothesizes that the gradual development of thalamocortical pathways and of reverberating circuits may account for the activation to shift to an earlier peak in the evoked response in later life. The activation in younger subjects is more variable (and is greatly affected by frequency and duration of stimulation) and may predominate in a later peak or component of the evoked response. Thus an ontogenetic study should essentially reveal which positive-negative component of the response "carries the message" or predominates in terms of amplitude as a result of thalamocortical activation. The gradual dampening and disappearance of several positive-negative component peaks after 3–4 wk of age may indicate that an inhibitory synaptic mechanism is involved; its absence earlier in life possibly accounts for the greater variability in the number, amplitude, and occurrence of secondary positive and negative components. As the neocortical (interneuronal) and thalamocortical connections are established, earlier positive-negative components become the most predominant wave (in terms of amplitude) in the evoked response as a result of this activation, and consequently the latency of the response is significantly shortened.

[6] G. Rose (1968a) found that a secondary EP of this type could be regularly elicited in neonate kittens following 1 flash, provided the stimulus (light) intensity was low.

Marty (1962) and Rose (1968*a*) have reported the presence of a double negative wave in the visually (and auditorily, Marty 1967) evoked response in the cat, rabbit, and rat, and this intriguing phenomenon is identical with the double negative wave here observed in the dog. In any single evoked response obtained during this particular age period, the negative component obtained earliest in life was preceded by a negative wave of variable amplitude, which in turn was separated by a positive wave of variable amplitude. This amplitude variability is emphasized, for this additional negative-positive component may appear only as a mere indentation on the ascending segment of the negative wave and then suddenly reappear dramatically with a pronounced increase in amplitude (see fig. 3.26).

With increasing age, this additional negative-positive component coalesces with the ascending segment of the ontogenetically older negative wave (the positive wave preceding this latter negativity gradually increases in amplitude with age while the negative component decreases in amplitude; see fig. 3.26).

Myslivecek speaks of a "simplification" of the multipeak or multicomplex visually evoked potential after 3 wk of age. One may speculate at this point as to the origin of these additional components during a discrete period in ontogeny. Their appearance may represent the inclusion of subcortical structures mediating sensory impulses, and the gradual disappearance may reflect integrative processes between these structures and in thalamocortical interrelationships. Following structurofunctional integration, the evoked response reflects a smooth and synchronous unitary response; before structurofunctional synchronization the different components of the complex system (including peripheral receptors) are not yet integrated, so that a multipeak or multicomplex response occurs.

Bernhard, Kolmodin, and Meyerson (1967) have shown that the surface negative evoked response to tactile stimuli is *preceded* by a positive wave in fetal sheep aged 65–70 days. This earlier positive component, they postulate, may be the result of a depolarization of afferents entering the cortical plate, which do not yet evoke postsynaptic activity; the late increase in negativity may indicate greater postsynaptic activation. Molliver (1967) also found an initial surface positive wave in the somesthetic cortex of the fetal sheep and dog which he proposes may be a summation of postsynaptic potentials in stellate cells and basal dendrites at the junction of the intermediate and pyramidal zones. He proposes other alternatives; that this early positivity is indicative of deep synaptic potentials or results from synchronous depolarization of presynaptic afferent terminals, and that the surface negative wave arises from postsynaptic activation of apical dendrites of pyramidal cells Molliver has shown that this initial positivity increases in amplitude up to 82 days of gestation and then *decreases* steadily until 100 days, whereupon it again increases. It is highly probable that in the postnatal studies of sensorily evoked potentials in the cat and dog (which are less precocial at birth than the sheep), this early positivity was not detected because of its decrease in amplitude during a particular period in ontogeny.

Fikova (1964) reported that the time of onset of spreading depression during development of the rat brain coincides with the maturation of neuronal cell bodies and dendrites. Kliavina and Obrastsova (1966) have found that the primary response to auditory stimulation in the rabbit is dependent upon the intensity of stimulation during ontogeny, which is an additional variable to be considered in evaluating development of evoked responses to external stimulation of various modalities.

Correlation on a structural basis for the gradual dampening (inhibition?) of after-discharges between 3 and 4 mo of age cannot be made, but recent behavioral studies on the development of delayed responsiveness in the dog show that an important event occurs around 16 wk, suggesting a phenomenon of internal inhibition in the Pavlovian sense (see chap. 5).

Zahlava, Chaloupka, and Myslivecek (1966) observed that the amplitude of the primary evoked potential of both auditory and visual cortical responses decreased in amplitude as the frequency of stimulation increased; this decrease in amplitude was inversely proportional to age. In pups immobilized with curare, the earliest responses to auditory stimulation were recorded at 6 days of age (in 2 out of 13 subjects), and they concluded that the most significant improvement in responsiveness to rhythmic acoustic stimulation occurred especially between the 10th and the 14th day of postnatal life.

Shagass and Trusty (1966) evaluated changes in somatosensorily and visually evoked potentials in adult human subjects during varying stages of sleep and wakefulness. Latencies and amplitudes of the first 12 peaks of each evoked response were calculated. They found that the late visual afterrhythm disappeared with the onset of sleep, and latencies became systematically more prolonged as sleep deepened. Amplitudes of initial components increased with deep sleep, and amplitudes of components following the initial ones tended to decrease. Also, responses during activated or REM sleep were indistinguishable from stage 1 of sleep and were significantly different from responses during wakefulness. Latencies of later components continued to be prolonged after waking from deep sleep, returning gradually to wakefulness levels.

The various behavioral states of sleep and wakefulness during recording sessions constitute an important ontogenetic variable and would account for the variability in amplitude in successive recordings recorded from the same unanesthetized but restrained subject on the same day (see fig. 3.23). Most of the peaks, however (both negative and positive), could usually be recognized in spite of amplitude changes. In comparison, however, changes in latency were insignificant.

Other variables such as the form, context, and character of the stimulus may greatly modify both visually and auditorily evoked responses (Sutton et al. 1967; John, Herrington, and Sutton 1967), and these effects may be complicated further by ontogenetic or perceptual limitations and the behavioral state of the subject.

The relative maturity of both visually and auditorily evoked potentials at 4–5 wk of age in the dog correlates chronologically with the cytoarchitectonic development of these regions (see chap. 4), and with biochemical, EEG, and reflex development (summarized in chap. 7). The end of the first month of life coincides with the onset of the critical period of socialization, when primary social relationships or emotional bonds are first established and the organism begins to interact, independent of maternal influences, with its environment. The neurophysiological and structural changes taking place during this time and underlying the socialization phenomenon suggest a period of integration when structural components of the CNS are intercalated and more complex behavior, dependent upon functionally adaptive perceptual and motor abilities, can be organized. This problem will be discussed in detail in chapter 7.

Summary

During the first 2 wk of neonatal life, there was little differentiation of EEG in relation to changes in overt behavior. During the 2d wk of life, slow wave activity was seen for the first time and was associated with the development of quiet sleep. Visually evoked responses were present shortly after birth, but auditorily evoked responses could not be evoked until the 2d wk of life. Both auditorily and visually evoked potentials were of long latency, which decreased rapidly during the first 21 days of life.

Between the 2d and 3d wk, the slow wave activity of quiet sleep was more clearly recognizable because of an overall increase in amplitude and synchrony. During this period, the spindlelike bursts of high amplitude, fast frequency activity present earlier in postnatal life disappeared. Between the 3d and 4th wk, alphalike activity could be evoked after occlusion of vision; the low amplitude, fast frequency components of wakefulness were not well developed, and were also clearly evident in activated sleep. Visually and auditorily evoked potentials attained relative maturity between 4 and 5 wk of age. During the 4th and 5th wk, the EEG developed the full range of activity that is present in the adult; it was during this period that sleep spindles and paroxysmal sleep patterns emerged. After 5 wk of age, only minor changes in amplitude and frequency of slow and fast activity occurred. In comparing the qualitative changes of the canine EEG during development with those of the human infant described in detail by Parmelee et al. (1967), many close parallels are found, indicating that both species undergo similar ontogenetic changes in the functional maturation of the CNS. Similar parallels in the structural development of the CNS will be described in the next chapter.

4

Structural and Functional Aspects of CNS Development

This chapter will describe various aspects of the gross and histological development of the CNS during postnatal development in the dog, and the effects of spinal cord transection and decerebration, which give us an indirect indication of structurofunctional interrelationships between various parts of the developing nervous system. Where pertinent, comparisons will be made with other species, including man.

The following topics are discussed:

1. The gross structural changes, in terms of brain weight and gyrus-sulcus patterning, that occur during early postnatal life.

2. Development of breed variations in brain and liver weights.

3. The effects of decerebration and spinal cord transection at different ages, the clinical signs of which will be correlated with the level of neurologic (reflex) development and structurofunctional integration of the CNS at a given age.

4. Malnutrition, or starvation per se, which represents the most devastating "environmental" influence on CNS and behavior development. Histological and neurophysiological findings from such influences in the dog will be presented (see chap. 6 for other "environmental-experiential" influences on CNS and behavior development).

5. Cell development (cytoarchitectonics) in various regions of the cerebrum of the dog and myelination of the CNS are described, and estimations of total lipid content of various brain regions are correlated with myelination.

6. Neocortical neuronal development in the motor, visual, and auditory cortices, presented from Golgi-Cox preparations.

7. The development of dendritic spines and their possible significance.

115

8. Glial cells—astrocytes and oligodendroglia, as revealed in Golgi-Cox preparations. These are classified and the development of these various cells is discussed in relation to neuronal development and myelination.

9. Myelination of the spinal cord. This is correlated with the development of neonatal reflexes and locomotor patterns described in chapter 2.

Each of the above topics receives separate discussion except sections 5 and 6, and relevant data from studies on other species are cited. Sections 5 and 6 are discussed together in order to contrast and compare the temporal sequences of neuronal development and myelination.

Gross Structure and Development of the Canine Brain

This study was undertaken to establish a reference index of normality in the gross structural characteristics of the canine brain in dogs of different breed and age and to correlate gross ontogenetic changes in the developing brain with changes in overt behavior.

References to developmental aspects of canine neuroanatomy are few. In the adult, cerebral convolutions have been described by Filiminoff (1923), Papez (1929), Sisson and Grossman (1960), Singer (1962), and Adrianov and Mering (1964), and certain aspects of the postnatal morphogenesis of the brain in different breeds of dog have been reported by Herre and Stephan (1955). Perkins (1961) and Phemister and Young (1968) have also reported some aspects of cerebellar development in this species.

Materials and Methods

Sixty-five brains were studied. Brains of 42 adult dogs from the following breeds were used: cocker spaniel, 10; Shetland sheepdog, 9; beagle, 9; basenji, 7; wirehaired fox terrier, 4. These dogs were all from moderately inbred strains.[1]

During the postnatal period of development, 26 brains were taken from dogs of different breeds at selected ages; sick or physically inferior dogs were not used in the study. There were 12 Shetland sheepdogs, 6 basenjis, 4 beagles, and 4 cocker spaniels. After age and body weight were recorded, each dog was killed by an intravenous barbiturate and the following records made from each brain obtained:

1) Length (between occipital pole and tip of prefrontal lobe) and width (greatest distance between temporal lobes).
2) Average brain weight (olfactory lobes were removed and the medulla was cut transversely at a point vertical to the posterior colliculus of the cerebellum before weighing; all brains were Formalin fixed).
3) Volume (by water displacement).
4) Gross development of the gyri and major lobes of the cerebral cortex.

Results

The Adult Canine Brain. All specimens were Formalin fixed. Immersion in Formalin causes an increase of up to 15% in weight; the average brain weights were therefore higher than in normal, fresh specimens. All measurements showed breed

[1] Most adult brain material was obtained from the collection of Dr. J. P. Scott, senior staff scientist, Jackson Laboratory, Bar Harbor, Maine.

consistency (table 4.1). The body-weight measurements were not of the dogs used, but were taken from average figures collected from several male and female dogs of each breed[2] and of the same strains from which the brains had been collected. The Shetland sheepdog, which was phenotypically a less uniform strain, had the greatest individual differences in brain and body weights. Gross differences in size and shape of the cerebral cortex of different breeds were apparent (fig. 4.1), although the basic patterns of gyrus and sulcus arrangements were similar in all of the specimens examined. The posterior sylvian gyrus showed breed and individual differences in width, but was always present; in all specimens, the ectosylvian gyrus formed a complete arch over the sylvian gyrus. In the cocker spaniel, and to a lesser degree in the beagle, accessory sulci were found, especially in the ectosylvian, suprasylvian, ectolateral, and lateral gyri.

The basenji had the most uncomplicated gyrus pattern; the ectosylvian gyrus was small and passed anteriorly for a short distance only, either being truncated or merging with the lateral gyrus. In the Shetland sheepdog, wirehaired fox terrier,

TABLE 4.1

AVERAGE MEASUREMENTS OF ADULT CANINE BRAINS

Breed	Brain Weight (gm)	Body Weight (kg at 52 wk of age)	Width (cm)	Length (cm)	Volume (cc)
Shetland sheepdog	60.31[a]	10.5	4.85	6.27	68
Cocker spaniel	79.44	9.23	5.36	6.71	78
Wirehaired fox terrier	68.66	7.7	4.86	6.5	70
Basenji	53.96	10.9	4.58	5.78	45
Beagle	72.75	10.6	5.07	6.45	72

[a] Greatest variations were found in this breed, weights ranging from 51.2 to 68.1 gm.

and cocker spaniel, this gyrus characteristically passed anteriorly as far as the post-crucial gyrus, merging with the suprasylvian gyrus.

In the beagle this ectosylvian gyrus was more variable, either uniting with the lateral or suprasylvian gyrus or passing directly to the postcrucial gyrus.

In the wirehaired fox terrier, the lateral gyrus was consistently divided by an entomarginal sulcus. In the cocker spaniel, accessory sulci in this gyrus sometimes united to form an entomarginal sulcus. No such patterns were seen in the other breeds.

The distance from the caudal end of the sylvian sulcus to the tip of the prefrontal lobe was greatest in the wirehaired fox terrier.

The Developing Brain of the Neonate. Length and width measurements were almost equal at birth, but with increasing age the increase in length was greater than the increase in width of the whole brain. The most dramatic changes in the length/width ratio occurred between the 3d and 4th wk, adultlike proportions being seen after 4 wk. The brain continues to grow rapidly up to 6 wk of age and then more gradually during the ensuing months of development. Brain volume studies (amount of displacement following immersion of brain in water contained in a graduated cylinder) also showed that a rapid increase in volume occurred up to approximately 6 wk, after which the volume fell within the adult average range.

[2] J. P. Scott, Jackson Laboratory, Bar Harbor, Maine. Unpublished data, 1960.

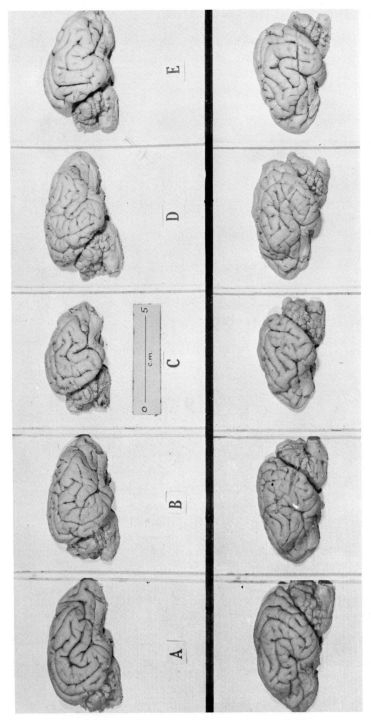

Fig. 4.1. Adult brains of fox terrier, *a*; beagle, *b*; basenji, *c*; cocker spaniel, *d*; Shetland sheepdog, *e*. Note relatively small size of basenji brain, but similar gyrus and sulcus patterns in all breeds. The apparently more complex gyrus-sulcus pattern in the cocker spaniel is due to the presence of accessory sulci.

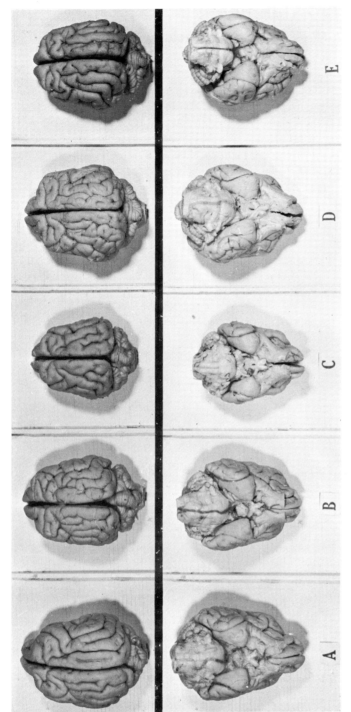

Fig. 4.1. *Continued*

The primary gyri and sulci were present at birth. The most marked developmental changes were the increased width of the cerebral hemispheres and the concurrent deepening of the sylvian sulcus and enlargement of the temporal and pyriform lobes (figs. 4.2, 4.3). Increase in length was associated with great enlargement of the frontal and occipital regions with thickening and increasing complexity of gyri; at birth the frontal and occipital lobes and caudal ends of the lateral and ectolateral gyri were poorly formed (fig. 4.2). By 2 wk of age, the superficial features

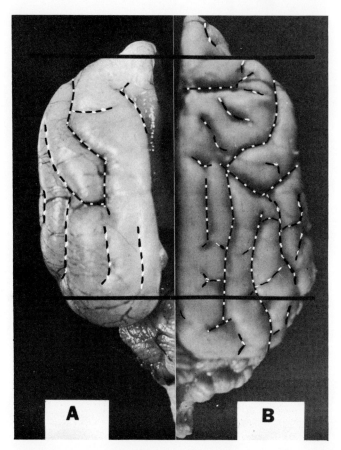

Fig. 4.2. Newborn (*a*) and adult (*b*) dog brains, the latter reduced in size to facilitate visual comparison. Note marked immaturity of gyrus-sulcus pattern and of frontal and occipital lobes.

of the cerebral hemispheres resembled the adult brain; mature patterns in relation to length/width ratios and relative sizes of the different lobes of the cortex were adultlike by 6 wk of age (fig. 4.3).

Summary and Conclusions

All five breeds examined presented similar major gyrus arrangements. Minor differences were apparent in certain details of gyrus and sulcus patterns, and these differences were found consistently among individuals of the same strain.

The developmental studies of the canine brain during the postnatal period showed that size, gyrus formation, and other characteristics were similar in the different breeds at birth. Development of the brain during the 1st wk of life was gradual, but, in the 2d and 3d wk, morphologic changes were more rapid, notably the development of gyri and sulci.

Development of Breed Variables in the Dog

Developmental studies of certain organs or systems in the dog are complicated by breed variables. Heredity and selection of breed types have given rise to a great variety of dogs differing widely in size, activity, and physiology (Stockard 1941).

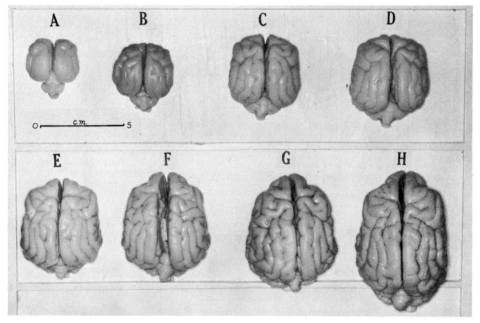

Fig. 4.3. Beagle brains at birth, 1, 2, 3, 4, 6, and 8 wk, and adult. Relatively mature gyrus development is not attained until after 3 wk of age. Note gradual development of frontal lobes, attaining mature proportions by 6 wk of age.

Some recognized breeds, showing wide deviation from the normal anatomicophysiologic constitution of the average dog, may be regarded as abnormal. Brachycephaly and achondroplasia are two of these more common abnormalities. This study was undertaken to investigate the degree of constancy of certain anatomical variables in three breeds of dogs of different ages. The results would give further indexes of normality which may be used in interpreting the origin of the domestic dog, where common features of different breeds may indicate a common ancestry. Degerbol (1927), using skull measurements as criteria of normality, studied prehistoric and modern Canidae. After comparing the data from a wide selection of present-day breeds with his archeological specimens, he found correlative evidence suggesting that these prehistoric remains were related to the modern domesticated dog. Indexes of normality may be applied comparatively to study ectotypes—for example, unusual domestic dogs of different or obscure origin such as the African basenji.

Materials and Methods

Three breeds of dogs, cocker spaniel, beagle, and Shetland sheepdog (with inbreeding coefficients 0.17–0.31, 0.12–0.45, and 0.22–0.38 respectively), were used in this investigation. All dogs were reared under the same standards of management and nutrition, and sick or physically inferior dogs were discarded from the experiment. Twenty-six dogs at selected ages were studied; total body weight, liver weight, and brain weight were recorded immediately after death by intravenous pentobarbitone. The brain weight did not include the olfactory lobes, and the medulla was cut transversely at a point vertical to the posterior colliculus of the cerebellum before weighing. The brain and liver weights were then calculated as percentages of the total body weight.

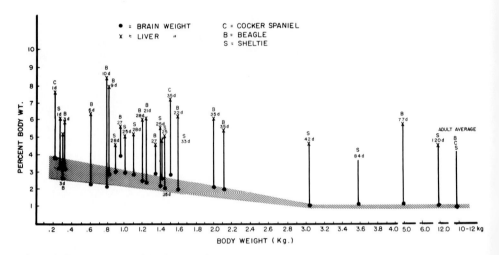

Fig. 4.4. Development of brain and liver as a percentage of the total body weight; there is little variability in brain weight in relation to body weight among various breeds, although the liver weight is subject to greater variability (see text for discussion). The ages of specimens are shown in days under the breed symbol.

Results

The brain weights and liver weights, each expressed as a percentage of the total body weight, were plotted (fig. 4.4). There was a definite correlation between the brain weight and body weight, but the liver weight was found to be considerably more variable. This great variation in liver weight may be influenced by genetic and prenatal nutritional factors (Fox 1966*d*), and in view of these variables the ratio of liver weight to body weight is not a reliable index of normality. These weights were plotted as percentages of body weight and not as changes in organ weight with age because the relationship between brain size and body weight was of primary consideration. It will be seen in figure 4.4 that irrespective of age there is a constant relationship between brain weight and body weight, whereas the liver weight is more variable. (Data plots are labeled with the age in days of the animal at the time of measurement.) Since the smaller body weights were taken from immature animals, the brain weight percentage of body weight may differ from that of an adult dog of the same body weight. This variation in the young animal is shown as a wide area of shading on the graph in the region of the earlier samples. By the age of 6 wk and after, when brain maturation is more gradual—after the almost explosive development between 2 and 4 wk—brain weight percentage of body weight is within the adult range of 1%. Sex differences were insignificant, and so the sex of the individual animals in figure 4.4 is not specified.

Discussion

Latimer (1942) studied the weight of the brain in 321 dogs of inconsistent breeds, many of which were mongrels of obscure origin. Body weights ranged from 4 to 30 kg. His results are summarized in table 4.2.

Latimer's data coincide well with the brain weight percentages in the adult specimens used in the present study, where a brain weight percentage of body weight was found to be 0.9% of an average 10 kg total body weight. From the results of the present investigation, and in the light of Latimer's findings, there appears to be

TABLE 4.2

TYPICAL BRAIN WEIGHT AS PERCENTAGE OF
TOTAL BODY WEIGHT FOR DIFFERENT
WEIGHTS OF DOGS

Body Weight	Brain Weight as % of Body Weight
4 kg	1.5
6 kg	1.1
8 kg	0.9
10 kg	0.8
12 kg	0.6
26 kg	0.4

SOURCE: Adapted from Latimer 1942.

a constant relationship between total body weight and the ratio of brain weight to total body weight. Irrespective of nutritional influences, the brain weight of the dog at birth is within the normal average range (Fox 1966d), and development of the organism is such that brain weight is spared at the expense of body and liver weights (see later). Liver weight and body weight are subnormal in the postnatal malnutrition syndrome; so brain weight, which is normal, when expressed as a percentage of the total body weight may be extremely high, indicating deviation from the norm.

Wide variations were not found in the three breeds studied, or in the sexes of each breed. To test the graph, brain weights of 4 wirehaired fox terriers, 9 beagles, 9 Shetland sheepdogs, 10 cocker spaniels, and 8 basenjis were reduced to a percentage of body weight and the results fitted perfectly with the anticipated result of 0.8 to 1% of body weight in all breeds except the African basenjis (with an inbreeding coefficient of 0.62–0.89), which were well below the expected range. For this breed, the average brain weight was 54 g and body weight was 10.9 kg. This discrepancy may be due to the fact that this breed of dog may be an ectotype, an atypical domestic canid, unrelated to the other breeds used in this study and presumably not included in the work of Latimer (1965).

During development in man, and similarly in several species of primates from the New World and the Old World, there is a constant relationship between brain weight and body weight (Dodgson 1962). There are marked differences, however, in brain-body relationships among different species of primates belonging to the same family, which may indicate differences in function and behavior more strongly than they indicate differences in evolutionary ancestry. Also, a great variety of blood groups are found in man, whereas only 5 types are recognized in the dog (Cohen and Fuller 1953). We may argue that the great morphological (e.g., brain-body relationships) and physiological (e.g., blood groups) and behavioral differences in the primate are characteristic of the primates, which are very diverse and highly organized mammals. Conversely, in the Canidae narrow variations in these anatomical and physiologic constants indicate a common ancestry, where behavioral similarity between different groups of Canidae (Scott 1954) is characteristic of a less diversely evolved mammalian species. Selective breeding by man has not caused sufficient variations to produce significantly wide deviations from the norm except in those breeds which are physiologically abnormal or anatomically atypical.

Summary

Brain weight and liver weight as a percentage of the total body weight was calculated in 26 dogs of 3 breeds, at different ages from birth to 5 years. A direct relationship between body weight and brain size was found, but liver weights were inconsistent. When testing the validity of the results with 5 breeds of similar size and type, one breed, the African basenji, was found to deviate widely from the norm. The evolutionary significance of these anatomical variables and constants is discussed, and the occurrence of diverse measurements in different breeds may be attributed to congenital or developmental abnormality or to a difference in natural selection or evolutionary origin.

Age Differences in the Effects of Decerebration and Spinal Cord Transection in the Dog

The diagnosis and prognosis of congenital, traumatic, or infectious diseases of the nervous system in neonatal animals is complicated because higher cortical structures are not developed, and so symptoms may not be seen until a later age. These problems have been described (Fox 1965d) in a developmental study of several strains of mice with various neurological disorders.

The purpose of this investigation was to determine the clinical effects of spinal cord transection and decerebration on reflex responses in dogs of different ages and to correlate these findings with changes in muscle tone and posture which occur during postnatal development. Some diagnostic criteria for developmental neurologic problems in the dog might therefore be established.

The levels of brain section at which decerebrate rigidity occurs have been described by Lovatt (1956) and Sherrington (1947); section at the thalamic or midbrain level does not cause rigidity, but section below the red nucleus and above the vestibular nuclei will cause rigidity. These criteria were used in the present study. Decerebrate rigidity is a facilitatory effect due to excitation of the reticulopentine formation and efferent reticulospinal tracts (Denny-Brown 1960). Decerebration eliminates the inhibitory effects from higher centers on spinal centers.

Materials and Methods

Twenty-two purebred dogs, reared under the same standards of management and nutrition, were studied. Decerebration was performed on 4 newborn (1 day of age), 2 1-wk-old, 2 4-wk-old, and 3 6-wk-old dogs under local (procaine) and general (Trilene) anesthesia. These ages were chosen specifically, for at these times changes occur in muscle tone during postnatal development. Periods of increased flexor tone followed by increased extensor tone and adultlike normal distribution of tone are seen at 0–3, 4–20, and 20 days onward respectively (see chap. 2, figs. 2.2, 2.3).

A small opening was made with a 0.25 mm dental burr 1 cm lateral to the parietal crest through the parietal bone on a line just anterior to the tympanic bullae. A silver probe was inserted and directed downward and slightly forward until the sphenoid bone in the floor of the cranium could be felt. The probe was then directed

TABLE 4.3

POSTOPERATIVE BEHAVIOR OF DECEREBRATE DOGS

1 Day Old	1 and 4 Wk Old	6 Wk Old
Strong rooting reflex	No rooting reflex[a]	No rooting reflex
Strong negative geotaxis	No geotaxis[a]	No geotaxis reflex
Fair righting reflex	Fair righting reflex	Weak righting reflex
Extensor rigidity in forelimbs	Extensor rigidity in forelimbs	Extensor rigidity in forelimbs
Slight flexor rigidity in hind limbs (normal)	Weak extensor rigidity in hind limbs but flexed at hip	Complete extensor rigidity in hind limbs
Normal Magnus reflex (tonic neck)	Fair Magnus reflex	Weak Magnus reflex
Normal labyrinthine reflex	Normal labyrinthine reflex	Fair labyrinthine reflex
Weak anterior opisthotonus— head occasionally flexed	Slight anterior opisthotonus— head and neck extended	Complete opisthotonus

[a] These reflexes normally disappear during 3–4 wk of age.

laterally in a sweeping movement, as in the leucotomy technique used in man (Walsh 1956). Lateral contact with the parietal bone on each side facilitated complete excursion of the probe. The incision was closed and the subject was allowed to recover overnight from anesthesia. It was observed subsequently for 12–24 hr before being killed, after which the site of the lesion was determined on postmortem examination. Recovery from anesthesia was rapid, but to reduce the effect anesthesia might have on the clinical symptoms, all subjects were examined the day following surgery.

The spinal cord was severed at the junction of the 1st and 2d lumbar vertebrae under local and Trilene anesthesia, using diathermy. Subjects were aged 1 day (2 dogs), 10 days (1 dog), and 14 days (1 dog), and the effects of spinal cord section were compared with earlier work on adult dogs. The spinal cords were removed at 6 wk of age and examined histologically to confirm complete transection at the site of the lesion.

Results

Before decerebration, the neurological status of the subject was determined as described earlier (chap. 2) to serve as comparison for responses observed postoperatively (table 4.3). These postoperative responses have been tabulated for clarity (table 4.3), and it is at once apparent what little effect decerebration has on the behavior of the neonate dog. Rooting and negative geotaxic responses were relatively unaffected in 1-day-old pups but were absent in older subjects. The body righting reflex was slow but apparently normal in 1-day-old pups but was more difficult to elicit in older pups, especially those 6 wk of age, in which it is normally strong. In all cases the lesion was accurately located just anterior to the pons, the cerebellum and medulla being left intact and the midbrain transected.

The pattern of decerebrate rigidity varied with the age of the subject; flexor dominance was marked at birth, followed by a gradual transition to the adult state of extensor dominance (fig. 4.5). Opisthotonus (back arching) increased with age.

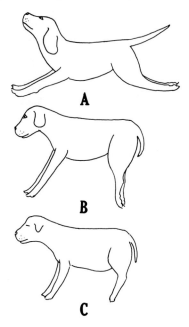

Fig. 4.5. Effects of decerebration at different ages (*a,* 6 wk; *b,* 1 wk; *c,* birth), showing gradual increase in extensor rigidity in the hind limbs, with extensor rigidity present in the forelimbs at all ages.

Section of the spinal cord at birth, 10, and 14 days of age caused complete flaccidity and lack of voluntary movement in the hind limbs. As crawling at this age is effected mainly by the forelimbs and the hind limbs are normally dragged behind, there was little loss of locomotion.

Immediately following spinal cord transection, reflex urination could be evoked by tickling the external genitalia, as in the normal neonate, but crossed extensor and pain withdrawal responses were difficult to elicit until the 1st or 2d day postoperatively. No significant differences were found between these dogs aged from 1 day to 2 wk. After the 3d day a mass reflex response appeared; pinching the tail caused inward flexion of the tail, adduction and extension of the hind limbs, and reflex urination. At this time also there was an increase in flexor tone in the hind limbs, which were adducted and slightly flexed. Seven days postoperatively, reflex urination, extensor, and pain withdrawal responses were easily elicited, but labyrinthine influences on the hind limbs (postural changes and Magnus or tonic neck reflex) were naturally absent. Normal standing occurred during the 3d wk after birth only in the forelimbs; the pup began to raise its body on the forelimbs and drag the hind limbs or pivot on them. Spinal cord section therefore did not alter the time sequence in the ontogeny of emergence of adult locomotor patterns. By 6 wk of age the locomotor pattern was similar to that reported in the adult dog with sectioned lumbar spinal cord, but the hind limbs were still held adducted and slightly flexed.

Discussion

Alterations in muscle tone and posture during postnatal development in the dog have been described (chap. 2). A period of flexor dominance from birth to 3 days of age was reported, followed by an extensor period from 4 to 20 days and then normal distribution of muscle tone after 20 days of age. Decerebration has a similar effect on the forelimbs at all ages, and reflex tests indicate that the cortical control of forelimb movements is well developed at birth in the dog. The hind limbs showed different postural rigidity patterns according to the age at which the dog was decerebrated. Flexion with little opisthotonus was seen at birth, and some increased extensor dominance was seen at 1 wk of age. At 6 wk there was extreme opisthotonus and posterior extension of the hind limbs as reported in the adult dog, indicating that in neonatal dogs cortical control of the hind limbs is quite different from that in the adult. Much of the reflexive behavior in the neonate was undisturbed by decerebration, suggesting that a great deal of the spectrum of neonatal behavior is controlled by subcortical centers (table 4.3).

Decerebration in adult animals causes exaggerated sensitivity of the stretch reflexes, which are most prominent in the extensor muscles that normally resist gravity. In the sloth, decerebration gives rise to flexion of the forelimbs, since the flexors are the antigravity muscles in this animal (Britton and Kline 1943). Since standing and adult locomotor patterns are not developed until 3–4 wk of age in the dog, so that the antigravity muscles and associated stretch receptors are not developed, the classical posture of extensor hypertonia is not seen in neonatal dogs, where fetal flexion predominates. Decerebrate rigidity is a release phenomenon and is caused by withdrawal of normal descending impulses inhibiting the stretch reflex (Walsh 1956). It has been found that the lesion must be higher than the pons to cause decerebrate rigidity in the dog (Keller 1945), and this was confirmed in the present investigation. Rigidity is also reduced if the vestibular nerves are destroyed (Sprague and Chambers 1953). In the decerebrate animal, stimulation of the bulbar reticular formation causes hypotonia and also inhibits the effects of direct stimulation of the cerebrum in intact subjects (Magoun and Rhines 1946). In man, the pathways from the reticular formation to the spinal cord that maintain spasticity are not fully developed until some time after birth; so the effect of brain lesions at birth may not be apparent for 12 mo or more (Kennard 1940). This may also be true in the dog, and would explain the variable states of decerebrate rigidity seen at different ages. The control over forelimb movements is superior to the hind-limb coordination; so the reticular pathways to the anterior limbs may be well developed in the young dog, for the effects of decerebration are similar for the forelimbs at all ages.

The difference in the strength of body righting, and labyrinthine responses where strong responses were found in younger subjects following decerebration, may be due to an age difference in the facilitation of these responses. These findings suggest that the lower centers in young animals respond differently after decerebration, since they are less under the control of higher cortical centers than in more mature subjects. Age differences in the responsiveness of these lower centers following decerebration may therefore be attributable to differences in release or disinhibition from higher neural control.

The effect of spinal cord transection in the adult dog has been described by Denny-Brown (1960). Immediately after transection spinal shock ensues, and the threshold of all spinal reflexes is increased after transection of the cord caudal to the midpontine level. Eventually there is recovery and return of spinal reflexes, and the limb flaccidity is replaced by flexor responses. Extensor reflexes later emerge and spinal stepping and reflex standing may be demonstrated (Denny-Brown 1960).

In contrast, the findings in neonatal dogs similarly treated are markedly different. In two of the subjects no spinal shock (as judged by the persistence of spinal reflexes) occurred, although the hind limbs were flaccid. Reflex urination was easily stimulated and could be elicited throughout the experiment. Electrical stimulation to cause bladder evacuation in adult dogs (Kantrowitz and Shamaun 1963) was found increasingly difficult 2–3 wk postoperatively and was thought to be due to spasticity of the external sphincter muscles. No flexor or extensor phases and no reflex stepping or standing could be demonstrated in the neonatal pups, although the hind limbs were held adducted and slightly flexed throughout the experiment. Muscle atrophy was evident by 6 wk of age and, although there was deterioration in the crossed extensor and pain withdrawal reflexes, no marked flexor or extensor rigidity as described in the adult dog was seen. Magnus (tonic neck) and labyrinthine responses (still present in the forelimbs) were absent in the hind limbs in all cases and served as reliable signs that the spinal transection was complete and no central impulses were reaching the hind limbs.

From these findings one may conclude that supraspinal influences on the lumbar spinal cord in the neonate are poorly developed and that consequently the innervation of the hind extremities and genitalia is mediated through local spinal synapses. Spinal shock is therefore minimal in the immature dog.

Spinal cord transection has been performed on young cats and dogs (Shurrager 1956) in a study designed to establish spinal conditioning or "motor learning." Spinal shock was seen only in animals old enough to walk, and not before this time. It was concluded that the effects of spinal cord transection were less serious in young animals, for although the local spinal response systems were established, the higher cord systems and brain centers were less developed, and the withdrawal of these effects by transection was less marked. The rate of performance (spinal conditioning and walking) was directly related to the amount of stimulation and inversely related to the age when transection was done. Exercise and training were undertaken to facilitate spinal walking and to control abnormal distribution of muscle tone in the hind limbs in these studies by Shurrager. This was not done in the present investigation: the hind limbs possessed good muscle tone, and the limbs were semiflexed at the hip and knee; this flexion was maintained throughout the experiment. Such abnormal distribution of muscle tone causes permanent displacement of the limbs (Fox 1966*d*) which may cause secondary skeletal changes and completely derange the emergence of adult locomotor patterns. Some regeneration in the spinal cord following transection has been reported by Freeman (1952), and the degree of regeneration was inversely proportioned to the age of the subject when the operation was performed.

The effects of cortical ablation on neonatal monkeys are also minimal. Corticospinal connections in the postnatal development of the monkey have been studied by Kuypers (1962) and it was observed that corticomotorneuronal connections are not established until some time after birth.

Similar results following decerebration in the kitten have been observed by Skoglund (1960*b*). Flexor dominance was seen in the newborn kitten, which was attributed to a deficit in the supraspinal control of spinal reflexes; that is, lack of inhibition of interneurons which inhibit extensor muscles. In older kittens, normal flexor-extensor balance was observed and the pattern of decerebration then resembled the adult. Although the cat is neuro-ontogenetically different from the dog in many aspects of development (Fox 1970*b*), we may conclude that alterations in muscle tone and posture, as exemplified by the effects of decerebration, undergo comparable changes in these two species during postnatal development.

From these observations we may draw two conclusions which may facilitate diagnosis of spontaneous neurological disorders in young animals. Extensive lesions of higher structures of the CNS (decerebration) may have little influence on behavior in the neonatal animal. As development progresses, however, behavioral organization becomes dependent on the integration of these higher levels of nervous activity and abnormalities in behavior will emerge.

The second point of interest is the lack of evidence for the occurrence of spinal shock in newborn animals following extensive lesions of the spinal cord. That spinal reflexes apparently are unaffected, and changes occur only in muscle tone (flaccidity) in the hind limbs, may be an aid to early diagnosis. The lack of "contrast" as spinal reflexes are "released" from supraspinal cortical influences is due to the immaturity of these higher structures. Only at a later age, when the hind limbs are under cerebral control after 2 wk of age, can a reliable diagnosis be made.

Finally, we may conclude that diagnosis and prognosis of possible neurologic disturbances in neonatal animals should be guarded and careful observations made, especially during the 2d–4th wk of age, when the most rapid changes in CNS development are taking place. The possible site of the lesions at various levels of neurologic development may therefore be determined by close observations of the chronological sequences of neuro-ontogeny (see also Fox 1965*d*).

The early plasticity of the immature brain, in terms of its ability to gain considerable functional and structural recovery following lesions of specific areas, has been noted by several workers (Sperry 1958; Wetzel et al. 1965; Fox 1966*a*). There are both species differences and ontogenetic limitations in the capacity of the CNS to compensate for ablation of particular areas, as exemplified by the work of Kling (1966). Further studies are indicated in this area, to identify critical periods after which experimental lesions have the same effect as in the adult. That an anatomical structure such as the brain has multipotentiality and plasticity during early development is little understood. To what extent afferent sensory stimuli from lower structures contribute to the reorganization of neocortical sensory and association areas remains to be evaluated.

Normal and Abnormal Growth Dynamics of the CNS and of the Internal Organs of the Dog

The prenatal development of certain internal organs in the dog has recently been reviewed by Latimer (1965), and the postnatal development of the brain in relation to body weight will be described later in this report. Differences in brain and liver weight in relation to body weight attributable to genetic (breed) differences must be considered; also, the effects of prenatal malnutrition associated with "runting" or competition for placental space have been discussed from the clinical standpoint (Fox 1966*d*), where the brain weight is relatively greater than normal because of reduction in body weight, and the liver may also be greatly reduced in weight.

Materials and Methods

The following investigation was undertaken on a series of physically normal dogs of various breeds (not including achondroplastic or acromegalic types) from which body, brain, liver, kidney, pancreas, and adrenal weights were obtained: the weights of bilateral organs were averaged for each subject. The length of the body from the dorsal tubercle of the atlas to the articulation of the first coccygeal vertebra (base of tail) and the length of the alimentary tract (from pharyngeal origin of esophagus to end of rectum, including measuring stomach along lesser curvature) were also calculated. These organ data were plotted against the body weight and further points added from a group of pups which had been raised under chronic starvation, being given only the daily feeding periods of 1 hr each with the mother from 3 days of age onward, until death. Biochemical data and evoked potential responses were also obtained from these subjects and from their littermate controls and have been reported in detail elsewhere (Myslivecek, Fox, and Zahlava 1967).

Results and Discussion

Data from the few samples of chronically starved subjects become significant when compared with the organ weights of normal subjects (figs. 4.6, 4.7, 4.8). With the exception of the brain weights and length of alimentary tract, all organ weights of the starved subjects were within normal range in relation to the reduced body weight; that is, reduction in size of these structures accompanied reduction in body weight. Brain weight and alimentary length, however, did not coincide in the normal proportion to body weight, indicating that these structures continue to grow at a somewhat greater rate than other internal organs subjected to chronic starvation.

The relationships of the various organ weights to body weight in normal subjects are presented in detail to serve as reference points for indexes of normality for physically normal dogs, of mixed breed but of uniform "mesocephalic" type.

Chronically starved mammals are characteristically pot-bellied and large-headed. These data support the layman's observations, but reveal an important concept on the adaptation of the organism to its environment. The genetically determined development of the body and internal organs ensures a definite ontogenetic pattern, where internal organs are in proportion to each other and to the body weight. These genetic influences are not rigid, however, for compensatory hypertrophy can occur adaptively through environmental influences. In this instance, starvation increased the size of the alimentary tract. Other internal organs which are

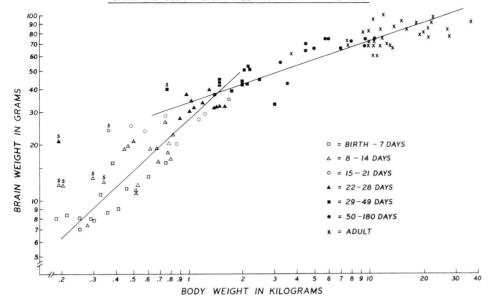

□ = BIRTH – 7 DAYS
△ = 8 – 14 DAYS
○ = 15 – 21 DAYS
▲ = 22 – 28 DAYS
■ = 29 – 49 DAYS
● = 50 – 180 DAYS
x = ADULT

Fig. 4.6. The growth curve of the canine brain (expressed in relation to body weight; age ranges are shown by symbols) shows a "break" at approximately 4 wk of age, after which growth is more gradual. Experimentally starved subjects (S) have brains heavier than normal in proportion to body weight (for discussion see text).

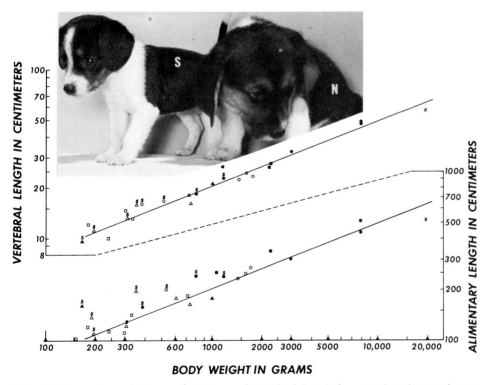

Fig. 4.7. Comparisons between alimentary and vertebral length in normal and starved pups (shown in inset at 6 wk of age). Starvation causes a "miniaturization" of the animal, in that vertebral length is in proportion to body weight. Alimentary length, however, is greater than normal in starvation. (S = starved, N = normal beagle.) In figs. 4.7 and 4.8 the age range is denoted by the same symbols as in fig. 4.6: S above symbol indicates starved subject.

reduced in size and are in direct proportion to body size are in contrast to the continual growth of the brain, which soon becomes out of proportion to body weight. This phenomenon suggests that the nurture of the developing brain is necessary because this organ attains functional maturity later in life than other organs and its most predominant component, the neocortex, is phylogenetically a newer and more elaborate structure in mammals. The nutritional demands of the growing brain may therefore be greater than those of other organs whose functional competence can

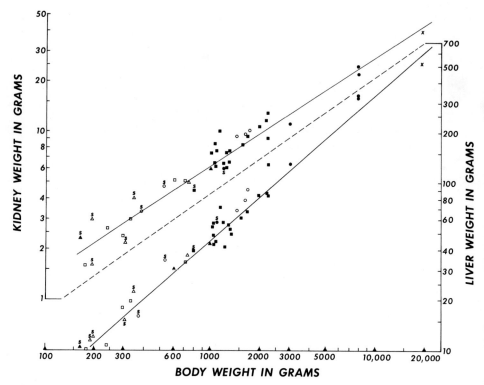

Fig. 4.8. Starvation causes miniaturization of liver and kidney; the weights of these organs (unlike the brain) are in proportion to the body weight.

adapt to undernutrition. The brain and alimentary tract under the influences of chronic starvation may show the respective phenomena of "priority" maturation and functional hypertrophy. Histologic examination and evoked potentials recorded from pups up to 3 wk of age showed that the developing CNS was retarded; but in older pups, structural and functional differences compared with controls were less marked (figs. 4.9, 4.10, 4.11). It must be added that many pups were unable to adapt to this vigorous regime of undernutrition, and high mortalities occurred during the first 10–14 days of life. The brain weight and alimentary length of two of these pups that died between 8 and 10 days of age were within normal range in relation to body weight, whereas starved pups of the same age, being more vigorous and active, showed the first indications of economic reduction in body size and size of other internal organs, and the brain weight and alimentary length were out of proportion to the body. These findings indicate that adaptation to starvation is accompanied by economic reduction in body weight and in weight of heart, liver, kidneys, pancreas, and adrenals early in life, whereas in those pups that did not adapt and which consequently died, brain growth and alimentary length were pathologically retarded. The ability to recover normal body proportions was not evaluated in this study. McCance and Widdowson (1951) found that children who must exist on an impoverished caloric intake can do so for prolonged periods of time by cessation of growth, which will be recouped later if the deprivation period is not of excessive length. Barnes (1965) has briefly reviewed some aspects of protein-calorie deficiency diseases (marasmus and kwashiorkor) and concludes that psychological (intellectual) and behavioral development may be impaired; the perpetuation of these

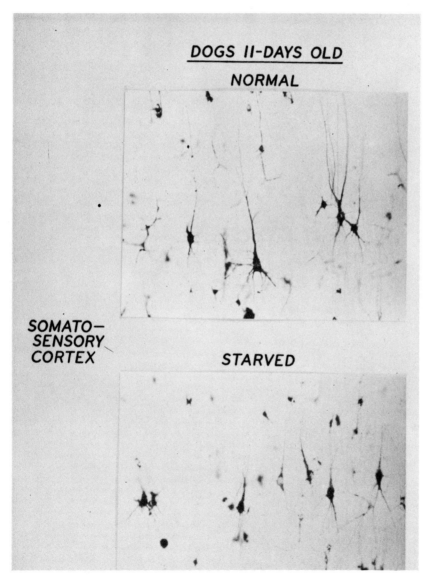

Fig. 4.9. Marked retardation of neuronal development in starved pup (Golgi-Cox; scale as in fig. 4.10).

effects and the extent of recovery following improved dietary intake (see Dickerson, Dobbing, and McCance 1967) require further investigation. Both myelination (Dobbing 1964, 1966) and learning abilities (Caldwell and Churchill 1967) in rats can be retarded by starving weanling rats or by prenatal malnutrition (dam on a protein deficient diet [Cowley and Griesel 1966]). Further studies on structural and functional changes in the CNS and other organs, as attempted in this study, are indicated, together with more information regarding such variables as the duration of starvation, extent of functional impairment, and capacity for recovery. Mourek et al. (1967) have shown also that starvation in the rat can retard ontogeny of EEG and cortical EP.

It is possible that the earlier in life the organism is exposed to such undernu-

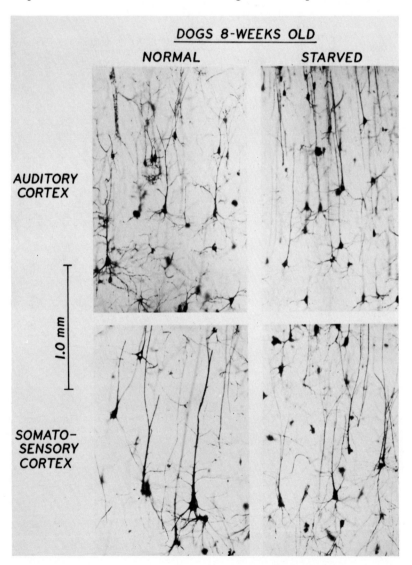

Fig. 4.10. Neuronal development in auditory cortex only slightly retarded in 8-wk-old starved pup, but motor cortex (Betz cells) shows greater growth retardation.

trition, the more severe the effect will be on those systems which are developing: in this regard, Davison and Dobbing (1966) postulate a vulnerable period in the development of myelin in the brain, which in the pig is during the initial postnatal period of maximal brain growth. Similarly, in the dog the initial period of most rapid brain growth, from birth to 4 wk (see fig. 4.6), may also be a vulnerable period; when myelination is proceeding rapidly, nutritional requirements are critical. Specific dietary restrictions of precursors of myelin would have the greatest effect on myelination during this vulnerable period, whereas a balanced diet, but in reduced quantity, could influence brain size but not necessarily affect myelination.

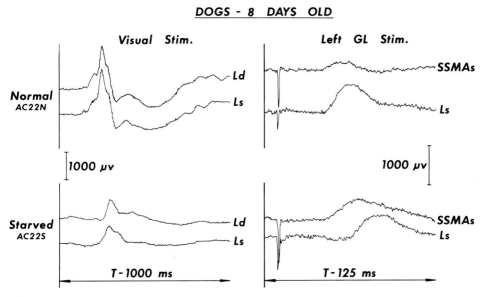

Fig. 4.11. Marked increase in latency of evoked response to visual stimulation and lateral geniculate stimulation in starved pup (from Myslivecek, Fox, and Zahlava 1966).

Postnatal Development of the Canine Neocortex

Introduction

In this section, the postnatal development of the cytoarchitectonic characteristics and myelination of the canine neocortex will be described. The postnatal development of the major gyri and sulci of the canine cerebrum has been described by Herre and Stephan (1955).

Sarkissow (1929) observed that the cells of the motor cortex in the dog are more developed at birth than those in other regions of the neocortex, and that the occipital region undergoes the most rapid postnatal development. Fox (1964e) reported rapid reduction in cell density from birth to 3 wk in both the frontal and occipital cortices of the dog; changes in cell density after this were more gradual. Haddara (1956) and Eayrs and Goodhead (1959), for example, have studied neuronal development and density changes with age in mice and rats, and Conel (1939–59) provides a detailed description of cytoarchitectonic development of the human cerebrum. The recent autoradiographic studies by Altman (1966b, 1967) on neuronal and glial development in the rodent CNS provide detailed information on the origin and migration of the precursors of these cells during ontogeny.

Fleschig (1894) first described the sequences of myelination of the CNS as occurring earliest in the spinal cord and later spreading into the medulla oblongata, pons, and midbrain, and finally into the telencephalon. Myelination is the process by which nerve fibers acquire a myelin sheath; this is a lipoprotein complex, and is formed in a coil around the nerve fiber, the process being modulated by glial cells (Luse 1956; Davison et al. 1966); in the peripheral nervous system, Geren (1954) correlated the Schwann cell with myelination in the chick embryo. Since the early observations of Fleschig, myelination has been investigated in several mammals.[3] Studies of various species include: rat (Watson 1903; Tilney 1933; Jacobson 1963), cat (Tilney and Casamajor 1924; Langworthy 1929; and Windle, Fish, and O'Donnell 1934), opossum (Langworthy 1928), sheep (Romanes 1947), guinea pig (Clark 1963), rabbit and hamster (Clark 1966), and man (Langworthy 1930, 1933; Conel 1939–59). A variety of techniques may be used to evaluate myelination of specific regions and tracts, using myelin stains for normal fibers, the Marchi stain for degenerating myelin sheaths, or the Nauta stain for degenerating axons. A detailed and classic series of studies on the myeloarchitectonics of the adult dog have been conducted by Kreiner (reviewed in 1966); these studies were concerned mainly with neocortical myeloarchitectonics, and no correlations were made with function or development.

Yakovlev and Lecours (1967) observe that in man there are great individual variations in myelination. The vestibular system and anterior (motor) roots are the first to myelinate. They found that the CNS begins to myelinate in a cephalocaudal procession from the level of the third cranial nerve (in those structures originating from the bilateral divisions of the neuraxis, namely the chordencephalon). Also, a caudocephalad procession of myelination occurs anterior to the level of the third nerve (in the forebrain or acrencephalon, which has a unibody origin and not a bilateral origin). Yakovlev and Lecours consider that stimulation in utero, initially by "floating" stimulation, causes early myelination of the vestibular nerves, and as the fetus grows and makes body contact with the amnion wall, cutaneous stimulation initiates myelination of posterior (sensory) spinal roots. These authors also describe myelinogenetic cycles in three distinct zones; the median (hippocampus and hypothalamus), paramedian (limbic), and supralimbic (cortex and related pallium) zones, in addition to caudocephalad and cephalocaudal sequences.

In this investigation, the temporal sequence of myelination of normal nerve fibers in the CNS of the dog will be described with particular regard to neocortical myelination. In this species, myelination has not as yet been described in any detail; Pampiglione (1963) notes that myelination of the cerebral hemisphere of the dog does not occur uniformly, but at 10 wk of age the staining is well distributed in the white matter of most convolutions. Harman (cited in personal communication by Scott 1963) observed that myelin is almost completely absent in the brains of newborn pups, except in those portions connected with certain cranial nerves, namely the trigeminal, the facial, and the nonacoustic portion of the auditory nerve.

---

[3] See also Caley and Maxwell (1968*a, b*) for EM descriptions of neuronal development in the rat cerebrum postnatally, and of neuroglial development.

The development of neocortical neurons and myelination of certain CNS structures and of the spinal cord will be described, and further correlations will be made between the results of this study and other aspects of postnatal development of the canine brain.

Materials and Methods

In this investigation, 9 brains from purebred beagles and shelties (Jackson Laboratory strains) were prepared in serial, coronal section and stained alternately with cresyl violet and Loyez's stain for myelin. Ages were 3, 10, 14, 21, 28, 35, 42, and 70 days and 1 yr. Sagittal sections from pups aged 4, 28, and 42 days and 9 mo were also prepared for comparison. All dogs were in good health and were reared under similar standards of management and nutrition. Photomicrographs were taken of the cell layers from the neocortical gray matter in the precruciate (motor), postcruciate (sensory), temporal (auditory), occipital (visual), and frontal regions, from the specific areas of these regions described in the cytoarchitectonic studies of the adult dog by Adrianov and Mering (1964). Cell counts of neurons from the same unit area (of layer V) of several photomicrographs were taken by three independent observers and their results were averaged. These data, therefore, serve to compare the neuronal densities in different regions in the same dog at a given age, and also show changes in density with increasing age. The development and differentiation of layers I–VI were determined by comparing similar regions with the cytoarchitectonics of the adult neocortex. Identification of these layers is facilitated by the fact that in most regions the cells of these various layers and sublayers can be differentiated on morphological grounds. Determination of myelination and identification of various tracts and subcortical structures was greatly assisted by reference to Singer's (1962) *The Brain of the Dog in Section* together with a complete set of coronal, horizontal, and sagittal serial sections of adult beagle brains which were used by Singer in his atlas and which were kindly made available for this study by Professor Yakovlev.

Results

a) *Cytoarchitectonic Development*

Occipital (Visual) Cortex (area occipitalis prima [O_1]) (fig. 4.12). This area, which occupies the posterior part of the marginal gyrus, is surrounded on all sides by area O_2. On the outer surface of the hemisphere, the borderline of area O_1 crosses the free surface of the postsplenial gyrus and passes medial to the postlateral sulcus. On the internal surface of the hemisphere the borderline extends over the free surface of the suprasplenial and splenial gyri, dips into the depth of the retrosplenial sulcus, and emerges on the free surface in the posterior part of the postsplenial gyrus (Adrianov and Mering 1964).

3–10 Days. At 3 days of age, the cell density in this area is greater than in any other part of the neocortex. The borderlines of the various cell layers cannot be determined until 10 days of age, when the paucity of cells in layer V can be seen. In layer V, however, both small cells and a larger single layer of Meynert cells can be distinguished. The palisadelike appearance of layer VI, composed of spindle-shaped, triangular cells arranged in columns, is clearly differentiated by 10 days of age.

2–Wk. Reduction in cell density is pronounced up to 2 wk of age, and by

3 wk, layers I, and the complex layers II and III and the very deep layer IV (divided into 3 sublayers by Adrianov and Mering) can be distinguished.

4 Wk–Adult. By 4 wk of age, these sublayers can be reliably recognized as follows: sublayer IV^1 is a narrow band composed of small irregular cells; layer IV^2 contains characteristically few cells, mainly large single cells of irregular or rounded form; and layer IV^3, which is the thickest of these three sublayers, is composed of mainly regular small round cells. By 5 wk of age, cell density in this area O_1 is within the adult range.

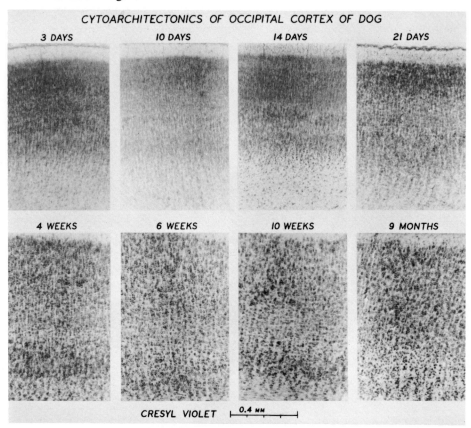

Fig. 4.12. Gradual reduction of cell density during first 3 wk of age, attaining adult level by 6 wk of age.

Frontal Cortex. This region lies on the medial surface of the hemisphere and occupies the superior section of gyrus proreus. Rostrally, this area borders areas F_2 and F_4; caudally, it borders subareas PrC_2–L_2 and F–L_2, and dorsally PrC_2 and F_2 (Adrianov and Mering 1964).

3–10 Days. The most striking features of the frontal area are the tightly compact arrangement of layer II cells and the large pyramidal cells of layer V^1, resting above the relatively clear zone of sublayer V^2, which can be recognized from 3 days onward. Layer VI can be recognized by 3 days of age as being composed of small, irregular cells which stain with less intensity than cells in layers II and III. The cells of this layer (VI) form small columnar aggregations which end abruptly at the boundary of gray and white matter.

2–3 Wk. Cell density rapidly decreases until 2 wk of age, and thereafter the reduction in cell density is more gradual. At 3 wk of age, the most predominant cells are large pyramidal cells which stain intensively and are located in layer V. By 3 wk, layer II, a very narrow layer composed of many small, predominantly triangular cells, can be distinguished from layer III.

4 Wk–Adult. Layer III_3 is discernible with the reduction of cell density at 5 wk of age. This layer is composed of small, rounded, and closely aggregated cells which do not stain as darkly as the adjoining cells of sublayers III_1 and III_2. Layer V consists of sublayer V^1, which contains large pyramidal cells, and sublayer V^2, with a few scattered, irregular, small and medium-sized cells, which lies directly below layer III. Layer IV, therefore, is not present in this area. Reduction in cell density together with increase in cell size and increase in thickness of these layers is more or less completed by 4–5 wk of age.

Temporal (Auditory) Cortex (area temporalis prima [T_1]). This area is in the posterior portion of the suprasylvian gyrus. Its posterior boundary extends along the base of the ectolateral gyrus, bordering area O_2. The lower boundary passes along the free surface of the ectolateral convolution and the anterior boundary extends into the depth of the posterior section of the suprasylvian sulcus. The superior boundary extends across the free surface of the suprasylvian gyrus (Adrianov and Mering 1964).

3–10 Days. Cell density is intense in this area at 3 days of age and undergoes the most rapid reduction during the first 2 wk of life. At 3 days, the most clearly recognizable features are the areas of rarefaction (paucity of cells in irregular foci) confined to layer V. By 10 days, the large pyramidal cells above this layer can be distinguished more clearly than at 3 days. These pyramidal cells belong to sublayer III^3, since layer IV is not clearly formed in this area, even in the adult animal. Above these large cells is a layer of smaller, sparser cells which make up sublayer III^2. Sublayer III^1 and layer II merge into each other and cannot be clearly distinguished on morphological grounds.

2–3 Wk. Layer II is characterized by predominantly small, pyramid-shaped cells, which are well formed at 3 wk of age. The deepest cell layer VI in some sections is separated by a light stria from layer V, and contains more cells than layer V, predominantly of mixed type (round, small, and medium polymorphic), often arranged in small columnar aggregations.

4 Wk–Adult. Between 4 and 5 wk of age the size and density of cells of the various layers attain relatively mature characteristics.

Precruciate (Motor) Cortex. Area precruciatus prima (Pr_1). This area lies on the external and medial surfaces of the cerebral hemisphere, occupying a small portion of the anterior and almost all of the posterior portion of the sigmoid gyrus. The cruciate sulcus separates it rostrally from parietal area PrC_2, and caudally the boundary with area Pc extends across the free surface of the marginal gyrus. On the medial surface of the hemisphere, the anterior section of the splenial sulcus separates area PrC_1 from the anterior limbic area L_2, and ventrally it is bound by the coronary sulcus (Adrianov and Mering 1964).

3–10 Days. At 3 days of age, the cells of this area are low in density compared with other regions of the neopallium; this reduction in density proceeds gradually during the first 3 wk of life. Most predominant in younger specimens are the large pyramidal (Betz) cells which are confined to layer V. Layer VI is distinctly separated from this adjoining layer as early as 3 days and is composed of irregular cells often arranged in columns and aggregations. Layer II, a narrow layer of small cells, layer III, a deep layer of cells divisible into 3 sublayers, and layers V and VI are well differentiated by 10 days of age. Layer IV is absent. The radial striations formed by cells of the upper layers are most clearly seen in the younger specimens. Occasional patches of translucence may be seen in the middle of layer III.

2–3 Wk. During this period there is a gradual reduction in cell density in all layers, especially in layer V, the component cells of which attain relatively mature proportions by 3 wk.

4 Wk–Adult. Although this region is relatively mature between 4 and 5 wk of age, the Betz cells of layer V continue to increase slightly in size up to 10 wk of age.

Postcruciate (Sensory) Cortex. Area postcruciatus prima (area Pc_1). This area occupies the posterior part of the coronal gyrus and the anterior section of the marginal gyrus (Adrianov and Mering 1964). At 3 days of age, this region is second only to the precoronal (motor) cortex as the most differentiated cortical region. The largest cells in layer V resemble the Betz cells of the precoronal area, both in size and form, although at 3 days of age they are less distinct than those in the precoronal area. The development and cellular differentiation of this area are essentially similar to area PrC_1, the greatest reduction in cell density occurring during the first 3 wk of life (fig. 4.13).

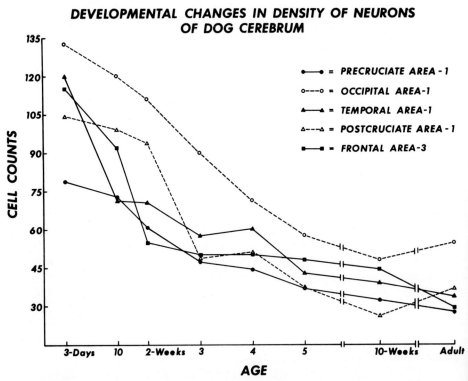

Fig. 4.13. Most rapid reduction in neuronal density occurs during the first 3 wk of life; relatively mature by 5 wk of age in most regions, cell density remaining highest in occipital area. (Precruciate area and postcruciate area = gyrus sigmoideus posterior and gyrus postcruciatus.) (Cell counts from an area of approximately 80 sq mm.)

Parietal (P_1) and *Limbic* (L_1 and L_2) areas were also studied. Cell counts were not taken, but the differentiation of the various cell layers was found to follow a pattern similar to that of the other areas described, there being rapid differentiation from 3 to 21 days of age and minimal changes thereafter.

b) Myelination of the Neocortex and Subcortical Regions

It is beyond the scope of this investigation to consider myelination of subcortical structures in detail. The following descriptions are based on comparative evaluations

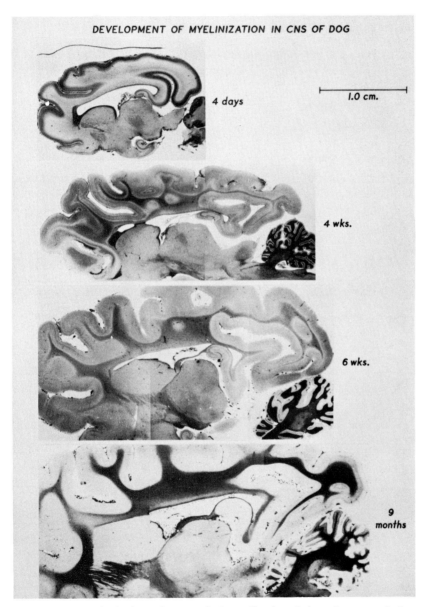

DEVELOPMENT OF MYELINIZATION IN CNS OF DOG

4 days

1.0 cm.

4 wks.

6 wks.

9 months

Fig. 4.14. General sagittal view of neocortical myelination, being absent at 4 days, predominantly in the sensory and motor regions at 4 wk, and more evenly distributed in the frontal and occipital regions at 6 wk.

of thalamocortical myelination; development of certain subcortical systems will be briefly described also. These findings are reviewed in a series of photomicrographs in which the major myelinated regions detectable histologically are shown to enable visual comparisons of the various ages studied (figs. 4.14–4.29).

3–10 Days. At 3 days of age, a few faintly myelinated fibers can be found in the internal capsule at the level of the caudate nucleus. The posterior commissure can be recognized at 3 days and most of its fibers are clearly myelinated, but by 10 days there is apparently no further increase in myelination. The inferior commissure of the colliculi contains a few myelinated fibers at 3 days, and by 10 days is more clearly recognizable. Several tracts in the CNS contain histologically detectable quantities of myelin, notably the tectospinal, tectobulbar, and fasciculus gracilis; the central tegmental tract, spinocerebellar, spinothalamic, lateral lemniscus, fasciculus longitudinalis medius, and median lemniscus are myelinated to a lesser extent (table 4.4).

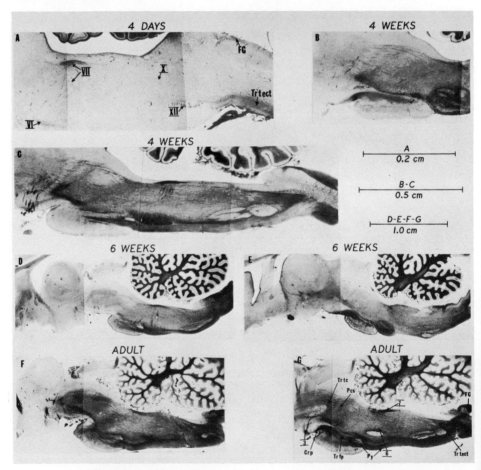

Fig. 4.15. General sagittal view of subcortical myelination; at 4 days, only the cranial nerves and fasciculus gracilis (*FG*) and tractus tectospinalis (*Trtect*) can be detected histologically. At 4 wk, all structures are well myelinated, with the exception of the tractus tegmentalis centralis (*Trtc*), crus pedunculi (*CrP*), pyramis (*Py*) and tractus frontopontinus (*Trfp*). At 6 wk these latter structures are well myelinated. (*Pcs* in adult = pedunculus cerebellaris superior.)

TABLE ... MYELINATION IN CANINE CNS

Tract or Region	3 Days	10 Days	2 Wk	3 Wk	4 Wk	5 Wk	10 Wk	Adult
Cortical								
Frontal (gyrus sigmoideus)	0	0	0	0	+	+	++	+++
Motor (gyrus postcruciatus)	0	0	0	+	++	++	+++	+++
Sensory (gyrus postcruciatus)	0	0	0	0+	++	++	+++	+++
Auditory (gyrus ectosylvius medius)	0	0	0	0+	+	+	++	+++
Visual (gyrus lateralis)	0	0	0	0	0+	+	++	+++
Limbic (cingulum)	0	0	0	0+	+	++	+++	+++
Thalamic radiations: specific	0	0	0	0+	++	++	+++	+++
nonspecific	0	0	0	0+	+	+	++	+++
Corporis callosi (truncus)	0	0	0	0+	0+	+	++	+++
Crus pedunculi (cerebri)	0	0	0+	+	++	++	+++	+++
Capsula externa	0	0	0	0	+	+	++	+++
Pyramis	0+	0+	0+	++	++	++	+++	+++
Genu capsula interna	0	0	0	0	0+	++	+++	+++
Commissure anterior	0	0	0	0	+	+	++	+++
Fornix	0	0+	0	0	0+	+	++	+++
Corticospinal and Corticobulbar	0+	+	+	+	++	++	+++	+++
Tr. tegmentalis centralis	0+	+	++	+++	+++	+++	+++	++++
Commissure posterior	+	++	++	++	++	+++	+++	+++
Tr. Spinocerebellaris	0+	+	++	+++	+++	+++	+++	+++
Fasciculus subcallosus	0+	+	+	+	++	++	+++	+++
Cerebellar peduncles: inferior	0	0+	+	+	++	++	+++	+++
middle	0+	0+	0+	+	+	++	+++	+++
superior	0+	0+	+	++	++	+++	+++	+++
Decussatio trapezoides	0+	+	++	+++	+++	+++	+++	+++
Tectospinal and Tectobulbar	+	+	++	++	+++	+++	+++	+++
Commissure colliculi inferior	0+	+	++	++	++	+++	+++	+++
Commissure colliculi superior	0	+	0+	+	++	++	+++	+++
Tractus spinocerebellaris ventralis	0+	+	+	++	+++	+++	+++	+++
Brachium superior colliculus	0	0	0	+	++	+++	+++	+++
Tractus spinothalamicus	0+	+	+	++	++	+++	+++	+++
Fasciculus gracilis	0+	++	+++	+++	+++	+++	+++	+++
Lateral lemniscus	0+	+	++	+++	+++	+++	+++	+++
Median longitudinal fasciculus	0+	+	++	+++	+++	+++	+++	+++
Median lemniscus	0+	+	++	+++	+++	+++	+++	+++
Cranial Nerves								
I	0+	0+	+	+++	+++	+++		
II	0	0+	0+	+++	+++	+++		
III	+++	+++	+++	+++	+++	+++		
IV	+++	+++	+++	+++	+++	+++		
V	++	+	+++	+++	+++	+++		
VI	+++	++	+++	+++	+++	+++		
VII	++	++	+++	+++	+++	+++		
VIII (nonacoustic)	+++	++	+++	+++	+++	+++		
VIII (acoustic)	0	+	++	++	++	+++		
XII	+	+	+++	+++	+++	+++		

0   No myelin
0+ Faint myelination of a few fibers
+   Light myelination of most fibers
++ Moderate myelination of all fibers
+++ Relatively mature myelination of all fibers
++++ Adult level of myelination

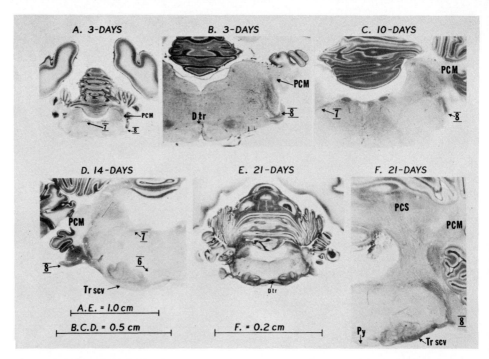

Fig. 4.16. Subcortical myelination at level of seventh pedunculus cerebellaris medius et superior (*PCM* and *PCS*) and genu of seventh cranial nerve. *PCM* and *PCS* poorly myelinated until 21 days, and cranial nerves VII and VIII and decussatio trapezoides (*Dtr*) are myelinated at birth. Tractus spinocerebellaris ventralis (*Trscv*) clearly myelinated at 14 days.

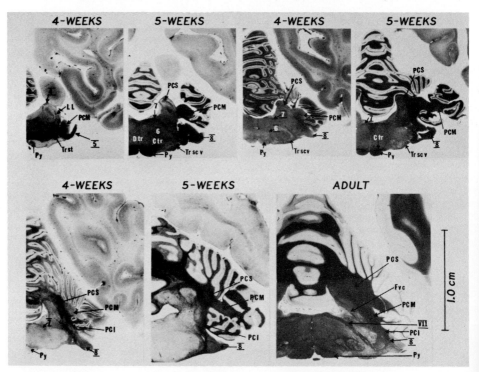

Fig. 4.17. Subcortical myelination at level of pedunculus cerebellaris medius et superior (*PCM* and *PCS*) and genu of seventh cranial nerve. *PCM, PCS,* and *PC* inferior, well myelinated by 5 wk; note increase in myelination of pyramis (*Py*) and tractus spinocerebellaris ventralis (*Trscv*) from 4 to 5 wk. (*Fvd* = fibrae vestibulocerebellares (et cerebellovestibulares) in adult, *Ctr* and *Dtr* = crus et decussatio trapezoidii in 5-week brain.)

The degree of myelination of these structures increases from 3 to 10 days, but myelination of other structures of the CNS during this period was not detected. Of the cranial nerves, V, VII, and VIII (vestibular division) are the most developed at 3 days, whereas nerves III, IV, and VI are less advanced; the lateral olfactory tract of the 1st cranial nerve is faintly myelinated at birth, but develops more definite myelinated fibers at 10 days. The optic nerve is nonmyelinated at 3 days, and only a few fibers are faintly myelinated at 10 days.

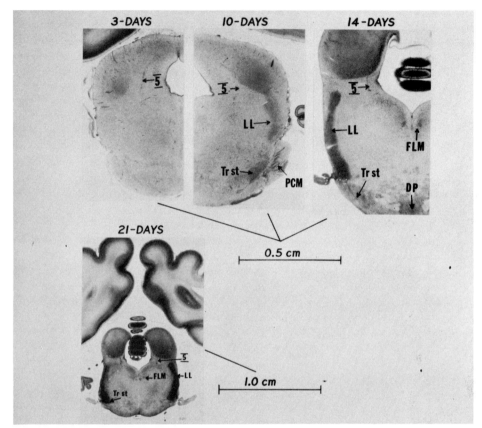

Fig. 4.18. Sections at level of lateral lemniscus and colliculi; only cranial nerve V myelinated at 3 days. With lateral lemniscus (*LL*) and tractus spinothalamicus (*Trst*) becoming myelinated after 10 days of age. Fasciculus longitudinalis medialis (*FLM*) and decussatio pontis (*DP*) clearly myelinated at 14 days.

2–3 Wk. At 14 days, the only detectable myelin above the level of the posterior commissure is in the faintly staining capsula interna and tractus olfactorius lateralis. These two regions are well myelinated at 3 wk of age, and it is at this age that the first myelinated neocortical radiations associated with gyrus lateralis, posterior sigmoid, and postcruciatus can be seen at the level of the anterior commissure, which as yet is nonmyelinated. The frontal area contains no myelin, but at the level of the 3d ventricle and faintly staining corpus callosum, the gyrus ectosylvius and gyrus lateralis contain faint myelinated radiations. Very faint strands of myelin can be detected in the optic radiations, although the optic nerve is well myelinated.

Between 2 and 3 wk of age, myelin develops in the thalamic radiations, cerebral peduncles, pyramids, and corticospinal and corticobulbar tracts (table 4.4).

4 Wk–Adult. By 4 wk of age, myelination of the lateral, ectosylvian, postcruciate, and posterior sigmoid gyri (or precruciate gyrus) is well advanced. Optic and auditory radiations can be clearly detected at 4 wk of age, but because of their intense staining, the postcruciate and posterior sigmoid gyri contain the most myelin. At 4 wk of age, myelin develops in the truncus corporis callosi and fornix, and a few myelinated fibers are present in the splenium of the corpus callosum. At the level of the interpeduncular nucleus, the crus pedunculi are well myelinated. Between 4 and 5 wk of age, a rapid increase in myelination occurs, so that by 5 wk, myelin can be detected in the frontal cortex and anterior commissure; the truncus corporis callosi and fornix are also well myelinated. The pyramids, poorly myelinated at 4 wk, now stain more intensely. Also, the sharp contrast between the darker staining, more rapidly myelinating sensorimotor region and other neocortical regions at 4 wk is less apparent at 5 wk, when these other regions stain with greater intensity. By 6 wk of age, myelin is evenly distributed throughout the neocortex (table 4.4), with the exception of the frontal region, which matures later. Myelination

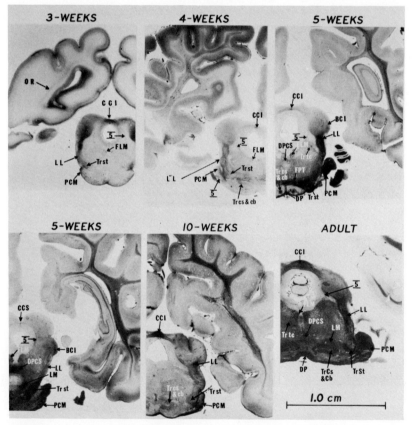

Fig. 4.19. Sections at level of lateral lemniscus (*LL*) and commissura colliculi inferioris (*CCI*). Optic radiation (*OR*) faintly myelinated at 3 wk, with *CCI, LL,* fasciculus longitudinalis medialis (*FLM*) and tracus spinothalamicus (*Trst*) also faintly myelinated. Tractus cerebrospinalis et cerebrobulbaris (*Trcs* and *cb*) first clearly myelinated at 4 wk, with myelin evident at 5 wk in the brachium colliculi inferioris (*BCI*), tractus tegmentalis centralis (*Trtc*), decussatio pedunculorum cerebellarium superiorum (*DPCS*), and decussatio pontis (*DP*).

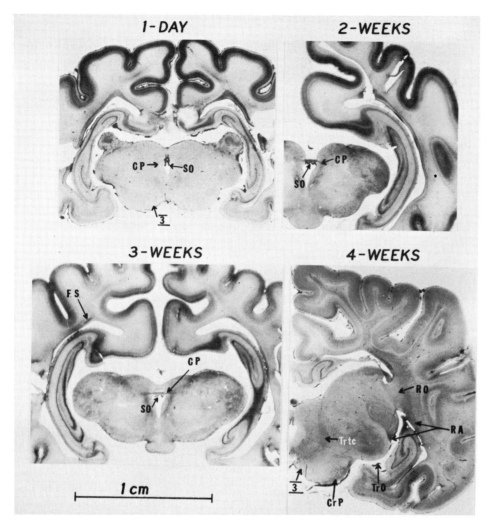

Fig. 4.20. Sections at level of subcommissural organ (*SO*) with commissura posterior (*CP*) very faintly myelinated at 1 day and increasing thereafter. Crus pedunculi (*CrP*), tractus opticus (*TrO*), and radiatio acustica (*RA*) et optica (*RO*) clearly myelinated only at 4 wk. Fasciculus solitarius (*FS*) well myelinated at 3 wk.

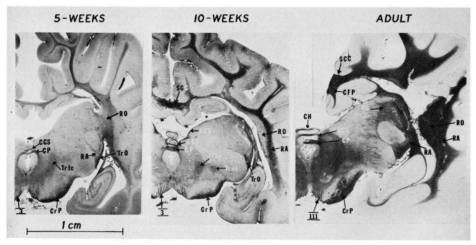

Fig. 4.21. Sections at level of subcommissural organ (*SO*) with all structures at this level clearly myelinated at 5 wk of age. (*TrO, RO,* and *RA* = tractus opticus, radiatio optica et acustica; *CrP* = crus pedunculi; *Trtc* = tractus tegmentalis centralis; *CCS* and *SCC* = commissura colliculi superioris; *CP* = commissura posterior; *Trst* = tractus spinothalamicus; *BCS* = brachium colliculi superioris; *CFP* = commissure fornicis posterior.)

of the neocortex continues more gradually after this time. In summary, myelination of the neocortex occurs most rapidly between 4 and 5 wk of age, in contrast to the paucity of detectable myelin before 4 wk.

Comparative Observations: Myelination in Man and Dog

Yakovlev and Lecours (1967) observe that in man the inner (vestibulocerebellar) division of the inferior cerebellar peduncle myelinates earliest, the most protracted myelination cycle being in the middle cerebellar peduncle, associated with the later functional integration of the cerebral hemispheres and cerebellum. Similarly, in the dog at 3 days of age there are faintly myelinated fibers in the inferior cerebellar peduncle. The superior and middle peduncles myelinate more gradually between 2 and 3 wk, myelination of the middle peduncle being more protracted (see table

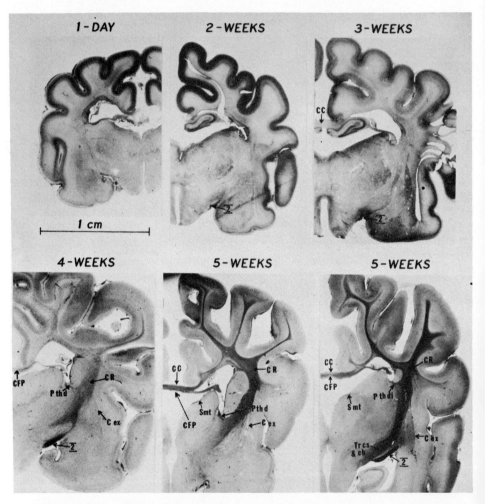

Fig. 4.22. Sections at midthalamic and optic nerve (2) level. Pedunculus thalami dorsolateralis (*Ptd*), corona radiata (*CR*), corporis callosi (*CC*) and capsula externa (*C ex*), clearly myelinated only by 4 wk. (*Smt* = stria medullaris thalami, *Trcs* and *cb* = tractus corticospinalis et corticobulbaris).

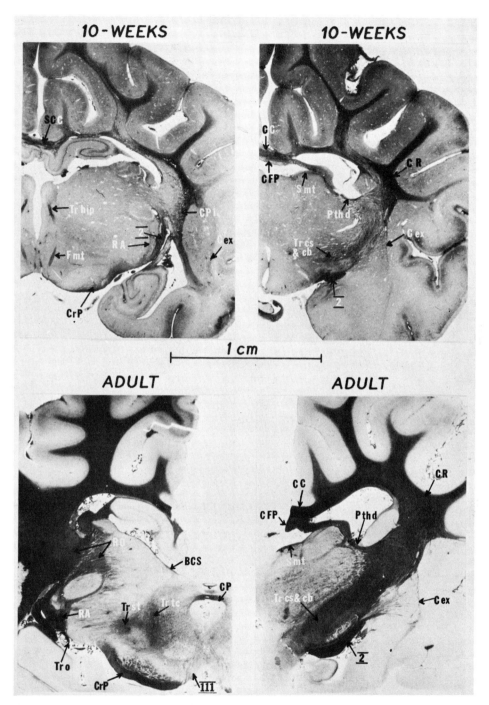

10-WEEKS

SCC
Tr hip
CPI
RA
C ex
Fmt
CrP

10-WEEKS

CC
CFP
CR
Smt
Pthd
Cex
Tr cs & cb
2

1 cm

ADULT

BCS
CP
RA
Tr st
Tr tc
Tro
CrP
III

ADULT

CC
CR
CFP
Pthd
Smt
Tr cs & cb
Cex
2

Fig. 4.23. Sections at mid- and posterior thalamic levels, showing structures similar to those described in fig. 4.12, with the addition of the crus posterius capsulae internae (*CPI*), fasciculus mammillothalamicus (*F mt*), tractus habenulointerpeduncularis (*TR hip*), brachium colliculi superioris (*BCS*), commissura posterior (*CP*) and tractus spinothalamicus et tr. tegmentum centralis (*Trst* and *Trtc*), corpus fornicis posterior (*CFP*), stria medullaris thalami (*SMT*) and sulcus corporis callosi (*SCC*).

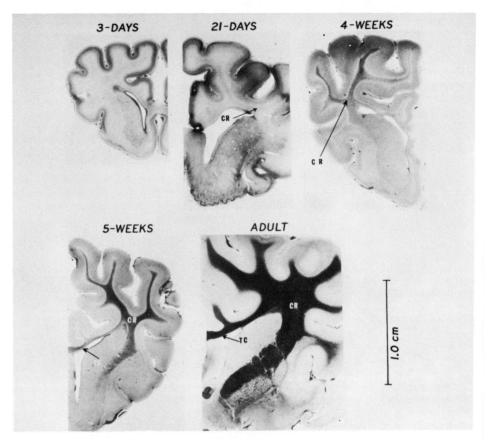

Fig. 4.24. Sections at level of caudate nucleus, showing sudden increase of myelin in corona radiata (*CR*) at 4 wk and myelination of the truncus corporis callosi (*TC*) at 5 wk.

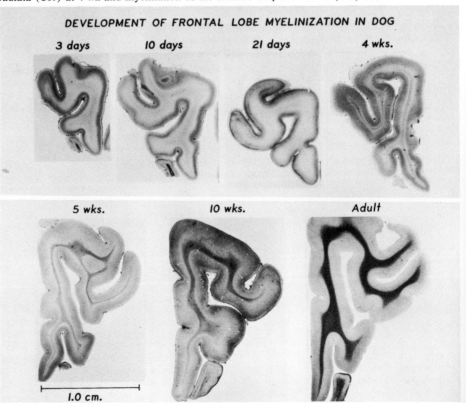

Fig. 4.25. First signs of histologically detectable myelin in frontal lobe seen at 4 wk, gradually increasing thereafter with increasing age.

4.4, fig. 4.27). In man, the slow myelination of the outer division of the inferior cerebellar peduncle, and similar myelination cycles in the brachium conjunctivum (superior cerebellar peduncle) and median lemniscus (i.e., fibers mediating general proprioceptive and exteroceptive somatic experiences), contrast with the more precocial myelination of the lateral lemniscus and median longitudinal fasciculus which mediate vestibular and acoustic stimuli. At birth and during the first 2 wk of life

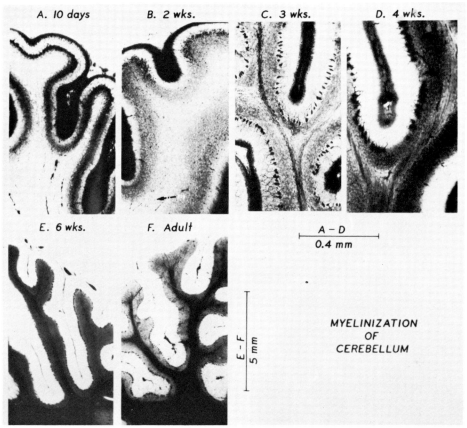

Fig. 4.26. Myelination of corpus medullare of cerebellum; a few faint fibers can be detected at 2 wk; relatively mature by 6 wk. Note Purkinje cells, which are variably stained by Ora's method.

in the dog, myelination of the median longitudinal fasciculus and lateral lemniscus is well in advance of myelination in the median lemniscus, middle cerebellar peduncle, and outer division of the inferior cerebellar peduncle.

Myelination of the reticular formation (increase in long collateral fibers and increase in the number of thin intrinsic fibers) is well advanced by 4 wk, but continues to increase gradually with age. A similar gradual increase in this region occurs in man (Yakovlev and Lecours 1967), and also in the median (periventricular) region, comprising the median thalamus, hippocampus, hypothalamus, and septal area, the fine, faintly myelinated fibers tend to increase with age. A comparable protracted myelination occurs in the periventricular region in the dog. In man, commissural and association fiber systems of the supralimbic division of the cerebral hemispheres have an extremely protracted cycle of myelination (Yakovlev and Lecours 1967). Not before 3 wk of age can myelin be detected in the corona radiata of the dog; with Loyez preparations, myelination gliosis preceding myelination (DeRobertis, Gerschenfeld, and Wald 1958) is particularly evident in the neocortical white matter. Myelination of the intracortical plexus is exceedingly protracted; at 4 wk of age (in the gyrus ectosylvius medius, see fig. 4.28) no myelinated fibers are present in the superficial cell layers. The length, number, and thickness of fibers in the deeper layers increase gradually with increasing age. Myelinated fibers first appear at 4 wk, but are very sparse in the supragranular layers until after 10 wk of age. Even in the adult dog, this fiber system comprises only a few delicate horizontal fibers.

In contrast to the protracted myelination cycle in neocortical association areas, the specific cortical analyzers in the dog mature earlier, first in the somatosensory (between 3 and 4 wk of age) and later in the visual and auditory (between 4 and 5 wk). It is of interest that in the human infant, Yakovlev and Lecours find that myelin first appears in the postcentral gyrus (somesthetic analyzer area) and then shortly after in the precentral gyrus (propriokinesthetic analyzer area).

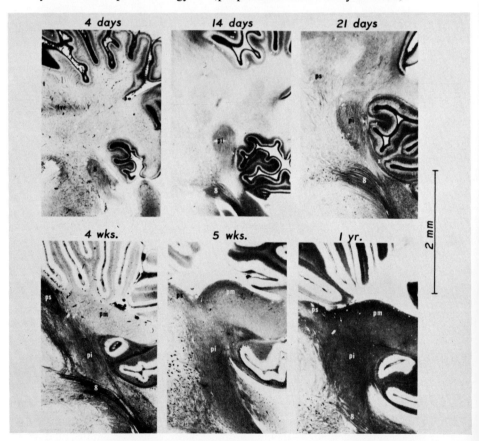

Fig. 4.27. Myelination of cerebellar peduncles (*pi, pm,* and *ps* = inferior, middle, and superior peduncles; *8* = vestibular nerve). Vestibular cerebellar fibers (*fvc*) faintly myelinated at 4 days. Inferior cerebellar peduncle myelinated at 14 days with gradual myelination of superior followed by middle cerebellar peduncles between 3 and 5 wk of age.

On the assumption that the thalamic fibers in the dog can be divided into specific and nonspecific fibers, a remarkable similarity between the myelination cycles of the corpus callosum and the specific and nonspecific thalamic fibers as described in the human infant by Yakovlev and Lecours was found in the dog (fig. 4.29). In these adjacent areas, intense myelination gliosis is present at 3 wk; by 4 wk, the first traces of myelin appear in the specific thalamic radiations. By 10 wk, the dog

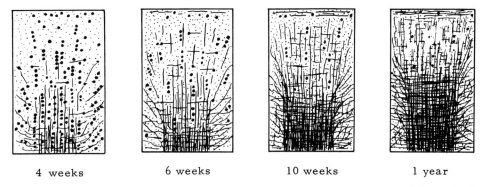

4 weeks   6 weeks   10 weeks   1 year

Fig. 4.28. Exponential myelination of intracortical plexus of dog (gyrus ectosylvius medius)

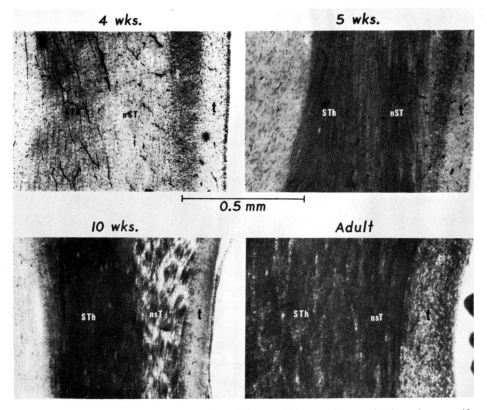

Fig. 4.29. Myelination of specific thalamic radiations (*STh*) precedes myelination of nonspecific thalamic radiations (*nST*). Myelination of tapetum (*t*) is more protracted. The *nST* at 10 wk has been cut at a slight angle; this artifact gives the impression that there is less myelin, but in fact the individual fibers are clearly thicker and more are myelinated than at 5 wk.

closely resembles the 3-yr-old human infant in that the specific thalamic radiations are heavily myelinated and the nonspecific radiations are only moderately myelinated. Also at 10 wk, the tapetum (the segment of the corpus callosum arching around the lateral ventricle) contains only a few myelinated fibers (fig. 4.29). In the 9-mo-old infant, these three adjacent fiber bundles are relatively equally myelinated, as in the 24-yr-old subject in Yakovlev's study.

Yakovlev and Lecours (1967) state that

> from direct inspection of the myelin sheath preparations of a whole brain section in the frontal or horizontal plane through about the middle of any adult brain, the myeloarchitectonic zones are recognizable: (1) a light staining periventricular, or *median* zone, including the median thalamus and the hypothalamus, the hippocampal rudiment and septal area, and the hippocampus; (2) a darker staining, prominently nucleate *paramedian* or limbic zone, bracketed by the Island of Reil laterad and the cingulate and parahippocampal gyri mediad and comprising the paramedian thalamus (lemniscal and limbic nuclei with the central median and medial dorsal nucleus), the subthalamic region, the internal capsule and pallidum and striatum with the amygdala and claustrum; and (3) a *supralimbic* zone, comprising the bulk of the white matter of the frontal, parietal and temporal lobes and respective opercula. These three myeloarchitectonic zones represent in the adult brain the ultimate elaborations of the three layers of His of the embryonal brain—respectively, the innermost matrix, the intermediate mantle or nuclear, and the outermost marginal or cortical layers. These three zones myelinate as different tectogenetic and myeloarchitectonic units and each exhibits a different cycle of myelination.

The most protracted myelination cycle is in the supralimbic zone, and the shortest in the paramedian limbic zone; the median zone is intermediate. Correlations with these classic details of myelination in the human infant from Yakovlev's laboratory with the present observations in the dog are difficult to make because of the rapid myelination in this species. It is comparatively significant that in the dog, the hippocampus and paraventricular structures (median zone) myelinate extremely slowly; at 4 wk of age, the hippocampus fimbria are faintly myelinated, and faint fibers are visible in the alveus. By 6 wk, the fimbria and alveus are moderately myelinated, attaining relative maturity by 10 wk (these data contrast with the early biochemical maturation of the hippocampus, Dravid, Himwich, and Davis 1965). Myelination of the median thalamic structures proceeds gradually, closely paralleling myelination of the hippocampus. Myelination of the paramedian zone (parahippocampal gyrus and cingulum) is well advanced by 5–6 wk of age; however, the truncus corporis callosi is well myelinated before myelination of the cingulum, which sharply contrasts with the reverse of this phenomenon reported in man by Yakovlev and Lecours. The posterior commissure of the fornix myelinates later than the truncus corporis callosi, the fornix being included in Yakovlev's median zone. In the dog, as in the human, the supralimbic zone shows the most protracted myelination cycle; it is phylogenetically the most recently evolved (and possibly, therefore, ontogenetically the most "plastic") CNS structure. Myelination of association areas such as the frontal lobe and the gradual increase in myelination of the intracortical plexus have been discussed earlier.

Yakovlev and Lecours conclude that

> the protracted cycle of myelination of the median zone of the forebrain appears to correlate with the protracted ontogenetic development of the reflex and behavioural patterns in the sphere of visceral motility and metabolic, enzymatic and hormonal

processes, which change slowly through the years of reproductive life. In contrast, the somatic motility of the outward expression of the internal states and movements of the body on the body itself such as mimicry, gestures, postural habitus, mannerisms and vocalization become definitive of the individual "makeup" by the end of the second decade and change little thereafter. The shorter cycle of myelination of the paramedian zone appears to correlate with the more rapid maturation of the reflex and behavioral patterns in the sphere of "innate" or "instinctive" movements conventionally assigned to basal ganglia and the "extrapyramidal" system. Also, the exponential myelination of the supralimbic division of the hemisphere and cerebral cortex correlates with the exponential maturation of the behavioral patterns in the sphere of motility of effective societal transactions—symbolized thought, language and manufacture, and of learning from individual experience.

In discussion (Yakovlev and Lecours 1967), Professor Yakovlev states that it is his belief that cycles of myelination of different fiber systems are highly species-specific. Those systems with special functional importance to a given species generally appear earlier, but have longer cycles of myelination, than those systems with more universal and less specific functions which differentiate later but have shorter cycles of myelination. He cites the earlier work of Filiminoff, who first drew attention to the early appearance and long cycle of architectonic differentiation of the hippocampus. It appears that the neural machinery of a function which biologically (and taxonomically) is most specific for the species emerges during development of the brain before (and not after) the neural substrate serving more universal functions, such as the hippocampal formation. Such structurofunctional correlations from anatomical data provide a valuable (if not the sole) approach to developmental neuroanatomy.

The conclusions of Yakovlev and Lecours, in relation to CNS and behavioral development, drawn from their neuroanatomical studies, find close agreement with Anokhin's (1964) theory of the heterochronous development of the CNS, which he elaborated on the basis of behavioral and neurophysiological evidence.

Lipid Content of Developing Brain

In order to provide some biochemical correlation with the histological development of myelin, estimations of the total lipid content of the following regions of the CNS were undertaken: medulla oblongata and pons; thalamus; cerebellum; neocortex. Purebred beagles were used to control for individual variability, two subjects being used for each age analyzed, and in each subject the brain was divided sagittally and analyses were run on both the right and the left sides. Subjects were killed with intravenous Nembutal and the brain was dissected into the various regions, which were weighed and then desiccated for 3 days in a drying oven at 160° C. Lipids were then extracted with chloroform methanol (3:1 using approximately 5 cc per g of tissue) in a water bath at 70° C. After 24 hr, the chloroform methanol mixture was removed and the remaining tissue desiccated, weighed, and then extracted twice more. Total lipid content was then calculated as a percentage of the dry matter content (figs. 4.30, 4.31).

Both total dry matter and total lipid content increased rapidly between the 2d and 6th wk of life, highest concentrations being found in the medulla and pons. Lipid increase in the cerebrum was marked during the 2d and 4th wk, there being a more gradual increase after 6 wk of age until maturity. These data find close agree-

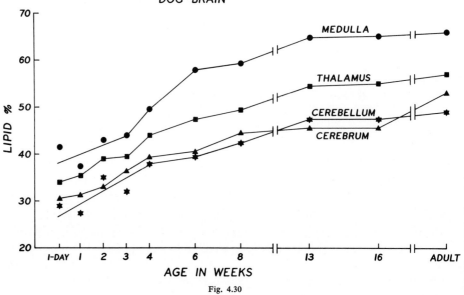

Fig. 4.30

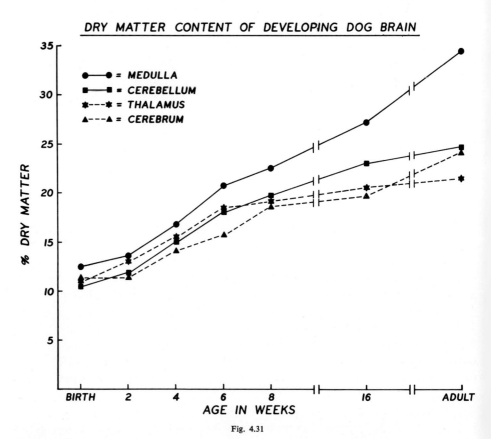

Fig. 4.31

Figs. 4.30, 4.31. Most rapid increase in dry matter content and lipid component of various brain parts occurs between 2 and 6 wk, highest values being obtained in the pons-medulla at all ages.

ment with the histologically determined rates of myelination, although total lipid analysis per se can give only an indirect indication of the rate of incorporation of certain lipids into the lipoprotein complex of the myelin sheath.

Development of Neocortical Neurons

Introduction

The postnatal development of dendritic structure in the neocortex has been investigated in the mouse (Kobayashi et al. 1963), the cat (Noback and Purpura 1961; Purpura et al. 1964) and the rabbit (Schadé 1960). In all three species the histological changes have been linked to electrophysiological maturation in both the spontaneous and the evoked EEG. Fox, Inman, and Himwich (1966) have described the development of neocortical neurons in the gyrus postcruciatus, and the following report is based on an extension of the observations to include development of the visual (gyrus lateralis), auditory (gyrus ectosylvius medius), and sensorimotor (gyrus precruciatus and postcruciatus) areas.

Materials and Methods

Samples from similar regions in the gyrus lateralis, gyrus ectosylvius medius, and gyrus precruciatus et postcruciatus were taken from both cerebral hemispheres of one purebred or crossbred beagle pup at each of the following ages: newborn (4 hr postnatal), 12 hr, 1, 2, 5, 7, 8, 10, 14, 21, 28, 30, 35, and 42 days; 8, 9, and 10 wk; and 2, 4, and 6 yr. Although the animals were of nonisogenic origin, they were all of the mesocephalic type and were reared under similar standards of management and nutrition. The Golgi-Cox method used in this work was essentially that of Sholl (1953). The descriptive anatomy of the development of the elements of the canine neocortex will be divided into age groups as follows: birth to 10 days, 14 to 30 days, and 5 wk to adulthood.

The criteria for determining the development of the neurons included:

1. Comparison of neurons (pyramidal and stellate) at different ages in the various layers of the neocortex from the areas studied. These layers may be divided as follows: the molecular or plexiform layer (layer I); the external granular layer of small pyramidal neurons (layer II); the external pyramidal (layer III); the internal granular (layer IV); the deep pyramidal or internal pyramidal (layer V); and the innermost multiform layer of irregularly arranged cells (layer VI). Layers II–IV in toto and layer V were selected for comparative studies. Layer VI, the deepest layer, was not included because the irregularity of cell arrangement and great variability in cell type did not permit accurate age comparison. It is interesting to note that the stellate or granular neurons which predominate in this layer (but are also present, although less numerous, in other layers) continue to multiply postnatally in the rat (Altman and Das 1965); they suggest that the cells may represent a plastic modulatory component of the CNS. The development and persistence of Retzius-Cajal (horizontal) cells, of layer I in these different regions has been described recently by Fox and Inman (1966).

2. The development of dendrites; that is, number, density and complexity of arborization. The three cortical regions studied will be described together, as only minor differences were detectable in the rates of development of the different layers. Where pertinent, these differences will be emphasized.

Results

Cortex from Birth to 10 Days. During this early postnatal period, differentiation of the neocortical neurons of the various layers was very gradual; the Betz cells of the motor cortex and comparable but slightly smaller cells of the sensory cortex were the most mature (see figs. 4.32–4.36).

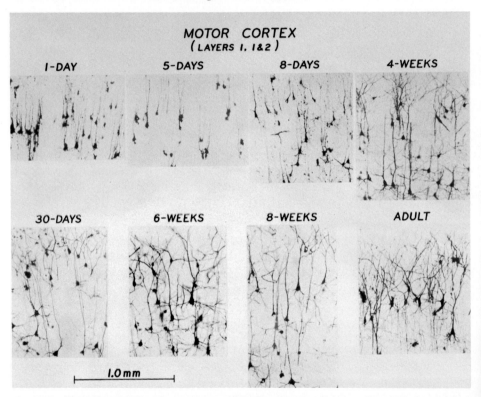

Fig. 4.32. Apical dendrites well formed at birth in neurons of layers I and II, but without collateral branches; relatively mature by 4 wk of age.

Layers II–IV. In the visual, auditory, and sensorimotor cortices at birth these layers are most distinct, being composed of predominantly closely packed, radially oriented, small pyramidal neurons; increasing numbers of these neurons develop double apical dendrites during this period. These dendrites pass upward and eventually develop arborizations in the molecular layer. Many of these small pyramidal neurons are, however, without basal dendrites at birth. In the visual cortex, the large neurons of layer V (Meynert cells) are more mature than the smaller pyramidal neurons of adjoining layers; and, similarly, in the auditory and sensorimotor cortices the large type of pyramidal neuron in layer III has relatively more elaborate apical dendrite development (fig. 4.36). In the sensorimotor region, by 1 wk, short and unbranched basal dendrites have appeared on most of the neurons of layers II–IV as well as on those cells with double apical dendrites. More rarely the cells also have a long basal dendrite: a slightly lesser degree of development is seen in the visual and auditory cortices at 1 wk of age. Collateral branches from the apical dendrites are present only on cells with basal dendrites, and as in the cat (Noback and Purpura 1961) some basilar dendrites appear before apical collaterals form. Stellate cells occur infrequently in these layers; their dendritic processes extend toward the molecular layer and the deep pyramidal layer.

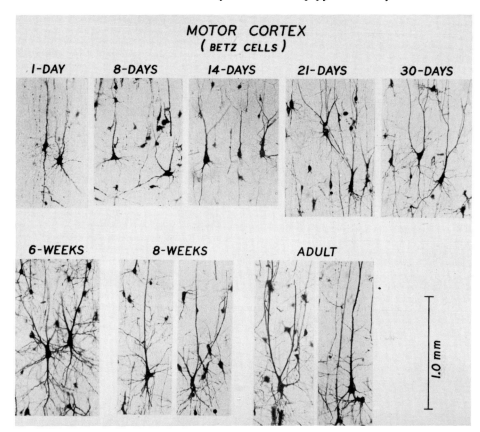

Fig. 4.33. Betz cells well developed at birth, with apical and basilar dendrites and collateral branches; relative maturity at 6 wk.

Layer V. The pyramidal neurons of this layer in the visual, auditory, and sensorimotor cortices are more developed at birth than those neurons in layers II–IV. The majority of the apical dendrites of the deep pyramidal cells arborize in a few terminal processes near the pial surface and in short apical dendritic collaterals in layers II, III, and IV, which they begin to reach by 1 wk of age in the sensorimotor cortex, and by 10–12 days in the visual and auditory cortices. The lateral spread of these collaterals is minimal at birth; so the cells give the gross appearance of rodlike radially oriented neurons. The basilar dendrites are, however, poorly differentiated at birth in many of these cells which resemble bipolar neuroblasts, with their apical dendrite directed toward the pial surface (fig. 4.34). Occa-

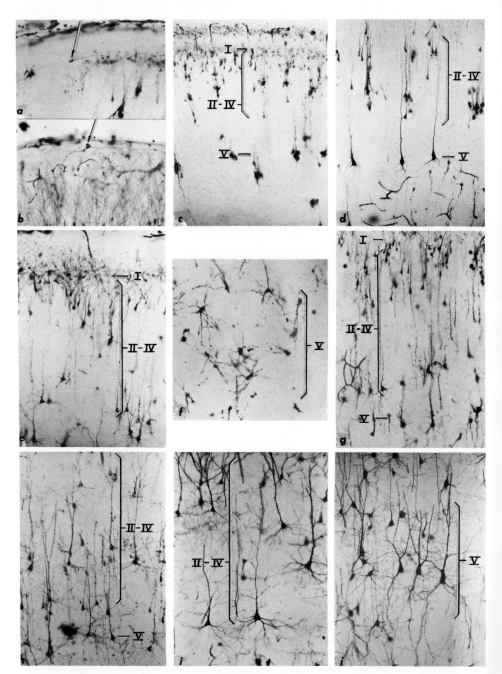

Fig 4.34. Figures are unretouched micrographs of Golgi-Cox preparations of cells from the gyrus pericruciatus of the immature dog. Pial surface is above each picture. All are at the same magnification (×220). Black roman numerals indicate various layers.

(a) Retzius-Cajal cell in neocortex of 7-day-old dog.

(b) Modified Retzius-Cajal cell (pyriform) in upper molecular layer of the neocortex of 6-wk-old dog.

(c) Note neurons of layers II–IV less developed than neurons of layer V of cortex of new-born dog.

(d) Note greater development of apical and basal dendrites and precocious maturation of neurons in layer V (7-day-old dog).

(e) Layers II–IV better differentiated than at earlier ages, with marked increase in basal dendritic growth (from 10-day-old dog).

(f) Well-formed deep stellate cells in layer V (from 10-day-old dog).

(g) Note increased dendritic elaboration in molecular layer and layers II–V (from 2-wk-old dog).

(h) Layers II–V with thicker and more elaborate apical and basal dendrites than in younger specimens (from 4-wk-old dog).

(i) Superficial pyramidal cells of layers II–IV at 6 wk of age.

(j) Deep pyramidal cells at 10 wk of age.

sionally, well-developed Betz cells can be found in the motor cortex at birth with elaborate basilar dendritic development and a short, branched apical dendrite. By 1 wk after birth the majority of the basilar dendrites, although more numerous, are still thin and unbranched, but by 2 wk branches are present in all cortical regions. Stellate cells are seen occasionally in layers I–V in all neocortical regions studied, and they predominate in layer VI (see fig. 4.34).

Cortex from 14 to 30 Days. The greatest differentiation of the neuronal elements of the neocortex takes place during this period, with more advanced arborization and thickening of dendritic processes accompanied by an increase in neuronal size. The large pyramidal cells of the sensorimortor cortex are outstanding in their size and dendritic development (fig. 4.33).

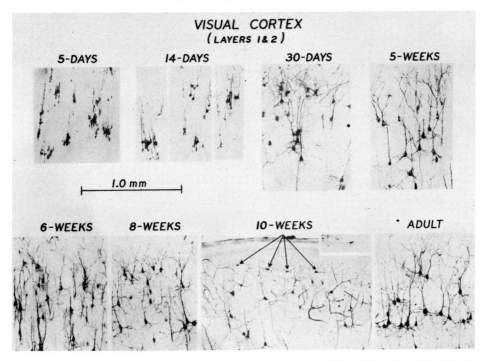

Fig. 4.35. Layers I and II less mature than in motor region at birth (cf. Fig. 4.33). Relatively mature by 30 days. Note unusual horizontal orientation of pyramidal neurons in 10-wk-old dog (typical Retzius-Cajal cell shown on insert).

Layers II–IV. All dendritic processes increase in thickness during this period, and most cells have well-developed basilar dendrites by 28 days. The apical dendrites of the pyramidal cells attain their adult complexity during this period, with many collateral branches. The axon of the more advanced pyramidal neurons may show collateral branches. By 4 wk the stellate cells have also developed more complex dendritic processes, which, however, are much finer than those of the pyramidal cells.

By 4 wk the neuronal elements of layers II–IV show greater differentiation, with marked "irregularity" between neighboring pyramidal cells, than was seen at earlier ages; that is, the rate of development and maturation of some neurons greatly exceeds that of others. This is especially apparent in the auditory region, where large pyramidal cells of sublayer III[3] are more developed than small pyramidal cells of this and adjoining layers. The collateral processes of the apical dendrites in these cells are increased also in number and length. The basilar dendrites show no further increase in number, but have grown longer, with more arborization. With the marked increase in length of apical and basilar dendrites which occurs during this period, the interneuronal space increases so that the various cell components of layers II,

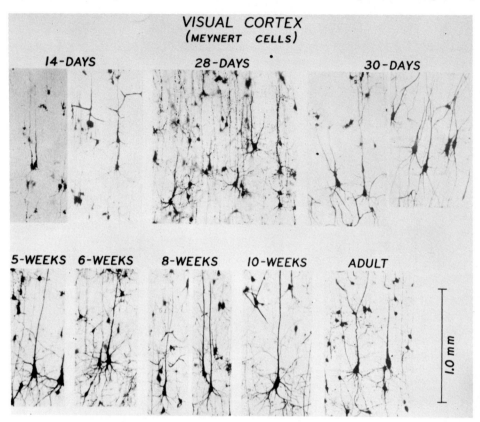

Fig. 4.36. Meynert cells of layer V relatively mature by 30 days

III, and IV can be clearly recognized; this increase in neocortical thickness and decrease in cell density can be confusing in that the large pyramidal cells of layer V, because of their position and close proximity to the poorly differentiated layers II–IV in younger subjects, may be mistaken for large pyramidal neurons of layer III.

Layer V. The basilar dendrites of the deep pyramidal cells in the sensorimotor region develop more slowly during the early part of this period than the pyramidal cells of layers II–IV, and attain relatively adult complexity by 5 wk of age. The deep pyramidal cells of the visual and auditory regions do not show such a marked distinction and parallel more closely the development of layers II–IV, with the exception of the large Meynert cells in layer V of the visual cortex, which are more elaborate than neighboring small pyramidal cells. Considerable maturation of the apical dendrites of the pyramidal neurons of layer V has taken place since birth.

Their dendrites have become thicker, with more collateral processes on the segments nearest to the cell body, and have developed spines on the branches of the apical dendrites. By 4 wk of age, the basal dendritic processes are both thicker and longer, with more branches (see figs. 4.33–4.36).

Cortex from 5 Wk to Adulthood. From the onset of this period there appear to be only minor developmental changes in the neuronal components of the three regions of dog brain studied, as compared with the more dramatic changes which occurred during the 2d to 4th wk of life. At 6 wk, the neurons appear to have their full complement of spinous dendritic processes. Throughout this period there is a slight thickening and lengthening of dendrites as well as an increase in the number of dendritic spines. One feature of the more mature cortex is the abundance of fine terminal dendritic branches.

Layers II–IV. The greater definition persists between the smaller pyramidal cells and the deeper, larger pyramidal cells of the submolecular layer present at 5 wk. The larger cells have more elaborate basilar dendrites than the smaller ones. The dendrites and collaterals of the pyramidal neurons and stellate cells, both apical and basilar, increase more gradually in length and thickness throughout this period.

Layer V. The large pyramidal neurons of this layer in both visual and auditory regions have numerous long branching basilar dendrites which are more elaborate than those of the submolecular pyramidal cells and which increase in thickness but not in number during this period. The apical dendrites on these pyramidal cells have fewer collaterals than those on the submolecular pyramidal cells and develop only a few more collaterals during the early part of this period. The large pyramidal cells of the sensorimotor cortex continue to increase in size into adulthood, but without any further increase in the complexity of dendritic arborizations (fig. 4.37).

Development of Dendritic Spines. In the cat, according to Noback and Purpura (1961), small bulbous outgrowths on the dendrites in early development are the precursors of the spinous processes of the mature neuron. In the dog, they were first seen in this investigation as rounded varicosities as early at 12 hr postnatally, on the most proximal portions of the dendrites of the large Betz cells of the motor cortex. They later developed on the dendrites of the larger pyramidal neurons of layer V in the auditory cortex, and on the Meynert cells in the visual cortex. Dendritic varicosities were seen last in the smaller pyramidal neurons of the upper cell layers II–IV. By 3 wk, these dendritic varicosities were present in all cell layers of the auditory, visual, and sensorimotor regions.

In the series studied, they were found to be most abundant on the apical and basilar dendrites in all cortical regions between 3 and 4 wk of age, but were less numerous at 5 and 6 wk of age. In the 10-wk-old subject and in the three adults examined, dendritic varicosities were markedly fewer in number (fig. 4.38); the absence of varicosities at all ages on the axon facilitates the recognition of this structure, especially when the basilar dendrites are numerous and have many arborizations. This apparent decrease in the density of dendritic varicosities may be due to elongation of dendritic processes occurring during the later phases of neuronal development.

Scheibel (1962) suggests that the dendritic spines make synaptic contact with corticopetal nonspecific (thalamic reticular) fibers, and that they are associated with the first signs of alpha activity and spindling in the kitten. Increasing maturation of this synaptic system in the late 2d and 3d wk coincides in time with (1) increasing effectiveness of fast reticular frequencies in producing cortical activation, (2)

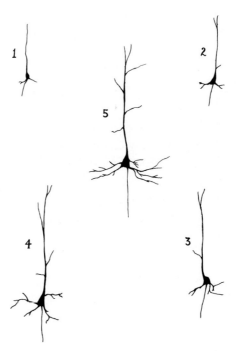

Fig. 4.37. Schema of development of deep pyramidal neurons in layer V of motor cortex. (1) birth; (2) 1 wk; (3) 2 wk; (4) 4 wk; (5) 6 wk. Note marked development from 14 to 28 days and increase in basal dendrites from 4 to 5 wk.

decreasing effectiveness of slow frequencies in producing this effect, and (3) rapid waning of the "habituation" or "fatigue" effect following one or two stimulations. Scheibel states that

> until recently, the role of dendrite spines or gemmules has been an anomalous one in the neurological literature. First described by Ramon y Cajal (1952), who believed that they were part of the synaptic mechanism of dendrites, the most common argument of their detractors has been that they represent silver or methylene blue artifacts owing to deposition of stain in extracellular spaces along dendrites or else are caused by fixation shrinkage of the tissue. Protagonists of these structures felt that, even if artifacts, they probably represent the remains of some type of specialized structure along the dendrites, while the more daring suggested that their presence *in vivo* served to increase the available postsynaptic surface area. Recent investigations by Gray (1959) with the electron microscope have clearly delineated the dendrite spine on cortical shafts and a specialized structure within characterized by sacs and dense bands. Analogous structures have more recently been demonstrated by Fox (1961) on the tertiary branchlets of Purkinje cells in the cerebellum, deeply indenting the adjacent parallel fibers. Such findings would seem to indicate that the spine system is a specific synaptic mechanism whose progressive maturation in the early stages of postnatal development bears an important relationship to functional development.

Also in the human infant, Conel (1952) observed that dendritic spines (or thorns, globules, bulbs, or pedunculated bulbs) are most numerous on the apical dendrites, less on basilar dendrites and collateral branches of apical dendrites, and least on terminal branches of apical dendrites; during development they increase in size and number and are in greatest quantity 2 yr after birth. Noback and Purpura (1961) reported that in the cat there was no significant difference in the time of appearance of spines on the basilar dendrites of the different types of pyramidal cells. However, Purpura et al. (1964) observed in the cat at birth numerous short protoplasmic projections resembling thin perisomatic dendritic ramifications (also observed in the neonate cat cortex) on the cerebellar Purkinje cells; also noted in

I Day M.   30 Day M.   6 wks M.   6 wks V.   10 wks V.   Adult V.

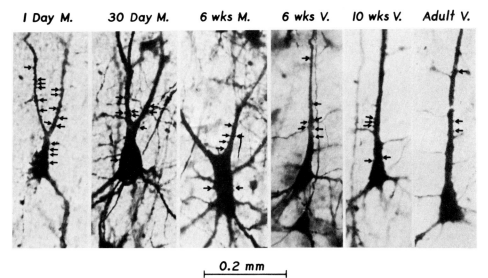

0.2 mm

Fig. 4.38. Gradual reduction in dendritic varicosities in motor (*M*) and visual (*V*) cortices of dog.

neocortical neurons of the dog in the present study, they appeared to be resorbed within 4–5 days. These authors also reported a "stripping" of dendrite spiny protuberances preceding the elaboration of secondary and tertiary rami and spiny branchlets on the Purkinje cells. A comparable "stripping" occurs in neocortical neurons in the dog during the first 4–5 wk of age (fig. 4.38).

Sarkisov (1966) cites A. M. Ivanitskii, who showed that the first appearance of the conditioning function in the rabbit coincides in time with the appearance of spines on the terminal ramifications of the apical dendrites of cortical cells. Spines first appear in the largest pyramidal cells of layer V in the specific cortical analyzers; pyramidal cells of layers II and III of the cortex have more spines than cells in deeper layers V and VI.

Pappas and Purpura (1961) have also studied these dendritic spines with electron microscopy and conclude that they represent specialized regions of axo-dendritic synaptic contact. Globus and Scheibel (1967*b*) have demonstrated a loss of spines on the oblique collateral dendrites of parietal cortical neurons following transection of the corpus callosum in neonate rabbits.

Discussion

The neuronal elements of the neocortex undergo gradual morphological differentiation during the first week of life, the Betz cells of the motor cortex being more developed then the deep pyramidal cells of the other regions studied. The layers of the cortex, although fairly distinct at birth, became more easily recognizable with increasing age as cell density decreases and apical and basilar dendrites increase in length.

The pyramidal neuron during early postnatal life first shows an apical dendrite which develops terminal branches at the same time that the basilar dendrites first appear. Collaterals of the apical dendrites nearest to the cell body then develop, followed by further branching of more peripheral collaterals of apical and basilar dendritic branches. In accordance with the findings in the kitten by Noback and Purpura (1961), stellate cells were infrequently seen in younger specimens, suggesting that they may be differentiated at a later age than the pyramidal cells of layers II–IV.

The deep pyramidal cells of layer V are more developed than the superficial pyramidal neurons at birth. Of the two groups of pyramidal cells, however, the superficial ones are the most differentiated by 2 wk. Because of their simplicity, the apical dendritic branches of layers II–IV mature earlier than the longer and more elaborate apical dendrites of the deep pyramidal neurons of layer V. From 2 to 4 wk, the most dramatic changes in the development of dendritic components occur in the somatomotor cortex, whereas the visual and auditory regions show the greatest development from 3–5 wk of age. After 6 wk changes are slower, involving terminal maturation of cellular elements, cessation of neuronal growth, and final organization of apical and basilar dendrites and their collaterals.

As had been formerly reported by Noback and Purpura (1961), more pyramidal and stellate cells were stained in older than in younger animals. The difficulty encountered not only in tracing the dendritic processes but also in obtaining an even impregnation of sections from immature subjects indicates an age difference in the staining properties of neural tissue. Ramon-Moliner (1961) has emphasized that impregnation decreases toward the surface of the cortex, and similar observations were made by Fox and Inman (1966). Van der Loos (1965) has presented a detailed discussion on the "improperly" oriented pyramidal cell in the cerebral cortex; this is another variable revealed in Golgi preparations. The discussion of Van der Loos pertains to dynamics of cell growth and orientation in the neocortical neuropil. Astrom (1967) has given a detailed description of neocortical development in the sheep fetus, using the Golgi method. He reports that the primitive bipolar pyramidal cells develop in the following sequence: terminal branches of the apical dendrites; descending and basilar dendrites from the cell body; branches on the apical dendrites; axon collaterals; spines on the apical dendrites. Development starts earlier in the marginal layer than in the pyramidal layer; in 12 g (48-day-old) fetuses the deep pyramidals were more developed than more superficial ones, and at this age, four cortical strata—the marginal, superficial, deep pyramidal, and stellate layers—can be identified. In 65–95 g fetuses, stellate and Martinotti cells develop in the pyramidal layer, possibly being associated with intracortical projections. Astrom lists the following sequence of cell layer development: marginal; deep stellates of layer VI B and large pyramids of layer IV and lower layer III; deep stellates in the internal granular layer; pyramids in layers V and VI; medium-sized pyramids in layer III; small pyramids in layer II; and finally the external granular layer. Afferent collaterals to the neocortical cells develop in the following sequence: descending collaterals from the horizontal layer to the deep pyramids and stellate cells; ascending projection fibers (possibly callosal and thalamic); ascending "oblique" fibers to the marginal and pyramidal zones; collaterals on axons from the pyramidal cells; recurrent axon collaterals to the marginal layer; ascending axons from the Martinotti cells.

The cytoarchitectonic studies in the dog indicate that the most rapid development of the different regions of the canine neocortex occurs during the first 3 wk of life. After this age changes are more gradual and by 5 wk cell density and comparative thickness and differentiation of cell layers resemble the adult. Some differences were found in the rate of development between the different neocortical areas studied. In most cases cell density was consistently greatest in the occipital area and lowest in the precoronal and postcoronal areas. The reduction in cell density was greatest in the frontal and temporal areas during the first 2 wk of life; cell density decreased more gradually in the occipital and precoronal areas during the first 3 wk of life. A sharp reduction in density in the postcoronal area occurred between 2 and 3 wk. The reliability of these different curves is questionable in view of the small sample size, but the overall data indicate that cell density undergoes the most rapid reduction during the first 3–4 wk of life; from 5 wk onward into adulthood, changes are minimal. As in other embryonic structures (Glücksman 1951; Levi-Montalcini 1964) cell death may occur in the developing cerebrum, but this is unlikely to account for the marked reduction in cell density as late as the first 2–3 wk of postnatal life in the dog. No conclusive evidence of postnatal neuronal degeneration was found in standard Nissl preparations.

In contrast to the slight and gradual regional differences in cellular development detectable histologically, the development of myelin in various cortical areas shows that there are dramatic differences in the rate of myelination occurring at 4 wk of age. The motor (precruciate) and sensory (postcruciate) regions show greater myelination than the visual (occipital) region, for example. Myelination of both cortical and subcortical structures continues until rather late in life, and may be regarded as a more continuous process than the relatively shorter period of neuronal cell development and maturation.

Golgi-Cox studies of the development of neocortical neurons in the dog correlate closely with these cytoarchitectonic data in that elaboration and arborization of the apical and basilar dendrites occurs during the first postnatal month. After 5 wk of age changes are more gradual, the essential feature in older subjects being an increase in thickness of dendritic processes, but no further detectable elaboration of arborizations takes place with increasing age.

Interdisciplinary Correlations. Biochemical correlation with these findings can be made insofar as the glycogen content and metabolism of the canine brain are within the adult range by 6 wk of age (Chesler and Himwich 1943; Himwich and Fazekas 1941), and resistance to anoxia decreases with age until 4 wk (Glass, Snyder, and. Webster 1944; Jilek and Trojan 1966). The DNA/RNA ratio, according to Mandel et al. (1962), reaches adult levels around 4–5 wk of age. Certain free amino acids (glutamic acid, glutamine, aspartic acid, and GABA) attain mature concentrations in the neocortex between the 30th and 40th days (Dravid, Himwich, and Davis 1965).

Pigareva (1964) reports that enzyme activity of the cytochrome system is similar in the visual, auditory, and motor regions of the dog during the first 10 days, and there is greatest differentiation in activity after 30 days. Adult levels are seen in the motor cortex at 10–15 days, and at 60–70 days in the visual and auditory cortex. Cholinesterase levels decrease with decreasing cell density and adult levels are seen by 15 days. Highest concentrations are seen during the first 10 days of life, associated with neuronal and glial differentiation.

Kiyota (1959) observes that insoluble protein increases with age in the dog in association with myelination and decreased hydrophilic property of the brain. Fox (1966*f*) has reported age differences in hydrophilic properties and effects of Formalin fixation on the dog brain; these findings may be correlated with Kiyota's observation that soluble proteins, which are very hygroscopic, decrease in concentration with age. The postnatal development of total lipids in various parts of the canine brain is most rapid between 3 and 6 wk, especially in structures containing mainly nerve tracts and few ganglia or aggregations of neurons. This increase closely parallels the rate of myelination detected histologically; Folch-Pi (1955) reports that in the mouse brain, lipid concentration increases especially during myelination.

Little information is available on specific aspects of regional development of the dog brain. Harman (1963) found that the cranial nerves in the dog associated with feeding and vestibular function are well myelinated at birth; Saltmann (1876) observed that neocortical lesions had minimal effects on motor function until several days after birth in the dog, and Dusser de Barenne (1934) was able to detect no effects of Fardic stimulation to the motor cortex until 9–11 days after birth in this species.

Postnatal Development of Oligodendroglia and Astrocytes

Introduction

The recognition of glial cells by various histological techniques is no easy task, for numerous cells show intermediate morphological characteristics, making their classification difficult. Attempts to classify these intermediate types in adult specimens have caused considerable confusion in the literature. One belief is that such cells are "intermediate" forms which may change into other forms and are thus "multipotential" (Ramon-Moliner 1958). The present investigation was undertaken to discover if such a "metamorphosis of multipotential cells" occurs during postnatal development, and also to provide normal information on the development of oligodendroglia and astrocytes and on their relationships with myelination and with the blood vessels and neurons of the neocortex.

Materials and Methods

Using the rapid Golgi-Cox method of Sholl (1953), samples from similar regions in the gyrus ectosylvius medius (auditory cortex), gyrus lateralis (visual cortex), and gyrus precruciatus et postcruciatus (sensorimotor cortex) were prepared from beagle and crossbred beagle dogs of the following ages: 4 newborn subjects, 1 subject each at 1, 2, 5, 7, 8, 10, 14, 21, 28, 30, and 42 days, 4 subjects at 35 and 70 days, and 7 adults ranging from 2 to 6 yr of age. The main advantage of the Golgi-Cox method is that both blood vessels and neurons and their processes, as well as various macroglial cells, are clearly stained, so that their interrelationships can be easily studied.

Results

The following classification of various cells stained in the neocortex was based on detailed evaluation of adult specimens, and is reviewed in figure 4.39.

1. *Components of the Neocortical Gray Matter*

a) Pyramidal Neurons. Clearly defined pyramidal cell body, apical and basilar dendrites, and an axon.

b) Stellate Neurons. Oval or rounded cell body with well-developed radiating branching dendrites and an axon.

Fig. 4.39. Neuronal and glial elements in canine neocortex revealed by Golgi technique. *a*, subpial astrocyte (note unmarked horizontal neuron to the right); *b*, deep fibrous astrocyte in white matter; *c*, protoplasmic and fibroprotoplasmic astrocytes; *e*, filamentous astrocytes; *f*, pyramidal and stellate neurons; *g*, "transitional" glia; *h*, oligodendroglia of gray matter; *i*, oligodendroglia of white matter (*BV* = blood vessel).

c) Horizontal Neurons (Fox and Inman 1966). Oval cell body and bipolar dendrites, which have occasional short branches toward the pial surface, under which these neurons are located.

d) Oligodendroglia. Small and large rounded cell bodies, with or without processes, frequently in satellite positions (perineural satellites) around large pyramidal neurons.

e) Astrocytes. 1. Fibrous Type. This form is characterized by a very irregular cell body and numerous thick, infrequently branching and radiating processes, often with one or two thick processes connecting with a blood vessel and attached by "end-feet" or by a thick collar.

2. Protoplasmic Type. Essentially this form consists of a rounded cell body from which radiate fine processes which, with the Golgi-Cox stain, possess flocculo-nodular inclusions which halo the cell body and appear as protoplasmic radiations or processes.

3. Intermediate Fibroprotoplasmic Type. This form differs from both 1 and 2 in that the radiating processes are generally thicker than in the protoplasmic astrocyte and possess short spinous branches; a few flocculonodular inclusions may be seen in varying quantities, but never forming a halo around the cell body as in the protoplasmic astrocyte. Unlike cell types 1 and 2, the cell body of the fibroprotoplasmic type is usually irregularly oval or rounded in shape. This type resembles the "mossy" cells of Ramon-Moliner (1958).

4. Filamentous type. This form of astrocyte is clearly distinct on morphological grounds, and unlike the other types is rarely associated with neurons, blood vessels, or oligodendroglia. The cell body is usually round or oval and varies greatly in size. Fine processes, often of remarkable length and without flocculonodular inclusions, radiate from the cell body and may form linear bundles which lie vertical or horizontal to the gial surface. Some astrocytes of this type have a more oval cell body with fewer processes, but these extremely long processes characteristically remain in a vertical or horizontal distribution.

2. *Components of the Neocortical White Matter*

a) Oligodendroglia. Oval and more rarely spherical cell bodies with unipolar or bipolar processes are frequently seen lying in the same plane as the myelinated nerve tracts in the white matter (interfascicular glia).

b) Astrocytes. Fibrous astrocytes (similar to those in the gray matter) are present in abundance in this region, being closely associated with blood vessels, and possibly make connections with the nerve fibers of this region. More rarely, intermediate fibroprotoplasmic and protoplasmic astrocytes are found in this region, but they tend to be more numerous at the intermediate region, where neuronal layer VI merges into the deep white matter of the corona radiata.

3. *Developmental Observations*

The difficulties in obtaining even impregnation of tissues from young subjects have been emphasized by Fox and Inman (1966). This is especially true of cell layers nearer the pial surface; deeper regions are more evenly impregnated. In spite of these ontogenetic variables, the large sample size of tissue specimens provided excellent preparations of various types of glial cells at different ages. However, as a result of these variables close comparisons of glial development between different regions of the neocortex were not possible. The regional differences that were detected will be described where pertinent.

a) Development of Oligodendroglia (figs. 4.40, 4.41)

1. Oligodendroglia of the Gray Matter. The cells in this region at birth can be recognized in their perineural satellite distribution around pyramidal neurons, which tend to stain in clusters with the Golgi-Cox technique. Connections with

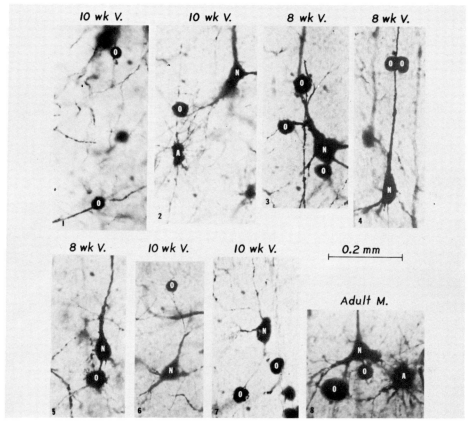

Fig. 4.40. Various morphological relationships between oligodendroglia (*O*) of neocortical gray matter, astrocytes (*A*), neurons (*N*), and nerve processes.

dendritic processes are not clearly evident until these processes are clearly formed between 2 and 3 wk of age. From this age onward, connections between oligodendroglia and basilar dendrites, in the form of terminal boutons or boutons en passage (as observed by Scheibel and Scheibel 1958) can be recognized. More rarely, the oligodendroglia may be found in close association with the apical dendrite, or connected by a thick process to the body of the neuron. These cells increase considerably in size with age, up to 4–5 wk, and in more mature specimens, a greater variability in size is evident.

2. Oligodendroglia of the White Matter. At birth, numerous small oligodendroglia are present in the white matter, being distributed in rows or columns among

the nerve fibers which will later become myelinated. These glial cells possess fine, short unipolar or occasionally bipolar processes, which increase in length and thickness with age, as the cell body of the oligodendroglia cell also increases in size up to 5–6 wk. Some variation in shape, but not in size, of these oligodendroglia was observed at all ages, some being spherical and others elongated fusiform or ovoid. Frequently, in all age groups, connections between oligodendroglia and with the processes of fibrous astrocytes were observed (fig. 4.41).

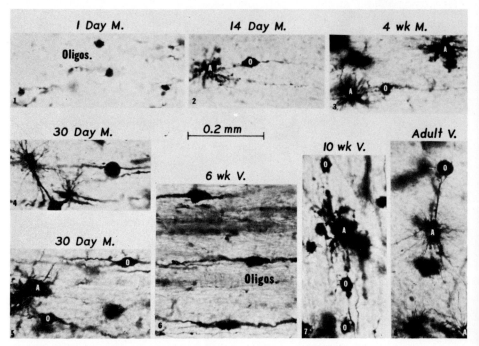

Fig. 4.41. Gradual development of oligodendroglia of white matter of neocortex, attaining relative maturity after 4 wk of age. Note intimate relationships between fibrous astrocyte processes (*A*) and oligodendroglia (*O*).

b) *Development of Astrocytes* (fig. 4.42)

1. Fibrous Astrocytes. Numerous small fibrous astrocytes with fine processes attached to blood vessels can be distinguished in the white matter in newborn subjects. These glial cells increase in size, and the number, thickness, and length of their processes also increase with age, attaining relative maturity between 4 and 6 wk. Occasionally, astroglial processes connect with the oligodendroglia of the white matter. Similar developmental changes occur in the fibrous astrocytes of the gray matter, where they are far less numerous and are often connected to one or more basilar dendrites of the pyramidal neurons. At the transitional zone between gray and white matter, basilar dendrites and axons of pyramidal neurons appear to make connections with fibrous astrocytes of the white matter. Many fibrous astrocytes in the white matter form interconnecting chains and ensheath blood vessels or lie between the fasciculi of the nerve fibers in close association with oligodendroglia, possibly making connections with some of the nerve fibers.

2. Protoplasmic Astrocytes. These glia, predominantly located in the gray

matter, tend to envelop the pyramidal neurons, and their precise relationship with the neuron is difficult to determine. The protoplasmic astrocytes attain mature proportions by approximately 5 wk of age, and are intimately related to the blood vessels of the gray matter and to the satellite oligodendroglia and dendritic processes of the neurons (fig. 4.43).

3. Intermediate Fibroprotoplasmic "Mossy" Astrocytes. Glial cells of intermediate type were observed in subjects of all ages. No obvious ontogenetic differences were observed, other than a gradual increase in size and in the number and thickness

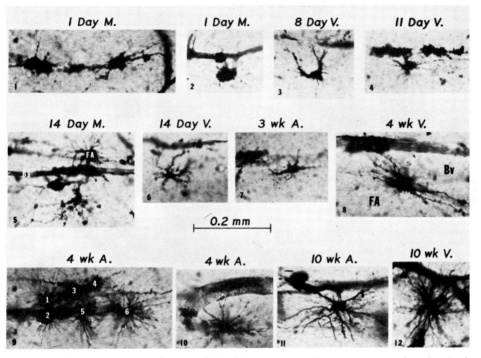

Fig. 4.42. Fibrous astrocytes of neocortical white matter attain mature proportions by 4 wk of age. Note astrocyte end-feet and cuffs around blood vessels.

of processes. These cells are distributed almost exclusively in the gray matter, being located beneath the pia, where they are attached to blood vessels by thick processes, and by finer processes to the pial tissue (subpial type) and also distributed in close relation with the apical dendrites of pyramidal neurons, where their processes emerge in a stellate pattern. Mention must be made at this stage of an unusual cell first observed in 4-wk-old pups. These cells are distributed in satellite positions around neurons, and closely resemble stellate neurons, but are lacking an axon. Possibly these cells are stellate neurons in which the axon was not revealed at the level of section, but morphologically they closely resemble the transitional astrocytes described in the dog by Hosokawa and Mannen (1963).

4. Filamentous Astrocytes (fig. 4.44). These cells can be identified in newborn subjects by their long, fine processes, which are especially aggregated vertical to the pial surface. The cell body is exceedingly small in young specimens but increases with age. The main characteristic of these cells is that they are most numer-

ous in the oldest subjects. Their vertical processes extend between layers I and VI of the gray matter and their horizontal processes often interconnect between adjacent cell bodies of other filamentous astrocytes. The cell bodies often vary greatly in size and may be found distributed in horizontal rows.

Some glial cells of the filamentous type, characterized by a rounded or oval cell body and extremely long processes, may occasionally be found in close association

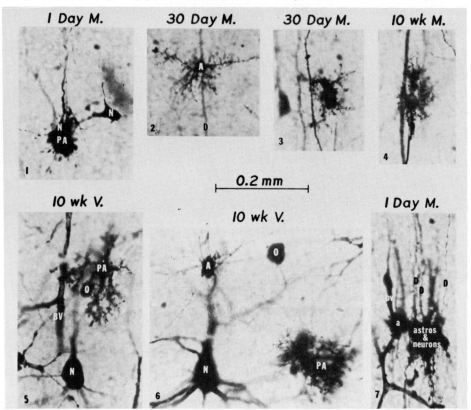

Fig. 4.43. Various relationships at different ages in neocortical gray matter between proto-plasmic or "mossy" astrocytes, neurons (1, 6, and 7), blood vessels (5), oligodendroglia (5), and apical dendrites (2, 3, and 4).

with the apical or basilar dendrites of pyramidal neurons, but generally they do not appear to make any anatomical connections with structures other than the processes of neighboring filamentous astrocytes.

Discussion and Conclusions

These developmental studies, although they did not reveal differences in the rates of development between different neocortical regions, clearly showed that the major types of glial cells of the adult are present in all ages from birth onward. In spite of the age variable associated with the reliability of the Golgi-Cox technique, no increase in the number of glial cells was observed with increasing age, with the exception of the filamentous astrocytes. That all glial types can be recognized in subjects under 7 days of age suggests that these cells are not "multipotential," for their location and relationships do not change during development. With increasing age, as basilar and apical dendrites of the pyramidal neurons and their collateral branches are elaborated, especially between 3 and 5 wk, dendritic connections between oligodendroglia and astrocytes are more frequently observed.

The progressive increase in the structural relationships between neurons and glia noted during early development finds close agreement with the observations of J. S. King (1966), who found a progressive increase in the morphological relationships of glial cell bodies and processes to neurons with ascension of the phylogenetic

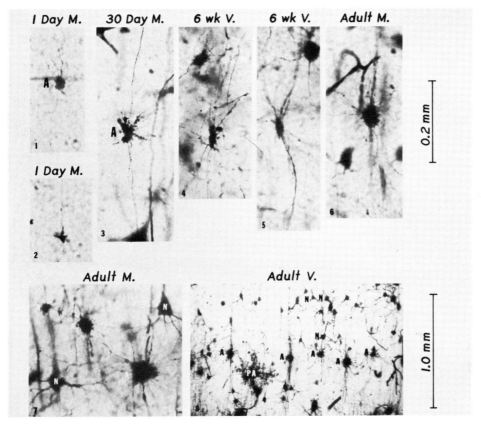

Fig. 4.44. Filamentous astrocytes in neocortical gray matters at various ages, characterized by extremely long vertical processes.

scale from fish to primate. At all ages, however, fibrous astrocytes have well-developed vascular connections; but with increasing age, as their processes become longer and more elaborate, connections with the oligodendroglia of the white matter are found. Fibroprotoplasmic astrocytes were not recognizable in the youngest specimens; only with increasing age, as their processes became elongated, were they more assuredly classified. Recognition of fibrous and protoplasmic astrocytes in the young subjects was facilitated by the different shapes of the cell bodies and thickness of processes in these two morphologically distinct forms.

It is beyond the scope of this study to indulge in speculations as to the various functions of the neuroglial cells, but some correlations can be made. Intimate morphological interrelationships between blood vessels, fibrous and protoplasmic astrocytes, oligodendroglia, and neurons suggest that there may be physiological associations between these components of the nervous system, in which structuro-functional concert the part played by microglia (Nakai 1963) must also be considered. The classic studies of Kuffler and Potter (1964) and of Kuffler, Nicholls, and Orkland (1966) have shown that there is a demonstrable functional relationship between glial cells, but their precise role in the integrative activity of the nervous system is still an open question.

The development of fibrous astrocytes associated with the cerebral vasculature which attain maturity between 4 and 5 wk of age may be correlated with the relative maturity of cerebral metabolism at this age (Himwich and Fazekas 1941) and resistance to anoxia (Jilek and Trojan 1966).

The development of oligodendroglia in the white matter parallels the gradual onset of myelination of the neocortex, which first begins after 3 wk of age and occurs most rapidly between 4 and 6 wk by which time the size of the oligodendroglia and the thickness of their processes closely resemble the adult form. Development of apical and basilar dendrites in the canine neocortex has been correlated with the maturation of the EEG (Fox, Inman, and Himwich 1966); possibly an underlying factor upon which mature electrocortical activity may be dependent is the establishment of dendritic connections between astrocytes and satellite oligodendroglia.

Most parameters of the developing canine brain attain adult characteristics by 6 wk, with two exceptions. Myelination (see earlier) continues more gradually after this time, and also the filamentous astrocytes become more elaborate in the number of their vertical and horizontal processes, and possibly their cell bodies increase in size, if not in number, with age. It is tentatively suggested that the more gradual development of filamentous astrocytes and of myelin (which may or may not be interrelated) may be associated with later changes in behavior in terms of the performance of complex tasks and improved learning abilities.

Postnatal Development of the Spinal Cord

Introduction

Studies on the maturation of adult locomotor patterns of limb-placing and of supporting reflexes and the disappearance of neonatal reflexes such as the crossed extensor reflex have indicated that by 4 wk the dog attains relative neurologic maturity (see chap. 2). These behavioral and neurologic observations may be correlated with morphological changes in the spinal cord, as studied in the kitten by Langworthy (1929), and the following study has been undertaken to determine the sequences of myelination of the spinal cord of the dog.

Maletta, Vernadakis, and Timiras (1966) have studied the pre- and postnatal development of acetylcholinesterase activity in the spinal cord, and they conclude that increasing activity of this enzyme is related to functional maturation of the spinal cord (see also Krnjevic and Silver 1966 for discussion of the development of this enzyme in the forebrain).

McClure (1964) has described the arrangement of the various tracts in the spinal cord of the dog (fig. 4.45), and his schema has been used to identify some of the structures studied in this investigation (see also Fletcher [1966] and Fletcher and Kitchell [1966] for additional anatomical studies on the canine spinal cord). The presence of several tracts found in other mammals has not been confirmed in the dog. These tracts include the ventral corticospinal, ventral reticulospinal, tectospinal, vestibulospinal, ventral spinothalamic, spino-olivary and fasciculus proprius (McClure 1964).

Materials and Methods

Spinal cords were removed as rapidly as possible from 12 healthy beagle dogs of the following ages: 1, 2, 10, 14, 21, 28, 32, and 35 days; 6, 10, and 16 wk; and one adult. Samples were dissected at C_3–C_6, T_9–T_{12}, and L_2–L_5, and after Formalin fixation for not less than 7 days were imbedded in celloidin and sectioned transversely at 20 μ. Alternate sections were stained with Thionine and with Ora's (1958)

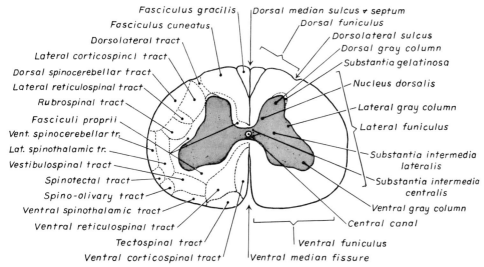

Fig. 4.45. Schema of spinal cord of dog in cross section, showing major tracts and funiculi (from McClure 1964, by kind permission of the author and W. B. Saunders Co., Philadelphia).

stain for myelin. (Additional sections from subjects aged 1, 7, 24, 32, and 35 days and 16 wk were treated with 5% trichloroacetic acid at 37° C for 24 hr before myelin staining [Reinis 1965], in an attempt to reveal masked immature myelin.) The Thionine preparations were used only to facilitate recognition of cellular components. The cervical, thoracic, and lumbar segments were examined for myelination of tracts in the dorsal, lateral, and ventral funiculi and for development of myelinated fibers in the dorsal, lateral, and ventral gray columns. Comparisons were made among the different ages.

Results

Cervical Spinal Cord (see fig. 4.46)

1–14 Days. Myelination in the dorsal, lateral, and ventral funiculi was not detectable at birth, with the exception of faint myelination in the tectospinal, ventral spinothalamic, spino-olivary, and spinotectal tracts of the ventral funiculus. By 1 wk, faint, ill-defined areas of myelination were detectable in the dorsal and ventral funiculi. At 2 wk, an interesting transitional phase was evident, in that the external tracts of the dorsal, lateral, and ventral funiculi were well myelinated, whereas the deeper tracts were as yet poorly myelinated (fig. 4.46). Thus, the myelin appeared later in the lateral corticospinal, lateral reticulospinal, rubrospinal, lateral spinothalamic, vestibulospinal, and ventral reticulospinal tracts than in the more superficial tracts. Also, at this time the median region of the dorsal funiculus occupied by the fasciculus gracilis was less well myelinated than the fasciculus cuneatus. The lateral corticospinal tract is outstanding as a nonmyelinated tract throughout this

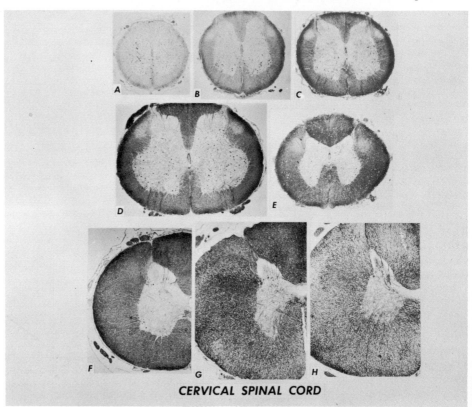

CERVICAL SPINAL CORD

Fig. 4.46. Cervical spinal cord of dogs at various ages, Ora's stain, showing gradual myelination of lateral corticospinal tracts (*x*) and earlier myelination of all other tracts in dorsal, lateral, and ventral funiculi; note transitional phase at 2 wk (see text). (*a*), 1 day; (*b*), 7 days; (*c*), 14 days; (*d*), 21 days; (*e*), 32 days (anterior to lumbar enlargement at 12); (*f*), 6 wk; (*g*), 16 wk; (*h*), adult.

period. A few fine myelinated fibers detectable in the ventral (motor) gray column at 1 day of age were by 7 days more distinct; the myelin sheath was clearly heavier than in the fibers in the dorsal (sensory) gray column. Prior treatment with trichloroacetic acid did not reveal significantly more myelin than was detectable in the untreated Ora's preparations. No myelinated fibers were found in the lateral gray column during this period. By 14 days, the dorsal gray column fibers were well myelinated but were still finer in diameter than those of the ventral gray column. Fibers of the ventral commissure were visible at 7 days and increased in thickness and density up to 5 wk of age.

21–42 Days. By 21 days of age, the deeper tracts in the dorsal, lateral, and ventral funiculi were evenly myelinated, with the exception of the lateral cortico-spinal tract and the fasciculus gracilis, which lacked much myelin until after 35 days of age. By 6 wk, myelination of the dorsal, lateral, and ventral funiculi was completed.

Increase in the number and thickness of fibers in the ventral gray column took place during the early part of this period, and relative maturity was attained by 5 wk of age. The fibers of the lateral gray column developed more gradually during this period than the fibers in the dorsal and ventral columns and did not mature until later.

6 Wk to Adult. Developmental changes after 6 wk were minimal, with the exception of the fibers of the lateral gray column, which increased in thickness and density until approximately 10 wk, when the adult level of development was seen. Although the cervical spinal cord increased in length and diameter with increasing age, further developmental changes were not detectable.

Thoracic Spinal Cord

The development of this segment of the spinal cord was essentially identical to the development observed in the cervical segment during the same age periods.

Lumbar Spinal Cord (see figs. 4.47–4.50)

1–14 Days. In the dorsal, lateral, and ventral funiculi no myelin was detectable at birth, although the superficial tracts in the ventral and lateral funiculi stained slightly darker than those in the dorsal funiculus. By 7 days of age, myelination of these funiculi was clearly evident, and at 2 wk the more superficial tracts contained more myelin than the deeper ones of the lateral and ventral funiculi. The deposit of myelin in the lateral and ventral corticospinal tracts was less advanced than in other tract areas.

From 1 day to 2 wk, the ventral gray columns developed well-myelinated fibers, which were clearly evident at birth and were more advanced than the fibers of the dorsal gray column. A few fibers were present in the ventral commissure at 7 days and increased significantly in thickness and number from 7 to 14 days of age.

21 Days–6 Wk. The funiculi continued to become myelinated during this period, with the lateral corticospinal tract being the last system in the dorsal funiculus to mature. The ventral commissural fibers were clearly evident at 3 wk and relatively mature between 4 and 5 wk of age. The lumbar spinal cord became relatively mature by 6 wk, although continuing to increase in length and diameter after this time.

The myelinated fibers of the ventral gray columns were most marked and easiest to identify. The fibers of the dorsal gray column were well myelinated by 3 wk but increased in thickness between 4 and 5 wk, so that they were of larger diameter than the fibers of the ventral gray column. By 6 wk of age, these fibers closely resembled those of the adult in their elaboration and thickness. The fibers of the lateral gray columns, as observed in the cervical spinal cord, developed more gradually and matured only after 6 wk of age.

6 Wk–Adult. Myelination was complete at the onset of this period, and the only detectable changes included further elaboration of the fibers in the lateral gray columns and an overall increase in the length and diameter of the lumbar spinal cord.

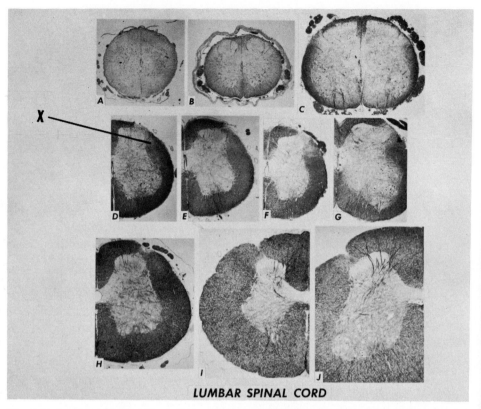

LUMBAR SPINAL CORD

Fig. 4.47. Lumbar spinal cord of dogs at various ages, Ora's stain, showing early myelination of funiculi and later myelination of lateral corticospinal tracts (*x*). (*a*), 1 day; (*b*), 7 days; (*c*), 14 days; (*d*), 21 days; (*e*), 24 days; (*f*), 32 days; (*g*), 5 wk; (*h*), 6 wk; (*i*), 16 wk; (*j*), adult.

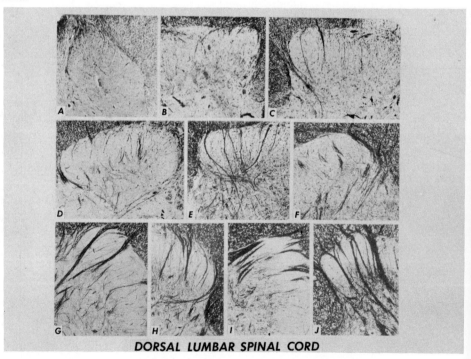

DORSAL LUMBAR SPINAL CORD

Fig. 4.48. Dorsal gray column of lumbar spinal cord of dogs at different ages, Ora's stain, showing relative maturity of dorsal fibers attained by 6 wk of age. (*a*), 1 day; (*b*), 14 days; (*c*), 21 days; (*d*), 24 days; (*e*), 32 days; (*f*), 5 wk; (*g*), 6 wk; (*h*), 10 wk; (*i*), 16 wk; (*j*), adult.

180

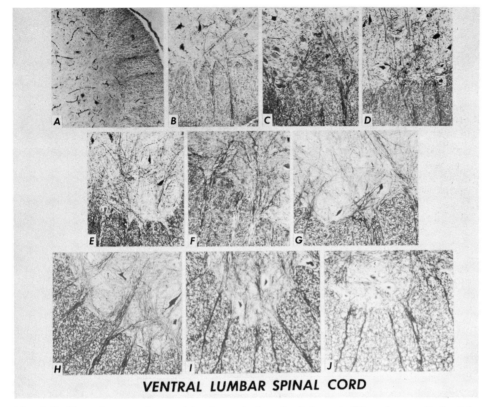

VENTRAL LUMBAR SPINAL CORD

Fig. 4.49. Ventral gray column of lumbar spinal cord of dogs at different ages, Ora's stain, showing earlier myelination than in dorsal horn (cf. fig. 4.48), and relative maturity at 5–6 wk of age. (a), 1 day; (b), 7 days; (c), 14 days; (d), 21 days; (e), 32 days; (f), 5 wk; (g), 6 wk; (h), 10 wk; (i), 16 wk; (j), adult.

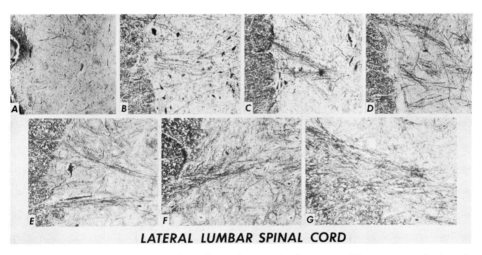

LATERAL LUMBAR SPINAL CORD

Fig. 4.50. Lateral gray column of lumbar spinal cord of dogs at different ages, Ora's stain, showing gradual increase in fiber number up to 10 wk of age. (a), 1 day; (b), 21 days; (c), 32 days; (d), 6 wk; (e), 10 wk; (f), 16 wk; (g), adult.

181

Discussion

These histological findings show that the spinal cord of the dog attains relative maturity at 6 wk of age, and that the fasciculus gracilis and lateral corticospinal tract are the last spinal structures to myelinate. The ventral (motor) gray columns show more advanced myelination than the dorsal (sensory) gray columns early in life, but with increasing age the fibers of the dorsal gray columns become larger than those of the ventral. The fibers of the lateral columns develop relatively slowly and do not become mature until after 6 wk of age.

Langworthy (1929) also observed that the fasciculus gracilis myelinates later than the fasciculus cuneatus in the kitten, and that the dorsal columns are fully myelinated by 38 days of age. In the kitten the lateral columns, however, are well myelinated by 14 days, whereas the corticospinal and rubrospinal fibers are poorly myelinated even at 35 days of age. Although it is difficult to make direct comparisons between these data and those of Langworthy, it would appear that the cat's spinal cord matures more rapidly than that of the dog, possibly 1 wk earlier. The observation of Langworthy that the ventral columns are almost completely myelinated as early as 8 days in the kitten could not be confirmed in this study of the dog, although there is agreement in that the ventral (motor) region matures at an earlier age than the dorsal (sensory) region.

Studies of the development of reflexes and locomotor activities in the cat (Fox 1968) and the dog (chap. 2) have shown that these activities mature in the cat approximately 1 wk sooner than in the dog. Moreover, comparisons of the development of neocortical neurons in the dog (Fox, Inman, and Himwich 1966), lead to the conclusion that they reach maturity approximately 1 wk later than in the cat (Noback and Purpura 1961).

The neurologic development of the dog, as determined by a series of reflex tests, shows a mature pattern by 4 wk of age. The disappearance of primitive neonatal reflexes such as the crossed extensor and Magnus reflexes in the hind limbs may be correlated with myelination of the ventral (motor) spinal cord; these reflexes disappear between 2½ and 3 wk of age, and adult postures, standing, sitting, and walking appear after this time and are well developed by 4 wk. Similarly coordinated movements in the hind limbs may be related to myelination of the ventral commissure. Forelimb placing reactions develop after 5 days of age, and hind-limb placing is first seen around 8 days. The ability to run and turn and coordinate the hind limbs develops later, toward 6 wk, and may be related to the more gradual myelination of the corticospinal tracts. In the same way, cortical control over certain superficial sensory reflexes may be related to myelination of the dorsal spinal cord; for example, reflex urination can be elicited until 3 wk of age, after which time it cannot be reliably demonstrated.

The effects of decerebration at different ages on the appearance of rigidity in the fore- and hind limbs of the dog indicate that mature decerebrate patterns of extension and opisthotonus are not seen until after 2 wk of age. Decerebration (see earlier) has a minimal effect in the newborn, although some change in muscle tonus in the hind limbs can be seen by 7 days of age. Rigidity in the forelimbs is seen before rigidity in the hind limbs. Similar observations of the kitten were reported by Langworthy (1929).

The rostral segment of the spinal cord is thought by Langworthy to develop sooner than the caudal segment, and this observation is supported by reflex studies in both the cat and the dog. Morphological differences in the rate of development of the cervical and lumbar regions were not quantitated in the present investigation.[4] However, between 1 and 2 wk of age the funiculi of the cervical region give the impression of staining slightly darker and, therefore, are possibly more myelinated than corresponding sections of the lumbar region of the same subjects. Also the ventral columns of the cervical cord tend to mature sooner than those of the lumbar. The greater differences in the neurologic development of the fore- and hind limbs may involve three factors: (1) gradual myelination of corticospinal tracts, which appears earlier in the cervical region; (2) visual and vestibulocerebellar control over forelimb movements, which develops before hind-limb control; and (3) experience (learning) and exercise, which are important in organizing reflex components of locomotion and in coordinating fore- and hind-limb movements. Buxton and Goodman (1967) similarly observed a more protracted myelination of the corticospinal tracts in young dogs. The initial ataxic gait, hypermetria, and muscular tremor in young quadrupeds may indicate a later maturation not only of corticospinal tracts but also of corticocerebellar and extrapyramidal connections. It is possible that myelination occurs in cycles, certain (often phylogenetically "older") systems myelinating sooner than others. Langworthy notes that

> when myelinization first begins, it continues rapidly for a time until a number of tracts receive their full component of myelin. Then a period of retardation seems to ensue so that final myelinization of the corticospinal, posterior column tracts and cerebellar connections does not occur for a considerable time. It may be that, just as Coghill found waves of cell-proliferation and maturation in the nervous system, waves of myelinization also occur.

Summary: Histological Development of the CNS and the Spinal Cord

The cytoarchitectonic development of the frontal, temporal, occipital, precoronal, and postcoronal areas of the canine neocortex was described. Differentiation of neuron layers and reduction in cell density occurred during the first 3 wk of life. By 4–5 wk, the cytoarchitectonics resembled the adult. Similarly, the development of dendritic components of neocortical neurons attained relative maturity by 5 wk. Myelination of neocortical structures took place most rapidly during 4–5 wk of age. Before 3 wk little myelin was detected histologically in the neocortex, but it was well developed in subcortical structures caudal to the posterior commissure. Therefore, at the time when cell development attained relative maturity myelination of thalamocortical structures was seen for the first time; after this initial wave of myelination, this process continued at a more gradual rate into adulthood. The development of various glial elements was closely correlated with neuronal development and myelination in the neocortex.

Myelination of the spinal cord occurred in an initial wave during the first 3 wk of life, during which time the dorsal and ventral funiculi were myelinated, with the exception of the lateral corticospinal tract. This tract did not become completely myelinated until 5–6 wk, and by that time the dorsal sensory and ventral motor roots

---

[4] See Bodian (1968) for account of development of ultrastructure of the spinal cord of fetal monkeys from the prereflex period to the period of long intersegmental reflexes.

were almost mature. The cervical cord myelinated a little sooner than the lumbar region, and also the ventral roots were myelinated earlier than the dorsal roots.

From these correlated aspects of CNS development it is clear that by the end of the first month of life, the most dramatic developmental events have taken place and adultlike structure and functional activity are attained. It is also at this time that electrocortical activity becomes essentially mature. By 5 wk of age, the EEG patterns of quiet sleep and activated sleep and the relative duration of activated sleep more closely resemble those of the adult; also, the development of visually and auditorily evoked potentials reaches relative maturity between 4 and 5 wk (see chap. 3).

In the dog, shortly after the first month of life, the most important events in CNS development have occurred. This time, when perceptual and locomotor abilities are sufficiently developed to permit adultlike function and interaction with the environment, approximates the onset of the critical period of socialization.

5

Developmental Aspects of Some Conditioned and Learned Responses

Education is nothing less than an essential and natural form of biological additivity.
In it we can perhaps catch a glimpse, still in the marginal, conscious state, of individual,
germinal heredity in process of formation: as though organic mutation at this stage took the
form of a psychic invention contrived by the parents and transmitted by them.

Pierre Teilhard de Chardin, *The Future of Man*

There are many categories or types of learning. By evaluating learning ability within
a given modality of stimulation or in a particular context where more complex learning processes are involved, we may gain some indirect knowledge of the functioning
of the nervous system. In cross-sectional studies of experimentally naïve subjects at
afferent ages, we may also gain some insight into the development of learning abilities and of the nervous system. This chapter concerns the latter point; learning in
one modality, olfaction, is investigated in order to evaluate such phenomena as
habituation, conditioning, and exposure learning. Several studies of the development
of various types of conditional responses will be reviewed and correlated with the
ontogeny of perception in different sensory modalities. More complex learning tasks,
namely visual (black-white) discrimination and reversal learning, and the ability to
delay a learned response are evaluated in dogs of different ages. The delayed-response test has been used by many investigators to assess the effect of brain lesions
(notably prefrontal lesions, Kurtsin 1968); these earlier studies of brain function
will be correlated with ontogenetic findings in the delayed-response test. Stability
(or retention) of a learned or conditioned inhibition of approach to a human being
will be studied in order to correlate age differences in retention. A possible sensitive period when psychophysiological trauma has its greatest effect at a particular
age may also be identified. The existence of such a period has been implied in earlier
socialization studies in the dog but has not as yet been convincingly demonstrated.

The last issue in this chapter is the development of exploratory behavior. Both
cross-sectional (naïve subjects) and longitudinal (subjects with previous experience) groups will be studied at different ages to evaluate the effect of previous
increments of experience on exploratory behavior.

185

Olfactory Responses in the Neonate Dog: Habituation and
Exposure Learning

Introduction

Using classical conditioning procedures, Fuller, Clark, and Waller (1950) were
unable to obtain stable withdrawal responses to a variety of stimuli until 3–4 wk
of age, and demonstrated clearly that such responses involving the centers of higher
nervous activity could not be established during early postnatal life in the dog.
However, Stanley et al. (1963) have demonstrated that conditioned avoidance to
quinine-flavored milk can be established in the dog during the neonatal period. More
recently Bacon and Stanley (1970) and Werboff (personal communication) have
shown that discrimination and reversal learning can occur in the neonate dog on
the basis of tactile cues.

Although Scott and Marston (1950) reported that olfactory responses do not
develop until after the "neonatal" period in the dog, Rosenblatt and Schneirla
(1962) have shown that in the kitten, olfactory responses play an important role in
neonatal behavior. The hippocampus is associated with the rhinencephalon and
adjacent structures (the limbic system). It seems probable that the newborn dog
has a well-developed and functional olfactory system, for Dravid, Himwich, and
Davis (1965) have shown that biochemically, the hippocampus is the most mature
region of the central nervous system of the dog at birth.

The following investigation was undertaken to determine whether the neonate
dog responds to olfactory stimuli and if an association of a specific olfactory stimulus with the nest environment (and mother) could be demonstrated. Positive data
would show if a form of olfactory conditioning or habituation-learning (or "exposure learning," Sluckin 1965) takes place during early postnatal life, as well as
illustrating the importance of olfactory responses in the behavioral organization of
the dog.

Materials and Methods

The following volatile agents were used to evoke olfactory responses: acetic
acid (5%), xylene, benzene, clove oil, and anise oil.

Thirty neonate dogs were employed in the experiment (physically inferior or
sick subjects were not used) in three test groups. The first group comprised 12 pups
from 2 litters, the mothers of which were smeared with anise oil over the mammary
area, the groin, axillae, and neck at the time of parturition. Anise was applied liberally to these regions twice daily throughout the test period, from birth to 5 days.
The other two groups whose dams were not treated with anise oil consisted of 12
pups from 1 litter which were tested only on the 6th day after birth, and 6 pups
from 1 litter which were tested daily from birth to 5 days.

The two unconditioned reflex responses described were used to ascertain the
pups' reactions to olfactory stimulation. When the head of the alert pup is stimulated
by contact with a warm object, such as the hand, the pup will "root" or crawl
forward, a thermotactile response. This has been described as the rooting reflex
(chap. 2). While the subject was actively rooting, the test series of olfactory stimuli
were randomly presented in turn on fresh cotton Q-Tips held approximately 2 cm
from the external nares of the subject (fig. 5.1*b*). Two responses were obtained

for each agent, and a normal rooting response without olfactory stimulation was elicited before and after each olfactory stimulus.

The second response was elicited by placing the subject on a solid tabletop without any thermotactile stimulation; in this "isolated" situation, the characteristic locomotion of the neonate is semicircular, the head being moved from side to side like an exploratory probe (James 1952*b*, fig. 5.1*a*). If the head touches any warm object, the pup will "root" toward it; if, however, no thermotactile stimulation is

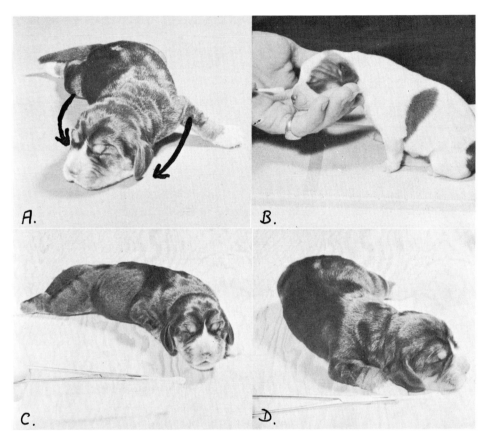

Fig. 5.1. (*a*), exploratory movements of pup—head swings from side to side; (*b*), stimulation of rooting reflex with impregnated Q-Tip in position; (*c*), positive orientation toward Q-Tip soaked with anise oil; (*d*), avoidance of xylene-impregnated Q-Tip.

presented, exploratory behavior continues. Under these conditions, the olfactory stimuli were randomly presented at intervals of 2 min, 2 responses being determined for each agent. The agent impregnated on a Q-Tip was held approximately 2 cm from the nose of the subject, and kept in this position by moving it appropriately as the head of the subject was moved from side to side in exploration. Avoidance or orientation toward the stimulus could then be determined (fig. 5.1*b*, *c*, *d*).

The strength of response was arbitrarily graded from 0 to 9 (0 = negative response or complete avoidance; 2.5, weak positive response; 5.0, moderate; and 9.0 strong positive) for the rooting and orientation reactions. Responses were scored by two observers. Results were averaged, for there was a high interobserver score correlation. Numerical data could then be analyzed statistically to compare reactions to different odors among the experimental and control subjects.

With noxious olfactory stimuli, the subject would stop rooting and twist out of the operator's hand. With noxious olfactory stimuli presented while the pup was isolated without thermotactile stimulation, the head, which was being moved from side to side in exploration, was violently turned away from the odor and the pup might crawl away from it. With less noxious stimuli no reaction was seen, as the odor had no effect on the exploratory head movements. A positive orienting response was seen when head movements ceased and the head was turned toward the olfactory stimulus, the body straightened out in line with the stimulus, and the subject crawled toward the stimulus ($= 9$). Moderate responses ($= 5$) were seen when the head only was turned toward the odor and no body-turning and locomotion occurred. Samples of frontal lobe and olfactory bulb were taken from 5 purebred beagles aged 1 day, 2, 4, and 6 wk, and adult, and stained to determine the development of myelin in the olfactory tract. The frontal lobe served as a control for comparing the qualitative differences in the staining properties of myelin in these two regions.

Results

All responses were averaged and reduced to the first decimal place to give an overall measure of the responsiveness of test and control groups (tables 5.1, 5.2). Individual differences among these groups were statistically insignificant. In the anisc-cxposed group, rooting in all cases was strong in the presence of anise, indicating that this agent was not obnoxious to the subjects (table 5.1) as compared to the controls ($p < .001$, Mann-Whitney U one-tail test). Clove oil, compared with other agents, was the least noxious ($p < .031$, sign test, Siegel 1956). In the control group tested from birth to 5 days of age (table 5.2), clove oil caused fewer avoidance reactions while rooting than did the other odors, including anise ($p < .031$). When these two groups were compared, anise oil had little effect on the rooting behavior of the first control group. In the second control group, tested only at 6 days of age, violent avoidance of all olfactory stimuli presented while the subjects were rooting was evident (table 5.2). Comparison of the two control groups showed that testing from birth caused some adaptation so that avoidance responses were less intense.

In no instances were orientation reactions to anise seen in the control groups, but in the anise-exposed group, orientation was strong (tables 5.1, 5.2). When the avoidance reactions to other olfactory stimuli presented during rooting and orientation are analyzed, the results show that all odors were avoided during orientation, whereas during rooting, avoidance did not occur in some individuals even with clove oil (and anise in control groups). This difference may indicate that during rooting, thermotactile stimuli predominate so that less noxious olfactory stimuli (normally causing avoidance when the pup has no thermotactile stimulation) are less effective in eliciting avoidance reactions. Thus, in the neonate in the nest environment, the sensory receptors enabling spatial and contactual localization of the dam by thermotactile stimuli will react maximally and overshadow olfactory stimulation. We may surmise that with stimulus deprivation the threshold of olfactory sensitivity was reduced in the "isolated" pup, but when the pup is in contact with a warm object, thermotactile stimuli possibly increase the threshold of olfactory sensitivity so that avoidance of noxious odors does not always occur.

The development of myelin (determined by intensity of staining) was marked in the olfactory tract (stria olfactoria lateralis) by 14 days of age, in contrast to slower myelination of the frontal lobe (substantia medullaris), which is minimal until 4 wk (see also chap. 4).

TABLE 5.1

AVERAGED OLFACTORY RESPONSES IN 2 LITTERS OF 6 PUPS

(Anise-exposed)

Odor	Day 2		Day 3		Day 4		Day 5	
	Root	Orient	Root	Orient	Root	Orient	Root	Orient
Cloves	1.0	0	3.0	0	1.0	0	2.0	0
Benzene	0.5	0	1.0	0	0	0	1.0	0
Xylene	0	0	0	0	0	0	0	0
Acetic acid	0	0	0	0	0	0	0	0
Aniseed	9	9	9	9	9	9	7.0	9
Control	9	0	9	0	9	0	9	0

NOTE: Root = response while rooting reflex is stimulated; Orient = orienting response toward odor. Strength of response is graded 0–9 (0 = negative, 2.5 = weak and variable, 5 = good, 9 = strong).

TABLE 5.2

AVERAGED OLFACTORY RESPONSES IN CONTROL GROUPS A AND B

Odor	Day 2		Day 3		Day 4		Day 5		Day 6	
	Root	Orient	Root	Orient	Root	Orient	Root	Orient	Root	Orient
Cloves	3.0	0	3.0	0	4.5	0	3.0	0	0	0
Benzene	0	0	1.0	0	0	0	1.0	0	0	0
Xylene	2.0	0	0	0	0	0	0	0	0	0
Acetic acid	0	0	0	0	0	0	0	0	0	0
Aniseed	2.5	0	1.5	0	1.5	0	3.0	0	0	0
Control	9	0	9	0	9	0	9	0	9	0

NOTE: Group A: 6 pups from 1 litter tested from day 2 to day 5 (habituated group). Group B: 12 pups from 1 litter tested on day 6 only (naïve group).

Discussion

These data support the observations of Engen et al. (1963) on the human neonate, in that increased refinement of response or adaptation to different odors occurs with age.

Scott (1963), in comparing myelination of cranial nerve of the neonate dog and the human infant, showed that the nerves concerned with feeding and cephalic stimulation (facial and trigeminal) are well myelinated at birth, and in this investigation it has been shown that the olfactory tracts become well myelinated during the neonatal period. These facts are correlated with the importance of head orientation to thermotactile stimuli, location of the teat, and the mechanics of sucking.

This investigation clearly demonstrates also that the neonate dog will react differentially to olfactory stimuli.

The age when positive conditioned responses can first be obtained is dependent upon the modality of the stimulus, as was stressed by Stanley et al. (1963). A conditioned response involving integration at a higher sensory level will occur at a later age than conditioned responses at a phylogenetically lower (rhinencephalic) level (Volokhov 1959a, b). The neuro-ontogeny of these various levels of higher nervous activity, when charted chronologically, clearly illustrates the

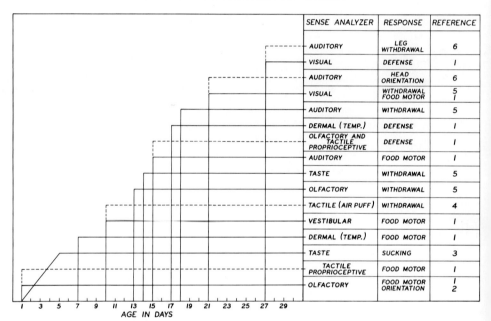

AGE OF FIRST APPEARANCE OF POSITIVE CONDITIONED RESPONSES IN THE DOG
(TIME OF STABLE CONDITIONING NOT INCLUDED)

SENSE ANALYZER	RESPONSE	REFERENCE
AUDITORY	LEG WITHDRAWAL	6
VISUAL	DEFENSE	1
AUDITORY	HEAD ORIENTATION	6
VISUAL	WITHDRAWAL FOOD MOTOR	5 1
AUDITORY	WITHDRAWAL	5
DERMAL (TEMP.)	DEFENSE	1
OLFACTORY AND TACTILE PROPRIOCEPTIVE	DEFENSE	1
AUDITORY	FOOD MOTOR	1
TASTE	WITHDRAWAL	5
OLFACTORY	WITHDRAWAL	5
TACTILE (AIR PUFF)	WITHDRAWAL	4
VESTIBULAR	FOOD MOTOR	1
DERMAL (TEMP.)	FOOD MOTOR	1
TASTE	SUCKING	3
TACTILE PROPRIOCEPTIVE	FOOD MOTOR	1
OLFACTORY	FOOD MOTOR ORIENTATION	1 2

AGE IN DAYS

Fig. 5.2. Age of first appearance of positive conditioned responses in the dog (time of stable conditioning not included). Note early emergence of food-motor responses at the rhinencephalic level and later development of withdrawal responses. References: (1) Volokhov 1959a, b; (2) Fox, present study; (3) Stanley et al. 1963; (4) Cornwell and Fuller 1961; (5) Fuller, Easler, and Banks 1950; (6) James and Cannon 1952.

gradual postnatal development of these systems (fig. 5.2). As these systems emerge, as exemplified by such conditioned reflex studies, the developing animal is able to establish certain specific stimulus response mechanisms at birth characteristic of neonatal behavior, which enable it to locate its mother and find shelter and nurture. At a later stage, as the locomotor system and organs of special sense develop, more complex responses are seen, including withdrawal, avoidance, and orientation responses which supersede the earlier responses. Thus neonatal behavior patterns are surpassed by more highly developed and complex activities, affording the animal greater maternal independence and increasing interaction within its environmental milieu. Zeval'd (1966), in an ontogenetic study of conditioned inhibition in the dog, concludes that there is a positive correlation between the "degree of excitation and concentration of inhibition," and the rate of formation of conditioned inhibition.

Development of the nervous system becomes more perfect as conditioned inhibition improves.

Nikitina and Novikova (cited by Lynn 1966) correlated the development of the cerebrum with habituation in the dog. They found that approximately 200 trials were required to habituate (or extinguish) the orienting reaction in pups between 3 and 14 days of age; only 15–20 trials were required between 40 and 60 days. They concluded that the cerebrum of the dog is mature by 8 wk, and that at this age the process of habituation is similar to that in the adult.

With this more gradual development characteristic of nonprecocial animals, the progression of neuro-ontogeny can be followed during postnatal life as contrasted with the precocial newborn animals, which interact rapidly with their environmental milieu at birth. Imprinting occurs in the latter group, since sensory development is more or less complete at birth. In nonprecocial mammals, such as the dog, some imprinting-like exposure learning can take place shortly after birth via the gustatory system (Stanley et al. 1963) and via the olfactory system, as shown in the present investigation. Long-lasting effects of similar olfactory experience in early life have been studied in the rat by Marr and Gardner (1965) and in the mouse by Mainardi, Marsan, and Pasquali (1965); subsequent social behavior, sexual preference, and responsiveness and care of young can be influenced by olfactory imprinting processes. Manning (1967*b*), in his studies of "pre-imaginal conditioning" in *Drosophila,* finds that flies raised on a medium containing geraniol show a reduced aversion to this odor when adult, and he concludes that this change is due to a form of habituation rather than to associative learning.

Summary

Pups exposed to anise oil applied to the mammary region of the bitch during the first 5 days postnatally showed orientation toward a cotton Q-Tip soaked in anise oil when removed from the nest environment. Anise oil was violently avoided by control subjects; reactions to a variety of other olfactory stimuli were also studied. These findings suggest that the neonate dog can respond differentially to odors and that habituation to an odor (which is avoided by controls) can develop at this early age; orientation responses to anise oil indicated that olfactory stimuli may play an important role in neonatal life, and the positive orienting responses observed support the concept that olfactory conditioning or "exposure learning" can be established during neonatal life.

Development of Visual Discrimination and Reversal Learning in the Dog

Introduction

The purpose of this investigation is to evaluate the oddity-problem solving ability to visual cues in the dog at ages ranging from 5 to 16 wk. Between 4 and 5 wk of age the dog attains relative structurofunctional maturity of the CNS (see chaps. 3 and 4); this time marks the onset of the critical period of socialization, which extends from approximately 4 to 12 wk of age (Scott 1962). Although the CNS is relatively mature at the onset of this period, more complex functions such as the development of delayed responsiveness are not elaborated until later in life. Thus the integration of perceptual and locomotor abilities and capacity to elaborate more complex responses may be a function of age, and this question will be examined.

Rajalakshmi and Jeeves (1965) have reviewed discrimination and reversal learning in several species, and they discuss a number of variables including phylogeny, ontogeny, genetics, and environmental factors, X-radiation, and brain lesions.

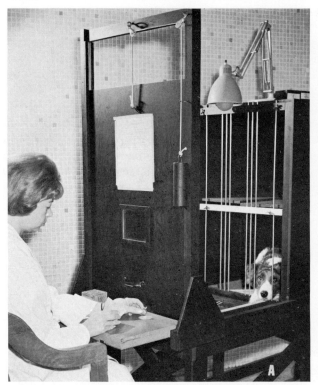

Fig. 5.3. Modified WGTA for use with dogs. Operator shown placing food under cube; subject responds appropriately.

Materials and Methods

A modified Wisconsin General Testing Apparatus (WGTA, Harlow 1949) adapted for testing dogs was used (fig. 5.3). The total length of the apparatus was 7½ ft. The compartment in which the subjects were tested was 4′ × 2′ × 3′. Eight adjustable metal bars were mounted on the front of the box, with 3 equally spaced openings 4 in wide. This allowed the subjects to displace the test objects with their noses, the bars being adjusted according to the size of the subject. A guillotine type of screen (40″ × 24″) with a one-way mirror (5″ × 5½″) prevented the subjects from seeing the experimenter during both initial and intertrial intervals. A stimulus tray (2′ × 1′) with 3 wells (2″ × 2″ × 1″) spaced 4 in apart was moved by a series of pulleys to the front of the cage where the subjects were, and then back to the experimenter, who remained behind the screen, which was raised a few inches to retrieve the tray. A light (150 w) was mounted above the apparatus to provide even illumination over the stimulus tray. The objects to be discriminated were 3 cubes measuring $3'' \times 3'' \times 2''$. For the initial discrimination 2 black cubes and 1 white cube were used; and for the reversal 2 white and 1 black.

Subjects: 20 pups were used in the study; 5 pups were assigned to each of the following age groups according to S's age: Group I (5 wk), Group II (8 wk), Group III (12 wk), and Group IV (16 wk). S's were housed in pens with other members of their age group.

At the appropriate age, each S was placed in the WGTA and given 15 shaping trials daily until criterion was reached. All dogs were placed on 23 hr food deprivation, being fed 1 hr after testing. The response to be elicited was pushing the cube with the nose to obtain a small piece of meat from a well in the tray under the cube. The differential cues resulting from the smell of the meat under the reward-cube were reduced by liberally smearing the undersurfaces of all three cubes and the tray-wells with meat. During trials, it was observed that when the subjects were responding correctly, they oriented visually to, and placed themselves between, the bars of the compartment in line with the correct cube as it was being presented on the sliding tray. Objectively, therefore, it would appear that olfactory cues played no part in this test procedure. Shaping consisted of presenting only the to-be-discriminated cube (white cube). Criterion was reached when S did not hesitate in responding, was alert and attentive during the intertrial interval, and approached the stimulus tray upon presentation in the direction of the cube.

After reaching shaping criterion, S's were given 15 trials each day in the initial and subsequent reversal discrimination tasks. Two black cubes and 1 white cube were presented in a systematically randomized order (right, left, and center). If the dog displaced either of the black blocks first, the tray was withdrawn for 5 sec and the error recorded; then the tray was pushed back again (correction technique, with a cutoff of 1 error per trial). The criterion of acquisition was arbitrarily set at 2 consecutive days of 85% or better correct responses.

Reversal discrimination began the day after the criterion for the initial task was reached. Two white cubes and 1 black cube were presented in a randomized order, using the same method as described above, with the exception that no reshaping to the black cube was undertaken. As soon as the criterion for reversal learning was reached (which was the same as the criterion level for the initial discrimination), the response was extinguished. The response was considered extinguished if S made no response in 10 consecutive trials on 2 successive days or received 300 extinction trials. Testing for spontaneous recovery began 2 days after extinction.

Results

The Kruskal-Wallis one-way analysis of variance showed a significant variance in the number of errors to criterion in the initial task within the entire population ($H \geq 9.2$ with $k - 1 = 3$ d.f., $p < .05$). The Mann-Whitney U test for small samples was used to make a between-group comparison. In the reversal task the H-value was 6.6 ($p > .05 < .10$) and so no group comparisons were made. However, with the subjects used as their own control, a comparison was made between initial task errors and reversal task errors. The results showed that all dogs in each of the groups made significantly more errors in the reversal than in the initial task ($X \leq 0$, $p = .016$, sign test).

No significance within the population in the number of days to shaping criterion, or in the number of trials to extinction, was found (see tables 5.3 and 5.4 for mean and range values). The spontaneous recovery measure showed that all dogs in each of the groups started responding to the correct stimulus within 3 days and the level of reacquisition or relearning was at the 80% level within 2 more days. The range of variability within groups on both the initial and reversal tasks is of interest; younger dogs made more errors with a much greater score range than older dogs, the same trend being seen in the reversal task (figs. 5.4, 5.5).

TABLE 5.3

SUMMARY OF DATA COMPARING DIFFERENT AGE
GROUPS IN VISUAL DISCRIMINATION TEST

Mean Number of Days to Meet Shaping Criterion	Mean Number of Trials to Meet Extinction Criterion
Starting at 5 wk—7.6 days (5–9)[a]	11 wk[b]—225 trials (195–240)[c]
Starting at 8 wk—11.8 days (5–7)	13 wk—177 trials (90–210)
Starting at 12 wk—3.1 days (3–4)	16 wk—183.7 trials (120–255)
Starting at 16 wk—4.3 days (3–5)	19 wk—146.2 trials (105–65)

[a] Range values in days.
[b] Actual mean age when tested for extinction in same subjects shown in left-hand column.
[c] Range of number of trials.

TABLE 5.4

COMPARISONS OF PERFORMANCES OF DIFFERENT AGE GROUPS
IN VISUAL DISCRIMINATION TEST

Mean Errors to Meet Initial Task Criterion		Mean Errors to Meet Reversal Task Criterion	
5-wk group (6.5 wk) 22.8 errors (10-38)	8-wk group (9.5 wk) 23.8 errors[a] (16-35)	5-wk group (9 wk) 84.0 errors (55-139)	8-wk group (11 wk) 67.3 errors[a] (42-103)
5-wk group (6.5 wk) 22.8	12-wk group (12.3 wk) 15.6[b] (9-21)	5-wk group (9 wk) 84.0	12-wk group (13.5 wk) 78.8[a] (49-95)
5-wk group (6.5 wk) 22.3	16-wk group (16.5 wk) 13.6[b] (7-18)	5-wk group (9 wk) 84.0	16-wk group (18 wk) 45.2[a] (31-58)
8-wk group (9.5 wk) 23.8	12-wk group (12.3 wk) 15.6[c]	8-wk group (11 wk) 67.3	12-wk group (13.5 wk) 78.8[a]
8-wk group (9.5 wk) 23.8	16-wk group (16.5 wk) 13.6[d]	8-wk group (11 wk) 67.3	16-wk group (18 wk) 45.2[a]
12-wk group (12.3 wk) 15.6	16-wk group (16.5 wk) 13.6[c]	12-wk group (13.5 wk) 78.8	16-wk group (18 wk) 45.2[a]

[a] Actual mean age when tested shown in parentheses.
[b] $p > .05$ between age groups.
[c] No significant difference between age groups.
[d] $p > .01$ between age groups.

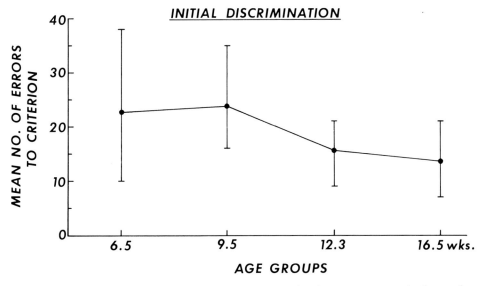

Fig. 5.4. Mean and range scores (5 dogs per age group), showing greatest range in the number of errors in the 6½- and 9½-wk-old pups, contrasting with the superior performances of the two older groups.

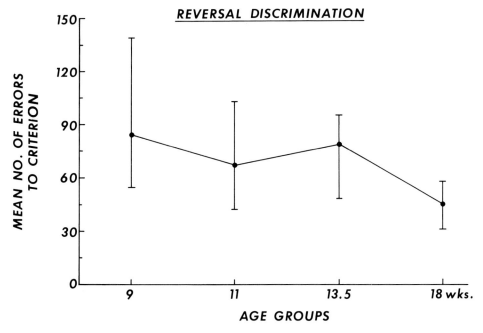

Fig. 5.5. Mean and range scores (5 dogs per age group) in task reversal; greatest range in youngest group at 9 wk of age, and range of variability in the number of errors to criterion decreases with age.

Discussion

In this study, the following points have been demonstrated:

1. Age is a significant factor in initial black-white discrimination.
2. Reversal training to criteria acquisition can be accomplished, and appears to be independent of age.
3. The range of variability in the number of errors in both the initial discrimination and reversal tasks and spontaneous recovery tends to decrease with increasing age.
4. All dogs, independent of age, made spontaneous recovery, reaching criterion 5 days after extinction.

Mackintosh (1965) views classificatory learning as important, for if animals do not classify stimuli appropriately, they are likely to develop errors. According to Mackintosh there is a direct relationship between attention and increased acquisition. In the present study, we noted that the dogs which were the most attentive (i.e., remained oriented toward the stimulus ray and did not move around inside the compartment) were the older dogs, which also made significantly fewer errors in the initial task discrimination.

That learning the "reversal task" is a difficult procedure at all ages confirms the observations of McDowell and Brown (1958), who found that in both normal and irradiated monkeys significantly more errors were seen on reversal of task than during the initial task acquisition in a similar oddity-test procedure.

Harlow and Hicks (1957) used 8 adolescent rhesus monkeys in the WGTA and the noncorrection techniques in their learning set problems of 2-object discrimination. They found that reward and nonreward operated in a parallel and constant manner throughout the entire course of the experiment. The curve functions looked almost identical. If, as Harlow and Hicks propose, reward and nonreward have equal potency, the difficulty in reversal learning is easily explained. Lipsitt and Serunian (1963) reported that the rapidity of oddity-problem solution (response to the odd color presented in 1 of 3 stimulus sources) was a function of chronological age, and indirectly of mental age, in the human infant. They did not go further to evaluate reversal of task discrimination. More rapid solution of oddity problems can be obtained by providing the subjects with several negative stimuli rather than just one, as reported in the canary by Pastore (1954) and in the chimpanzee by McCulloch and Nissen (1937); there was a more pronounced response to the oddness of color than to shape or pattern in the latter study. In the present study, differences between age groups in both discrimination and reversal were not so marked as observed in the delayed response test (see later). We may surmise, therefore, that this latter test is much more complex, and correct responses are more dependent upon maturation and improved learning ability. Harlow (1959) stresses that this progressive improvement with age is independent of special experience; that is, it is a matter of maturation, not of learning by practice. In the monkey, Harlow found that performance on oddity-principle problems improved with age, although several different oddity problems were presented over a given time. In the dog, the greater variability in the youngest subjects in the number of errors to criterion in both the initial discrimination and the reversal suggests that the majority are unable to elaborate correct responses within the same time period utilized by more mature subjects. This ability of initial discrimination appears to be well developed in dogs by 12 wk of age. Although all age groups had difficulty in the reversal discrimination, the best results again were obtained in the oldest age group at 18 wk.

Summary

Oddity discrimination (1 white "correct" object vs. 2 black objects) was studied in four groups of dogs, aged 5, 8, 12, and 16 wk at the onset of the study, in which a WGTA apparatus was used. The findings were as follows:

1. There was a marked difference between the 5- and 8-wk-old dogs compared with the 12- and 16-wk-olds in the mean number of days of training before criterion level was reached, the 5- and 8-wk-old dogs requiring significantly more trials.
2. In the initial discrimination task, the range of variability in the number of errors decreased with age.
3. In the reversal test (1 black vs. 2 white objects), the greatest variability was also found in the youngest age groups.
4. In the number of trials to extinction, there was a marked difference between the youngest and oldest subjects, indicating that extinction was equally more difficult for the youngest and equally more easy for the oldest to accomplish.

These findings are discussed in relation to earlier studies on discrimination learning in other species, and to the development of learning ability.

Development of the Delayed Response

Introduction

The purpose of this investigation was to determine the possible existence of age differences in delayed response of the dog. The delayed response test was originally described by Hunter (1913) for use in evaluating the behavior of rats and dogs; many variables are present in such a test, notably secondary reinforcing stimuli and diverting stimuli (Walton 1915), and the test itself may range in method through choice without delay, simple delay with choice, and delay with choice (Konorski and Lawicka 1959). These more recent studies of Konorski and Lawicka (1959) attempt to provide a physiological (conditioned reflex) interpretation to the analysis and classification of delayed reactions.

Fuller and Gillum (1950) found no difference attributable to breed variations in dogs tested over extended periods, but found great individual differences. Maximum delays were in the region of 4½–5 min. They reported that visual fixation had no effect and that the intervening variable of practice had only a minimal effect on performance. Using a correction technique, Thompson and Heron (1954) found a significant difference between normal dogs and those reared in a restricted environment (mean response times 300 sec and 25 sec respectively after 300 trials). Mishkin and Pribram (1956) reported that frontal lesions in monkeys caused significant deficits in delayed response; the significance of the ontogenetic development of the frontal lobes will be correlated with the behavioral observations in the dog in this present study (see Brutkowski 1965 for general review of the functions of the prefrontal cortex in animals).

Materials and Methods

An 8-sided behavior arena (8′ × 8′) was used for testing. The walls were painted gray and were 7 ft high with 10 (12″ × 15″) one-way windows for observation. Three boxes (18″ × 12″) painted black were placed 6 ft to the left, 9 ft in front, and 6 ft to the right of the start box. The boxes on the left and right had doors that could be lowered to prevent the dog from gaining access to the inside. The box in the center was a "neutral box." At one end of the arena

BEHAVIOR ARENA : DELAYED RESPONSE TEST

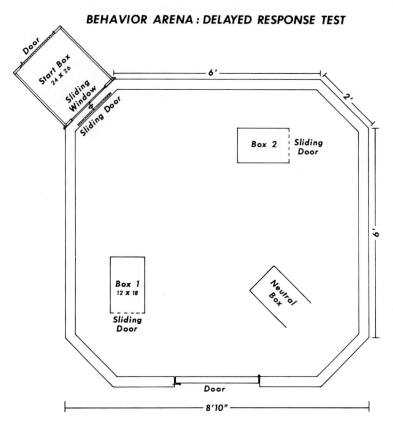

there was a start box (24″ × 26″), which was used to hold the dog during the delay period. Two doors, one with a plywood front and the other with a Plexiglas front, were attached to the front of the start box and could be raised or lowered (fig. 5.6). A Colortran lighting system was used to provide equal illumination and wattage throughout the arena (2,500 w).

Twenty-one naïve mongrel dogs were placed in 4 groups (5 per group, except 6 in the 12-wk group) according to their respective ages—4, 8, 12, and 16 wk. All pups were reared under the same standards of management and nutrition and were kept in numbers of not less than 4 per pen. After the dogs became accustomed to the arena, three measures were taken.

1. *Days to Shaping Criterion.* Each subject was placed in the start box and the plywood door was raised so that the dog could look out into the arena. The ex-

perimenter was standing by either the right or the left box with a dish of meat, which he placed inside the box while the dog observed. The Plexiglas front was raised, allowing the dog to come out into the arena. When the dog ran over to the box where the experimenter was and ate the food, the trial was terminated. The dog was taken out of the arena and placed back in the start box and the process was repeated. After the dog came out for three consecutive trials without coaxing, the process was switched to the other box, using the same method. Then the dog was allowed to look out of the start box for 10 sec, after which the plywood door was lowered, leaving the dog in total darkness for 3 sec. Then both doors were opened and the dog was allowed to come to the box where the experimenter was and eat. After 4 consecutive runs, the dog was ready for testing. A total of 8 shaping trials were run each day. All dogs were fed only one meal 1–2 hr after testing, to ensure that they would be hungry the following day. Each subject was allowed to control the amount of food given (Purina Dog Chow), being allowed to feed ad-lib, that is, being fed to appetite. Feeding in proportion to body weight is less reliable because of great individual differences in the amount of food consumed at one time. Younger pups require more frequent daily feedings than older ones (Fox 1966*d*) and rationing in proportion to body weight may result in underfeeding, as contrasted to ad-lib feeding to appetite where the subject controls its food intake.

2. *Delay Time Measure.* The same process described above was used, except that after the dog had looked out for 10 sec, the plywood door had been lowered, and the delay time was started, the experimenter left the chamber. Delays started at 3 sec, then 5 and 10, increasing by 5 sec every time the dog made 4 consecutive correct runs. If the dog made an incorrect response, he was allowed to correct himself on the first 2 days. For the remaining time, a noncorrection technique was used. Eight trials were run per day for 13 days. The selection of the correct $(+)$ and incorrect $(-)$ box was done by assigning each box a group of numbers. By randomly drawing a number after each trial, one box was designated $+$, the other $-$ depending on which group the number was in. The "correct" box was the box where the experimenter stood (in full view of the dog) and placed the meat inside. If the dog (after the appropriate delay time) came out of the start box and ran to the box where the experimenter had been and went around to the rear without going to either of the other two boxes first, the subject was allowed to eat the food and no errors were noted. If the dog went to the $-$ box first or the neutral box, a door slid down over the $+$ box, preventing the dog from eating.

3. *Response to the Neutral Box.* If the dog went to the incorrect box and then checked the box in the center, he was given a double error. The center box was the neutral box throughout the experiment. The experimenter never stood by or placed any food in this box.

Results

Behavioral Observations

4-Wk Group. This group required a great deal of coaxing to come out of the box, times ranging from 6 sec to 360 sec. In most cases, it took almost 3 days before all the dogs would come out. After shaping to one of the boxes, the dogs developed a position preference to that box and would not switch. Approximately 20 to 30 trials were required to get the dogs to associate the experimenter with the food. The successive approximation method was used for the first 3 to 4 days; pups appeared to lose interest after 8–9 trials, and would run around and explore the chamber more than older pups.

8-Wk Group. This group was much more active than the 4-wk group and was highly aroused throughout the experiment. A position preference developed, but was generally broken after 4–5 days of testing. This group, like the 4-wk group, made continual errors and showed little ability to profit from mistakes.

12-Wk Group. These pups rapidly learned the correct sequence and paid little attention to irrelevant cues. They were highly aroused while in the start box in darkness, jumping against the glass screen and vocalizing. They did not run around the chamber but stayed with the experimenter during shaping and appeared to profit from mistakes.

16-Wk Group. Several dogs in this group had to be coaxed out of the start box and were not as aroused or as attentive to the experimenter as were the other groups. This group had an unexpectedly high number of errors compared with the 12-wk group, and several days were required before testing criteria were met.

TABLE 5.5

KRUSKAL-WALLIS ANALYSIS OF VARIANCE

Measure	H	DF $(K-1)$	p
Days to shaping	12.6	3	$< .01$
Delay time	16.6	3	$< .001$
Response to neutral box	15.7	3	$< .01$
Total number of errors	18.3	3	$< .001$

Test Scores

The Kruskal-Wallis one-way analysis of variance was used to show a significant variance within the entire population for the measures of shaping, delay time, responses to neutral box, and total number of errors (table 5.5). Group comparisons were then made on each of these separate measures by using the Mann-Whitney U test for small samples. Analysis of the data (tables 5.6 and 5.7) comparing the age groups shows statistically significant differences in the mean number of total errors to both incorrect and neutral boxes, there being a gradual reduction in the number of incorrect responses, with the exception of the 16-wk group. Responses to the neutral box decreased with age, and the differences between the 12- and 16-wk groups were not significant. Comparing the slopes of the two curves, the most rapid inhibition of reaction toward the neutral box occurred between 4 and 8 wk, and between 8 and 12 wk, marked reduction in reactivity toward the incorrect box was seen (fig. 5.7). A gradual decrease in the number of days required to reach shaping criterion correlated with increasing age, except that the 16-wk group was similar to the 8-wk group. Mean delay time increased significantly with age, but the 12-wk-old pups were significantly superior to the 16-wk group ($p < .01$). The average delay time did not increase during successive days of testing up to the 6th day in the 4-wk-old pups, but thereafter some improvement was noted (fig. 5.8). The 8-wk group showed little improvement until the 4th day, and thereafter delay

TABLE 5.6

SUMMARY OF DATA COMPARING AGE GROUPS
IN DELAYED RESPONSE TEST

Mean Days to Shaping Criterion		Mean Delay Time (sec)	
4 wk 11.0 (10-11)	8 wk 7.6^c (7-8)	4 wk 2.8 (0-5)	8 wk 13.0^a (0-20)
4 wk 11.0	12 wk 3.8^c (3-5)	4 wk 2.8	12 wk 51.3^c (35-60)
4 wk 11.0	16 wk 9.0^c (8-10)	4 wk 2.8	16 wk 34.0^c (20-45)
8 wk 7.6	12 wk 3.8^c	8 wk 13.0	12 wk 51.3^c
8 wk 7.6	16 wk 9.0^a	8- wk 13.0	16 wk 34.0^b
12 wk 3.8	16 wk 9.0^c	12 wk 51.3	16 wk 34.0^b

NOTE: Range shown in parentheses.
^{a} Not significant.
^{b} $p < .05$.
^{c} $p < .01$.

TABLE 5.7

SUMMARY OF DATA COMPARING AGE GROUPS
IN DELAYED RESPONSE TEST

Mean Response to Neutral Box		Mean Total Errors	
4 wk 13.4 (4-21)	8 wk 4.4^b (2-6)	4 wk 66.6 (58-73)	8 wk 44.6^b (36-53)
4 wk 13.4	12 wk .16^c (0-1)	4 wk 66.6	12 wk 9.3^c (1-18)
4 wk 13.4	16 wk 1.2^c (0-3)	4 wk 66.6	16 wk 29.0^c (24-38)
8 wk 4.4 (2-6)	12 wk .16^c	8 wk 44.6	12 wk 9.3^c
8 wk 4.4	16 wk 1.2^b	8 wk 44.6	16 wk 29.0^c
12 wk .16	16 wk 1.2^a	12 wk 9.3	16 wk 29.0^c

NOTE: Range shown in parentheses.
^{a} Not significant.
^{b} $p < .05$.
^{c} $p < .01$.

DELAYED RESPONSE TEST OF DOGS OF DIFFERENT AGES

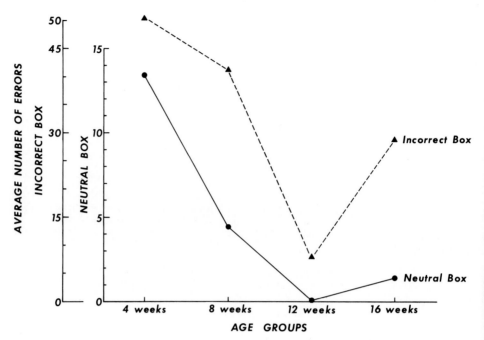

Fig. 5.7. Gradual reduction in number of responses to — or incorrect and neutral boxes with increasing age up to 12 wk followed by sudden increase of incorrect responses at 16 wk.

DELAYED RESPONSE TEST OF DOGS OF DIFFERENT AGES

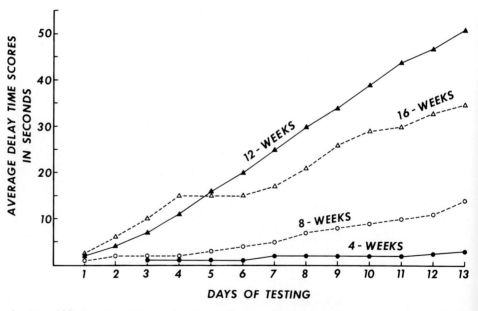

Fig. 5.8. Ability to delay response increases with age, with the exception of low scores at 16 wk

time increased rapidly. Both the 12- and 16-wk groups developed an increasingly longer delayed response from the 1st day of testing up to the 5th consecutive day. At this point (delay time 15 sec), the 12-wk pups continued to increase their delay time in a linear fashion, whereas the 16-wk pups were much slower (fig. 5.8).

Discussion

The highly significant differences attributable to age clearly show the gradual development of delayed reaction or the ability of the dog to delay its response to a learned but variable stimulus situation. The delayed response involves both long-term memory (learned food-motor approach pattern) and short-term memory (remembering for a short time span which box contains the reward), and also the *ability to inhibit* inappropriate responses to nonreward boxes and other extraneous stimulus variables (Konorski and Lawicka 1959) and, in addition, to inhibit or perhaps eliminate or discard the short-term memory trace of the preceding trial. Thus a complex functional integration of perceptual, motor, excitatory, and inhibitory elements of behavior is involved in the delayed reaction, which underlies the establishment of a fixed action pattern or learned response (long-term memory) to the food-reward situation, coupled with a highly adaptive and labile (short-term memory) response. The gradual improvement in delayed reaction time up to 12 wk of age can be correlated with the development of internal inhibition which follows periods of generalization and specialization of reflex components of behavior (Tuge 1961). Stelmak'h (1959), in an ontogenetic study of external inhibition of a motor-alimentary conditioned reflex, showed that external inhibition is poorly developed and unstable until 4–7 wk. Before this age (20–25 days), pups are deficient in internal inhibition and tend to be generalized in their reactions to positive and negative stimuli. A similar second phase of incompetence or instability, in that external inhibition is absent and extra stimuli cause generalization of the conditioned reflex, is seen around 8–12 wk of age, followed by gradual improvement to adult abilities of inhibition by 4–6 mo. Troshikhin and Kozlova (1961), in studying the development of the pup's ability to show the correct conditioned response to reversal (or "switching") of the conditioned stimuli, found that mobility declines with age, and the range of individual variation increases with age in untrained controls. In dogs tested continually, no training effect was observed until 4 mo of age, and the rapidity of switching declined continuously from 25 days to 4 mo. After 4 mo of age, switching occurred more readily than in controls, that is, they showed a definite training effect. Their findings show that pups from 1 to 2 mo of age have the greatest mobility of nervous processes. Without training, mobility (reversal ability) decreases and individual differences increase around 3–4 mo, when the typological properties of the nervous system are taking shape in each individual. Subsequent development leads to the formation of inertia in some dogs and mobility of nervous processes in others. Such a hypothesis finds close agreement with the observations of Stelmak'h. The age discrepancies in later generalization and reduction of internal inhibition observed in these separate investigations are due to different reactions studied, the delayed response being more complex and therefore emerging in older subjects.

It must be noted that adult dogs perform better than 12-wk-old pups in the delayed response test. Eight adult male dogs were tested in this laboratory, and mean delay times of 30, 75, and 120 sec were obtained after 60, 100, and 125 trials, giving 10 trials daily. Vince (1961) has shown that problem-solving abilities are superior in older birds, and attributes the inferior abilities of younger birds to lack of internal inhibition (or extinction of unreinforced response). Tasks requiring directed rather than superabundant activity give the advantage to older animals; conversely, younger animals may perform better under conditions where greater responsiveness and highly exploratory behavior are facilitatory.

Few changes in the CNS can be correlated with this dramatic change occurring at 4–5 mo of age. At this time, a marked reduction in amplitude of the EEG of the alert dog occurs (Pampiglione 1963), and in addition, afterdischarges or secondary and tertiary waves are reduced or absent in visually evoked potentials at this age. Similarly, Venturoli (1962) found that the frequency of EEG waves increases rapidly up to 4 mo, and more gradually thereafter. Thus some rather abrupt neurophysiological changes occur later in life, around 4 mo, which may be regarded as "terminal maturational processes." Such abrupt changes in the functional organization of the CNS may account for the unexpected findings at this age in the present study. We must bear in mind, however, that delayed socialization (Pfaffenberger and Scott 1959) can influence trainability, as these pups were outside the age when socialization can be most readily accomplished. This argument, however, would not account for the similar number of days required to train the 8-wk-old pups to criterion, as 8 wk is around the optimum time for socialization. A third possibility is that at 16 wk, the animals are less responsive and less exploratory (as in Vince's observations in birds); but in this case such an argument, suggesting that increased internal inhibition causes impairment of delayed reactivity, would not account for the high number of reactions toward the incorrect and neutral boxes.

Perhaps at this age in the dog there is, in the Pavlovian sense, an imbalance in excitatory and inhibitory processes (Pavlov 1927). Elaboration of many activities follows definite patterns of excitation (or generalization) followed by inhibition. The "balance" at 12 wk is such that pups can delay their responses rather well; but as noted, with a single exception, they are still inferior to adults. It is conceivable, therefore, that pups at 4 mo are in a state of "imbalance"; certainly around this time definite neurophysiological changes, suggesting a terminal stage of maturation, are taking place.

Luria (1961) presents evidence that the early predominance of excitatory processes over inhibitory processes in the human infant is gradually balanced as internal inhibition develops in association with later development of the frontal lobes. EEG activity in this region in man is not mature until 12 yr (Lindsley 1960). Myelination in the frontal lobes of the dog is extremely slow compared with other neocortical regions (see chap. 4), and it is probable that the later development of the frontal region is related to the slow emergence of internal inhibition, as it is in the human infant. Psychopharmacological studies using classical conditioning in adult dogs, frontal lobectomized adults, and pups aged 5 wk show that there is close similarity between the behavior of young pups and that of frontal lobectomized adults (Jilek and Fox 1965).

Motivation: Drive and Reward Variables. The experiment has one important variable—the degree of hunger in different subjects, which may vary with age and among individuals of the same age and cause differences in motivation, thus influencing the validity of the delayed-response data. Because of this variable, each pup was allowed to control his own food intake at the one meal given after testing by ad-lib feeding. There are age differences in the nutritional requirements of the dog, and in the number of daily feedings that are necessary (Fox 1966*d*), and it is conceivable that because of the greater nutritional demands of the younger pups their motivation may differ considerably from that of older pups. Their inferior performance in the delayed-response test did not indicate that this might be the case.

Other variables include the reward value of the food obtained following correct responses in the test, and also the reward value of being released from confinement in the start box, which acts as a secondary reinforcer, and which may differ with age. Also, age differences in perceptual and locomotor abilities are to be considered. Many such variables are inherent in any ontogenetic study and cannot be adequately controlled since the subject itself is changing through successive days of testing.

Berkson (1962), in studying food motivation and delayed response in gibbons, found that food deprivation affects both correctness of response and the number of trials the animal will perform, and delay interval can limit the proportions of correct responses under conditions of high motivation. In rats, delay in being rewarded does not affect the hunger drive, but weakens the incentive factor (food), according to Hamilton (1929). Miles (1959) found that in squirrel monkeys, the proficiency in discrimination learning is not influenced by the degree of hunger, and performance on a two-choice discrimination is relatively independent of drive magnitude. In view of Miles's findings, it is possible that different degrees of hunger in various pups in the present investigation is a less significant variable than expected, although the number of trials the animal will perform and the number of correct responses, according to Berkson, is dependent upon the level of food deprivation. That motivation is not completely controlled by equal periods of food deprivation is, therefore, an important variable, and equalizing the degree of food deprivation in individuals differing in age and nutritional status is a difficult and controversial problem.

In contrast to this difficult delayed-response test, age differences are not so marked in simple oddity-task discrimination and reversal learning in the dog, but there is a greater range of variability in subjects at 5 and 8 wk of age (see earlier). Harlow (1959) concludes that increased learning ability is demonstrated in two ways: most simple problems are mastered with increasing speed as the individual matures until it reaches the point of greatest maturity for the functions involved, and increasingly complex problems fall within the ability of the animal as it matures, independent of special experience. Thus, it is a matter of maturation rather than of learning by practice.

Summary

These observations indicated that the acquisition of adaptive behavior patterns to the experimental situation in which the delayed response was elaborated improved with age up to 12 wk. This may be correlated with the development of internal inhibition, and with the phasic, sequential evolution of excitatory and inhibitory processes in the elaboration of acquired activities. That learning ability did not improve directly as a function of age was supported by the observations of Sedlacek et al. (1961) and Stelmak'h (1959), who proposed that reflex acts, which are originally generalized, undergo inhibition and that they later become specialized and adaptive units of behavior. The inferior abilities observed at 16 wk compared with the 12-wk group might have been due to lack of homogeneity between groups or to the presence of one of these ontogenetic phases which, owing to lack of internal inhibition, prejudiced the elaboration of the delayed responses.

Differences in Approach/Avoidance Behavior: Age and Socialization Variables

Introduction

Approach/avoidance as a natural phenomenon in the ambivalence of behavior in both young and adult animals has been extensively reviewed in terms of classical psychology by Miller (1961) and elaborated further by Schneirla (1965) to embrace ontogenetic and ethological concepts. In the adult dog, Krushinskii (1962) has found that early experience and inheritance may alter the intensities of approach and withdrawal responses in different breeds and crossbreeds of dog. Bacon and Stanley (1963) and Stanley (1965a) have shown that the dog running toward a human for contact reward is much like a rat running for food, but because the dog is a highly social animal, the presence of a human can act as an incentive and be of reward value (see also Stanley and Elliot 1962; Stanley, Morris, and Trattner 1965). Moreover, their investigation showed that pups with decreased human contact (the "unsatiated" group) ran faster toward the observer than those with human contact just before the experiment (the "satiated" group). With these considerations in mind, the following experiment was designed to investigate the possible existence of age differences in the effects of aversive (electroshock) conditioned inhibition on approach behavior of the dog to a human observer. The age groups studied were selected to coincide with the early, middle, and late parts of the critical period of socialization (Scott and Marston 1950), in an attempt to provide further information on the processes underlying this age-limited phenomenon of socialization. In view of Scott's (1962) observations that social isolation overnight is an effective means of causing emotional arousal, we employed this to induce the pups to leave the start box and run toward a passive human. Genetic variables were not controlled, but early experience variables were controlled insofar as all animals were reared under similar conditions before testing.

Materials and Methods

A total of 41 dogs (beagles and crossbred shelties and mongrels) in good physical condition were used in the investigation. All dogs chosen were reared under similar standards of management and nutrition and were cared for on a strict schedule by laboratory personnel who were not involved in the testing procedures (no handling; fed twice daily; pens cleaned every 2 days). Treatment was assigned to randomly selected pups, using the split-litter technique, and littermates were housed together in numbers of not less than 4 per litter. Control and shocked subjects were tested in the following age groups: 5–6 wk (8 shocked and 6 control), 8–9 wk (8 shocked and 7 control) and 12–13 wk (8 shocked and 4 control). The apparatus consisted of a start box (18″ × 22″ × 24″), which was opened by a pulley operating a sliding "guillotine" gate which led into a runway. The runway consisted of 3 ft high sides and was 6 ft long. At the end opposite the start box (the "reward" end), the observer was seated. Before each daily test all subjects were isolated from each other overnight. Testing was done at the same time each morning. Ten trials were given daily for 5 consecutive days and then repeated 7 and 14 days after the last trial. An assistant handled the dogs between trials, but no handling was done by the observer (or "shock" or "reward" human). The time each subject spent in the start box when the door was open and the time taken for the subject to reach and touch the extended hand of the observer were recorded. As soon as the pup touched the extended hand, its left ear was held for 5 sec. The interval between trials was 60 sec, during which time the subject was replaced in the start box by the assistant and released after 60 sec. Shocked subjects received 200 μamp electroshock for 5 sec on the left ear when they touched the extended hand of the

TABLE 5.8

CONDITIONED AVOIDANCE IN THE DOG AT DIFFERENT AGES

(Averaged Scores from Trials 1–5)

MEASUREMENTS	5–6 WK		8–9 WK		12–13 WK	
	Shocked 8[a]	Controls 6	Shocked 8	Controls 7	Shocked 8	Controls 4
Time in box (sec)	10.5	1.1	6.2	2.9	2.7	2.6
Approach time (sec)	43.5	6.0	30.8	14.4	16.2	6.3
No. shocks received	15.5	....	23.5	....	39.5	....

[a] Number of dogs.

operator, but were not shocked on the "recovery trials" 1 and 2 wk after the last consecutive trial day. Nonshocked controls were handled similarly, with the observer's hand holding the left ear for 5 sec.

Some subjects could not be used in this study because they refused to leave the start box at the first trial. It was therefore necessary to discard extremely fearful dogs. One pup in the 5–6-wk age group, 3 in the 8–9, and 1 in the 12–13-wk group could not be used in the experiment. This variable was unavoidable and illustrates the great individual differences in normal approach/withdrawal behavior in this species.

Results

From the averaged daily scores for approach running time, marked differences in the three age groups are apparent (figs. 5.9, 5.10). Control subjects in the youngest age group, in spite of inferior locomotor abilities, approached significantly faster than those in the 8–9-wk age group ($p = .071$, Mann-Whitney U two-tail test at .05 significance level), and statistically insignificant differences between the 5–6- and 12–13-week-old controls were apparent ($p = .086$, table 5.8). By the 3d day of testing, most subjects in all groups reached a stable response level. Data from trials 2–5 were statistically analyzed, the first trial being regarded as a shaping period for these approach times. Shocked subjects differed significantly in approach times compared with their controls in the 5–6- and 8–9-wk groups ($p < .05$ and $p < .05$

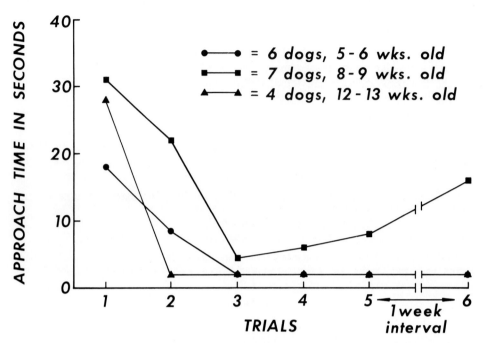

Fig. 5.9. Average approach times are significantly slower in the 8–9-wk-old dogs than the sustained short approach times of the 4–5- and 12–13-wk groups.

AVERAGE APPROACH SCORES IN SHOCKED DOGS

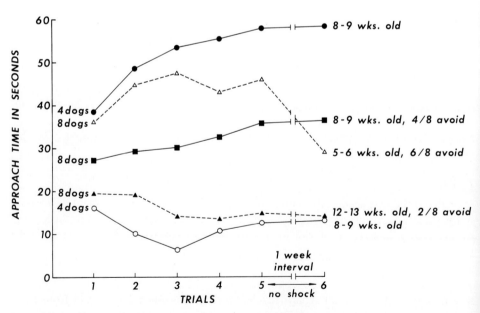

Fig. 5.10. Slow approach times in 5–6-wk group followed by recovery after 1 wk contrasted to consistently short approach times of 12–13-wk group. Results for 8–9-wk group have been divided to show consistent approach in half and avoidance with no recovery in remaining subjects.

respectively, Mann-Whitney U two-tail test), but the 12–13-wk shocked subjects did not differ significantly from their controls ($p = .086$). In the 5–6-wk subjects the majority (6 out of 8) learned to avoid shock by not approaching the observer, but showed dramatic recovery (7 out of 8) on the subsequent retests without shock 1 wk later. In contrast to the rapid recovery of the 5–6-wk-old pups, 4 pups in the 8–9-wk shocked group did not approach when retested (fig. 5.10). Attempts to "rehabilitate" these 8-wk-old dogs by using food reward or running the dog with a control subject were ineffectual. Averaging the individual time scores of the pups that approached and others that avoided in the 8–9-wk age group, a marked similarity was apparent between the 8–9-wk "approach" pups and the 12–13-week group, and between the 8–9-week "avoiding" pups and the 5–6-wk group (fig. 5.10). Ambivalence of the approach/avoidance pattern was seen by the 3d trial day, when stable approach or avoidance responses were established. In the 12–13-wk group, nearly all the subjects (6 out of 8) constantly ran into shock. This was not attributed to changes in sensitivity to shock, because increasing the intensity to 500 ma for a duration of 15 sec, although provoking intense distress vocalization, in no way reduced the approach tendency in later studies with these dogs. Consequently, the total number of shocks received was greatest in the 12–13-wk group. Also in the 12–13-wk group, the shortest times spent in the open start box were recorded (table 5.8). Statistical analysis (Kruskal-Wallis one-way analysis of variance by ranks) of the number of shocks received in each group revealed a significant difference between the 5–6-wk and 12–13-wk groups ($p < .05$). The 8–9-wk group, because of the ambivalence of approach/avoidance, was not statistically significant when the total number of shocks received was compared with the other age groups.

Discussion

The similar reactions of the dogs receiving shock in the 5–6-wk-old age group may be due to the delayed appearance of individual differences in behavior of young animals until several weeks after birth. By 7–8 wk, avoidance behavior emerges and overshadows approach responses; it is so strong that if socialization with man is prevented until after 4 mo of age, intense avoidance of all human beings occurs (Freedman et al. 1961). From the ambivalence of results in the 8–9-wk group, in that some shocked subjects approach and others avoid, we may postulate that either socialization with man has only been partially established in some pups at this age or that the intensity of approach behavior varies among individuals. This latter explanation would fit Krushinskii's concepts of the balance and varying intensities of approach and withdrawal responses in adult dogs (which he termed the active and passive defensive reflexes). However, ambivalence is not seen in the 12–13-wk group, and the stronger approach into shock may indicate an increment in socialization or emotional attachment to man and represent an anxiety-reduction mechanism. This marked difference in the 8–9-wk shocked subject suggests that by this age some pups have developed strong attachment to man, whereas other individuals having similar exposure to humans have not yet developed strong attachments and therefore avoid shock. Individual (genetic) differences in timidity, perceptual ability, and pain sensitivity may be involved. The slower approach scores of control subjects in the 8–9-wk group support the observations of Freedman et al. (1961) that avoidance behavior (or fear of a passive handler) emerges around

7–8 wk of age. Similarly, according to Scott (1962), fear of novel objects develops at 7 wk. As all subjects were reared in litter groups and had contact with humans only during feeding, the data from the shocked subjects imply that emotional attachment to man increases up to 12–13 wk of age. Thus, in light of the critical period of socialization hypothesis, exposure to humans results in socialization during 3½– 12 wk of age. There is a gradual increment in emotional attachment with increasing age during this period, which accounts for the strong approach behavior in pups receiving shock at 12–13 wk. Ambivalent results in the 8–9-wk group may indicate that fewer pups at this age are fully socialized than older pups which have been exposed for a longer period to the scheduled human care by laboratory personnel. The rapid "recovery" of conditioned avoidance in the 5–6-wk pups compared with the poor recovery rates in the 8–9-wk pups that avoid shock may be due to unstable conditioning or inferior retention in younger subjects. This may indicate that traumatic experience has the greatest effect around 8–9 wk of age, retention being unstable in younger pups. It may be argued that recovery from shock-avoidance is greatest in the youngest age group because retention of the conditioned response is less stable. Conditionability (assessed by the number of trials required to produce a stable response) is essentially similar in all age groups, however. When correlating these observations with the running times of the control subjects, we may postulate that traumatic avoidance learning is facilitated in those subjects in which avoidance behavior is at maximal intensity. Thus, there is greater retention and stability of the conditioned response in accordance with the behavior (or Pavlovian "nervous typology") of the subject. If avoidance behavior varies in intensity at certain times, conditioned avoidance reactions should therefore be more readily established in naïve subjects at certain ages. Stelmak'h (1959), using Pavlovian conditioning (motor alimentary), found that at 3 wk of age there is no external inhibition of the CR, whereas between 3½ and 6½ wk marked inhibition can be established. From 8 to 12 wk of age, external inhibition is again difficult to establish. In periods in which there is avoidance behavior, external inhibition is strong; but in periods where avoidance behavior (or passive defensive reflex) is weak or absent and approach behavior predominant, inhibition of the CR is difficult to produce. He concluded that generalized inhibition at 3 wk is due to insufficient maturity of the cerebrum, and as inhibition increases avoidance behavior emerges. A similar pattern is essentially evident in the present investigation, where conditioned inhibition of approach behavior is best established at 8–9 wk, being unstable in the younger 5–6-wk age group and difficult to establish in the older 12–13-wk group. Comparable results were reported by James and Binks (1963), who find that chickens are capable of escaping from shock at birth but do not learn to avoid shock until after 3 days of age. In comparing our data with those of Stelmak'h, the ages when these different reactions occur do not coincide, but the basic pattern is evident. These differences may be attributed to the different responses evaluated in these two investigations. The findings of Stelmak'h (1959) support the ethological studies of Freedman, King, and Elliot (1961), who observed that avoidance behavior develops after approach behavior (in accordance with Schneirla's theory [1965]), reaching greatest intensity around the 2d mo. Familiarization (habituation) and socialization to strange objects and subjects (novel stimuli or human beings) can be readily accomplished at this time, but if delayed until after 3 mo socialization is extremely difficult to establish. These data support the general concept that there is an "anxiety" period or time when avoidance behavior reaches maximal intensity in the ontogeny of nonprecocial mammals (Schneirla 1965; Spitz and Wolf 1946). This phenomenon is variable among different individuals, and inherited factors may be involved, which in turn may also modify learning and the effects of early experience. A similar anxiety or fear period has been recognized in precocial animals, and in birds it develops after the initial phases of imprinting and following. Sluckin (1965) and Hinde (1966) postulate that this fearfulness of unfamiliar objects indicates that the young bird has, through exposure learning, developed the ability to recognize and to respond adaptively to sudden changes in its environmental milieu. In this context, it is interesting to note that Brown (1964) found that there is a critical period at around 5 days of age (as contrasted with the 1st day for social imprinting), at which time chicks learn the stimulus properties of motionless objects in their environment; that is, a process akin to exposure learning and attachment to their home environment. A comparable mechanism of "exposure learning" underlying the development of fearfulness may also be present in nonprecocial mammals such as the dog. The appearance of this fear of the unfamiliar and sensitivity to environmental stimuli occurs later in life because perceptual development is more gradual in the dog. Comparable observations have been made by Sackett (1966b), who found that isolation-raised monkeys between 2½ and 4 mo of age showed marked disturbance in operant control of visual stimuli when a picture of a "threatening" monkey was presented; this sudden emergence of fearfulness may suggest that an innate releasing mechanism is operating. This change in responsiveness may be a function of improved perceptual abilities or of gradual maturation of higher levels of CNS activity (Bronson 1965). A sudden decline in open-field activity may not be due to fearfulness, but may actually arise from a cumulative effect of the total influx of novel stimuli as sense modalities mature (Thiessen 1965). Similar to Thiessen's observations in mice, Frankova (1966) noted that there is a sudden decrease in exploratory behavior in the rat between the 20th and 25th days of age.

Rosenblum and Harlow (1963) report that surrogate-reared monkeys spend more time on their surrogates than do controls if they are given intermittent aversive stimulation (air blast) while in contact with their surrogates. Their results are in contrast to expectations based on Miller's formulation of approach/withdrawal behavior. These observations, where the monkeys are more emotionally attached to their surrogates if traumatized while in contact with the surrogate, support the present findings in the 12–13-wk-old shocked pups, which approached the human faster than younger age groups receiving nociceptive stimulation. Fisher (1955) concluded from studies of differentially raised wirehaired fox terriers that the process of socialization is not inhibited by punishment, and may even be speeded up. The age variable in the development of emotional attachment and the problem of anxiety reduction after nociceptive stimulation in heightening emotional attachment are to be considered in the ontogeny of social behavior. In this experiment the effects of shock inhibition of approach behavior are found to vary with the age of the subject. This variability is related to the emergence of learned responses, which become stabilized and underlie the development of emotional attachments during the critical period of socialization.

Summary

Control subjects received approximately 5 sec contact and shocked subjects received 5 sec electroshock, provided they approached the observer and made contact with his extended hand. In the control subjects, slowest approach responses occurred in the 8–9-wk-old group. Traumatic experience (shock) had its greatest effect (i.e., slowest recovery rates) in the 8–9-wk age group, in those shocked subjects that developed avoidance responses. Half of the pups in this age group did not avoid shock, however, but approached instead. This ambivalence was attributed to individual differences in the effects of human contact before testing which had socializing effect in some. Shock did not cause avoidance in older subjects 12–13 wk of age, suggesting an increment in socialization or emotional attachment to man. Similar treatment at 5–6 wk caused avoidance, but there was rapid recovery when the dogs were retested without shock, indicating poor retention or unstable conditioned avoidance.

Development of Exploratory Behavior

Introduction

Berlyne (1960) has pointed out that one common type of exploration is inspection. Various types of objects or stimuli seem to evoke a response of approaching, with visual stimulation playing a major role and olfactory, auditory, or tactual stimulation also being shown to have importance. The one basic property of inspective locomotor exploration is novelty. In the rat, for instance, a preference is shown to "new" objects over previously exposed ones (Berlyne 1950).

In higher mammals the frequency of both play and exploration seems to reach a peak during childhood, with each species having its own maximal age period (Welker 1961). As age increases, external stimuli seem to lose their potency for initiating exploration. Welker has suggested that the motivation of exploratory and play behavior must depend upon stimulus novelty, habituation of responses with increased exposure to stimuli, recovery of habituation, and stimulus preferences and aversions. Age and phylogenetic differences should be related to these points.

Although a great deal of work has been done with a wide range of species regarding both exploratory and play behavior (Fowler 1965; Welker 1961; Barnett 1958; Berlyne 1966; Burgers 1966), very little investigation has been done with the canine species, especially developmentally. The present discussion examines the ontogeny of exploratory behavior in the dog under two standard conditions of measurement, longitudinal and cross-sectional. An attempt is made to elucidate ontogenetic and experiential variables which may enhance or modify the development of exploratory behavior in the dog.

Materials and Methods

An 8-sided behavior arena approximately 8′ × 8′, equipped with one-way windows for observation, which was previously described in the delayed response study, was used for all testing. Two groups of 57 dogs (35 beagles and 22 mongrels) were tested: litters were split and the subjects were randomly placed in one of two groups (cross-sectional or longitudinal) after being divided into groups according to sex and breed. Male and female mongrel and beagle subjects were assigned as evenly as possible among the various groups to avoid any experimental bias attributable to an excessive number of one sex or breed in any one group. The subjects were handled (being taken to and from the arena) only just before and after testing. All subjects received the same standards of management and feeding and were weaned at 4 wk and 4 days of age. They were on ad-lib feeding 2–3 hr before testing, and the time of testing was the same for all animals. Subjects were raised together in litter groups of no less than 3 and no more than 6 in $3'6'' \times 10'$ pens. During routine cleaning and feeding they were not handled by laboratory personnel, nor were they allowed out of their pens. No manipulatable objects were in the pens, other than a fixed water bowl and a food bowl which was placed on the floor. The pens were indoors, and each pen faced the same direction so that pups received similar visual and auditory experiences while in confinement. A timer switch provided 16-hr illumination, which was distributed evenly over all the pens.

In the longitudinal group 16 dogs (3 male and 3 female beagles and 6 male and 4 female mongrels) were tested as outlined below and retested at 5, 8, 12, and 16 wk in the following manner: on day 1, reactions to a handler were evaluated. The subject was placed in one corner of an empty arena with the experimenter in the opposite corner, who then called and coaxed the pup to come to him (approach). The pup was ranked on the following scale: 3 = strong approach (25 sec or less to come to and remain by experimenter); 2 = moderate approach (over 25 sec, but under 120 sec, and not remaining with experimenter); 1 = no approach (stayed in corner).

In the second test (following) the pup was placed in the center of the arena and the experimenter walked around trying to get the pup to follow. In the third test (recovery), contiguous with the second test, the experimenter suddenly turned and walked toward the pup, clapping his hands loudly to inhibit following; then the experimenter walked around trying to make the subject continue to follow.

All three tests (approach, following, and recovery) had a time limit of 2 min, and the method of ranking scores was the same for each test (see Fox 1968 for further details of this test).

On day 2, each pup was placed singly in a start box ($6'6'' \times 3' \times 2'6''$) with three 8″ wide, 14″ high openings spaced 12″ apart on a hinged iron-mesh door through which the pup could see the arena. The stimuli in the arena consisted of two standard size rat cages ($1' \times 1'6'' \times 1'6''$), one of which contained an adult albino rat, an Eveready 6-v battery that emitted a flashing red light every .5/sec (the entire battery being covered with cloth), a plastic toy pup ($2' \times 1'4''$) taped to the floor, a mirror ($1'3'' \times 2'$) mounted on the wall, and a speaker covered by a wooden box ($1' \times 1'6''$). The speaker was hooked to an amplifier from a Grass stimulator model S4, 115 v, that emitted a click every .5/sec. (The spatial relationships of these stimuli are shown in fig. 5.11.)

Four observers standing behind one-way windows took one or two of the five following measures during the 15-min test period for each subject. There was no control for observer bias, since the measures and criteria were rather straightforward.

Time Out of the Start Box. After placing the subject in the center of the start box, the experimenter left the arena. The time taken by the pup to come completely out of the start box and into the arena was recorded. If the pup did not come out within a 10-min period, it was taken from the start box and placed in the center of the arena. The test was stopped at this point. Observations were continued, however, for 5 more min.

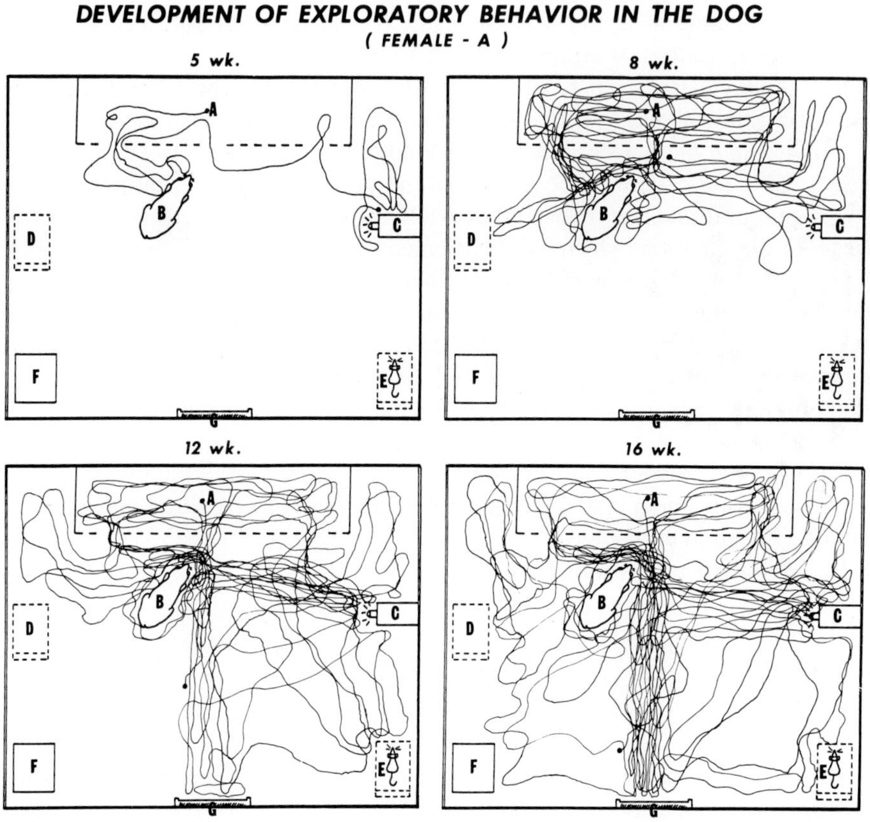

DEVELOPMENT OF EXPLORATORY BEHAVIOR IN THE DOG
(FEMALE - A)

Fig. 5.11. Activity of same subject at various ages during 15 min observations in arena

Vocalizations. The total number of barks and yelps for the 15 min period was recorded.

Activity. The total number of 30.5 cm squares, marked on the arena floor, that were crossed by the pup was assessed by setting the criterion of one-half or more of the body in each square to be counted as one.

Frequency of Interaction with Stimulus. Each time the pup came within 5 cm or less of any one of the stimuli in the arena and was oriented toward it, the object was recorded as having been approached once.

Duration of Interaction with Stimulus. Each time the pup came to the stimulus and remained there for 3 or more sec actively interacting (licking, chewing, smelling, etc.), the time was recorded until the pup left the stimulus.

The cross-sectional group comprised five independent groups of dogs that were tested only once at either 5 (1 male and 2 female beagles and 3 male and 1 female mongrels), 8 (2 male and 2 female beagles and 2 male and 1 female mongrels), 12 (2 male and 1 female beagles and 3 male and 3 female mongrels), or 16 wk of age (3 female and 1 male beagles, 3 male and 3 female mongrels). There was also an unrelated adult group of 8 dogs (1 male and 1 female beagle, 3 male and 3 female mongrels) with a mean age of 2 years. Females were non-estrous. The testing procedure in these subjects was the same as in the longitudinal group. In both groups, no attempt was made to control for odor on the individual stimuli, but odor-trails possibly laid by the footpads of the subjects were eliminated by washing the arena floor with Airkem deodorant between tests.

TABLE 5.9

CROSS-SECTIONAL GROUP

Age	Percentage of Animals Not out of Start Box in 10 Min	Percentage of Same Animals with Low Approach Scores
5 wk	43% (3/7)	100% (3/3)
8 wk	29% (2/7)	50% (1/2)
12 wk	33% (3/9)	33% (1/3)
16 wk	60% (6/10)	50% (3/6)
Total	34% (14/41)	57% (8/14)

Results

The approach scores to the human observer (initial, following, and recovery) were analyzed using the method of variance partition of ranked data (Winer 1962). For the measures of activity, vocalization, and time out of start box, the data for both groups were analyzed by nonparametric statistics (Siegel 1956). Level of significance was set at .01 for all tests.

Cross-sectional Group. Approach scores, activity, and vocalization were not significant across any of the age groups ($F = 1.4$, $H = 5.0$ and 4.9). Time out of start box, measured in seconds, did show a significant overall variance across ages ($H = 22.0$). The adult group had the shortest time out of the start box (between-group comparisons made by Mann-Whitney U test).

A 5×6 factorial design revealed that no relationship existed between various age groups and stimuli as to number of times they were approached (age $\times$ stimuli, $F = 1.2$). The time spent with the various objects did show an interaction effect between age and stimuli ($F = 2.5$). Here the 5-wk group spent more time with the rat in the cage than with any of the other stimuli, with the exception of the toy pup and the flashing light. The 8-wk group spent more time with the flashing light than with the rest of the test objects. After 8 wk of age no differences were seen (between-group comparisons made by Duncan range test).

Table 5.9 compares the percentage of animals that did not come out of the start box in 10 min with the percentage of those same animals that had low approach scores. Of the 14 dogs that did not come out of the start box. close to 60% had low approach to the human observer on the day before being tested for exploration to novel stimuli; 85% of these 14 animals did not interact with any of the stimuli when taken from the start box and placed in the center of the testing arena.

Longitudinal Group. The approach score measure revealed a nonsignificant chi-square value for differences across ages of retesting ($X^2 = 5.5$) (see fig. 5.11). The Freedman two-way analysis of variance for K-related sample did yield a significant chi-square for the measures of activity and vocalization ($X^2 = 15.0$ and

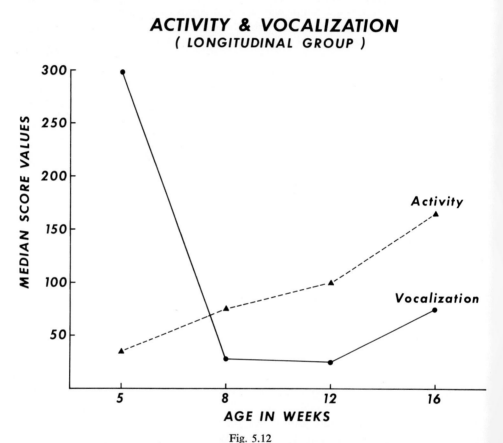

Fig. 5.12

11.2 respectively). By 16 wk there was an increase in activity when compared with other ages of retesting. Vocalization dropped significantly after 5 wk and no between-retesting age differences were noted. Figures 5.12 and 5.13 compare the two measures for both groups. Vocalization scores were markedly skewed but declined across retesting ages. Activity scores were positively accelerated with increasing age. In contrast the cross-sectional group showed a great deal of variation, low activity scores and high vocalization scores being obtained from most subjects after 8 wk of age (fig. 5.12). The significance of this will be discussed subsequently. Time out of start box revealed no differences across age ($X^2 = 6.7$).

Frequency and duration of interaction with stimuli were analyzed by using a $4 \times 6 \times 16$ repeated-measure factorial design. Both of these measures yielded significant interactions between age and stimuli ($F = 7.4, 4.4$). Only the toy pup was approached more than any of the other stimuli at 5 and 8 wk, and at 12 wk the mirror was included. By 16 wk the mirror was the only stimulus approached more than the other objects. More time was spent with the toy pup and flashing light at 5 and 8 wk, whereas at 12 and 16 wk there was a switch, more time being spent with the mirror.

Table 5.10 compares all measures using correlation coefficients. A t-test for

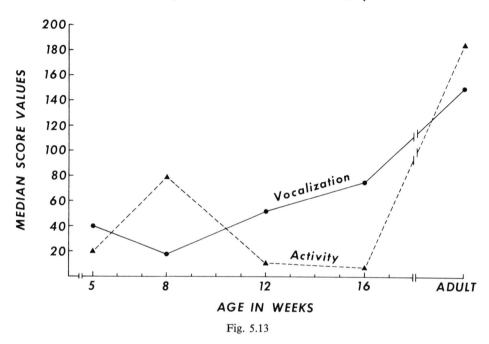

ACTIVITY & VOCALIZATION
(CROSS-SECTIONAL GROUP)

Fig. 5.13

zero correlation was then done with level of significance again set at .01. At each age of testing and retesting, those subjects that showed the highest activity scores were the same subjects that approached more objects and spent less time in the start box. After 5 wk those subjects that approached the various objects also were the ones that remained and interacted with the stimuli. The most sociable pups, as determined by the reaction to human test, tended to be the more exploratory individuals and also showed the lowest time in the start box.

No differences were seen between breeds or sexes on any test measures. With a larger sample size, though, the influence of breed and sex on exploratory behavior might be revealed, as Dykman, Murphree, and Ackerman (1966) have shown with two strains of pointer.

Qualitative Observation (*Both Groups*). The following qualitative observations from the longitudinal group are briefly summarized to give some intimation of differences in reactivity at different ages. At 5 wk of age, most pups wagged their tails at the toy pup and flashing light. Only one pup showed approach/withdrawal (A/W) to click and flashing light, and only one pup interacted with all stimuli.

At 8 wk, several pups showed approach/withdrawal ambivalence (A/W) to the rat and to the mirror, although the toy pup and flashing light were approached by most subjects. Some pups climbed onto the light during play and clasped it and showed copulatory pelvic thrusts. One pup looked at the light from a distance of 2 ft and began pelvic thrusting.

By 12 wk the mirror was most readily approached, although some dogs showed an initial A/W before making a positive approach. Both toy pup and flashing light were investigated. One subject "pointed" to the rat, and one was highly aroused by the click.

At 16 wk of age, reactions similar to those at 12 wk were observed, notably high interest in the mirror, with some initial A/W ambivalence. Both toy pup and flashing light were investigated; one subject mounted the light and showed pelvic thrusts. One subject spent the last 6 min of the test jumping up against the arena walls attempting to escape. No such reactions were observed at earlier ages, other than distress vocalization.

TABLE 5.10

COMPARED MEASURES BY RANK CORRELATION

(Longitudinal Group)

MEASUREMENTS	AGE (wk)				
	5	8	12	16	Total
Activity: Objects approached	.86[a]	.68[a]	.89[a]	.82[a]	.89[a]
Activity: Time in box	−.70[a]	−.20	.28	−.20	−.60[a]
Activity: Vocalizations	.17	.54	.36	.52	.39
Activity: Interaction time	.47	.55	.74[a]	.70[a]	.70[a]
Vocalization: Interaction time	−.10	.12	.58	.62[a]	.25
Vocalization: Interaction frequency	.26	.49	.46	.52	.50
Vocalization: Time in box	−.50	−.20	.10	.10	.37
Objects Approached: Interaction time	.28	.77[a]	.87[a]	.75[a]	.79[a]
Interaction Time: Time in box	−.30	−.50	.25	−.20	−.50
Objects Approached: Time in box	−.50	−.50	.25	−.20	−.50
Approach score: Interaction frequency					.55
Approach score: Interaction time					.34
Approach score: Vocalization					.39
Approach score: Activity					.62[a]
Approach score: Time in box					−.73[a]

[a] $p = .01$.

TABLE 5.11

MEAN STIMULUS INTERACTION FREQUENCIES IN 5-WK-OLD
ISOLATION-RAISED AND CONTROL PUPS

Group	Toy Pup	Flashlight	Mirror	Activity (Squares)
Isolates (N = 6)	10.8 (7-13)[a]	7.1 (5-11)	4.1 (1-7)	174 (91-260)
Controls (N = 5)	5.8 (3-7)	5.0 (3-8)	0.6 (0-1)	129.5 (82-191)

[a] Range of scores is shown in parentheses.

In contrast, adult dogs from the cross-sectional group showed a very brief interaction with every stimulus and intense interaction with the mirror. Most adults jumped up at the walls of the arena and attempted to escape. Several showed A/W to the mirror, rat, and flashing light. Only in adults was a standing-up reaction seen; they would stand up on their hind legs in the middle of the arena and appear to scan the arena visually. No similar reaction has been observed in younger dogs.

An interesting displacement or compromise reaction between turning away, preparatory to withdrawing, and turning toward the stimulus to explore it was observed in a number of dogs, especially at 12 and 16 wk of age and in adults. The subject rapidly turned its head laterally away from the stimulus toward which it was oriented and looked at its flank (see chap. 2).

In several pups aged 8 wk, spontaneous self-play was observed while the animal was in the middle of the arena and not in contact with or oriented toward any stimulus. This self-play resembled a vacuum activity and possibly resulted from the animal's being aroused by the novelty and complexity of its environment, but not being fearful.

A number of older subjects, from 12 wk onward, predominantly in the cross-sectional group, would curl up and apparently go to sleep during the observation period. They remained either in a corner of the start box or in a corner of the arena, if they had come out of the start box voluntarily or had been removed after remaining in the start box for 10 min. When first placed in the start box, these dogs were extremely inactive, and would often shiver, defecate, and urinate. Once they had assumed a sleeping posture, they were easily aroused by a sudden noise but would promptly appear to go back to sleep again. This reaction, possibly displacement sleep as a result of intense arousal, has been described by Pavlov and his school as occurring in certain dogs during conditioning (hypnoticlike state), and has recently been discussed by Delius (1967), with other displacement activities, in relation to arousal and conflict.

In three litters from the longitudinal group, social dominance hierarchies were determined at 17 wk of age using the bone-in-pen test (Scott and Fuller 1965; see also Fox 1968). In two of these litters a female was found to be the dominant individual, and data from the exploratory tests showed that these two dogs ranked lowest in attraction scores to the handler and in exploratory activity and time out of start box. From this small sample it may be that socially dominant animals are not necessarily the most friendly toward humans or the most outgoing and exploratory.

Discussion

The stimuli chosen for this study were arbitrarily selected according to modality and complexity. Complexity was subjectively thought to be as follows, in ascending order: empty cage, click, flashing light, toy pup, rat in cage, mirror. Reactions might be based on complexity, but stimulus preference might depend on earlier associations. Thus the mirror was correctly predicted as being more stimulating than the rat in the cage, or any of the other stimuli in older dogs, and the flashing light and toy pup were preferred over the click and empty cage at all ages. Exploration may be a function not only of novelty and previous experience but also of stimulus distance and complexity (see also Hinde 1954 and Schneirla 1965).

Because of the proximity of certain stimuli to the start box (toy pup and flashing light) it may be argued that younger pups would approach these objects more readily and would not perceive or respond to objects at a greater distance (such as the mirror or rat in cage). Some pups at 5 and 8 wk of age did, however, respond to these more distant stimuli. The possibility of position familiarity as well as stimulus familiarity was undoubtedly involved in the longitudinal group.

To investigate this problem further, one group of 5-wk-old pups was tested in the arena after 1 wk of partial social and sensory isolation (following the method described in chap. 6). All 5-wk-old isolates reacted more to the mirror than did nonisolates at this age (table 5.11), supporting the hypothesis presented in chapter 6 that isolates, on initial emergence from isolation, are highly aroused and appear to interact with abnormal perceptual (peripheral or central?) filtering processes. This may suggest, therefore, that with increasing age in normal pups there is an increasing preference for more complex stimuli, in accordance with the central excitatory state (or arousal) and perceptual filtering processes; exploratory behavior and stimulus preferences may reflect the degree of input necessary to maintain perceptual homeostasis, or in Berlyne's (1960) terminology, the quest for intermediate arousal potential.[1] Individual differences (and breed differences, Krushinskii 1962; Melzack 1952; Mahut 1958; Fuller and Clark 1966a; and Gregory 1967) in exploratory behavior may therefore reflect innate differences in the organization of the autonomic and central nervous systems.

It may be postulated that gradual development of peripheral receptors would result in a greater input, so that the organism must develop filtering processes to exclude irrelevant information and to inhibit nonreinforced responses (i.e., internal inhibition). In this regard, both Thiessen (1965) and Frankova (1966) observe a drop in exploratory activity, in infant mice and rats respectively, which is closely correlated with opening of the eyes and startle reactions to sound. Thus greater input results in a decrease in activity, which may reflect a homeostatic process to counterbalance the increased input. Activity subsequently increases, conceivably because perceptual filtering mechanisms are operating. However an isolation-raised animal, having had little exploratory experience, is incapable of separating (or filtering) relevant from irrelevant cues on the basis of previous experience; immature but normally raised animals are somewhat similar in their behavior to such isolation-raised subjects (Thompson and Heron 1954). It is significant that Sackett (1966a) finds that with increasing age infant monkeys prefer more complex stimuli, whereas isolation-raised subjects prefer less complex stimuli. He postulates a process involving paced increments of environmental complexity.

Even though the longitudinal group had a mere 15-min exposure to the novel stimuli and arena at widely separated intervals, this exposure was highly effective in facilitating subsequent exploratory behavior compared with the cross-sectional group. Although distress vocalization was high in all 5-wk-old pups, approach/ withdrawal ambivalence was rarely seen until 8 wk; in the longitudinal group this A/W ambivalence predominated at this age and persisted subsequently, but it was

---

[1] Mason (1967) has shown how the degree of arousal influences the organization of behavior during different stages of development in chimpanzees. He speaks of a "general motivational state" and describes how the animal attempts to maintain optimal levels of arousal in various social situations.

more frequently seen in the cross-sectional subjects.[2] It may be argued that the behavioral deficits manifest in the cross-sectional group after 8 wk might be due to inadequate socialization and lack of handling, and not principally to experiential deprivation. This is improbable in view of the findings, that pups raised under the same conditions as the cross-sectional subjects in the present study showed clear evidence of a strong emotional attachment to man by 12 wk of age (see chap. 6, p. 249).

We are unable to account for the high interaction with the caged rat observed in some of the 5-wk-old subjects from the cross-sectional group. Also, distress vocalization scores were less in this age group than in subjects of the same age in the longitudinal group. In both groups however, there was a marked decrease in distress vocalization between 5 and 8 wk of age, indicating that earlier in life separation from littermates was more disturbing, as shown by Elliot and Scott (1961) and Ross et al. (1960). Between 5 and 8 wk of age there was a marked increase in activity, in contrast to this decline in distress vocalization; but in contrast to the longitudinal group, activity subsequently declined in the cross-sectional group and distress vocalization again increased.[3] These differences in the two groups clearly illustrate that previous experience in the arena facilitates subsequent exploratory activity and reduces the stressfulness of the situation in the longitudinal group. In sharp contrast, the cross-sectional subjects, having had no previous experience, show a dramatic decline in activity, especially at 12 and 16 wk of age, together with an increase in distress vocalization. The high activity and vocalization in the adults were associated with attempts to escape from the arena.

These findings imply that the so-called normal rearing conditions of the laboratory, in which litters of pups are raised in relatively large (4' × 12') pens, produce severe deficits in exploratory behavior in a novel environment, and reflect an experiential decrement of rearing in an "impoverished" environment. The effects of such treatment may be aggravated by genetic factors in certain breeds or strains (Fuller and Clark 1968). Subjects from the longitudinal group, however, have an experiential increment as a result of previous exposure to novel stimuli. Thus exploratory experience and familiarity facilitate subsequent exploration. The duration of interaction tends to fall with increasing age in the longitudinal group, but frequency does not, indicating that objects that were preferred earlier in life are still investigated, and that although their releasing power may be little altered, some habituation occurs so that older animals are less stimulus-bound. In this regard, Welker (1956) found that in older (7–8 yr) chimpanzees, the response to novel objects waned more rapidly than in younger (1–2 yr) subjects, and that the latter were more cautious in their initial responses. In the cross-sectional group, after 8 wk of age, the frequency and duration of interaction with various stimuli were similar

---

[2] Fuller (1967) has observed such A/W ambivalence and even more bizarre behavior in isolation-raised dogs when first placed in a novel environment: an overwhelming fear response to novelty may be operating.

[3] Recent studies of wild canids (Fox 1971a) have shown that distress vocalization is consistently inhibited after 4–5 wk when subjects are placed in an unfamiliar environment. At this age in the domesticated dog there is great variation, some individuals vocalizing constantly, others remaining silent. These comparative findings indicate that distress vocalization may be a poor indicator of emotional arousal at this age in canids, and therefore may account for the sample differences in vocalization scores in the longitudinal and cross-sectional groups.

at different ages, suggesting that habituation processes after 8 wk are relatively mature. Nikitina and Novikova (cited by Lynn 1966), using conditioning techniques, report that habituation in the dog attains mature levels by 8 wk of age, thus supporting these behavioral observations.

Menzel (1963) has observed the effects of repeated exposure of isolation-raised chimpanzees to novel objects; such cumulative experience resulted in an increase in exploration (grasping and manipulating), as was observed in the longitudinal group in the present study. Fuller and Clark (1966*b*) conclude that the postisolation depression in dogs raised in isolation is due not to perceptual deficits but to a blocking of approach and contact responses by preemptive aversive reactions to unfamiliar stimuli. We may draw similar conclusions from the data obtained from the cross-sectional group. At this point we may hypothesize that exploratory behavior and preference for stimuli of varying complexity depend upon (1) degree of development of peripheral receptors and filtering processes, (2) innate (genetic) differences in organization of neural substrata (central and autonomic nervous systems which influence the central excitatory state), (3) quantitative and qualitative experiences earlier in life, in addition to stimulus properties of novelty and complexity as emphasized by Berlyne (1960). Basically, therefore, differences in exploratory behavior between individuals are the result of different genotype-environment interactions and differences in the level of development of the CNS of the organism; age, genotype, and experiential differences are therefore contributory. As proposed by Hebb (1949) and subsequently confirmed in many studies involving "handling" (Levine and Broadhurst 1963; Denenberg 1964) or environmental enrichment (Forgus 1955) of various strains of mice and rats in early life, such early experiences influence subsequent exploratory behavior and emotional reactivity or fear. Under conditions of strong fear, exploratory behavior can be completely suppressed (Montgomery 1955). Halliday (1966) has demonstrated that motor activity per se may be nonspecific and not directly related to exploratory behavior but related to early rearing conditions (handling). Montgomery (1953) showed that activity deprivation had no influence on exploratory behavior; both restricted and exercised rate showed approximately the same amount of maze exploration; exploratory behavior cannot be explained in terms of an activity drive. Nissen (1930) reported that rats would cross an electrified grid in order to explore a complex maze; thus some "drive" to explore and to manipulate (Harlow, Harlow, and Meyer 1950) must be involved, such activities possibly being rewarding in themselves.

Ontogenetically, there may be a critical period for the onset of exploratory behavior which most probably occurs at the onset of the critical period of socialization (Scott 1962), which is characterized by the organism's having relatively mature perceptual and motor abilities. This period of perceptual and motor integration, implying a structurofunctional integration not only within the CNS but also between the organism and its environment (Hebb 1949; see also chap. 7), marks the onset of exploratory behavior and the organism's gradual integration with its environment. If such environmental interaction is restricted (as was disclosed in the present investigation under "normal" laboratory rearing conditions), the experiential decrement affects the organism's subsequent exploratory behavior and its preference for complexity. An organism exposed to a relatively complex environment early in life presumably becomes familiar with certain aspects of this environment; as its perception improves, more of this environment (facilitated by previous associations) is perceived and reacted to. Also on the basis of previous experience the organism can select (perceptual filtering) which stimuli are relevant, and can therefore organize its response patterns appropriately. An older but naïve animal, in similar circumstances, would have no reference points or associations, and if raised under impoverished conditions would not have the perceptual mechanisms elaborated to filter relevant from nonrelevant information. Thus all objects may be intensively investigated, so that such a subject appears to react like an immature organism (Thompson and Heron 1954), or the sudden increase in perceptual input causes excessive arousal and disrupts exploratory behavior (see chap. 6). This excessive arousal or "overload" may be manifest behaviorally as high frequency, short duration interaction with stimuli (chap. 6) or complete inhibition of exploratory behavior and avoidance of novel stimuli in older subjects (Fuller 1967). No such disturbances occur in animals having had previous experience, and their behavior may be so organized as to balance the amount of exploration with the amount of stimulation or input (i.e., perceptual-motor homeostasis).

In conclusion, some of the variables to be considered in evaluating exploratory behavior in animals will be briefly reviewed. There are age limitations on what the animal is able to perceive and respond to. There may be some perceptual selection as a result of previous experience reinforcement or association which may sensitize the organism (in terms of an image to search for or perceptual set), and behavior is patterned in accordance with its appropriate motivational category. Thus a motivational component may be added to the set or tuning of receptors and effectors. Certain components of a particular sensorimotor system may be precociously matured (i.e., "innate" receptor-effector specificity) independent of previous experience (Anokhin 1964). A novel stimulus may evoke intense arousal and the resulting central excitatory state may reflect the stimulus-complex releasing power of a given stimulus. The response or motor output will be a function of the stimulus-complex releasing power and central excitatory state, and will be affected by the degree of internal or reactive inhibition, this being influenced by previous experience and the individual nervous typology of the subject. Indeed, all reactions may be inhibited completely by a stimulus which has a high stimulus-complex releasing power but which evokes fear or withdrawal and consequently a high reactive inhibition which reduces the motor output.

The degree of stimulation or input sought by the animal in maintaining perceptual homeostasis is a function of its previous experience; if the set-point is low, as in an isolation-raised (or institutionalized) animal, the amount of stimulation required will be low, and the animal will show a preference for a less complex environment and less stimulation. Excessive stimulation (and therefore arousal) may be controlled by withdrawal or by self-directed arousal/anxiety-reducing reactions. An animal with a higher set-point will necessarily seek more stimulation, and to compensate for inadequate stimulation (as in certain species of captive wild animals) will develop repetitive stereotyped activities—"leerlauf" reactions—exaggerate or hypertrophy normal patterns, or vary these patterns and develop new patterns which may become highly stereotyped (Morris 1966).

Summary

On the basis of their reactions to various novel stimuli placed in an arena, the exploratory activity of 57 dogs was evaluated in the same subjects at 5, 8, 12, and 16 wk of age (longitudinal) or in subjects aged either 5, 8, 12, or 16 wk or adult (cross-section). In the longitudinal group, exploratory activity and preference for more complex stimuli increased with age. In the cross-sectional group, activity decreased markedly at 12 and 16 wk, indicating that "normal" laboratory rearing conditions can modify exploratory behavior, possibly as a result of experiential deficits. This effect was not attributable to inadequate socialization. Displacement and compromise activities, including flank-gazing and reactive sleep, are described and the effects of experience which may modify the ontogeny of behavior are discussed. It has been shown in this paper that rearing conditions may dramatically influence exploratory behavior. Experience before 12 wk of age in a novel environment appears critical for the subsequent development of qualitative and quantitative differences in exploratory behavior in naïve and experienced subjects.

6

Effects of Differential Early Experience on Behavioral Development

Transplanted by man into a thinking layer of the earth, heredity, without ceasing to be germinal (or chromosomatic) in the individual, finds itself, by its very life-centre, settled in a reflecting organism, collective and permanent, in which phylogenesis merges with ontogenesis.

Pierre Teilhard de Chardin, *The Phenomenon of Man*

Handling and Isolation

Introduction

A variety of stimuli and treatment methods have been used, differing in modality and intensity and thus differing in the degree of stress exerted upon the organism, to assess the effects of early experience or environmental variables on subsequent development (e.g., starvation stress or time of weaning, Novakova 1966; electroshock, Denenberg 1962*b*).

"Handling" and Stressful Stimulation in Early Life. The behavioral effects of "handling" or gentling, which essentially lowers body temperature (Schaefer 1963), and cold exposure or mild electroshock instigated either prenatally (Thompson and Sontag 1956; Thompson 1957; Broadhurst 1961; Denenberg 1963) or at specific times postnatally, have been reviewed by Beach and Jaynes (1954), King (1958), Thompson and Schaefer (1961), Denenberg (1962*b*, 1968), Levine (1962*b*), Ferreira (1965), and Morton (1968). Handling during the neonatal period results in animals that are more docile and less emotional (Levine 1957) and that possess superior learning abilities for certain test situations (Denenberg and Bell 1960; Bernstein 1957), although excessive stimulation in early life may cause a decline in learning performance because the animals become so phlegmatic that their motivation is deficient ("Yerkes-Dodson" law, Denenberg 1964);[1] animals also have heavier adrenal glands and elevated corticosteroid levels following handling or elec-

---

[1] Wilson, Warren, and Abbott (1965), for example, found that handled cats required more trials to learn an avoidance task, but made fewer errors than controls in a Hebb-Williams maze.

225

troshock (Levine 1962*a;* Ader et al. 1968), (although in later life novel or fear-evoking stimuli cause a lesser elevation of corticosteroids in handled rats or in the offspring of handled mothers than in nonhandled controls, Levine 1967); increased brain weight (Vernadakis et al. 1967), greater survival rates in stressful situations and to tumors[2] (Bovard 1954; Levine 1957; Ader 1965; Ader and Friedman 1965), and accelerated sexual maturation (Morton, Denenberg, and Zarrow 1963). Early postnatal development of locomotor patterns may also be accelerated (Gard et al. 1967). A wide variety of drugs (hormones, steroids, and tranquilizers, etc.) given prenatally or postnatally may affect the development of the brain and behavior (Jewett and Norton 1966; Thompson and Olian 1961; Curry and Heim 1966; Fuller, Clark, and Waller 1960; Zamenhof, Mosley, and Schuller 1966; Eayrs 1961; Pfaff 1966; Harris and Levine 1965; Werboff 1966; Schapiro and Norman 1967). The effects of ionizing radiation have recently been reviewed by Hicks and D'Amato (1966) (in this regard, Strobel, Clark, and MacDonald [1968] have found a sensitive period between 7 and 9 days of incubation in the chick, during which radiation has an effect on the later development of approach behavior; treatment before or after this period has little or no effect). The possible effects of the immune tolerant state have been explored by Kamarin (1967) in relation to imprinting in chicks.

Peters and Murphree (1966) found that young (2-mo-old) rats recovered faster (5 wk) in terms of exploratory activity and defecation, following only one 90 v shock for 2 sec, than similarly treated rats aged 7 mo (still abnormal after 6 mo). They emphasized that their results show the greater resilience of young animals and the need for caution in interpreting research and theories on early experience. Variables such as "early plasticity," immaturity, and instability of learning or conditionability should also be considered, and the limitations of the testing procedures should be used to evaluate the effects of such treatment, which may have different effects on subjects of different ages.

The various effects of rearing rats in an "enriched" or free environment have been described and confirmed by many researchers;[3] superior learning abilities, greater brain weights, and cortical thickness and elevated cholinesterase levels, for example, have been reported. These effects are compared with the "control" subject raised in a standard laboratory cage, which makes one question the "normality" of standard rearing conditions of laboratory animals. Handling and the effects of photic stimulation on acetylcholinesterase activity and protein metabolism have recently been reported by Kling, Finer, and Nair (1965) and Talwar et al. (1966).

Early handling, either prenatal (DeFries et al. 1967) or postnatal (or maternal deprivation, Newell 1967), also has a differential effect on animals of different strains or genetic backgrounds (King and Eleftheriou 1959; Levine and Broadhurst 1963; Joffe 1965*a, b*). Freedman (1958) reported that there are distinct breed differences in the effects of permissive versus disciplinary rearing in dogs; the interactions between genotype and experience may, therefore, produce wide variance among genetically different members of the same species. The age at which handling

---

[2] Not verified, however, by Otis and Scholler 1967.

[3] Hebb 1947; Levine and Alpert 1959; Rosenzweig et al. 1962; Bennett et al. 1964; Diamond et al. 1966; Diamond, Linder, and Raymond 1967; Tapp and Markowitz 1963; Geller, Yuwiler, and Zolman 1965; Forgus 1955, 1956; Singh, Johnston, and Klosterman 1967; and Gibson and Walk 1956.

is undertaken and the modality and intensity of stimulation can result in widely differing effects, suggesting that there are certain sensitive periods when a particular type of treatment has a maximal effect (Denenberg 1964, 1968; Denenberg and Kline 1964). Haltmeyer et al. (1966) have shown that the early postnatal effects of handling (which are blocked if the nest is kept at 35.5° C) are associated with ACTH release of corticosteroids. There is a decrease in effects of ACTH around 7 days, associated with a slightly earlier decrease in pituitary function. These data support the notion that the effects of handling are most clearly demonstrated during the first few days of life, after which a refractory period follows. Environmental factors influencing emotional and exploratory behavior of the organism may be transmitted to successive generations of offspring, in mice at least (Ressler 1966): these findings have been confirmed in Denenberg's laboratory (Denenberg and Rosenberg 1967).

Paulson (1965), Klosovskii (1963), Meier (1961), Wilson, Warren, and Abbott (1965), Peeler (1963), and White and Castle (1964) have studied the effects of supranormal stimulation on a variety of parameters, including EEG, visually evoked potentials in the duckling, vestibular neuron size in the dog, EEG activity and behavior in the cat, and ontogeny of the grasp reflex in the human infant. Excessive auditory and photic stimulation of the rat during pregnancy (Geber 1966) and photic stimulation of the chick during incubation in the egg (Tammimie and Fox 1967) can result in structural defects of the developing organism. The borderline between beneficial stimulation and stressful stimulation needs further clarification in regard to the intensity and modality of stimulation and possible existence of behavioral disturbances in the absence of any obvious teratologic anomaly.

Social and Sensory Deprivation and Subnormal Stimulation. As early as 1871, Darwin observed that the domesticated rabbit had a smaller brain than its wild counterpart and concluded that this was due to breeding under restricted environmental conditions.

Considerable research in recent years has been focused on the effects of rearing young animals under varying degrees of sensory and social isolation, which may range from complete social isolation (animals reared singly in soundproof boxes with no visual or auditory stimulation from their peers) to partial social isolation (animals reared singly without tactile access, with or without visual access, but with auditory access to peers and with olfactory stimulation owing to exposure to odors). Sensory isolation, or deprivation, may vary similarly in intensity, depending on the number of modalities that are experimentally blocked or denied stimulation, the age at which treatment is instigated, and the experience of the animal before isolation (Hymovitch 1952; Lessac 1966). Nyman (1967) has shown that problem-solving abilities in the rat are related to early experience during an experientially optimum critical period. He concluded that more experience during a less critical period may have results similar to that of less experience during the critical period, and that subsequent experiences in maturity do not compensate for earlier experiential deficits. Early social deprivation or isolation in phylogenetically diverse species such as fish (Shaw 1962), rats (Griffiths 1961; Moyer and Korn 1965), chickens (Padilla 1935; Siegel and Siegel 1964; Ratner 1965), dogs (Thompson, Melzack, and Scott 1956), rabbits (Scherrer and Fourment 1964), and songbirds (Thorpe

1964) can result in the emergence of a wide variety of behavioral and neurophysiological deficits or abnormalities in later life. Depression following maternal separation has been observed in infant monkeys (Kaufman and Rosenblum 1967). Krech, Rosenzweig, and Bennett (1966) found that in rats reared in social isolation or in an impoverished environment, brain weight and acetylcholinesterase activity were less than in controls or subjects reared in a complex environment. They did not observe the stressful effects of long-term isolation reported by Hatch et al. (1963). With findings similar to the behavioral observations of Fuller and Clark (1966*a, b*), Krech, Rosenzweig, and Bennett reported that rearing rats in pairs did not protect them from the cerebral changes caused by experiential impoverishment. In monkeys, stereotyped movements, self-directed and autistic behavior, inferior learning abilities, fear of novel objects, and unpredictable emotional reactions to slight environmental changes have been observed, and abnormalities in sexual and maternal behavior have been described by several investigators.[4] Ourth and Brown (1961), Casler (1961), Bowlby (1951, 1952, 1958), and Sackett (1965) have reviewed these problems in relation to child development. Kruijt (1964), in his studies on the development of social behavior in the Burmese jungle fowl, found that rearing males in partial visual isolation caused severe deficits in agonistic and sexual behavior; occasionally bizarre self-directed activities (including courtship) were seen. More drastic effects arose from complete visual isolation.

Shaw (1962) found that the type of environment in which the animal is restricted may produce widely different effects. In platyfish, she showed that those which were socially isolated in clear tanks and could see outside (but no other fish) were almost normal contrasted to the severe deficits in social behavior in fish raised alone in glass tanks with frosted or opaque sides. One may conclude that the organism is capable of creating to some extent a self-generated environment under conditions of isolation and deprivation. Along these lines, Morris (1966) proposes that the animal in a deprived environment either makes more variable the appetitive behavior available to it (e.g., cats will fling and catch or pounce on a piece of meat) or abnormally increases the amount of fixed consummatory activity (e.g., bears and ungulates overeat). These compensatory activities become stereotyped, and Morris concludes that ritualization in nature and stereotypy in zoo animals are similar, as both are the result of physical or psychological inhibition (e.g., fear/aggression/sexual conflicts in nature). Although these observations have been made primarily on animals that have had experience in their natural environment before captivity, similar mechanisms may be operating in animals which are born in captivity or are raised experimentally under deprived conditions that do not provide the normal range of stimulation for the development of normal behavior patterns (by "normal" we imply such factors as the context of their occurrence, frequency, direction, and motivation). Isolation may result in spontaneous regression of certain innate, species-characteristic behavior patterns. In both dog and monkey, isolation rearing results in many symptoms which resemble those of autistic children (Fox 1966*h;* Berkson and Mason 1964). Hyperactivity and stereotyped behavior are frequently seen in

---

[4] Seay, Hansen, and Harlow 1962; Berkson and Mason 1964; Harlow and Harlow 1962; Harlow, Harlow, and Hansen 1963; Harlow, Dodsworth, and Harlow 1965; Harlow et al. 1966; Jensen and Tolman 1962; Mason and Green 1962; Menzel 1963; Sackett, Porter, and Holmes 1965; Mitchell 1968; and Mitchell et al. 1966.

wild animals raised, but not born, in captivity (Hediger 1950), and also in animals reared under standard laboratory conditions (Fox 1965c). Berkson and Mason (1964) found that novel stimuli increased the level of stereotypy in the chimpanzee, and it is well known that sudden stimulation (e.g., loud noises) increases stereotyped behavior in laboratory animals. This increase is attributed to a high level of arousal or excitation produced by the stimulation. Disturbances in routine, which constitutes changes in stimulation, also increase stereotypy, but with learning or habituation to regular changes, some decrease in arousal and stereotypy occurs (Menzel 1963). Levy (1944) regarded stereotypy as an activity resulting from restraint of movements, and Hines (1942) postulated a mechanism for reducing anxiety.

Social and Sensory Isolation in the Dog. Thompson (1954) and Thompson and Heron (1954) reared pups in a restricted environment (partial social isolation) from 4 wk until 7–10 mo of age. These dogs were hyperactive (highly exploratory) in novel situations and were less competent to solve a simple maze problem. They also showed diffuse reactions to novel stimuli which control subjects either avoided if menacing or approached if apparently innocuous. These inappropriate responses to possibly noxious stimuli were thought to represent abnormal development of normal fear reactions, and Melzack (1952) and Melzack and Scott (1957) found that restricted dogs were unable to perceive and appropriately respond to (i.e., avoid) painful stimuli. Clarke et al. (1951), Angermeier and James (1961), Melzack (1962), Melzack and Burns (1963), and Lessac (1966) have also reported the effect of early sensory deprivation on later behavior and perception in the dog, and Burdina, Krasuskii, and Chebykin (1960) investigated the effects of restricted versus free-range rearing on the behavior and conditioned reflex activity of dogs. Lessac (1966) emphasized the importance of evaluating the effects of isolation on behavior already developed before isolation; he concludes that isolation is an invalid technique for studying normal behavioral development because of demonstrable destructive effects upon behavioral and perceptual organization. His subjects were not isolated, however, until the relatively late age of 12 wk. Krushinskii (1962), Fuller (1964, 1966, 1967), and Fuller and Clark (1966a, b) in long-term studies on the effects of isolation on canine behavior, found that there were genetic differences in susceptibility to the effects of isolation in the different breeds studied (generally the timid breeds were more affected than the more aggressive or outgoing breeds). These studies on the effects of domestication on the development of socialization in the dog have been discussed by Fox (1965a), and the effect of early experience on the later trainability of border collies has been explored by Boyd (1964). Dogs reared under partial social isolation between the ages of 4 and 16 wk developed an "isolation syndrome," characterized by extreme activity-reduction in the intensity of social contacts and decreased manipulative behavior (Fuller 1964). Fuller emphasizes that these results are of psychiatric interest because the isolation-syndrome dogs showed some symptoms similar to those of so-called autistic children. Fuller's data indicate that the events surrounding the emergence from social isolation are critical to the origin and persistence of the syndrome as a mass-fear response. The slow recovery from the syndrome does not indicate the time lag in the learning of new responses, but rather indicates the gradual removal of a rigid activity pattern of intense avoidance behavior.

Materials and Methods

This experiment was designed to determine the effects of differential rearing on several aspects of behavior and development of the dog. Forty-six dogs were studied. A total of 8 control, 8 handled, and 8 partially socially isolated pups were used in the initial study. A second series of 12 pups (all beagles) was selected on the split-litter basis and reared in isolation, 6 being used as controls. Evoked potentials to auditory and visual stimulation and EEG recordings were taken with skin electrodes (modified Michele wound clips), then amino acid analyses were run on specific brain regions. A third group of 10 pups was implanted with chronic electrodes at 3 wk of age, and at 4 wk 6 of these were isolated and the remaining 4 served as controls. EEG and evoked potential recordings were made on these subjects before and after isolation to determine the recovery of EEG and behavior following isolation. Handling was carried out from the first day after birth until 5 wk of age (a total of 35 hr of handling). The handling procedures consisted of 1 hr of stimulation daily, comprising 10 min photic stimulation in a light- and soundproof box, with a flashing light stimulus at 0.16 intensity and approximately 1 sec frequency; 10 min labyrinthine stimulation consisting of 5 min anteroposterior and 5 min bitemporal tilting at an approximate frequency of 1.5 sec through an excursion of $45°$ from the horizontal; 10 min auditory stimulation, 2 min each at 1, 10, 10^2, and 10^3 cycles/sec at an intensity of 1.0 v and duration of 1.0 msec. This was followed by 1 min exposure in a cold room at $37°$ F, 5 min in a centrifugal rotator at approximately 45 rpm, and 10 min handling, during which time a series of reflexes were evoked, including the Magnus, rooting, righting, geotaxic, pain, and panniculus reflexes (see chap. 2). By eliciting these reflexes, the rate of reflex development could be assessed and compared in different treatment groups. The subjects were then placed in a water bath at $80°$ F and were immersed for 15 sec, during which time they would swim; this was done during the first 3 wk. Subjects were then rubbed dry with a hand towel and groomed with a soft brush for 10 min, and received 2 min general cutaneous stimulation with an air jet ($60°$ F). From 3 wk of age onward the handling period was increased to include 10 min play with the operator. After this handling period, they were returned to the mother. Control subjects were kept under typical rearing conditions with the mother, having frequent scheduled human contact or twice-daily feeding and cleaning routines. All subjects were weighed and heart rates were recorded at weekly intervals while the pup was lying quietly in the hands of the investigator. The pups were weaned at 4 wk of age, received gamma globulin and piperazine anthelmintic, and were reared singly in metabolism cages in the animal house environment. At this time, subjects for rearing in social isolation were selected; these subjects had previously been raised in the same manner as the control or mother-reared animals. Social isolation subjects were placed in a quiet darkened room (illumination approximately 0.5 ft-c), housed in single cages, and fed and cleaned twice daily with minimal contact with the handler (approximately 1.5 min daily). It was decided to rear these pups for only 1 wk in social isolation (from 4 to 5 wk of age), to compare with observations of other workers who socially isolated their subjects for much longer periods after weaning. It must be emphasized that social isolation was only partial, for auditory and olfactory stimuli from the subject itself and from other dogs in the isolation room were not eliminated, as they were in most earlier social isolation or deprivation studies with dogs. Control and handled subjects were reared in single cages in the animal-house environment and control subjects had approximately the same amount of human contact daily as the isolation group. At 5 wk of age, the subjects were tested singly in a behavior arena equipped with one-way windows to enable the experimenter to observe the animals without being seen. The arena contained cloth bedding from the mother of the pups and, in another corner, a brightly colored child's toy. The reactions of the subjects were observed for 5 min when they were first placed in the arena, and observations continued for 5 min more after these objects had been removed. The objects were then replaced for 5 min more of observation. The observers, with stopwatches, independently recorded the duration of certain activities of each pup throughout each of the three 5-min observation periods, and time scores were then averaged for each group. The activities observed and time-scored were as follows:

1. *Specific Interaction with Stimulus.* Duration of interaction with either cloth or toy, including approach, play, chewing, licking, carrying, and lying beside or running around the object, was recorded.

2. *Nonspecific Exploratory Activity.* The time spent exploring the arena was recorded, including sniffing and licking walls and floor and jumping up at walls, looking up at walls (visual), and attention to extraneous noises (air-conditioner turned on as sound blanket). During this activity period, pup never approached cloth or toy.

3. *Random Activity.* The time spent sitting or pacing the arena without any overt reaction to cloth or toy or attention toward walls, floor, or extraneous noises was recorded.

4. *Distress Vocalization.* As a level of emotional arousal, the number of distressful yelps and the duration of distress vocalization was recorded by one observer only while the other observer noted what else the pup was doing (random or nonspecific exploratory activities). There was a high correlation between distress vocalization and nonspecific exploratory activity.

After this 15-min testing period, the subject's approach to a passive observer in the arena was determined, and then approach and following response were assessed while the observer walked around the arena. The ability of the pup to negotiate a simple wire-mesh barrier placed between him and the observer was next used to assess detour behavior. Four trials were allowed, and if the subject was able to come around the barrier to the observer one end was blocked; if there was an end preference, the preferred side was blocked first. The time taken to pass around the barrier and the number of trials required were recorded. Finally, the social interaction of these differentially reared subjects was observed when they were placed together in the arena, which still contained the cloth and toy. After 5 min of observation, the experimenter entered the arena and observed the effects of the presence of a human on the group behavior of the pups. After these behavior observations, EEG recordings were taken on a Grass 6-channel recorder or on an Offner 8-channel type R dynograph. EEG recordings were also taken and evoked responses to visual and auditory stimuli of various frequencies were recorded on a computer of average transients (CAT 400 B) and monitored on an oscilloscope via a Grass 6-

channel EEG recorder. Recordings were taken while the subjects were lying quietly awake and also while they were asleep in a darkened room; they were retained in a copper-gauze box lined with foam rubber. For evoked potential recordings, subjects were restrained in a towel-swaddle and tape. Selected subjects were then killed and several organs were dissected and weighed in the cold room at 37° F. The brain was dissected for amino-acid analysis and for histological examination, and the adrenal glands were dissected and prepared for epinephrine and norepinephrine analysis. Some tissues were also prepared for lipid analysis.

Results

No significant difference in body weight gain was observed in the different groups, nor were significant differences in organ weights or in total brain weight observed. When subjects were tested at 3 and 4 wk of age by a variety of reflex tests employed to determine the degree of reflex development (see chap. 2), no significant differences were observed. Some handled pups, however, showed slightly superior coordination while standing and walking at 4 wk. Histological examination of motor, occipital, and frontal cortex and vestibular neurons revealed inconsistent differences in neuronal size, but no differences in cell density were observed. Vestibular neurons in 4 handled subjects were significantly larger and contained more chromatin than those in control or isolated pups, and the total population of neurons observed in serial sections contained fewer small-sized neurons. The Meynert cells of the fifth layer in the occipital cortex and those of the fifth layer in the frontal and auditory cortices (large pyramidals) appeared larger in 3 handled pups compared with litter-mate controls, and contained more Nissl substance. Heart rates were recorded in the control and handled groups only, because it was not possible to take resting heart rates at 5 wk of age in the social isolation reared pups, as they were hyperactive and had tachycardia. The marked differences between the handled and control groups were apparent from the 2d wk onward (fig. 6.1). Normally there is a decrease in heart rate from 2 wk of age onward, owing in part to an increase in vagal tone (Fox 1966c), which was seen in the control subjects; but in the handled group, carioacceleration was seen from 2 wk of age onward, and at 5 wk the heart rates in all handled subjects were greater by 60 beats/min, indicative of greater sympathetic tone. Glutamic acid, glutamine, GABA, and aspartic acid were estimated in the cerebral cortex (gray matter), superior colliculi, thalamus-hypothalamus, caudate nucleus, and hippocampus-amygdala (Agrawal, Fox, and Himwich 1967). Significant changes between control and isolated groups were found in the superior colliculi, thalamus-hypothalamus, and caudate nucleus, with practically no changes in the cerebral cortex. The apparent changes in the level of glutamic acid, GABA, glutamine, and aspartic acid in cerebral cortex and hippocampus were not significant, with the possible exception of GABA in hippocampus-amygdala ($p < .05$). However, partial social deprivation had a pronounced effect on glutamic acid and GABA content of thalamus-hypothalamus and caudate nucleus, with glutamic acid increasing in the thalamus-hypothalamus ($p < .01$) and decreasing in caudate nucleus ($p < .001$). The changes in glutamic acid resulted in the proportional increase of GABA in the thalamus-hypothalamus and its decrease in the caudate nucleus. Glutamine, which is usually considered to be in dynamic equilibrium with glutamic acid, was high in the superior colliculi ($p < .02$) and caudate nuclei ($p < .005$) of the control group, the decrease in isolated group being statistically significant. The average percentage of epinephrine per adrenal gland was found to be 63% ± 9 in the handled group and 56% ± 7 in the controls, there being no change in the total amine content of the adrenals owing to handling but a significant increase in epinephrine. An increase in triglyceride content of the kidney and adrenals and a decrease in the liver was found in the handled pups compared with their controls, which may indicate an increase or change in lipid metabolism as a result of early handling.

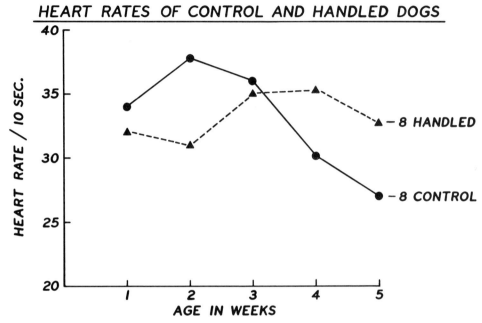

HEART RATES OF CONTROL AND HANDLED DOGS

Fig. 6.1. Normal reduction in heart rate occurs between 2 and 3 wk in controls, but this effect is not seen in the handled pups, in which a sustained tachycardia develops. (Heart rates are averaged for each group; all handled subjects showed little individual variance after the 3d week, tachycardia being present in all subjects.)

Behavioral Observations. Extreme differences were not found among individuals in the same group, and this surprising uniformity facilitated comparisons among the 3 differentially reared groups. These data have been summarized in table 6.1. Generally, the handled pups were hyperactive, highly exploratory, very sociable toward humans, and dominant in social situations (e.g., play) with their peers. The handled subjects showed the greatest distress vocalization immediately after the handler had entered the testing arena and removed the cloth and toy. In contrast, the control subjects were little distressed by this interference but showed great emotional arousal when first put into the arena. The socialization subjects showed little emotional arousal in any of the test situations. Control subjects reacted more to the cloth stimulus than to the toy, whereas handled and social-isolation pups were somewhat similar in their reactions to both cloth and toy. The time spent with these specific object stimuli was in contrast with the random and nonspecific exploratory activity of the various subjects; random activity was characterized by the pup's running around the arena in an aimless or nondirected fashion, and nonspecific exploratory activity was seen when the subject intently explored the floor, walls, and door of the arena. Random activity was greatest in the isolation groups, whereas the control group showed a high-level random activity when the stimulus-specific objects were present in the arena (excitation effect?). In contrast, the handled group showed increased random activity when these specific stimuli were removed. This increase in random activity in the handled group when the arena was empty was correlated with the greater distress vocalization at that time. Nonspecific exploratory activity was greatest in the handled group when the cloth and toy were in the arena, but was greatest in the control group when the arena was empty. This increase in nonspecific activity in the control subjects was associated with their high interaction with the cloth when it was present in the arena; control subjects were, therefore, stimulus-bound throughout, and when the stimulus was removed they showed an increase in

TABLE 6.1

OPEN-FIELD BEHAVIOR IN DIFFERENTIALLY REARED DOGS

(Isolation from 4 to 5 Wk, Handling from Birth to 5 Wk)

ACTIVITIES	SPECIFIC STIM.		RANDOM	EXPLORA-TORY (Non-specific)	DISTRESS (Vocaliza-tion)	DETOUR SUCCESS RATES		
	Cloth	Toy				Side Pref.	R. Closed	L. Closed
Control 8	78.0 .... 76.0	37.2 .... 7.4	32.5 *68.0* 34.0	152.3 *232.0* 182.6	27.2 *2.3* 10.0	R. 1.8 L. 2.3	41.5	41.5
Handled 8	52.5 .... 49.75	38.25 .... 47.0	22.0 *183.0* 13.0	187.25 *117.0* 190.25	17.2 *75.5* 8.5	R. 1.6 L. 2.2	93.0	96.5
Isolated 8	47.0 .... 24.7	32.6 .... 42.5	51.25 *136.25* 96.0	169.15 *163.75* 136.8	1.4 *3.5* 0.1	R. 1.1 L. 2.1	23.0	28.0

NOTE: Figures in italics indicate observations when cloth and toy are removed from arena. All figures represent average time in seconds during three 5-min test periods, in which arena is full, then specific stimuli removed and replaced after 5 min.

nonspecific exploratory behavior (in contrast with the diffuse reactions of the isolates). The level of nonspecific exploratory activity in the social isolation group was similar in the three test situations, and when assessed with the total random activity it shows the relative hyperactivity of this group. In the barrier test situation the handled pups performed best in that they required the fewest trials to negotiate the detour, whereas the control pups reacted more slowly and showed distress vocalization in this situation (table 6.1). In the control group, therefore, emotional arousal in this situation prejudiced problem-solving ability. The isolation subjects, in 4 out of 6 cases, were unable to negotiate the barrier; 2 were able to solve the detour problem but, unlike other subjects, did not come directly around to the observer but wandered off toward the toy or cloth. They behaved like the control pups in that they became hyperactive and would run along the barrier "pushing" with their noses; but, in contrast, they were nonvocal. In the social situation (group behavior observations), in all cases the handled pups were dominant during play and were the first to leave the group to approach the observer when he entered the arena. The control subjects were the most subordinate but would interact constantly with the group and not leave the group, in contrast to the isolation-reared pups, who would frequently leave the playful group and either indulge in "self play" (e.g., tail chasing) or approach the cloth or toy. During aggressive play-fighting the controls were most subordinate and the isolation pups were intermediate in that they would fight with the handled pups to a greater extent. When 2 handled pups from the same litter were present in the group, it was observed that these subjects would frequently leave the group together and explore the test arena and indulge in aggressive play away

Fig. 6.2. Control (*C*) pups show strong approach and following responses, in contrast to the slow approach and following of isolates (*I*), which do not indulge in play but make contact with inanimate play objects.

from the control and isolated pups. Approach behavior toward the observer standing in the arena (cloth and toys still present) and following response as the observer walked around the arena were greatest in handled pups. Control pups were slower to approach and follow, but in no instance did any pup actively avoid the observer. In contrast, the isolation-reared pups often showed passive avoidance behavior (fearful crouching), and those that did follow only did so for a short distance and were easily diverted; they would approach the cloth or toy as they came into the vicinity of these objects (fig. 6.2). Throughout the test procedures, vocalization in the isolated group was at a very low level: socialization processes may therefore be important in developing and reinforcing vocal behavior and distress vocalization.

EEG Results. EEG recordings were extremely difficult to take in the isolation pups. The recordings were originally to be taken when the animals were in a similar behavior state. To achieve this, it was decided to record when the pups were lightly asleep in the arms of the observer and could be aroused by a loud noise. Successful recordings were obtained in all control and handled pups, but in the isolation subjects it was almost impossible to get good recordings. These animals would not rest for one moment and were constantly alert. Successful recordings were obtained in 2 of these subjects in the first group while they were lying quietly awake. In other series of pups, with chronic electrodes, excellent EEG recordings with few move-

SLEEPING EEG OF HANDLED AND CONTROL 5-WEEK OLD PUPS

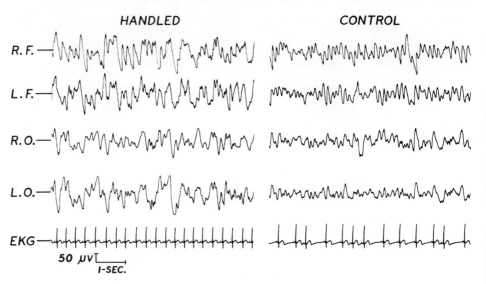

Fig. 6.3. Greater amplitude in handled pup during quiet sleep compared with control, and faster heart rate contrasting with the arrhythmic heart rate of the control.

ment artifacts were obtained, and evoked responses to visual and auditory stimulation (frequencies 0.1, 0.4, 1, 2, 4, 8, and 16 per sec) were successfully obtained using the swaddling method described in the EEG section (chap. 4). EEG recordings of all the handled pups showed a greater amplitude during light sleep than those of the control subjects (figs. 6.3, 6.4). As amplitude increases with age, it may be presumed to be an indication of greater maturity in the handled subjects. No differences in amplitude or fast frequency components were observed between the handled and the control pups in the alert state.

EEG recordings in all isolation-reared subjects when they were first removed from isolation showed the presence of 14–16 cycles/sec variable amplitude (50–100 μv) activity, which was frequently synchronous in all channels (fig. 6.4). Also, desynchronization with faster components and overall decrease in amplitude was evident. In some pups, this rhythmic 14–16 c/sec activity was paroxysmal, occurring at frequencies varying from every 4 to every 15 sec, and varying in duration from 0.5–2.0 sec. In one subject this activity was continuous, being most predominant over the occipital regions. All subjects were highly alert during recordings. This rhythmic activity decreased in frequency in some pups on the 2d day, but in others it persisted for over 7 days (figs. 6.5, 6.6). This activity was found to correlate with behavior, for in those pups that remained hyperactive and alert (i.e., slow recovery from isolation) it was seen to persist for several days after emergence from isolation. No attempts were made to quantify these EEG findings. They were essentially utilized qualitatively to correlate with overt behavior (hyperactivity) in each individual on emergence and during recovery from isolation.

Occlusion of vision by placing a hand or towel over the eyes of an alert 5-wk-old pup causes synchronization of EEG with the appearance of medium amplitude slow wave, 3–4 c/sec, activity. Similar phenomena are seen in older dogs, but are not seen in tense, nervous dogs (i.e., highly aroused) or during nociceptive stimulation (e.g., by pinching the interdigital web, chap. 4). In all controls, this activity

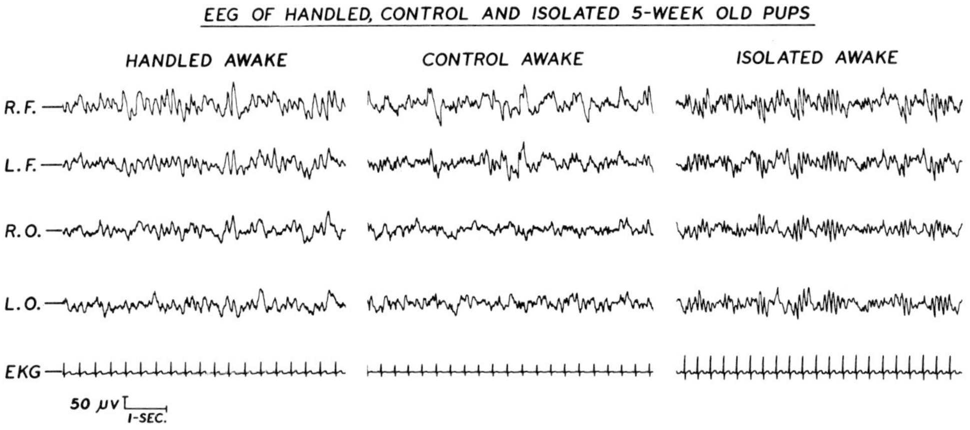

EEG OF HANDLED, CONTROL AND ISOLATED 5-WEEK OLD PUPS

HANDLED AWAKE   CONTROL AWAKE   ISOLATED AWAKE

Fig. 6.4. Skin electrode recordings from right and left frontal and occipital regions; no differences between alert handled and control pups, but synchronous bursts of rhythmic activity in isolate.

was seen after occlusion of vision, but it was not seen in the isolates on the first day. Its absence was attributed to intense arousal in the extremely alert isolation-reared subjects, but it appeared on subsequent days, again occurring earlier in the less aroused pups (fig. 6.7).

In all isolated subjects, evoked potentials to photic stimulation were consistently of shorter latency (to peak of first positive wave) than in controls at 5 wk (table 6.2). This difference was approximately 30 msec ($p < .001$, Mann-Whitney U one-tail test), but by 6 wk, the difference was insignificant, latencies of control and isolates being similar, with few exceptions. These exceptions were the "slow recovery" isolates, in which latencies only 5 msec shorter than those of controls were found at 6 wk; these differences were statistically insignificant (figs. 6.8, 6.9). These observations need further confirmation, in view of the heterogeneity of subjects, which in the dog is an almost insurmountable problem. For example, the control latencies of this study (75 msec $\pm$ 15 msec) contrast sharply with latencies described for normal 6-wk-old dogs (55 msec) in chapter 3. With such individual and interlitter variability in the dog, it is clearly imperative to employ the split-litter tech-

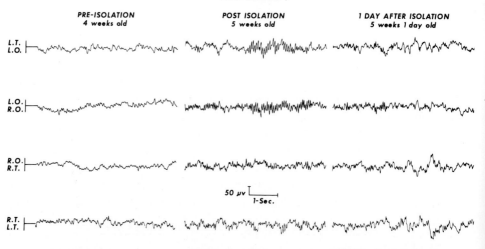

EEG RECORDINGS OF ISOLATE BEAGLE - 3
(FAST RECOVERY)

PRE-ISOLATION
4 weeks old

POST ISOLATION
5 weeks old

1 DAY AFTER ISOLATION
5 weeks 1 day old

L.T.
L.O.

L.O.
R.O.

R.O.
R.T.

50 µv
1-Sec.

R.T.
L.T.

Fig. 6.5. Chronic electrode recordings from right and left temporal and occipital regions showing presence of 14–16 c/sec activity on emergence from isolation and rapid disappearance of this activity after 1 day.

EEG RECORDINGS OF CONTROL & ISOLATE - 2 PUPS
(SLOW RECOVERY)

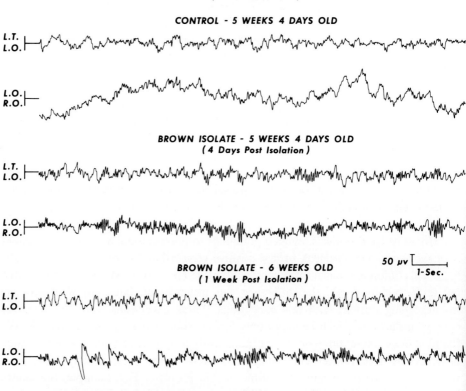

CONTROL - 5 WEEKS 4 DAYS OLD

L.T.
L.O.

L.O.
R.O.

BROWN ISOLATE - 5 WEEKS 4 DAYS OLD
(4 Days Post Isolation)

L.T.
L.O.

L.O.
R.O.

BROWN ISOLATE - 6 WEEKS OLD
(1 Week Post Isolation)

50 µv
1-Sec.

L.T.
L.O.

L.O.
R.O.

Fig. 6.6. Chronic electrode recordings showing presence of more persistent 14–16 c/sec activity in isolate, predominantly in occipital regions.

nique in assigning subjects to "experimental" or "control" treatments. Data of EP development in chapter 3 were collected from a different selection of unrelated subjects, which may in part account for these latency differences.

Discussion

The observations obtained from the handled group of pups indicate that in this experiment handling causes increased adrenal activity (reflected in the ontogeny of the heart rate and adrenal percentage of norepinephrine at 5 wk), confirming the

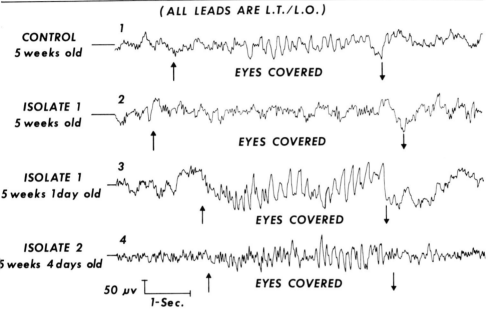

Fig. 6.7. Absence of synchronous slow wave activity in isolate when first removed from isolation, but rapid recovery thereafter. Recording from left occipital and temporal regions, chronic electrodes.

TABLE 6.2

AVERAGE LATENCIES OF EVOKED RESPONSES IN
CONTROL AND ISOLATION-REARED PUPS

(Peak of First Positive Wave)

Group	VISUAL (0.4 Sec, Chronic Electrodes)			AUDITORY		
	4 wk	5 wk	6 wk	4 wk	5 wk	6 wk
Controls (N=4)	75	75 (76)[a]	74	55	45	45
Isolates (N=6)	75	45[b] (55)[a]	73	55	55	46

[a] Surface electrode subjects in parentheses.
[b] $p < .001$.

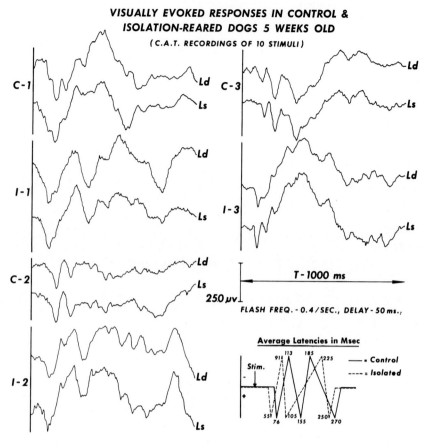

Fig. 6.8. Recordings taken with surface electrodes over left and right gyrus lateralis showing consistently shorter latencies in isolates (*I*) than in littermate controls (*C*).

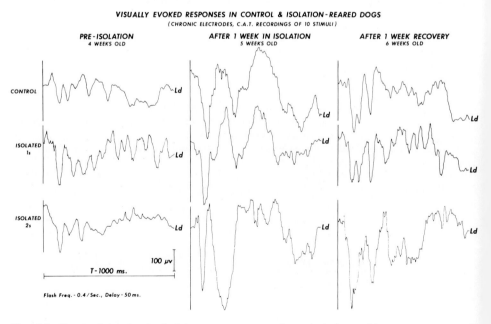

Fig. 6.9. Shorter latencies in isolates on emergence from isolation, with return to normal latencies after 1 wk.

observations by other workers on the effects of the early handling in the rat and mouse reviewed earlier in this paper. The only significant neurologic finding was slightly superior locomotor ability and equilibratory coordination in the handled pups. We may surmise that reflex development in the dog normally proceeds at a maximal rate postnatally and is little affected by stimulation or exercise in this experiment. However, the general behavior and electrocortical activity of the handled group compared with the control group shows marked differences, in that the EEG is more mature as amplitude during quiet sleep increases with age (chap. 4). Handled animals show similar changes in their behavior patterns, as reported in handling studies in other species; they perform superiorly in the problem-solving situation (the barrier test) and show less emotional arousal in this situation. In group behavior, the handled pups are the dominant individuals and show the greatest attraction or attachment to man. The isolation-reared pups, in spite of being isolated for such a short period of time at the early part of the critical period of socialization, behave similarly in certain respects to pups reared in social deprivation for much longer periods. They are hyperactive, show diffuse reactions to novel objects, and pay more attention to their physical environment than to their littermates when tested in the group situation. They have the lowest emotional attachment or attraction for man and show the most inferior problem-solving abilities. Fuller (1966) noted an impairment of place learning in isolation-raised beagles, but concluded that problem-solving ability was not *permanently* impaired by restricted rearing. In monkeys, however, Harlow (1965*b*) found that learning ability apparently was not impaired by isolation rearing. This is a surprising observation; one would expect that learning would be adversely affected because isolation-rearing conditions restrict experience and manipulation, and emergence from isolation is characterized by avoidance or fear of novel objects. The isolation-raised animal must be carefully handled to reduce these emotional reactions which may interfere with learning; otherwise false interpretations may be drawn from studies of learning abilities in emotionally disturbed subjects.

It is pertinent that in isolation-reared dogs, the persistence of fast-frequency EEG activity is correlated with the frequency of this activity when the subject is first removed from isolation and with subsequent duration of abnormal behavior.

As in the observations of Fisher (1955), pups reared in social deprivation isolate themselves from the group and play in a solitary fashion (self-play). It is interesting that such profound changes in behavior following this short period of isolation result in symptoms similar to those described in pups reared in isolation for much longer periods. In contrast, abnormal fear reactions and maladaptive approach and avoidance responses are not observed in these isolation subjects, whereas Fuller (1964) reported such abnormalities in pups isolated for up to 16 wk. This is to be expected because by 5 wk of age the approach behavior is normally at maximum intensity and avoidance behavior is poorly developed (Freedman, King, and Elliot 1961). Long-term isolation (partial social deprivation) results in inappropriate avoidance or approach responses to novel stimuli. On emergence from long-term isolation, exploratory behavior is overshadowed by mass avoidance behavior and fear of novel stimuli. Long-term isolation rearing, therefore, causes deficits in the establishment of fear responses, and by 16 wk of age the capacity for long-lasting fear responses is developed (Fuller and Clark 1966*a, b*). There is also a lack of response to social stimuli (autism) and inhibition of aggressive behavior. Waller

and Waller (1963) reported that they were able to reconstitute normal social behavior in asocial, isolation-raised ducks by forcing the isolates to associate with normal ducks in a small pen.

The general picture, therefore, of a pup emerging from isolation is one of an
organism reacting maximally to a relatively enriched environment and having height-
ened sensitivity to extraneous stimuli. It might be said that such animals are reacting
without operation of their afferent filtering systems, or in the Pavlovian sense, without internal inhibition. Hutt et al. (1965) have emphasized in their telemetered
EEG studies of autistic children, showing behavior patterns very similar to isolation-
reared animals, that the EEG manifestations of constant desynchronization suggest
a state of chronic reticular arousal. In the autistic child, either socioemotional or
neurological (e.g., deafness) factors may be involved in the genesis of the syndrome.
Stereotypy, impairment, or absence of speech and impaired pain perception are
symptomatic. Isolation-reared dogs show stereotypy, minimal or no vocalization,
and impaired pain perception (Melzack and Scott 1957). In the dog, more prolonged isolation results in greater sensory and motor deficits and more severe and
persistent behavioral anomalies, including emotional hypo- and hyperactivity and
fear of the unfamiliar. Genetic factors are also involved, as some breeds are more
susceptible to isolation rearing than are others (Krushinskii 1962; Fuller and Clark
1966*b;* Murphree and Dykman 1966; Dykman, Murphree, and Ackerman 1966).
The hypothesis that chronic reticular arousal is a possible underlying factor in
autism, as advanced by Hutt et al. (1965), is supported by the observations of
Lindsley et al. (1964). In long-term dark-reared monkeys, Lindsley and co-workers
observed

> definite reversal or paradoxical effects from light stimulation or absence of stimulation,
> in which the cortical electrical activity, which normally reflects changes induced in the
> reticular activating system, was made to block not at the presence of light but at the ab-
> sence of light, and to show synchronized rhythms not when it was dark but when there
> was light.

They suggest that these phenomena are due to malfunction of regulating and adapt-
ing mechanisms in the hippocampus and reticular activating system. Photic stimulation produces markedly enhanced evoked potentials, possibly because deprivation
causes increased sensitization. Similarly, Scherrer and Fourment (1964) observed
hypersensitivity of the unspecific system as reflected in the intense and sustained
arousal reactions to light, sound, and tactile stimuli in isolation-raised rabbits. Melzack and Burns (1963, 1965) note marked and sustained desynchronization of
EEG, with a significantly greater proportion of high frequencies, in isolation-reared
dogs released from isolation. Average evoked visual and auditory responses are of
lower amplitude in these subjects when placed in an unfamiliar environment. In
contrast, Baxter (1966) failed to show any detectable EEG abnormalities in the
spontaneous EEG of dark-raised cats, but found reduction in flicker-induced potentials at all frequencies of visual stimulation utilized. Baxter's study emphasizes
that differences in methodology, species studied, and parameters measured may
produce varying and apparently conflicting results.

These earlier findings on the effects of isolation are in part confirmed in the
present investigation and lend support to the general concepts of environmental
adaptation and stimulus-dependent homeostasis of the CNS. Without adequate

stimulation for a prolonged period, when suddenly confronted with an enriched environment and stimulation of many modalities, such isolation-reared animals are unable to adapt to what constitutes a "normal environment." A state of acute reticular arousal occurs, characterized by increased sensitivity to visual stimulation and marked desynchronization of the EEG (with bursts of fast-frequency activity) accompanied by intense behavioral arousal. The views of Melzack and Burns (1963) support this general hypothesis; they postulate that the isolation-reared animal resembles a neural model in which failure to filter out irrelevant information on the basis of previous experience leads to excessive arousal, which in turn interferes with the mechanisms that normally act in the selection of cues for adaptive response. Following short-term isolation, rapid behavioral adaptation occurs, with the gradual recovery of normal EEG and EP. Permanent behavioral abnormalities have been reported by earlier workers in long-term isolation-reared animals. If isolation extends beyond the period of integration (see chap. 7), adaptive behavioral processes are no longer plastic, but become rigid and stereotyped. Recovery in the "normal" environment is then protracted, and complete adaptation may never occur, as a state of chronic arousal ensues. In the present study it is conceivable that the effects of isolation, if extended over a longer period, may be made more permanent; but as social isolation was discontinued earlier in the critical period of socialization, the effects are transient. Thus, early plasticity affords greater adaptability. Sackett (1965) forwards a complexity dissonance preference theory to account for the abnormal behavior of isolation-raised monkeys. He assumes that behavioral development proceeds by a gradual process of paced increments in environmental complexity. Inappropriate pacing of environmental complexity during development thus disrupts the patterns of development so that the organism will seek or prefer visual and manipulatory stimuli of low complexity. As Hutt et al. (1965) have postulated, Hebb (1955) formulates that with intense arousal specific attentiveness decreases and behavioral disorganization ensues. Thus an animal emerging from isolation cannot cope with a complex environment, and the disorganized behavior is a result of intense arousal.

The effects of handling or stress in early life influence behavior via the neuroendocrine system, and, provided the stress is not sufficiently intense to produce irreversible pathophysiological reactions, animals so treated may be superior in several aspects to nontreated subjects of the same age.

Summary

The effects of handling from birth to 5 wk and isolation from 4 to 5 wk were studied and compared with the behavior of control subjects raised under normal conditions. Differences in behavior, heart rate, and EEG activity were evident in the three differentially reared groups of dogs and were attributed to the effects of handling and isolation in the experimental groups as compared with the control groups. Emergence from isolation was characterized by intense behavioral arousal, abnormally short latencies of visually evoked potentials, and marked desynchronization of the EEG, with paroxysmal or continuous rhythmic 14–16/sec activity. Recovery was generally rapid, and by 7 days after emergence from isolation behavior and EEG activity were apparently normal. These findings were discussed in the light of earlier studies on the behavioral and neurophysiological effects of isolation rearing, and the isolation syndrome was described in relation to autistic behavior in the human infant. Preliminary biochemical data (adrenal and CNS analysis) are included, and some correlation in the differentially reared groups is shown. These data in part support simliar findings in other species reviewed in this study.

Effects of Restricted Socialization on Behavioral Development

Introduction

This experiment was designed to determine the effects of rearing dogs under varying schedules of restricted socialization with their own species on their later social behavior toward human beings and toward their littermates. Sackett, Porter, and Holmes (1965) and Sackett et al. (1967) have shown that hand-reared monkeys have a greater preference for man than for other monkeys and that there is a gradient of preference dependent upon the increment of peer-socialization. Green and Gordon (1964) observed similar differentiated behavior in maternally reared and maternally deprived monkeys; the latter subjects responded at a lower level to a variety of stimuli when tested in the Butler box (Butler 1957*b*). Physical contact, grooming, vocalization, and play are the most important elements involved in developing the mother-infant affectional system and peer relationships in monkeys (Harlow 1962). Ingel and Calvin (1960) have shown that isolation-reared pups also develop attachments to surrogate objects, as reported in the monkey by Harlow, and it is generally accepted that the provision of food is of less significance than these other factors in the development of emotional bonds (Stanley 1965*a;* Brodbeck 1954). There are marked species differences in the effects of group versus isolation rearing; Candland and Milne (1966) have shown that social preferences in chickens and cats, but not in guppies or rats, are influenced by early environmental experiences such as group versus isolation rearing, with or without certain inanimate stimulus objects.

Freedman, King, and Elliot (1961) have shown that if dogs reared together are denied human contact until after 12 wk of age they show strong avoidance of human beings and are "wild dogs." Pups given contact with man between 4 and 10 wk of age develop social responses to their handlers and to other human beings. In view of these findings, the hand-reared subjects in the present experiment were isolated from their peers until 12 wk, which is approximately the end of the critical period of socialization, during which primary social relationships are established (Scott 1962; Scott and Fuller 1965).

It was decided to reverse the study of Freedman, King, and Elliot (1961) and to restrict dogs from contact with their own species until 12 wk of age. Two control groups were included in the design; one group was nursed by the mother and weaned normally at 8 wk, and an intermediate group was weaned at 3½ wk. With such programmed life histories, subjects would have varying increments of socialization with their own species, and might show varying deficits in the development of social behavior patterns.

A battery of tests was used to determine the effects of this differential early experience; differences between groups might be found and attributed to the effects of restricted early social experience.

Methods

Rearing Procedures. A total of 17 dogs from 4 litters were studied, half being purebred beagles, the rest mongrels. Sick or physically inferior pups were not used. Pups were randomly assigned to three groups, using the split-litter technique (table 6.3). Six pups were successfully hand-reared from 3 days of age, after they had received adequate maternal antibodies via the colostrum. They were incubator reared and had scheduled contact with human beings, being given 6 daily 8–10 min periods of contact for feedings with Esbilac, a synthetic bitch-milk formula, and for cleaning and reflex stimulation of urination. Hand-rearing was successfully accomplished using the methods recently described by Fox (1966*d*). Body weights were checked regularly before the first morning feeding to ensure that weight gains were within the normal range. At 3½ wk these subjects, designated isolates (IIs), were weaned and placed in separate metabolism cages which were screened to allow

TABLE 6.3
LITTER DISTRIBUTION OF DIFFERENTLY
TREATED GROUPS OF PUPS

Litter	Hand-Reared II	Early-Weaned CI	Normally Weaned CCI
Beagle litter I	2	1[a]	1[a]
Beagle litter II	2	1	1
Mongrel litter I	1	2	1
Mongrel litter II	1[a]	2	2
Total	6	6	5

[a] Not used in dominance test at 15 wk of age because of mild bronchopneumonia.

neither visual nor tactile contact between the subjects. Other pups which had been reared with the mother and which were weaned at 3½ wk and designated control isolates (CIs) were placed in separate cages. The third group of pups, designated control-control isolates (CCIs), were removed from the mother at 8 wk and similarly isolated (see table 6.3).

Treatment while in Isolation. The room in which the pups were isolated contained only the experimental dogs; it was well lighted and the temperature was maintained at 70° F. An extractor-fan ventilation system provided adequate ventilation of the cages and also acted as a sound blanket, considerably reducing extraneous noises. All dogs in isolation were cared for only by the experimenters, having contact for approximately 6 min daily during two periods of cleaning and pan-feeding. The dogs were never handled or petted during this period of isolation except during the arena activity and approach response tests at 5 and 8 wk of age (see below). The pups were removed from their separate cages at 12 wk, and after a series of behavior tests were placed in their original litter-groups and raised together in large pens.

Test Procedures. The following tests were employed:

1. Daily Reflex Tests. Tests were conducted on all groups from birth to 3½ wk to determine differences in development attributable to nutrition or maternal

stimulation. The following reflexes were tested, using the same methods of evaluation as described earlier (chap. 2): Crossed extensor, Magnus, fore- and hind-limb
placing, body righting, urination, labial, and rooting reflexes, and equilibration and
locomotor coordination. Responses were assessed as strong and stereotyped in the
neonate, weak and variable, and absent or adultlike for each individual dog tested.
The emergence of adultlike responses and disappearance of neonatal reflexes were
thus evaluated chronologically so that developmental differences in the different
groups of subjects could be determined.

2. Approach Responses. Responses to a passive observer were recorded to
determine locomotor ability and approach time. Five trials were given at 5, 8, and
12 wk of age, and the subject was released after 60 sec delay in a start box and the
time recorded for the pup to touch the experimenter, who was seated at the far end
of a 6-ft runway. On reaching the experimenter, the pup was allowed 5 sec contact
with the extended hand of the "reward object," and then was replaced in the start
box for 60 more sec by a second observer, who recorded the approach times.

3. Activity. Activity in a $12' \times 12'$ behavior testing arena with one-way observation windows, and time spent interacting with (sniffing, chewing, playing with,
approaching, carrying, running around, or lying beside) a variety of novel stimuli
over a 10-min period for *each* subject were observed at 5, 8, 12 wk of age. These
novel stimuli consisted of a $2' \times 3'$ mirror mounted at floor level, a child's toy, and
cloth bedding from the mother's pen. Two independent observers recorded the time
spent by each subject with these novel stimuli: their records were then averaged to
reduce individual bias. A third observer recorded the number of 1-ft squares marked
on the arena floor covered by each subject during the test period.

At 12 wk, the following tests in the sequence shown were employed:

1. Distress Vocalization in Confinement. Pups were confined by a wire-mesh
screen in one corner of the behavior room, and their distress vocalization was noted
while alone, while in the presence of a dog (their mother), and while in the presence
of a human being, for periods of 3 min each. Constant distress vocalization was
rated as 2, intermittent weaker vocalization rated 1. Again two observers made recordings and their scores were averaged.

2. Social Preference. The pup was released from a start box, with immediate
visual access to an anesthetized adult dog in one corner of the arena and a passive
human sitting in the opposite corner. A solid screen separated these passive subjects
(modified Y maze). The time spent with each stimulus and the number of contacts
was recorded over a 3-min period by two observers.

3. Social Behavior. Following these tests, differently reared pups in every possible combination of pairs (II and II, CCI and CCI, CCI and II, CI and II, etc.)
were observed for approximately 10 min each, and then pups from the entire litter
were observed all together. Both observers recorded if either of the pups showed
any of the following activities when together: vocalization, barking or yelping, tail
wagging, licking, biting, chewing each other, play, including chasing, or fighting with
aggressive biting and chasing. It was also noted which pup appeared more aggressive
(constantly on top of peer, holding scruff of neck and "pinning" or holding down
with paws) during play and also during fighting. When observations were terminated, the pups were placed with littermates in large pens and observed at frequent
intervals during the ensuing days of group rearing and peer interaction.

4. Open Field Test. On the first and subsequent days after they were grouped at 12 wk of age, the pups were observed en masse in an open field outdoors. Play behavior, fighting, group-coordinated or allelomimetic behavior (keeping together in a "pack") and approach and following behavior toward the observer were noted. The presence or absence of these activities in each individual was noted.

5. Dominance Tests. At 1 and 3 wk after grouping (i.e., at 13 and 15 wk of age), pups were tested in pairs for dominance over food in the form of a rib-bone. They had been given no food for 24 hr before testing. Each individual was tested with every peer for a dominance rating. Scores were obtained for each successful "covering" of the bone and not allowing the peer to approach. Five trials were given for each pair; the bone was removed from the dominant dog and then returned after a 1-min time interval. A score of 2 denoted complete control over the bone in one trial, 1 was scored if the dog first had the bone and then lost it to its peer, who also scored 1, and 0 was scored for no retrieval.

6. Visual Motivation. At 3 wk after socialization (15 wk of age), pups were tested in a Butler box, where nose-pressing on a clear Plexiglas window would open an opaque shutter to give the pup visual access to its peers in their pen opposite. One hr of habituation to the shutter operating was followed by 1 hr with the shutter held open, and the number of times the pup pressed the Plexiglas plate as it observed its peers was recorded. Preliminary trials showed that with increased arousal, the subject would more frequently press the Plexiglas screen in an attempt to reach its peers. This was followed by 1 hr with the shutter operating; that is, the Plexiglas plate was covered by the screen, preventing the pup's visual access to his peers unless the Plexiglas plate was pressed, releasing the shutter. All presses were recorded in a Leigh-valley behavior recording unit to give activity measures when the window was open and the pup could see its peers and when the window was covered and the pup had to press to see its peers.

Results

1. *Daily Reflex Tests.* Tests failed to reveal neurological deficits in development which could be attributed to nutritional factors in the hand-reared group. Reflex development was similar in all groups with two exceptions: the hand-reared pups showed persistent sucking and rooting responses toward humans even at 4 wk of age, but were standing earlier than CIs and CCIs. They also developed a "stand-crawl" locomotor pattern between 2 and 3 wk which was attributed to the lack of "rooting" stimulation due to paucity of maternal stimulation.

2. *Approach Times.* Approach scores were similar in both IIs and CIs, whereas the CCIs approached more slowly at all ages (fig. 6.10), notably at 5 and 8 wk of age. Statistical analysis of the approach times (Mann-Whitney U one-tail test at 0.05 significance level) showed a close similarity in the CI and II groups at 5, 8, and 12 wk of age ($p = .01$ at each age). A statistically significant difference in the CCIs over the IIs ($p = .01$) and the CIs ($p = .029$) was found in approach times at 5 wk of age and at 8 wk. By 12 wk, the CCIs still differed from the IIs ($p = .029$) and from the CIs ($p = .01$). These slower approach scores in the CCIs may have been due to a lesser attachment to man; that is, approach and contact with the human in the runway has a different reward value, being more rewarding for pups having a greater increment of socialization with man during isolation rearing.

3. *Activity in Testing Arena with Novel Stimuli.* All dogs showed similar interaction times with the child's toy and dog-litter cloth (table 6.4). No statistically significant differences in activity scores or interaction times with the cloth and toy were found in the cumulative records of each group from the tests at 5, 8, and 12 wk, with one exception. The CI pups interacted significantly more with the cloth than did pups of the other two groups ($p = .008$ over CCIs, and $p = .032$ over the IIs, Mann-Whitney U one-tail test at .05 significance level). This may indicate that early weaning may influence the pup's reactions to certain objects having particular qualities of odor and texture. All dogs were hyperactive and highly aroused by these objects and interacted with them at a high rate. II pups, although they spent the

MEAN APPROACH SCORES OF DIFFERENTIALLY REARED DOGS

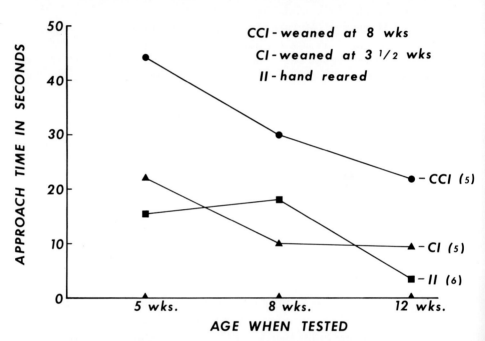

Fig. 6.10. Consistently slower approach times in CCI pups contrasted to fast approach times in CI and II pups to a "human" reward.

TABLE 6.4

CUMULATIVE ACTIVITY AND INTERACTION TIMES (SEC)
IN BEHAVIOR ARENA

Objects	CCI	CI	II
Mirror	15– 60 (36.5)[a]	0– 60 (21)	0–25 (6)
Toy	6– 58 (30)	8– 77 (42)	5–70 (33)
Cloth	7– 61 (23)	17–140 (67)	11–85 (36)
Activity[b]	43–111 (77)	43– 84 (62)	41–76 (61)

[a] Range and average interaction times in sec.

[b] Range and average activity scores = number of 1-ft squares covered during test.

same amount of time with these objects, were nonvocal an⸍
lation, but instead ran at them and into them. CCIs were
whereas CIs tended to be intermediate, as some were silent aᵖᵘ⁻
were vocal and oral. Before contact with their peers at 12 wk, tⁱᵃˡ,
that the CCIs were most active and consistently approached theᵉʳˢ
behind it with tail wagging and excited vocalization ($p = .008$, s⸍ᵈ
level over CIs). Analysis of the reactions of the CI and II pups r⸍
cally significant differences between these two groups: both ha⸍
times.

4. *Distress Vocalization.* All three groups of pups had high di⸍
tion scores when confined and in the presence of a human being. ⸍
were emotionally aroused when confined and in the presence of their
ences in distress vocalization scores when in the presence of a humaι

TABLE 6.5

SOCIAL PREFERENCE SCORES FOR DIFFERENTIALLY
REARED DOGS

Group	INTERACTION PREFERENCE		DISTRESS VOCALIZA-TION SCORE	
	Human	Dog	Human	Dog
II	122.0 sec (70-155)	19.0 sec (0-45)	10	2
CI	99.5 sec (57-129)	25.5 sec (0-45)	10	2
CCI	97.0 sec (57-159)	40.0 sec (0-82)	10	8

NOTE: Significantly higher interaction times with dogs in CCI group; all groups show strong attraction to man.
Distress vocalization significantly increased in presence of human for all groups, but only in CCI when in the presence of their dam.

when in the presence of the bitch were compared statistically for each group, using
the one-tail sign test at the .05 significance level. No statistically significant differences in distress rates were found in the CCI pups. In the CI and II pups statistically
significant differences were found ($p = .031$ and .031 respectively), indicating that
the presence of the dam evoked less distress vocalization than in the CCI group
(table 6.5).

5. *Social Preference.* As in the previous test, all dogs showed a high preference
for a passive human being. Only the normally reared CCI pups had a higher interaction time with a passive dog in contrast with the lower scores of CI and II pups
(table 6.5). Statistical analysis (Mann-Whitney U one-tail test at .05 significance
level) of the differences in interaction time with man and with dog for each group
showed a slight trend indicating that the differences were less in the CCI. The II
group spent significantly longer with man ($p = .001$), as did the CIs ($p = .004$)
and also the CCIs ($p = .008$). This graded trend in statistically significant differences in interaction times clearly demonstrates intrinsic differences in the three
groups of pups investigated.

l Behavior Observations. The CCI pups tended to group together, hav-
teraction with more mutually compatible behavior patterns, and were
e toward their peers (fig. 6.11*c, d*). IIs were lacking in responsiveness
rs (fig. 6.12*c, d*), appearing asocial, were nonoral and submissive (fig.
d on no occasion initiated play—always the CCI attempted to initiate
onses. IIs in pairs were hypoactive, constantly in contact and maintaining
position for extended periods of time (fig. 6.12 *a, b*). CIs as a group were
liate; some individuals would initiate play with IIs but were initiated into

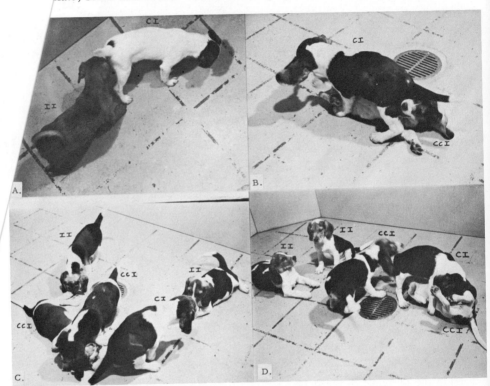

Fig. 6.11 *a,* Strong anogenital orientation in II pup; *b,* CI pup showing normal aggressive play behavior; *c* and *d,* strong interaction between CCI and CI pups; CIs are less active and less socially aroused.

play by CCIs. The term "initiated" implies that pup which ran toward its peer and more actively solicited play responses. The IIs would frequently leave the group and cease to interact socially with their peers. The CCIs would leave the IIs alone, as they were deficient in play activity patterns or would not respond playfully. Two male IIs spent the 1st day of group testing mounting and pelvic thrusting on their peers of either sex, and showed no other social responses (fig. 6.11*a*). The CCI pups were oral; they chewed each other roughly, but no severe fighting occurred. The 2d and 3d days after socialization were marked by the increased vocal behavior of the II pups and their ability to fight back. The II pups tended to bite back aggressively when CCIs were being playful, which may account for the later dominance of IIs over others. CCIs also showed strong nuzzling approach to humans, and would lick and nibble an extended hand, but this was rarely found in the IIs in spite of hand-rearing (this oral behavior is probably a social greeting activity and may have developed from soliciting food from the mother). CIs, when in pairs, tended to play together intermittently, first clinging together like paired IIs and then breaking off and chasing like normal CCIs. Clinging and passive postures were never seen in CCIs. IIs tended to circle each other like neonates while maintaining chin, neck, and forepaw contact (fig. 6.12*a, b*).

By 3 wk following socialization the deficits of the IIs were less apparent, although 3 beagles remained relatively nonoral and nonvocal in approach to man.

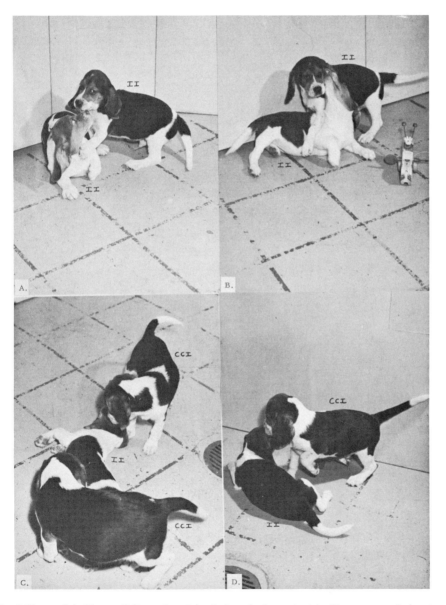

Fig. 6.12 *a* and *b*, Hypoactivity and sustained close body contact in II pups; *c* and *d*, extreme passivity exhibited by II pups in presence of normal littermate CCIs.

Recovery was generally rapid in all CIs and IIs, although finer differences which could only be subjectively determined were seen, in that the IIs were less playful and more aggressively aroused by the playful activities of their peers.

This lack of playfulness and peer-manipulation and interaction may have long-term effects on sexual behavior, especially in the male dog, and would be worthy of further investigation.[5]

7. *Open-Field Observations.* During the 1st week of freedom outdoors, the CCI pups tended to keep together, showing the strongest allelomimetic or pack behavior. The II pups initially would leave the cohesive group, engaged in either self-play or exploration, and "get lost" in their own activities. These pups would wander off as far as 100 yd from the group and display no signs of distress. Occasionally the group would move off, leaving behind a CCI pup: the latter would quickly become distressed and hasten to return to the group. Group-coordinated behavior, therefore, appeared deficient in the II subjects. The CI pups were intermediate, some individuals being indistinguishable from CCIs whereas others resembled IIs. By 3 wk, however, the litters were more intradependent, and allelomimetic activities were apparently "normal."

8. *Dominance Tests.* Tests for dominance indicated that although the CCIs were dominant at the end of the 1st week of socialization, by the end of the 3d week of group-rearing there was a change in the hierarchy which remained stable on later observations, thus indicating recovery of the II pups that in some instances became dominant. This recovery was attributed to the aggressive behavior and the general tendency for IIs to bite (protectively?) during play. One II from one litter and one CCI and one CI from another were not retested at 15 wk because these pups developed mild bronchopneumonia.

9. *Visual Motivation.* Although the scores were low for most dogs in this test, statistically significant differences between the different groups demonstrate that the CCIs were the most motivated for visual contact with their peers when visually deprived. The CCIs press rates were significantly higher than the IIs when the shutter was open ($p = 0.001$) and also when the shutter was closed ($p = .002$). The CIs also had significantly higher press rates than the IIs in both of these circumstances ($p = .008$ and $p = .002$ respectively, Mann-Whitney U one-tail test).

It was significant that press rates were higher when the shutter was open, giving the pup visual access to its peers, for emotional arousal was increased at this time and general activity was accompanied by attempts to get out of the box. Emotional arousal was therefore greatest in the CCIs under these conditions. There was great variability among differences in press rates when the shutter was closed, the II pups showing the least tendency to develop this operant activity (table 6.6).

10. *Activity in a Strange Environment* (*in the presence of adult beagles*). Although the mean scores of the three groups of pups were similar, the high number of contacts (approaching a strange adult in the pen) made by the CCIs was in contrast

[5] Since the completion of this study, two hand-reared female IIs (beagles) have been bred and both have successfully nursed and raised a litter of pups.

to their timid and submissive posture. The IIs were the least submissive in their posture. We may surmise the normal approach to an adult is necessarily submissive and that IIs essentially lacked the normal approach responses to adults. These observations, however, did not prove statistically significant. Results were inconsistent owing to greater individual variability within groups than was found in other tests.

Discussion

This investigation has shown that hand-reared pups (IIs), although emotionally attached to humans, behave the same toward human beings as do pups that are weaned early (CIs) or weaned normally (CCIs), but they show marked deficits in responsiveness to their own species. Fox (1965a) has discussed similar phenomena in the owner-pet relationship and it is widely recognized that overindulged pups reared with restricted contact with their own species may become human-dependent and develop asocial behavior toward other dogs.

TABLE 6.6

AVERAGE BUTLER-BOX PRESS
RATES PER HR

Group	Window Open	Window Closed
II	3.0 (0-15)	0 (0-1)
CI	12.5 (1-52)	13.0 (1-27)
CCI	27.0 (15-56)	57.0 (0-300)

NOTE: Pups were given a 1-hr pretest habituation period.
There is significantly greater operant behavior in CCI pups, indicating that the sight of their littermates is more rewarding for them than for the II pups; the early-weaned CI pups tend to be intermediate.

Social preference tests demonstrate that pups of all three treatment groups are extremely sociable toward handlers, and in a stressful situation, when placed behind a barrier to cause emotional arousal, they are equally vocal in the presence of a human. Only the normally reared dogs (CCIs) respond significantly more than other groups when confronted by their dam in this situation.

When first exposed to their peers at 12 wk of age, the isolated hand-reared subjects are nonaggressive and nonvocal and show no growling or excited yelping. Aggressive behavior appears, however, and by 15 wk, some of these dogs are dominant over their peers. Uyeno and White (1967) similarly found that isolation-raised rats were dominant over group-raised rats, using an unusual underwater dominance test to evaluate these differences. Rosen and Hart (1963) found that isolation rearing reduced dominance in *Peromyscus maniculatus bardii* but not in *P.m. gracilis;* so genetic variables influencing such experiential effects are also involved. Fisher (1955) observes that fox terriers, when reared in *isolation* from 3 to 16 wk of age, are submissive, develop no fighting behavior, and play in a solitary fashion when placed with their peers. Our findings demonstrate, however, that dog-deprived pups do recover rapidly, although deficits in social behavior are apparent early in their socialization at 12 wk.

The variable of maternal influences, where mothers may produce different behavior in their pups by postnatal "transfer" of some of their behavior, was not controlled in this experiment. It is a common practice to wean pups earlier if they are nursed by a timid or overfearful bitch, and this problem is worthy of further investigation.

If in this study the hand-reared pups had been given more than only food-contact with the handlers, such as play and other modalities of stimulation, it is conceivable that they would have shown more social behavior and emotional attachment toward their peers. Harlow (1962) emphasizes that grooming and play with the mother monkey and peers are more important factors in the development of normal social behavior than mere nurture. With this background, a purely objective point must be added; the hand-reared pups appear "loveless" toward humans, and this may be due to lack of reinforcement of social releasers such as barking, tail wagging, paw raising, and genital-olfactory exploration.

This study has shown that many aspects of behavior must be reinforced or learned by social interaction with the subjects' own species, and that the young animal has great abilities to learn and consolidate some aspects of behavior which are deficient after restricted socialization with human beings only. Foley (1934) observes that self-grooming and related "social" grooming disappeared in a long-term isolated chimpanzee. We may conclude that innate behavior patterns, if not socially reinforced, will undergo regression or modification under conditions of deprivation (Lorenz 1965). Thorpe (1964) has discussed these problems and emphasizes that the developing organism learns early in life to recognize its own kind, and because of its own behavior patterns, which act as compatible social stimuli, is in turn accepted by its own kind. Hand-rearing in this study causes some reduction of these social responses, for normally reared pups tend to aggregate and play together, whereas the hand-reared pups are ignored. When two hand-reared pups are first introduced, there is no active play. Passivity and close body contact and occasional licking or tail wagging are observed, but vocalization, play-biting, and fighting are not seen. With time, however, these pups show some recovery. Possibly with more extended isolation the ability to recover would be more severely affected, as has been reported in the monkey by several investigators.

Few studies have been undertaken on the effects of rearing animals of one species with members of another related species (Denenberg, Hudgens, and Zarrow 1966). These authors have reported the effects of rearing mice with rats, and Fox (see later) has observed differences in social behavior and social preference in dogs reared with cats and also evaluated the importance of habituation in interspecies socialization. Cairns and Johnson (1965) have recently reported the effects of extended isolation of young lambs from other sheep, coupled with continuous exposure to an alien species, which in their experiment was the dog. Kuo (1960) demonstrated that socialization in early life can reduce interspecies aggression in a variety of species that normally have a prey-predator relationship (although Cairns and Werboff [1967], found that rearing dogs with rabbits did not eliminate interspecies aggression). Thorpe (1964) has reviewed several reports showing that behavioral characteristics of one species may be transferred from one to another if the young animal is reared with a member of another species. There is evidence that rearing different breeds of dogs together may cause some "transfer" of traits from one breed to another (Scott and Bronson, personal communication). Social experience in the dog between 4 and 12 wk of age greatly influences subsequent behavior, and these observations have been incorporated in the critical period of socialization hypothesis (Scott 1962, 1963). The work of Freedman, King, and Elliot (1961) gives much support to this hypothesis, and these problems have been reviewed by Fox (1965*a*).

In differentially reared chickens (Baron, Kish, and Antonitis 1962), the effect of social isolation or social contact is modified by social experiences; social isolation following an early period of social contact reduces the effects of early social contact, and social contact following an early period of social isolation reduces the effects of early social isolation if short periods of social contact have been previously permitted. Thus increments of early experience may facilitate later social responses, and short-term isolation has lesser effects due to greater plasticity and adaptability of the organism, facilitating more complete socialization.

Harlow (1965*b*) reports that social potentials are destroyed if monkeys are isolated from birth to 6 or 12 mo, but not if they are isolated for only 3 mo or given social contact from birth to 6 mo and then isolated until 1 yr of age. These observations are supported by the findings in the early-weaned (CI) group, for few behavioral deficits were observed, although considerable individual variability was noted. Gottlieb (1965) emphasizes that parentally naïve ducklings and chicks have a marked preference for the parental call of their own species, a reaction which is highly resistant to change by learning or by previous experience with parental calls of other species. The observed resistance to change by previous experience is supported by the finding that hand-reared pups are not overly attached to human beings and recover rapidly from their behavioral deficits after only a few days of socialization with controls. Kunkel and Kunkel (1964) observed perpetuation of infantile behavior in adult male guinea pigs reared in social isolation. These observations lend support to the observations that neonate-like neck and body contact behavior are the major social responses in 12-wk-old hand-reared pups when they are first introduced to each other. Play activities of normal 12-wk-old pups are not present or "released" by the behavior of the reciprocal social interactor. Ellis and Pearce (1962) report that isolation-raised locusts react less toward live decoys than do group-reared controls, spending less time near them and moving more slowly. Similarly, the hand-reared and early-weaned pups frequently leave the social group and react significantly less toward their mirror reflections; normally reared pups rarely leave the social group and react strongly when confronted with a mirror (see also subsequent section on mirror responses in cat-raised dogs).

The adaptive survival value of innate behavior patterns is to promote rapid socialization with like species and is a phenomenon similar in many respects to imprinting in precocial animals (Sluckin 1965). These innate patterns disappear if no social reinforcement is present, or may become fragmented and incorporated in atypical behavior patterns which are not characteristic of the species. Thus learning and the socioenvironmental milieu have great influence on the ontogeny of behavior. It is hoped that this investigation will provide further background for more detailed studies on the critical factors underlying the development of social relationships and species identity.

Summary

The effect of varying decrements of socialization of the dog with its own species was studied in dogs reared under three different conditions: (*a*) hand reared and socially isolated from peers from 3 days to 12 wk (IIs); (*b*) weaned early at 3½ wk and socially isolated until 12 wk (CIs); and (*c*) weaned at 8 wk and socially isolated until 12 wk (CCIs).

At 12 wk, when run through a battery of tests and in subsequent observations up to 15 wk, the IIs showed the greatest deficits in social behavior and reactions to their own species. The CCIs were most reactive toward peers, the IIs least reactive, and the CIs intermediate. All groups showed similar attraction scores toward human beings. The IIs were nonvocal, nonoral, nonaggressive, and passive with peers when first put together. They rapidly became aggressive toward their peers following socialization and rarely engaged in group play. They tended to wander off alone and engage in self-play or to manipulate inanimate objects. CCIs grouped together and showed strong interaction attributed to mutually compatible behavior patterns. The CIs were intermediate, some individuals behaving like IIs and others appearing much like CCIs. These findings were discussed in relation to the critical period of socialization, during which primary social relationships are established.

Behavioral Effects of Rearing Dogs with Cats during the Period of Socialization

Introduction

Few studies have been undertaken to evaluate the effects of rearing an animal with an alien species on its later social behavior and ontogeny of species-specific behavior patterns. Hediger (1950) observed that if animals are reared from early infancy with an alien species, including man, sexual responses may be directed toward these alien species; and where reproductive processes are compatible, as between alpaca and vicuña, hybridization may occur. There are several reports of various animals' becoming socialized to human beings as a result of restricted rearing under conditions of captivity; they may become overattached to human beings and direct their later sexual activities or social preferences toward their handlers and show varying degrees of social incompatibility with their own species. Such observations have been made on several species of hand-reared birds (Lorenz 1935; Klinghammer 1967), sheep (Scott 1958*b*), in the dog under conditions of domestication (Fox 1965*a*), and in the monkey (Sackett, Porter, and Holmes 1965; Sackett et al. 1967; Pratt and Sackett 1967). Denenberg, Hudgens, and Zarrow (1964, 1966) and Hudgens, Denenberg, and Zarrow (1967) reported the effects of rearing mice with rats, and Cairns and Johnson (1965) and Cairns and Werboff (1967) evaluated the effects of rearing lambs with dogs and dogs with rabbits. Kuo (1960) found that socialization in early life of a variety of species which normally have a prey-predator relationship greatly reduces interspecies aggression. Thorpe (1964) has reviewed a number of reports that have shown how song patterns may be modified to some extent by rearing birds with an alien species. Generally the basic song characteristics are unaffected. Thus, interspecies socialization and restricted intraspecies socialization may result in the following behavioral changes:

1. Social preference for alien foster-parents or foster-peers through socialization or imprinting processes.

2. Reduction of normal social reactions to the foster species, such as aggression and prey-predator relationship.

3. Interspecies sexual behavior, with hybrid offspring if physiologically compatible.

4. Asocial reactions to own species, but recovery possible if experiences with alien species do not cause regression or inhibition of its species—specific behavior patterns.

5. Innate or phylogenetically determined species-specific behavior patterns may be unaffected by rearing with an alien species, and those behavior patterns and activities which are only partially phylogenetically determined may not emerge with typical species-specific characteristics. Those activities and behavior patterns which depend more on ontogenetic contingencies of reinforcement (see Skinner 1966) will be more severely disrupted, especially where there is a greater phylogenetic "distance" between the alien species that are raised together.

Materials and Methods

Because their physical size is comparable to that of cats, purebred Chihuahuas were used in this study. A problem with using this breed is that only 2–3 offspring are normally born, and neonatal mortalities and obstetrical problems are frequently encountered. Also, the birth of pups had to be approximately synchronized with the birth of a litter of kittens to permit cross-fostering. Ideally, the pups were 5–7 days older than the kittens, because they attain relative maturity in terms of reflex development and CNS maturation I wk later than the cat (Fox 1971*a*). Four pups were raised singly with a litter of 4–6 kittens, together with their mother, from 25 days to 16 wk of age; that is, throughout the critical period of socialization (Scott and Marston 1950). No problems were encountered in the cats' accepting the pup. Within a few hours the pup would be feeding from one of the teats of the cat, and when introduced to semisolid foods, had no difficulties in supplementing its diet at this early age. The female cat was removed and the young were weaned at 8 wk. Control pups in numbers of not less than 2 were weaned at 8 wk of age and raised together. A series of tests were run on both experimental and control dogs at 16 wk, and in social behavior observations, the foster-cats and a litter of cats of approximately the same age but without previous experience with dogs were used. After these observations, the cat-raised dogs were housed with their own species and their conspecific resocialization in terms of social reactivity was evaluated over several weeks.

The following tests were employed in an 8-sided behavior arena ($8' \times 8'$) equipped with one-way windows for observation and photography, and with a floor marked in 1-ft squares so that activity scores could be recorded:

1. *Reaction to Mirror.* A $1\frac{1}{2}' \times 2'$ mirror mounted on one of the walls of the arena, 1 in above the floor was used to test the control and experimental pups' reactions to their own reflection when they were alone in the arena for 5 min. The number of times they approached the mirror, duration of interaction, vocalization, and activity were recorded by four observers during this period.

2. *Reactions to Littermates.* The cat-raised dog was then placed in the arena with littermates of its own species, and the reactions and interactions of both control and experimental dogs, in terms of play and play fighting, aggressive fighting, submissiveness, vocalization, and group-coordinated activities (running around the arena together) were observed for 15 min.

3. *Reactions to Own Species in Presence of Alien Foster-Species.* Following the above test, the foster-kittens of the pup were placed with the other dogs in the arena and similar observations were conducted for 15 min more.

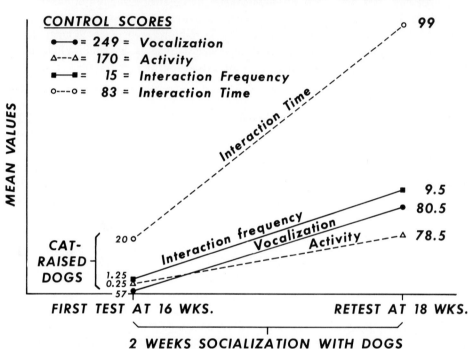

MIRROR TEST
AVERAGED RESULTS IN CONTROL & CAT-RAISED DOGS

Fig. 6.13. Low interaction scores with mirror (own reflection) in cat-raised dogs, but marked recovery following 2 wk living with dog-raised dogs.

4. *Reactions of Nonsocialized Alien Species.* The behavior of dog-raised pups and of cat-raised cats was then observed to provide some information as to the reactions of the cats that had no previous experience with dogs.

5. *Reaction to Man.* The individual social reactions—approach, following, submissive postures, and greeting responses—were tested in the control and experimental dogs.

Results and Discussion

All cat-raised dogs showed minimal reactions to the mirror, and their number of interactions and interaction times were extremely low (fig. 6.13). Vocalization was minimal and tail wagging was rarely seen except in a submissive position. In contrast, control subjects were highly aroused by their reflection in the mirror and had long interaction times. They were consistently vocal, tail wagging was continuous, and they would jump up at the mirror and paw, scratch, or dig at it. They also moved to the sides of the mirror, possibly attempting to reach behind it. Reactions of cat-raised dogs increased significantly during subsequent socialization with their own species (fig. 6.13). One cat-raised dog only approached the mirror at the end of the first test observations when it heard the observers' voices. This apparent arousal stimulated the dog to approach its reflection in the mirror, the dog being nonvocal and passive and wagging its tail in a submissive position.

These observations lead to the conclusion that socialization influences the development of species and self-identity. Cat-raised dogs, having had no experience with their own species, were consequently nonreactive to their own reflection, but became more reactive as they were subsequently socialized with their own species.

1. *Reactions to Littermates.* Cat-raised dogs were submissive and passive toward their species-peers (whereas with their alien-peers in rearing quarters they were always active and playful). These pups were nonvocal and the tail-wagging response was inhibited or presented with the tail held low in a submissive position. These reactions are very similar to those observed in hand-reared dog-deprived pups (see earlier).

The control pups, after intensively investigating the cat-raised dog and after futile attempts to solicit play responses from it, began to explore the arena together (group-coordinated behavior) and to play with each other, while the cat-raised dog remained passive and rarely moved around the arena (see figs. 6.14, 6.15).

2. *Reactions to Own Species in Presence of Alien Foster-Species.* As soon as the dog-exposed kittens were placed in the arena, the cat-raised dog approached them and showed tail-wagging greeting responses. These cats were intensively investigated by the control pups, and were frequently rather roughly chewed, nibbled, and pawed. They remained passive, but as soon as play responses were solicited, the cats began to react playfully, showing piloerection, pawing the pups, and jumping over them; both alien species chased each other around the arena. These cats would back up into one corner of the arena and leap onto the control pups as they ran by. The cat-raised dog became much more reactive and exploratory to the other dogs as soon as the cats had been placed in the arena, but on no occasion was active play or play-fighting seen between cat-raised dogs and control dogs. One cat-raised dog began to show defensive aggression, as it attempted to bite and bared its teeth as control dogs persisted in vigorously soliciting play.

These observations dramatically showed that although the cat-raised dog was relatively asocial toward its own species, the cats that had been socialized with one dog interacted well with strange dogs and thus generalized their social reactions from earlier experiences with only one member of the alien species.

3. *Reactions of Nonsocialized Alien Species.* Two groups of Chihuahua pups and two litters of 3 cats each were observed together (for the first time) at 16 wk of age. In both instances, pups actively investigated the cats and then attempted to solicit play. Cats remained passive, but if they attempted to escape, this reaction

released playful chasing by the pups. As the pups pawed and chewed the cats more vigorously, the cats withdrew to the corners of the arena and assumed defensive-threat postures. Surprisingly, 1 cat of the 6 actively played with the pups and spontaneously chased them and allowed them to chase it, to roll it over, and to chew and pull vigorously on various body appendages.

These differences in social interactions between cat-raised cat and dog-raised dog suggest that the dog generalizes its social reactions in terms of investigation

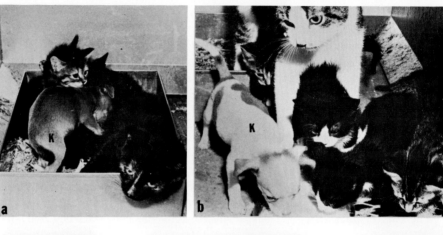

Fig. 6.14 *a* and *b,* Chihuahua pup being nursed and feeding with cat littermates; *c,* transient passive reaction to mirror in cat-raised dog (*k*), whereas normal (*n*) dog-raised dogs react vigorously and frequently (*d* and *e*).

followed by spontaneous play or at least attempts to solicit play from the alien species. Similar reactions in cats are more dependent upon previous social experience, and they do not generalize their social reactions as the dogs do unless they have had previous social experience with the alien species.

4. *Reactions to Man.* Normal approach and following responses were present in cat-raised dogs, and vocalizations, tail wagging, and submissive hind-leg raising and urination were present. The normal licking-chewing response to an extended hand is a species-specific social gesture in the dog, which they do to each other as a facially and orally directed greeting gesture (facial-lingual greeting, Fox 1971*b*). In cat-raised dogs, the strong oral tendency to chew was absent; the extended hand was gently licked, and even when engaged in play, in contrast to con-

trols, no biting was noted. This social nuzzle-nibble greeting response may be a social greeting gesture emancipated from the facial and orally directed food-soliciting responses of pups toward the mother. Only occasionally will a bitch vomit food for pups after 4–5 wk of age, whereas in wild Canidae, such as *Lycaon* (Kuhme 1965), regurgitation of food is a normal response. Possibly in the dog this initially food-soliciting response has been emancipated into a form of social greeting. That it is almost absent, in terms of nibbling and oral manipulation, in cat-raised dogs

Fig. 6.15 *a,* Two cats raised with dog (*k*) play spontaneously with dog-raised dog; *b* and *c,* passive and submissive behavior of cat-raised dogs (*k*) on first encounter with dogs of same age raised together (*n*); *d,* dog-raised dogs actively playing whereas cat-raised dog avoids social interaction and stays with its foster-kittens; *e,* cat-raised dog (*k*) does not interact socially or show allelomimetic behavior with controls (*n*).

(and also in hand-raised dog-deprived dogs, see earlier) suggests that this species-specific response is in part ontogenetically determined. Lack of adequate contingencies of reinforcement or possibly social inhibition (as cats do not normally chew and nibble each other on the ears, face, and lips) may have contributed to the repression of this social response in cat-raised dogs. Recovery was quite rapid, however, for the oral chewing response was evident in all cat-raised dogs after they were with their own species for 7–14 days. Similar recoveries were noted in some hand-raised dogs when they were resocialized (see earlier).

Recovery. The resocialization to their own species was apparently well established after 2 wk. This is not surprising, since many species-specific behavior patterns were preserved in the cat-raised dogs; also, while living with the cats they had plenty of opportunity to indulge in play activities.

When the mirror reactions of the cat-raised dogs were tested 2 wk after they had been removed from their cat foster-peers and housed with a group of 6 dog-raised Chihuahuas of approximately the same age, there was a marked increase in reactivity. Vocalization scores, activity, frequency of interaction, and duration of interactions increased in all subjects (fig. 6.13). Tail wagging was observed in all subjects, but they tended to be less demonstrative in front of the mirror than controls, who frequently jumped up against the mirror and scratched vigorously with their forelimbs. One cat-raised dog repeatedly approached the mirror, wagging its tail, and sat quietly looking at its reflection for long periods, occasionally pushing with its nose. When observers began to talk outside the arena at the end of the observation period, all pups now oriented toward the direction of the extraneous stimulation, became generally aroused, and wagged their tails. This reaction contrasted with the reaction seen in the first test, when the pups approached the mirror at the sound of a human voice (which, incidentally, was not coming from anywhere near the mirror). Thus socialization with the same species resulted, within a 2-wk period, in a marked improvement in species recognition in terms of reactivity to a mirror image, and in an improved ability to recognize that the human voice was not associated with the mirror image. Why the latter association was made earlier is not clear; possibly the effect was one of response generalization, the subject responding to its mirror image because of its inability to recognize the type of responses characteristic of its own species. In other words, the dog, being unable to recognize its mirror image, and not knowing how it would respond, reacted as though the mirror image were speaking to it.

Conclusions

These observations have shown that the development of "species identity" (or self-recognition) is dependent upon the species to which the animal is socialized, and this socialization effect influences later social preferences for the same species or alien foster-species. Earlier studies with hand-raised dogs have shown that experience from birth to 3½ wk, that is, before the onset of the critical period of socialization, has some effect on subsequent behavior. The rapid resocialization of the dogs reared with cats throughout the critical period of socialization indicates that certain phylogenetically determined, species-specific behavior patterns which are not severely affected by restricted early social experience may facilitate subsequent socialization with the same species. Socialization with an alien species in cats facilitates their social reactivity and play interactions, but without such previous social experience, cats will rarely interact spontaneously with dogs. In contrast, dog-raised dogs interact spontaneously with cat-raised cats and actively attempt to solicit play. In the formation of affectional bonds in adult life, the contribution played by "early experience" of those bonds established during the infantile period of primary socialization or imprinting has received little detailed study. It appears that the filial social bonds established in early life facilitate the formation of sexual bonds in later life, although there are certain exceptions. Warriner, Lemmon, and Ray (1963) find that male pigeons prefer to mate with birds whose color is similar to that of the parents who reared them, and Schutz (1965) noted that female mallards do not become sexually imprinted toward other species but will mate with mallards independent of their early experience. However, in many species Schutz observes that although individual attachments are formed during the imprinting period around 16 hr of age, species-attachments may not develop until 30 days, and sexual attachment to members of the opposite sex does not come about until 5 mo of age. Apparently, in sexually dimorphic species sexual imprinting is found only in males, whereas in the sexually isomorphic, both sexes are imprinted. Rearing male (but not female) mallards together through the time when species bonds are formed, that is, until at least 75 days of age, Schutz found that they became homosexual, even in the presence of females. An internationally known breeder of shih-tzus (a breed of dog originating in China) reported to the author that one of his stud dogs (a golden) purchased from another kennel refused to breed with some of his bitches that had a black and white coat color. Successful breeding occurred in bitches that had a golden coat color. This male had apparently come from an entirely golden-coated line, and it is conceivable that this early experience greatly modified his subsequent sexual preference. Breeders of numerous varieties of dog have stressed that an "odd colored" pup in a litter, such as a merle or harlequin, "keeps to itself" or is "ignored by the majority," and, if there are two or three such pups, they usually stay together and are especially found sleeping together. These observations may be erroneous and arise from a perceptual bias on the part of the breeder: however, the case of the shih-tzu is certainly more convincing, and may suggest that coat type (even though the dog is supposedly colorblind) may be a significant variable in the social behavior of the dog. Hinde (1966) has critically reviewed several experimental and anecdotal observations on the later sexual preferences of animals modified by their early filial relationships; in many cases the later experiences during the juvenile period around the onset of sexual maturity can overrule the preferences established earlier in life. Hinde concludes that "the most economical hypothesis is that the influence of previous experience on later choice of a sex partner is only a special case of greater readiness to respond to a familiar stimulus. Thus experience in early development is merely one of the factors determining choice of a sex partner." Pratt and Sackett (1967) have found that monkeys raised under different conditions of social contact choose as social partners those monkeys that have been raised under the same conditions and have received the same intensity or amount of social contact in early life. Similar observations were made in isolation- and hand-raised pups (see previous section), in that subjects that had had similar social and perceptual experiences tended to remain and interact together. How important these incremental effects of experience are on the individual's later choice of a sexual partner with similar previous experience (and conceivably, therefore, a similar behavioral repertoire with comparable deficits or idiosyncrasies) remains to be evaluated.

The social environment, in providing contingencies of reinforcement and actual conditioning and subsequent organization and direction of behavior, plays a major role in behavioral development. In addition to providing "love objects" such as the parent figure or peers, which are associated with socialization and the development of affectional bonds, the social environment also provides reinforcement, which can organize the developing organism's repertoire through conditioning and also provide motivation through reinforcement or reward. Rheingold, Gewirtz, and Ross (1959) have clearly shown the importance of the social environment or milieu in the conditioning of vocalizations in the human infant. The extent to which habituation influences the developing organism's reactions to its social milieu remains to be evaluated.

Habituation, exposure learning, and attachment to the inanimate components of the social milieu (locality imprinting) may play an additive role during the process of socialization and development of primary social relationships. Also, the acquisition of species-specific rituals, or culturally acquired response patterns in man, should be considered; Gesell (1954) stresses the importance of distinguishing between maturation and acculturation, for the culture or social milieu acts as a mold for the matrix of maturational processes directing the development of behavior.

Age Differences in the Effects of Visual Deprivation

Introduction

Stimulation is a necessary prerequisite of normal growth and development, and it is generally recognized that without adequate stimulation of one modality, such as vision, in early life, degeneration of receptors and afferent pathways may occur, together with deficits in behavioral development (Riesen 1961*b*, 1966; Wilson and Riesen 1966). The *stimulus-dependent* nature of development of structurofunctional components of behavior is, therefore, a generally accepted fact. Held and Hein (1963) also emphasize that multiple afferent feedback plays an important role in the organization of visually guided behavior. The work of Hubel and Wiesel (1963) and Wiesel and Hubel (1963*a, b,* 1965) has shown that monocular occlusion of vision in the kitten produces structural and functional changes only if it occurs early in life; similar treatment at a later age produces insignificant changes. In their studies, however, vision was occluded for a relatively long period of 3 mo. The present investigation was undertaken to determine if any changes could be detected in the dog following visual deprivation for a short period of 5 wk. Fox (1966*g*) has presented the hypothesis that various units within a given system of the CNS are developed and organized during an early postnatal period of integration. It is at this time that the organism is dependent upon stimulation for the consolidation of structurofunctional components (through a process akin to learning) of a given system. Lack of stimulation during this sensitive period of integration would possibly cause severe deficits within that system, whereas similar treatment at a later age, when integration is completed, would have minimal effects. Similarly, excessive stimulation through various systems may be effective only during and immediately after structurofunctional integration, since before this the system is not operationally "open"; that is, there may be ontogenetic limitations of "sensitive" periods.

Materials and Methods

Subjects. A total of 29 dogs were used in this study. They were of mixed breed (sheep-dog type) and were maintained under similar standards of management and nutrition. Eight subjects were used in the first group, whose eyes were occluded from 1 day to 5 wk of age. In the second group, 6 had occlusion from 5 to 10 wk of age. Four littermate controls were used in each group. In addition, 3 adults had their vision occluded for 5 wk, and 4 adults were used as controls.

Treatment. The experimental design consisted of binocular occlusion of vision in dogs for a period of 5 wk. Vision was effectively prevented by securing a foam-rubber pad across the eyes with adhesive tape. To prevent the pad from slipping backward, loops of adhesive tape were passed under the throat. Self-adhesive gauze bandage was then applied around the occiput and extended to the base of the nasal bones. Then several layers of bandage were used to encircle the neck. The subjects were unable to dislodge the foam-rubber pad from over the eyes. This method was chosen in preference to suturing the eyelids, for a considerable amount of light can enter through the thin tissues of the eyelids. Difficulty was encountered in pilot studies in ensuring that the youngest pups received adequate food from the mother; lack of cephalic stimulation disrupted the rooting reflex and prevented the pups from orienting and locating the nipple. It was therefore essential to use attentive and cooperative mothers, and in addition the pups were placed on the nipple at regular times for 1 hr twice daily and were allowed to feed without competition with littermate controls, who were removed at these times. At 3 wk of age the difference in weight between blindfolded and control pups ranged from 50 to 150 g, but by 5 wk of age, after 2 wk on solid food, which supplemented the bitch milk, these differences were eliminated. Studies on the effects of chronic starvation on the neuronal and visually and auditorily evoked potential development in the dog (Myslivecek, Fox, and Zahlava 1967) have shown that neuronal dendritic development and ontogeny of evoked potentials are severely retarded during the first 2–3 postnatal wk. By 4–6 wk of age, however, dendritic development and evoked potentials were similar in experimental and control subjects. The second group of pups in which vision was occluded between 5 and 10 wk of age were introduced to solid food at 3½ wk and weaned from the bitch at 5 wk, as were their controls. No difficulties were encountered by these pups in taking solid food when their vision was occluded. Adult dogs, after a short period of 1–2 days, ate normally and maintained excellent health.

Tests. After 5 wk occlusion of vision, the following procedures were carried out:

1. Sedation and analgesia sufficient for surgery was obtained with Fentanyl and Droperidol (Innovar-Vet, McNeil) given intramuscularly.
2. Removal of bandages, saline lavage of eyes, and application of atropine eyedrops.
3. Following local anesthesia with procaine, a midline incision was made over the cranium, and the temporal muscles were reflected. Trephine holes were made with a dental drill approximately 1.0 cm lateral to the midline over the occipital cortex, and stainless steel needle electrodes were inserted into the posterior segment of the right and left lateral gyri of the visual cortex. Accurate placement of electrodes was confirmed later on dissection. A similar electrode was placed in the frontal region over the frontal sinus and served as an indifferent lead. A ground connection was made with an alligator-clip electrode placed on the interdigital web of a forefoot, which was moistened with saline.
4. A Grass photostimulator placed 2 in from the subject provided binocular photic

stimulation. Illumination intensity was set at 16, flash duration at 10 μsec. Each recording epoch consisted of 10 flashes at a frequency of either 0.4/sec or 1.0/sec, with a delay of 50 msec at the onset. Stimuli were applied at intervals of 2–3 min and were repeated 4 times at each frequency. The evoked responses were monitored on an oscilloscope and fed into a CAT model 400B by means of a 6-channel Grass model III electroencephalograph. The average of 10 evoked potentials was computed and recorded on a Moseley X-Y plotter. The head was supported with sandbags to ensure that the eyes were kept directly in front of the light source.

5. After these recordings were completed, subjects were killed with intravenous Nembutal and the brain was removed immediately in a cold room at 4° C.

The left gyrus lateralis of the occipital lobe was dissected and prepared histologically using Thionine, and rapid Golgi (Sholl 1953) impregnation techniques. Hematoxylin and eosin preparations were made of the retinas and the optic nerves were stained by Ora's method for myelin. Occipital cortex, superior colliculi, and caudate nucleus were dissected from the brain and immediately homogenized separately in ice-cold perchloric acid, using a Branson sonifier for biochemical analysis.

Estimations of noradrenaline (NA) were done according to the method of Bertler, Carlsson, and Rosengren (1958). Dopamine (DA) was determined using the methods of Carlsson and Waldeck (1958) as modified by Carlsson and Lindquist (1962). Values are expressed as μg/g wet-weight tissue.

Results

Averaged Visually Evoked Potentials. The greatest variability in form of evoked potential was seen in the youngest group of pups, visually deprived from birth to 5 wk. In many of these 5-wk-old subjects, summated evoked potentials were not observed after 10 stimulus presentations, and yet after 10 more stimulus presentations, clear evoked potentials were obtained. Asymmetry between left and right recordings and variation in amplitude were also observed. A commonly occurring response was seen as a low-amplitude negative wave of relatively long duration, which might or might not be followed by a positive wave (fig. 6.16). This type of evoked response is characteristic of the normal pup aged 2–10 days (chap. 4). In some visually deprived 5-wk-old pups, a relatively mature positive wave predominated but had a peak latency 10–20 msec longer than that of controls and varied in duration and amplitude. In all 5-wk controls, the predominant wave of the averaged evoked potential was a positive wave which did not vary in amplitude, duration, or latency in successive recordings in the same subject. The extreme variability and inconsistency of evoked responses in the visually deprived pups of this age group did not enable peak latencies to be calculated with sufficient reliability to show the average differences in latencies between the control and visually deprived subjects (fig. 6.16).

In pups visually deprived from 5 to 10 wk of age, the extreme variability in evoked potentials seen in the youngest group was not observed (fig. 6.17). In all subjects, evoked potentials were reliably elicited, and differed only slightly from those of the controls. The average peak latency of the primary positive wave was 56.0 msec in the visually deprived pups and slightly shorter in the controls, 51.0 msec.

Averaged evoked potentials from visually deprived adults were composed of normal positive and negative wave components, and no variability between stimulus presentations to the same subject was observed (fig. 6.17). The average peak latency of the primary positive wave was 55.0 msec in visually deprived subjects and 65.0 msec in controls.

Histological Findings. Neuronal and dendritic development in the visual cortex, determined by Sholl's rapid Golgi-Cox method, was relatively well advanced in the pups visually deprived from 0 to 5 wk of age (fig. 6.18). The majority of large cells of Meynert in layer V of the neocortical gray matter were less developed than in

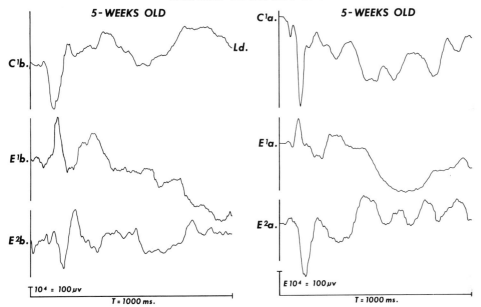

Fig. 6.16. Abnormal evoked potentials in litters *b* and *a* (vision occluded from birth to 5 wk), showing predominance of negative component in E[1]b and E[1]a, and longer latency, long duration of positive component in E[2]b and E[2]a.

the controls; dendritic development of some of these neurons was markedly arrested, whereas other neurons had elaborate basilar dendrites, but the cells were generally smaller and the dendritic arborizations were fewer and thinner. The smaller neurons of other layers of the visual cortex were well developed in the deprived subjects, but the apical and basilar dendrites, although as elaborate as those in the controls, were generally not as thick. It is unfortunate that these marked qualitative differences in neuronal development could not be supported by such quantitative data as the number of dendritic spines. In all subjects, few dendritic spines were detectable; this may be due to histological technique or some species-tissue variable.

Thionine preparations from separate tissue blocks from the visual cortex revealed that the Nissl content of many cells, notably in the Meynert cells in deprived pups (0–5 wk), stained less intensely and was less granular than in controls.

No structural differences were detectable histologically in the visual cortices of control animals and pups visually deprived from 5 to 10 wk of age, or in adults deprived for 5 wk (fig. 6.18).

Signs of retinal degeneration were observed in only two pups of the youngest age group, in which the rod and cone layer was reduced and the ganglion layer contained small, poorly developed cells.

No histological differences in the degree of myelination of the optic nerves or optic chiasma were observed in the youngest age group, with one exception, or in older subjects (fig. 6.19). Signs of demyelination were evident in one of the visually deprived pups of the youngest age group.

Biochemical Findings. A significant increase (compared with controls of the same age) of noradrenaline was found in the colliculi of deprived pups of the youngest age group only (table 6.7), and also only in this group was there a significant increase of dopamine in the colliculi following visual deprivation. In the

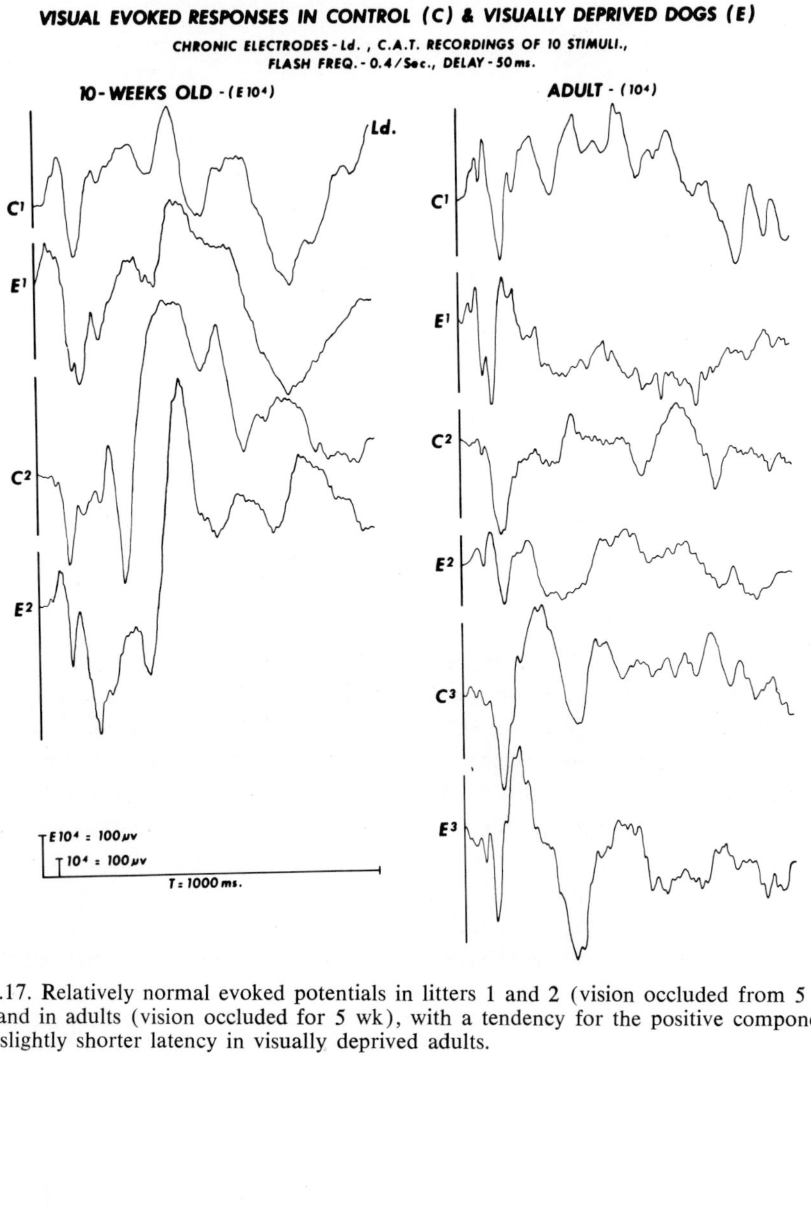

Fig. 6.17. Relatively normal evoked potentials in litters 1 and 2 (vision occluded from 5 to 10 wk), and in adults (vision occluded for 5 wk), with a tendency for the positive component to be of slightly shorter latency in visually deprived adults.

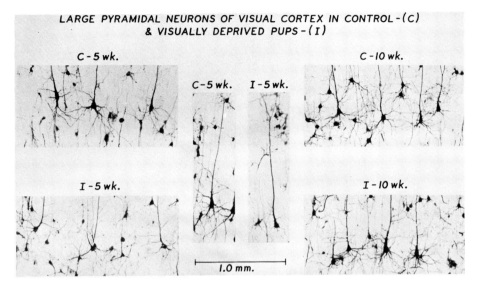

Fig. 6.18. Golgi preparations showing marked reduction in neuronal size and dendritic arborization in pups visually deprived from birth to 5 wk, whereas subjects treated from 5 to 10 wk have no histologically detectable retardation of development.

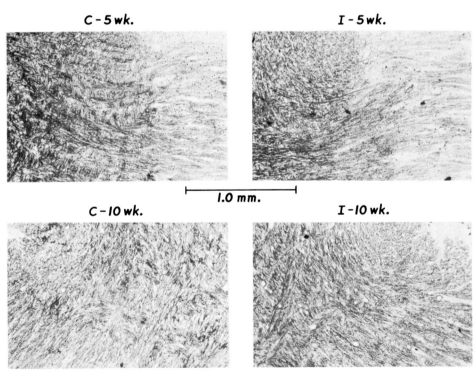

Fig. 6.19. Myelination (Ora's method) is little affected by visual deprivation during early or late postnatal life.

caudate nucleus of visually deprived adults and pups treated from 5 to 10 wk there was an increase in dopamine compared with controls which approached statistical significance. No increase was found in the youngest visually deprived group. If these data are compared among the three age groups, the biochemical effects of visual deprivation are similar in the 10-wk-old and adult dogs but are significantly different in the youngest age group (table 6.7).

The amine levels (table 6.7) found in the occipital cortex are so close to the sensitivity of the method that it is only possible to state that increases were found in the isolated dogs of all ages for both NA and DA, with the exception of 5-wk occipital cortex.

TABLE 6.7

RESULTS OF BIOCHEMICAL ANALYSIS OF BRAIN REGIONS IN VISUALLY DEPRIVED DOGS

CHEMICAL		CONTROL			EXPERIMENTAL		
		Superior Colliculi	Caudate Nucleus	Occipital Cortex	Superior Colliculi	Caudate Nucleus	Occipital Cortex
Noradrenaline	5 wk	.098[b](±.09)	.071	.038	.400[b](±.14)	.049	.064
	10 wk	.305	.028	.047	.265	.045	.070
	Adult	.372	.042	.089	.429	.034	.160
Dopamine	5 wk	.342[a](±.03)	3.640	.078	1.167[a](±.39)	3.450	.039
	10 wk	1.770 (±.42)	3.490[c](±1.10)	.025	1.970 (±.69)	4.570[c](±.57)	.104
	Adult	.658 (±.15)	9.520[d](±2.30)	.078	.412 (±.10)	10.470[d](±1.60)	.141

NOTE: μg/g wet weight tissue (SD in parentheses).
[a] $p < 0.001$.   [b] $p > 0.01$.   [c] $p = 0.1-0.05$.   [d] $p = 0.05-0.01$.

Discussion

These findings show that visual deprivation for 5 wk only, early in postnatal life, can produce marked anatomical, electrophysiological, and biochemical changes in the CNS. In contrast, similar treatment after this early postnatal period has a minimal effect. These data indicate that at a certain time during development, the visual system is particularly sensitive to stimulation; that is, a sensitive period exists when the CNS is dependent upon stimulation for normal development. This sensitive period lies within the short postnatal period of integration (see chap. 7), and it is during this time that the most dramatic events in the development of the CNS occur. Both auditorily and visually evoked potentials and neuronal development in the visual and auditory cortices attain relative maturity by 5 wk of age (chaps. 3, 4).

It is surprising that the development of neocortical neurons was so advanced in the visual cortex of the pups visually deprived from birth to 5 wk of age, and that myelination had not been significantly retarded in the optic nerves. Gyllenstein, Malmfors, and Norrlin-Grettve (1966a) similarly observe that myelination of the optic nerves of visually deprived mice is apparently normal, and thus independent of stimulation. These data emphasize that a particular system or component of a system may develop independent of exogenous stimulation; however, as soon as such component parts of a system attain sufficient maturity for structurofunctional integration with other components, stimulation may then be essential for subsequent organization and consolidation.

Thompson and Schaefer (1961) have discussed these problems and conclude that primacy, plasticity, differentiation, and critical periods in development represent the most crucial characteristics of the young organism. Hubel and Wiesel (1963) have demonstrated in a series of neurophysiological studies in the kitten that if visual stimulation is denied, neuronal disorganization ensues—thus stimulation is essential for the maintenance, development, and maturation of neural systems. They believe that the visual system is already well organized at birth and that monocular visual occlusion causes disruption of already established pathways. However, myelination of the visual pathways and neocortical neuronal development is minimal at birth in the dog, and there is no evidence to suggest that the visual system is well organized at birth in this species. We believe, therefore, that visual deprivation early in life produces pathodevelopmental retardation rather than disruptive changes or disorganization. In the absence of function, continued structural development is impaired.

Gyllenstein, Malmfors, and Norrlin-Grettve (1966b) have shown that long-term visual deprivation in the mouse can affect other sensory systems; they reported alterations in the auditory cortex which may indicate a compensatory hypertrophy of this system to adapt to the deficits of sensory deprivation in another system in order to maintain perceptual homeostasis (or optimal afferent input) in the CNS. These observations on the interrelationships between different systems and on the afferent "tonus" or perceptual homeostasis of the CNS are worthy of further investigation.

The function of biogenic amines in visual perception is currently of much interest. Drujan, Diaz Borges, and Alvarez (1965) have shown that nonillumination of the retina in frogs, toads, and rabbits causes an increase in retinal dopamine. Himwich, Davis, and Agrawal (1967) have studied the biochemical and electrophysiological maturation of the superior colliculi in the rabbit and reported data on the development of biogenic amines in these structures. Biogenic amine concentrations showed the greatest fluctuations between 12 and 14 days, at the time when the eyes open, and they postulated that this may be related to the amount of visual stimuli the young received after the eyes were open.

Sprague (1966) has shown in cats that the contralateral superior colliculus and occipital cortex mediate visually guided behavior. Even though significant changes were not found in the occipital cortex in this present investigation, significant increases occurred in the superior colliculi in the 5-wk-old visually deprived animal both for NA and DA (table 6.1), which may reflect the creation of a stress on the normal development of visual perception, or possibly indicates a disuse phenomenon.

The results of this investigation demonstrate essentially qualitative changes following visual deprivation early in life. The capricious nature of the rapid Golgi-Cox method tends to reduce the number of adequately impregnated neurons and dendritic processes with spines. Only too frequently, spines are not visible even though the neuron and dendritic processes are well impregnated. As emphasized by Globus and Scheibel (1966), only a percentage of neurons are suitable for quantitative study. The important quantitative findings of Valverde (1967) and Globus and Scheibel (1966, 1967a, b), who reported a marked reduction in the number of dendritic spines following visual deprivation,[6] eye enucleation, or lesions of the lateral geniculate, remain to be reevaluated in terms of critical or sensitive integrative periods during ontogeny. Coleman and Riesen (1968) have shown clear evidence of shorter dendritic length of layer IV stellate cells in the primary visual cortex of cats reared in darkness until 6 mo of age, and similar decrements in dendritic fields in the upper pyramidal cells; they found no significant effects in layer V pyramids of the striate cortex.

Appel, Davis, and Scott (1967) have suggested that an increase in the activity of messenger RNA in the brain may result from environmental changes; they found that brain polysomes decreased in rats deprived of light and increased in those stimulated with light. Significant changes in body weight, cholinesterase activity, and sensory conditioning were found following manipulation of visual complexity in rats during early life (Singh, Johnston, and Klosterman 1967).

Further studies should be directed toward identification of integrative periods of various systems sensitive to the absence of stimulation during their ontogeny. Absence of qualitative stimulus components may produce qualitative and quantitative changes within a given system and also affect systems sensitive to quite different modalities of stimulation, as shown by Gyllenstein, Malmfors, and Norrlin-Grettve (1966b). Conversely, as demonstrated in the present investigation and by Gyllenstein, Malmfors, and Norrlin-Grettve (1966a), other components of a given system apparently may mature independent of stimulation. Thus the maturation of components of a given system, and subsequent functional integration of the system with the entire complex of the CNS, may be either independent or partially or wholly dependent upon stimulation. These relationships between the developing organism and the environment await further rigorous investigation.

Addendum: Bilateral Ocular Enucleation

The effect of *bilateral ocular enucleation* on myelination and neuronal development was evaluated in 10 dogs (5 operated upon at birth and examined histologically at 5 wk, and 5 operated on at 5 wk and examined at 10 wk of age). An equal number of littermate controls were used. Auditorily evoked potentials were recorded in these subjects under Fentanyl and Droperidol (Innovar-Vet, McNeil) before death. Similar evoked potentials were recorded in both control and blinded subjects; clear "nonspecific" negative waves were detected in the visual cortex (gyrus marginalis, see fig. 6.20), indicating that nonspecific thalamocortical connections were functional in the visual cortex of blinded subjects (i.e., polysensory input to visual cortex). Myelination (Ora's stain) was only slightly protracted in the visual cortex of pups blinded at birth, compared with controls, and no differences were detectable in the older group of dogs. Neuronal development (Sholl's Golgi-Cox method) was relatively well advanced in the visual cortex of pups blinded at birth, although many of the larger pyramidal and Meynert cells of layers III and V were smaller than in controls and had fewer collateral dendritic processes, which were more delicate but were not grossly lacking in spinous processes (see fig. 6.21). No dif-

---

[6] Schapiro and Vukovich (1970) have conversely demonstrated an increase in dendritic spines and in the number of cells stained by the rapid Golgi-Cox technique following multimodality stimulation of rats during early life: increased afferent input may therefore influence neuronal development as revealed histologically by the Golgi-Cox technique.

ferences in neuronal development were detectable in the 10-wk-old group. Demyelination was extensive in the optic nerves and chiasma in all blinded subjects in this older group. In the younger age group, the optic nerves of blinded pups were of smaller diameter than those of controls and contained no detectable traces of myelin (except in one dog, in which delicate, faintly myelinated fibers were present in one of the optic nerves). However, at the age of examination there was no demyelination of the optic chiasma in these subjects (fig. 6.22), suggesting that myelination continued independent of afferent input, thus masking the effects of

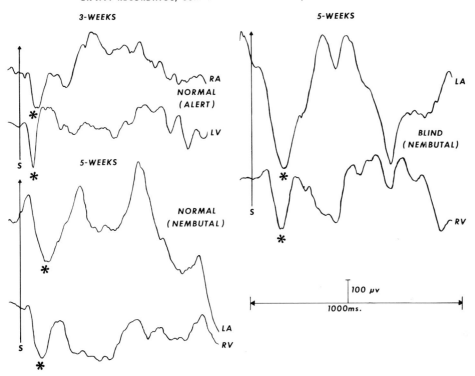

Fig. 6.20. Marked positive wave (*) evident in both visual (gyrus marginalis) and auditory (gyrus ectosylvius medius) cortices following auditory stimulation, in normal and blind pups.

degenerative processes and contrasting sharply with the complete demyelination of more distal segments of the optic nerve. These findings imply that myelination occurs in discrete (unrelated?) cycles in different regions of the visual system, and that regions more centrally situated are less dependent upon afferent input than are more peripherally located regions that are more directly connected with the receptor.

Cragg (1967) has presented preliminary observations on changes in the visual cortex of rats subjected to light deprivation and exposure to light following deprivation. He found that exposure to light may promote the formation of new synapses of small diameter in the deeper layers of the visual cortex, and that synapses already formed in the more superficial layers may grow slightly larger. Cragg concludes that it is now necessary to discover how long a period of initial exposure to light is required for these synaptic changes to be most clearly recognized. Exposure to light presumably causes an increase in neuronal activity, which may then produce synaptic changes.

Tsang (1936)[7] has reviewed earlier conflicting studies on the effects of peripheral lesions on the structure of the visual system. In his studies, he found that the degree of degeneration was proportional to the duration of the lesion (ocular enucleation), being most extensive in the colliculi, minimal in the visual cortex, and intermediate in the lateral geniculate. In rats blinded early in life, the results were more underdevelopment than positive degeneration. Enucleation at birth or 13 days in the rat induced about the same degree of degeneration in 7 mo.

Lesions of the visual system and occlusion of vision at different ages in the present study revealed some of the ontogenetic phenomena which must be considered in the development of the CNS; namely, stimulus-dependent and independent

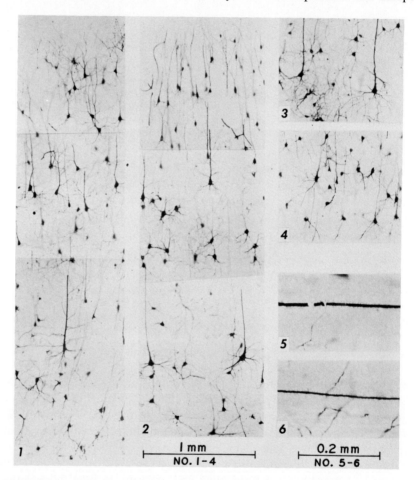

Fig. 6.21. Visual cortex of control (1) and blind (2) pups at 5 wk of age, showing fewer and finer dendrite collaterals in blind pup. In many regions, Meynert cells were smaller in blind subjects (4) than in controls (3); apical dendrites were more delicate (6) than in controls, although differences in dendrite spines were not observed.

[7] See also Berger 1900.

maturation; trophic degenerative changes associated with disuse atrophy; and trans-neuronal degeneration following lesions of the afferent system. Lesions produce marked degenerative changes, whereas lack of stimulation alone produces less extensive or less rapid changes. Impaired afferent input in the mature organism eventually results in degenerative changes, and in an immature organism, such treatment has an even greater effect within the same time period because, in addition, development is retarded and integration is inhibited or delayed.

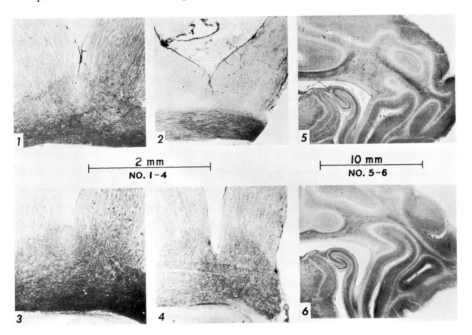

Fig. 6.22. Myelination of optic nerves and chiasma in control pups at 5 wk (1) and 10 wk (3) compared with 5-wk-old pup blinded at birth (2) and 10-wk-old pup blinded at 5 wk of age. Note marked demyelination of optic nerves in 2 and 4 and granular appearance of demyelinating chiasma in 4, whereas chiasma is unacected in 2. Myelination of visual cortex in 5-wk-old control (5) and in 5-wk-old pup blinded at birth (6).

However, some components of a complex sensory system may develop independent of stimulation (as in the myelination of optic nerve) and may therefore increase the potential for recovery and restoration of function in spite of degeneration and retardation. The effects of stimulation (or exercise, both qualitative and quantitative) in a fully integrated and functional system, before impairment of afferent input, must be considered in evaluating the potential for recovery following restoration of input in subjects of different ages.

Summary

Visual deprivation in dogs during the first 5 wk of life resulted in marked structural, biochemical, and electrophysiological changes which were not apparent in dogs similarly treated between 5 and 10 wk or for 5 wk in adults. These findings are discussed in relation to the period of integration, when structurofunctional relationships of neural elements begin to reach adultlike levels of organization. It was postulated that lack of stimulation of one modality during this period would result in a marked arrest in the development of the sensory system so treated. This hypothesis was partially confirmed; although there was complete visual deprivation, some neuronal and myelin development had occurred independent of visual stimulation. Visually evoked potentials were markedly abnormal in the youngest age group only. The findings suggest a "sensitive" period, in the pathodevelopmental sense, when development of a particular system is retarded if stimulation is inadequate. This period corresponds to the period of integration, during which structurofunctional organization of component systems of the CNS occurs. The effects of binocular enucleation are also discussed.

7

Discussion and Conclusions: Integrative Development of the CNS and Behavior

The data from this study of various aspects of the developing brain and behavior have been reviewed in figure 7.1 in an attempt to illustrate schematically the chronologically similar patterns of development of various parameters of the CNS. The rate of attainment of adult structural complexity or function is depicted and it will be noted that development continues at a more gradual rate after 5–6 wk of age. It is evident from this schema that during the transitional period and early part of the critical period of socialization (described by Scott and Marston 1950), these dramatic developmental changes occur. Biochemical data on glycogen metabolism (Himwich and Fazekas 1941), amino acids (Dravid, Himwich, and Davis 1965), DNA/RNA (Mandel et al. 1962), and lipids (chap. 4), correlate respectively with the data of Jilek and Trojan (1966) on the increasing resistance to anoxia with increasing age[1] and the findings reported in this investigation on the development of neocortical neurons, maturation of EEG, and myelination. The development of stable conditioned responses to various sensory modalities follows a clearly defined ontogenetic sequence and reflects the gradual evolution of more complex perceptual mechanisms as the CNS develops (fig. 5.2). Relatively mature conditioned responses at higher levels of central nervous function can be obtained by 4 wk of age. More complex tasks, however, such as the delayed response (chap. 5), are not easily accomplished until much later in life.

---

[1] These findings on the greater resistance to anoxia in the newborn, together with those of O'Neill and Duffy (1966) on alternate metabolic pathways in the newborn brain, suggest an adaptive process enabling the organism to withstand an extended period of anoxia without incurring any deleterious changes in the CNS, as might occur at the time of birth.

277

In early postnatal life (discussed in chap. 2) taxes and kineses predominate in the organization of behavior; as the organism matures, innate behavior patterns and later learned responses are elaborated and in turn predominate over earlier components of behavior. This closely resembles the evolutionary schema of Dethier and Stellar (1964) which depicts the gradual organization of behavior in phylogenetically diverse species. This does not imply that phylogenetic recapitulation is taking place during development, but rather that the organization of behavior contains elements of earlier systems of behavioral organization. Interaction at these various levels of behavioral organization occurs during the gradual emergence of mature behavior patterns at the onset of the socialization period.

The experiments of differential early experience in chapter 6 tend to support the critical-period hypothesis in that experience in early life during the critical period can greatly modify subsequent behavior patterns and social relationships.

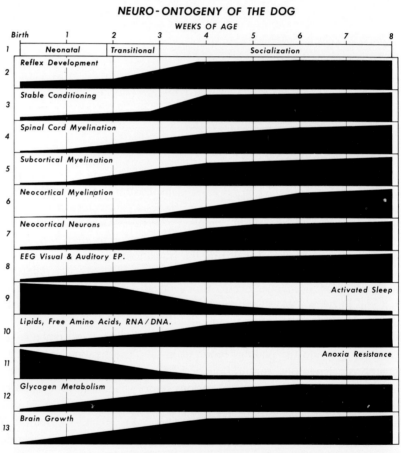

Fig. 7.1. Schema showing approximate rates of development of various parameters of the CNS: relative maturity in these parameters is attained between 4 and 5 wk of age. References: (1) Scott and Marston 1950; (2) chapter 2, this volume; (3) James and Cannon 1952, Cornwell and Fuller 1961, Fuller, Easler, and Banks 1950, Stanley et al. 1963, Volokhov 1959*a, b,* and chapter 5, this volume; (4–7) chapter 4; (8–9) chapter 3; (10) Dravid, Himwich, and Davis 1965, Mandel et al. 1962, and chapter 4; (11) Jilek and Trojan 1966; (12) Himwich and Fazekas 1941; (13) Fox 1964*e,* Fox 1966*c.*

The findings on the effects of isolation rearing provide intriguing information which finds close agreement with observations by other workers on a variety of animals, including man. The experimental design of providing the developing organism with specific stimuli, excessive stimulation, an enriched environment, or lack of stimulation of various modalities, and therefore experimentally controlling the environment and programming the quality and quantity of stimulation the subject receives, has gained wide use in ethology and related fields. Although the various treatment methods have not yet been standardized, thus making possible conflicting or misleading conclusions, valuable information regarding the development of innate and acquired behavior patterns and of the organization of the central nervous system has been reported. The importance of a multidisciplinary approach in determining biochemical, neuroanatomical, and neurophysiological changes underlying behavioral modifications as a result of experimental treatment has been shown in the research of Denenberg (1962a, b, 1964), Levine (1962b), and Bennett et al. (1964). Biochemical changes in the developing brain have only recently attracted more intensive investigation, and at present it is often difficult to discuss the findings of biochemical changes detected in the CNS in relation to behavior, for these relationships are often unknown. Close correlation with observed changes in behavior and of the structure and electrophysiological activity of the brain may facilitate future neurochemical and psychopharmacological studies and analysis of the important role that biochemical changes have on the development and function of the CNS and consequent behavior.

Genetic and Environmental Considerations

The possible contribution of genetics to the variability of behavior is now being evaluated at the molecular biochemical level by several investigators in an attempt to find the causal factors underlying both normal and abnormal ontogeny of structure and function (McClearn and Meredith 1966) (see fig. 7.2). In this regard, Marler and Hamilton (1966) lucidly state that "demonstrations of unchanging developmental patterns in a varied environment are a first step toward establishing contributions of the genotype to sensory development." Earlier studies in behavioral genetics have evaluated the end effects of gene action modifying biochemical function, and are of importance in determining what gross differences do exist between closely related species or between individuals of the same species. In this investigation no attempt has been made to evaluate genetic influences, but the significance of the genotype-environment interaction has been discussed. Another important variable, maternal influence, was not investigated in this study on postnatal development of the dog. The behavior of the mother may influence the development of the offspring (Reading 1966) through reciprocal interaction and reaction and vice versa (Barnett and Burns 1967), especially if she is overfearful or aggressive in the presence of human beings.[2] King (1966) and Cairns (1966) have presented useful reviews of certain aspects of attachment behavior and infant-mother relationships in animals; it must be remembered that the presence of the offspring and their solic-

---

[2] Also, litter size can influence behavior; Seitz (1954) found that small litters of rats were less active, hoarded less food, and were more emotional than were rats from larger litters. He also found that maternal behavior was disrupted by very large litters.

itous care-seeking and food-begging behavior not only may stimulate maternal responses, but may also cause profound endocrine changes in the mother, such as the production of crop milk in even foster-parent birds (Hansen 1966). The possible postnatal transfer of reactions from the mother to the offspring is worthy of further investigation. It should be emphasized, however, that in the selection of brood-bitches used in this study (and of sires), subjects with abnormal behavior patterns (such as fearfulness in the presence of human beings) were not included. Another maternal variable is prenatal ("intrauterine environmental") influences, which have been reviewed in chapter 6. That environmental influences affecting the dam during gestation or before mating may subsequently affect the offspring, and possibly subsequent generations, and have a different effect according to the parental strain is

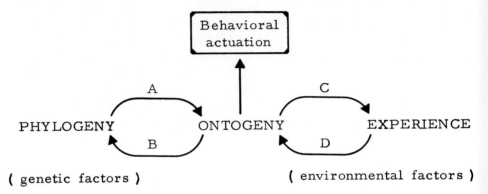

Fig. 7.2. Interrelationships between genetic and environmental factors which through reciprocal interaction can influence ontogeny. Ontogeny in turn can influence phylogeny via selection (*B*) as a result of environmental influences (*D*). These interreactions result in behavioral actuation, or the expression of the overt behavior phenotype. *A*, Phylogeny influences ontogeny path of gene action, consisting of structure-coding and regulation of phylogenetically selected genotype. *B*, Ontogeny influences phylogeny—selection, adaptation. *C*, Ontogeny influences type of environmental experiences, e.g., too immature to perceive; also critical periods. *D*, Experience influences ontogeny—may accelerate, disrupt, reorganize, etc.; also endocrine effects, e.g., handling.

an important consideration (i.e., genotype-environment interaction, Thompson and Olian 1961; Cooper and Zubek 1969; Levine and Broadhurst 1963; Ottinger, Denenberg, and Stephens 1963; Henderson 1966; Joffe 1965*a*, *b*; Weir and DeFries 1964). Denenberg and Rosenberg (1967) have recently discussed the significance of nongenetic transmission of information. As far as possible, brood-bitches used in this study were housed under careful supervision in whelping quarters during the last 3–4 wk of gestation to minimize or at least standardize to some extent these environmental influences. With the evidence from the literature that prenatal influences can modify behavior, it would be of great interest to attempt transfer of fertilized ova between closely related but behaviorally different strains, such as the Maudsley reactive and nonreactive strains of rat and Dykman's withdrawn and friendly German pointers. Thus the genetic, environmental, and maternal interactions and qualitative and quantitative contributions to behavioral differences might be evaluated, as used in studies in mice by DeFries, Weir, and Hegmann (1967) and earlier by Ginsburg and Hovda (1947). As early as 1935, Maier and Schneirla emphasized that all behavior is the product of the interaction of heredity and environment; Klopfer and Hailman (1967) state that this subtle formulation has been overlooked in ontogenetic studies and especially in the involved arguments on "instinctive behavior" versus "learned behavior" which have arisen over the last 20 years (see also Hailman 1969).

Two other variables which may affect the behavior of the offspring have been reported; Elens, Mouravieff, and Heuts (1966) find that the age of the parents when they are bred may influence the learning abilities of the offspring in mice, and Meier (1964) and Meier and Garcia-Rodriguez (1966) have shown that the mode of birth (cesarean versus normal delivery) may affect subsequent behavior, independent of anesthetic or drug effects.

Handling rodents during pregnancy can affect the behavior of the offspring (Denenberg 1963; Denenberg and Rosenberg 1967), and again the neuroendocrine changes occurring in the mother (in addition to her subsequent direct maternal influences on the offspring) constitute an internal environmental change, which modifies epigenesis and the genotype-environmental interaction. It is probable that neuroendocrine changes in the mother as a result of environmental stimuli (e.g., gentling or electroshock) have some direct effect upon the developing fetal neuroendocrine system. Thus a primary genetic influence is not present, although the genotype may increase or decrease susceptibility to such effects. Within this frame of reference to maternal influences, Ounsted and Ounsted (1966) have presented some interesting data (and references cited) regarding maternal regulation of fetal growth. The velocity of placental growth may be enhanced by antigenic dissimilarity between mother and fetus, and also by the prepotent force of the maternal genotype, which acts as a maternal regulator constraining intrauterine growth. This maternal regulator is also a function of the degree of growth constraint imposed on the mother when she herself was a fetus; that is, possibly the setting of the maternal regulator is predetermined. Ounsted and Ounsted also suggest the applicability of fertilized ova transfer to determine maternal influences in experimental animals.

Development in Relation to the Environment

Anokhin (1964) concludes that "it is true that the systemogenetic type of the maturation and the growth is the most marked for those functional systems of the organism which must be mature exactly at the moment of birth. They are evidently inborn, the preparation for their consolidation is preformed, and, in fact, in the process of the ontogenesis, they correspond demonstrably to the ecological factors of that species of animal" (fig. 7.3).

Schneirla (1965) suggests that as a result of natural selection individual situation-canalizing factors insure that the newborn animal will be presented with stimuli in the environment (i.e., incidental situation-structuring by species mates) in accordance with its characteristics of receptor and other structural-functional specialization, and this forms the basis of Anokhin's hypothesis of systemogenesis. Genetic regulation of development of CNS systems follows a heterochronous pattern, for example, and this selective preformation of particular systems is specifically adapted to certain environmental factors which in turn have influenced development indirectly through phylogenetic selection or reinforcement (Anokhin 1964). Ontogenetic processes are more plastic and affect later modification of behavior; many

genes or potentials are not expressed because of lack of contingencies of reinforcement during ontogeny (Skinner 1966). Scott and Fuller (1965) state that in learning situations, high motivation must be maintained in a problem-solving situation in
order to bring out the maximum genetic capacities of the organism. Reinforcement,
as a result of maintained motivation through success, is thus modified by the genetic
capacity of the organism.

In Schneirla's (1965) discussion of approach/withdrawal processes in development, he emphasizes that these are part processes of a single homeostatic system

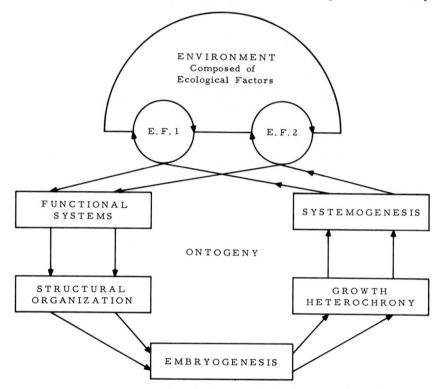

Fig. 7.3. Schema (after Anokhin 1964) demonstrating relationship of systemogenesis in evolutionary development of functional adaptation to environment.

in which parasympathetic-approach (A-processes) and sympathetic-withdrawal (W-
processes) represent the polar components. The stimulus intensity determines which
component will predominate in terms of overt behavioral response, the response
being adaptive in bringing about homeostasis. Schneirla clearly illustrates that ontogenetically, the parasympathetic-approach process (or component) develops before
the emergence of the sympathetic-withdrawal process, and supports this fact with
several examples, such as imprinting and the following response. The necessary reinforcement for the fixation of approach-type responses to low intensity stimuli rests
in the A-processes they elicit, and such reinforcement is available on new bases for
the later discriminative and reactive specialization of approach mechanisms through
contiguity and selective learning.

It is surprising that in elaborating the approach/withdrawal hypothesis

Schneirla failed to show the correlation between his hypothesis and the evidence from Russian work on the ontogeny of conditioned reflexes. In the ontogeny of conditioned reflexes to various modalities, positive approach (e.g., food-motor) responses can always be elaborated *before* the emergence of negative avoidance responses. Even at the level of unconditioned (spinal) reflexes, excitation precedes inhibition (Coghill 1929; Tuge 1961; and Sedlacek et al. 1961), and the development of internal inhibition at various levels of sensorimotor integration occurs at different ages at ontogenetically determined periods.

The phenomenon of excitation and inhibition underlying the development of approach-withdrawal processes has more than a species-preserving, homeostatic function. Perceptual homeostasis during the excitatory phase insures that the organism will *seek* stimulation, and in relation to quantitative input is important for providing optimum interaction so that the genetic capacity of the organism can be fully exposed. Arousal, excitability, and high motivation for exploratory behavior insure that the developing organism will seek out and receive maximal stimulation and optimal experience; Vince (1961) has shown that excitatory processes predominate over inhibitory processes in young animals as compared with older ones. Volokhov (1959*a, b*) has shown that this excitation and inhibition are evident in the ontogeny of conditioned reflexes to various modalities, involving at first the phylogenetically lower sensorimotor systems and later more complex, higher sensorimotor systems which develop at different times postnatally in nonprecocial animals such as the dog.

Another variable which was not considered by Schneirla in discussing aversive stimuli in causing sympathetic arousal and avoidance, is the influence of *socialization*. It was shown in chapter 5 that age is an important variable in determining stability of a learned response (in this case, conditioned avoidance) and that in a socialized animal, painful stimulation, predicted to be aversive, can actually reinforce approach behavior. Therefore, the variable of of socialization and the establishment of an emotional bond modifies the predictability of behavior in terms of stimulus intensity and aversive stimuli. Rosenblum and Harlow (1963) have found a similar phenomenon in surrogate-raised monkeys. We may surmise that because the animal has developed an emotional bond during the approach period, aversive social stimuli after the avoidance period do not generally disrupt the emotional bond, because through previous experience, approach to the mother-object was rewarding. Approach under aversive stimulation may therefore be an attempted form of adaptation and anxiety reduction. This provides an additional dimension to Schneirla's notion that intense withdrawal-evoking stimuli which cause arousal of withdrawal processes may motivate the animal to seek out and approach withdrawal-process-reducing (anxiety-relieving) stimuli; the balance between sympathetic and parasympathetic arousal is therefore restored. These autonomic mechanisms may play a major role in the process of socialization and need further investigation. In precocial birds, arousal through anxiety has been found to speed the process of imprinting (Hess 1964). Harlow et al. (1966) observe that mother monkeys that have been raised in isolation treat their offspring with indifference and may severely injure them; regardless of this, the infant monkey will repeatedly approach and attempt to cling to the mother and feed. In spite of disruption of the mother-infant bond, the infant has a "built-in" mechanism which insures that it will seek maternal contact, and this mechanism is so resistant to change that under abnormal circumstances, as in Harlow's experiments, it may prejudice the survival of the organism.

During a period of maximal excitation of a particular system, the developing organism seeks stimulation and through exposure learning (Sluckin 1965) develops a positive conditioned response or approach behavior, as in following and imprinting, for example. The mechanism by which inhibition and selective, qualitative regulation of input stimulation are subsequently integrated into the system is not clear. It may be a genetically regulated mechanism which is triggered during ontogeny as soon as an optimum level of response-patterning of the positive component or approach process has been elaborated, or it may occur at a fixed age, independent of the level of positive approach response patterning. Isolation rearing (social deprivation) can extend the period of imprintability and thus delay the onset of avoidance (to the unfamiliar) which heralds the termination of the imprintable period in birds (Sluckin 1965); thus the time of onset of inhibition may not be entirely genetically predetermined, but may also be a function of amount of experience (learning) and the level of development and elaboration of response patterns during the earlier, excitatory phase.

The importance of the excitatory/approach period in establishing normal social relationships and in the animal's later developing appropriate approach or avoidance responses to novel stimuli as the inhibitory period develops is demonstrated in social-isolation studies (see chap. 6). Because the avoidance period is dependent upon what the organism learns during the approach period, lack of experience during this initial period results in severe restriction of subsequent socioenvironmental interactions, and the postisolation syndrome is characterized by perpetuation of maladaptive avoidance behavior as a mass fear response (Fuller 1964, 1967), although some objects which are avoided by normal subjects may be approached (Melzack and Scott 1957). Because of this imbalance between approach/avoidance processes and inadequate development of inhibition, a chronic state of arousal ensues, with "neurotic" behavior patterns emerging because of imbalance or conflict between approach and avoidance (see also Miller 1961).

During the normal processes of socialization, a "fear" period or increasing tendency to avoid the unfamiliar develops in both human (Spitz and Wolf 1946) and canine (Scott and Fuller 1965). This is correlated with previous experience, the establishment of primary social relationships, and subsequent development of improved perceptual, discriminative abilities in terms of recognition of the strange or unfamiliar. The presetting of approach processes before avoidance insures the survival of the organism by bringing about socialization with its own species, and the development of species identity and imprinting to its native environment. Restricted experience during the excitatory-approach period can severely disrupt or selectively inhibit socialization to related or nonrelated species. Subsequent experience or exposure is important in *maintaining* those primary social relationships which are established during the initial approach-period of the critical period of socialization, for in both wolf and dog, isolation or reduced contact with human beings after the critical period may result in desocialization or disruption of the social bond with man.

It must be emphasized that genetic differences in behavior greatly modify these natural processes of development, although these extreme genetic differences in the dog may prejudice survival in the wild state. Both Fuller and Clark (1966*a*, *b*) and Krushinskii (1962) have shown that isolation rearing has a greater effect on breeds which are naturally more passive, timid, or withdrawn, and a lesser effect on the more aggressive, outgoing breeds. Dykman, Murphree, and Ackerman (1966) have been able to selectively breed the extremely withdrawn, inhibited type and to study hybrids of the two strains (Murphree, Peters, and Dykman 1969). The Pavlovian interpretation of the two extreme types of dog (the overreactive and the nonreactive) would be that there are imbalances of excitatory processes over inhibitory processes. The genotype, therefore, greatly influences the way in which the animal will react, interact, and develop in its perceptually individualized environment. An organism with a balance between excitatory and inhibitory processes will develop normally and show the usual ontogenetic phases of excitation-approach, inhibition-avoidance. The studies on the development of exploratory behavior (between 5 and 16 wk of age) in the dog (see chap. 5) reveal that the majority of subjects interact with more complex stimuli as they mature after 8 wk of age, indicating that as perceptual abilities improve with age, more complex stimulation is sought, or is more rewarding. Great individual differences were found in a few subjects that were nonreactive at 5, 8, 12, and 16 weeks of age, whereas other subjects from the same litter (having had the same experience) become increasingly reactive with increasing age. Because the majority of subjects became more reactive with increasing age, this was considered the normal pattern of development of exploratory behavior, a function of improved perceptual and motor abilities. A few subjects either were hyperexploratory at all ages (the "overfriendly" type) or reacted less and less as they matured. These three types of reaction in the minority of subjects suggest a genotype-environment interaction, where the acquisition and development of exploratory activities is influenced by the innate balance between excitatory and inhibitory processes. Extremely withdrawn subjects did not show an initial period of excitation-approach-exploration, and developed under a self-imposed environmental deprivation. Less severely affected subjects became more withdrawn as their perceptual abilities improved.

Benjamin (1961), in discussing the psychiatric implications of innate and experiential factors in child development, lucidly states that "not only can innate differences in drive organization, in ego functions and in maturational rates determine different responses to objectively identical experiences; but they also can help determine what experiences will be experienced and how they will be perceived."

It is of interest to note that one pup (a Chihuahua), which as early as 3½ wk of age showed a withdrawal response to human beings and to strange dogs of the same age, showed similar responses at 6 mo of age, although its littermate was normal. These two pups were raised together, and it was observed that a dependency-relationship developed; the withdrawn pup would begin to interact with other pups or to explore the arena only when in the presence of its peer, and would cease to interact as soon as its littermate was removed. Similar observations have been made by several workers with young rats and monkeys, in that their exploratory behavior when they are in a novel environment increases only when their mother is present (Thompson and McElroy 1962). Also, in cat-raised Chihuahuas (described in chap. 6), extreme submissiveness and passivity was seen when pups were first introduced to dog-raised peers, but social exploration and interaction was triggered as soon as the foster-peer kittens were placed with the other pups in the behavior arena.

It is significant that the behavior of cat-raised pups was very similar to that of human-raised pups, in that they were nonreactive toward their mirror reflection, vocalization was reduced, and oral chewing-greeting gesture was absent, although normal tail wagging and submissive leg raising were present. There was also a marked preference for the species with which they had been raised, and the initial phase of passivity and submission was followed by defensive-aggressive behavior as the control pups attempted to solicit play. The capacity for recovery of normal social behavior when subsequently raised with their own species was remarkable, compared with the greater deficits observed in human-raised pups.

Developmental Stability and Species (Phenotypic) Uniformity

In studying the development of some aspect of behavior in a particular species, several workers have noted the following phenomenon; that in spite of individual differences (see also Hirsch 1963), subjects progress through similar developmental stages provided they are raised under similar environmental conditions. A particular predetermined event (sexual maturity, emergence of fear response) in development may occur relatively late in life; such an event is genetically determined and species-specific, but its time of manifestation may be accelerated or delayed by previous experiences (such as "handling" stress or isolation rearing). In such delayed ontogenetic phenomena, it becomes increasingly difficult to determine to what extent experiential-environmental influences make their appearance. Altman (1966a) distinguishes three models of neural programming or patterning of behavior: fixed morphogenetic programming, which occurs without individual experience and is in general impervious to alterations by experience; modifiable epigenetic programming, which consists of essentially inborn components but which also necessitates individual experience for its proper realization; acquired transectional programming, in which new behavior schemata are formed on the basis of individual experience, with minimal employment of inborn elements. In these three models we see varying increments of environmental influence on the genotype and especially on the developing phenotype, which emphasizes the point that species uniformity is not necessarily entirely genetically determined but is also influenced by the socioenvironmental milieu and the type of ecology (and cultural influences in man).

Periods of Integration

The developmental changes in the nervous system and behavior demonstrated in the dog tend to fall within a fairly discrete period between the 3d and 4th to the 5th wk of life. This period does not coincide with the overt periods of behavioral development, and on the basis of these correlations, a period of integration of component elements of the CNS is evident.

This concept has been tested experimentally by disrupting the ontogeny of the visual system through visual deprivation in pups during and after the period of integration (see chap. 6). It was argued that such treatment during the period of integration would cause more severe disturbances than if similar treatment was instigated at a later age. This hypothesis was in part confirmed in the present investigation, but it was remarkable that myelination and dendritic development of neocortical neurons were well advanced in subjects treated during the period of integration. Thus the developing nervous system and behavior may not be entirely dependent upon stimulation. In this regard, Coghill (1929) observed that in *Ambystoma,* exercise did not appear to be essential for the development of mature swimming movements; similarly, Grohmann (1938) concluded that restriction of exercise during early development had little effect on the subsequent flying ability of pigeons. Crain's laboratory has shown that the development of electrical activity and of the growth patterns of brain tissue in culture follow relatively normal sequences of ontogeny, thus revealing a high degree of independence from regulating influences from adjacent structures. Crain and Bornstein (1964) conclude that "the self differentiation and maintenance of such functional integrity in an explant measuring less than 1 mm sets obvious limits both to the anatomical complexity required to account for similar bioelectric phenomena *in situ* and to the role of extrinsic factors, e.g., sensory input and peripheral field influences in cerebral ontogenesis." Crain, Bornstein, and Peterson (1967) also observed that the development of electrical activity in cultures of nervous tissue was not affected by drugs that inhibit electrical activity. These observations are reminiscent of Carmichael's observations on the effects of Chloretone on the development of motility in salamanders. Similarly, Purpura and Housepian (1961) found that isolated blocks of cortical tissue left in situ developed relatively normal electrical activity and neuronal-dendritic complexity, except that more axon-collaterals were formed. These data lend strong support to the contention that the "units" or component parts of a given neural system develop independently until a critical stage is reached; at this time, when structural organization and integration of component parts occurs, operationally functional systems are formed. The critical stage marks the time when such an integrative process occurs. The directing mechanisms controlling and modulating these structurofunctional interrelationships remain to be elucidated, but it is remarkable that functional interneuronal junctions can develop in vitro between cells in completely separate explants (Crain and Peterson 1965). In this regard we must recall Sperry's (1958, 1963) theory that the orderly patterning of synaptic associations in the CNS may be determined by biochemical affinities specific for each component part of the CNS. From Jacobson's (1969) findings, it would appear that the specificity of neural connections within the visual system, for example, is established at a particular period in embryonic development. Before this period, the system appears to be plastic and capable of reorganization following surgical disorganization. The process of integration of developing components of this system would therefore be essentially predetermined once the stage of development is reached when neural connections become specified. This concept of a period of integration of neural components also embraces the notion of integration and adaptation of the organism to its environment. It is at this time that almost adultlike perceptual and locomotor abilities allow more complete interaction of organism with environment.

Normal behavioral development is dependent upon environmental stimulation, exposure learning, and maturation, and also reflects the stimuli that were or still are present. The interaction of genetic and environmental influences modifies and selects behavior, and both inherited and acquired modifications of structure and function allow adaptation of the individual (ontogenetically), and of successive generations (phylogenetically) (fig. 7.2).

Stimulation (either exogenous or endogenous) may or may not be essential for the development of a particular action pattern and underlying neural system. The period of integration represents a sensitive time in development when the organism becomes receptive to and dependent upon such stimulation for further development or refinement of a particular action pattern.

The foregoing remarks on various aspects of development have been schematically reviewed in figure 7.4 to show the ontogenetic relationships between the major events and variables which have so far been identified in neuro-ontogeny and behavioral development.

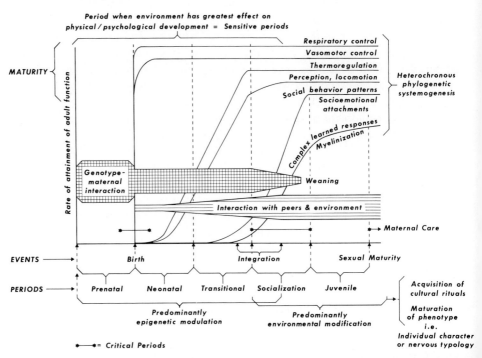

Fig. 7.4. Schema of developmental phenomena in a nonprecocial animal. This schema shows the ontogenetic relationships of various developmental phenomena; sensitive periods (Denenberg 1964); critical periods and socialization (Scott 1962); epigenetic modulation (Waddington 1961); integration period (see present discussion); and heterochronous phylogenetic systemogenesis (Anokhin 1964).

The later development of individual character or nervous typology has recently been demonstrated in the dog by Kozlova (1964). Only after 6 mo of age do individual differences appear in the excitability and equilibration of behavior, which apparently reflect individual differences in the typological peculiarities of the nervous system. Bronson (1965) has presented a developmental schema of the CNS in terms of the organism's reactivity to the environment, which is dependent upon the level of maturity of the CNS and the type of learning possible at different ages. His schema closely resembles the more specific schema of Sedlacek et al. (1961) in regard to the ontogeny of unconditioned and conditioned reflexes. Bronson's schema (fig. 7.5, slightly modified) is self-explanatory. When level I matures, for example, the integrated structures of the brainstem and reticular formation permit learning to occur at the simple conditioned-response level, and the organism's behavioral repertoire at this age essentially comprises arousal, orientation, approach, and withdrawal reactions. Environmental stimuli at this age or level of development, for example, prenatal or early postnatal handling, gentling, or electroshock-stress in the rat, can have profound effects on subsequent CNS development and behavior. Handling in early life not only causes some changes in arousal (Henderson 1964) in later life, but also in emotionality (a function of level II integration). Bronson restricts the early handling effects as influencing the organism via level I, but direct effects through an influence on the hypothalamus and limbic system may also occur

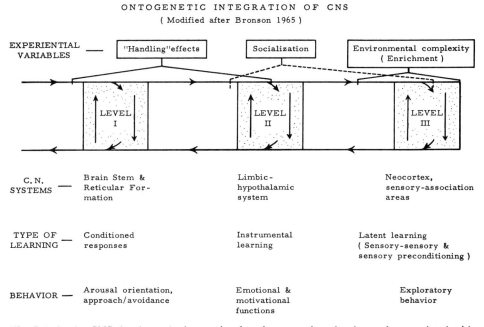

Fig. 7.5. As the CNS develops, the integrative function at various levels can be correlated with the type of learning, behavior, and experiential variables that can be effected.

at the same age. Subsequent development of levels II and III and their integration, reciprocal excitation, and inhibition (a necessary oversimplification at this point of discussion) may be disrupted or modified by environmental influences upon the initial organization and integration of level I structures. Bronson also restricts the second critical period (socialization) to level II structures, but it has been shown in this study on the perceptual development of the dog that relative maturity of level III structures is associated with the onset of the critical period of socialization. Identification of the third critical period (fig. 7.4), at which stage of development the environment influences the development of neocortical sensory-association areas, is strongly supported by the studies of Bennett et al. (1964) and others. A similar ontogenetic relationship between the level of functional development of the CNS and the effects of environmental influences on development has been formulated independently from these observations of Bronson (see fig. 7.4). Bronson does not, however, stress the significance of Anokhin's observations on the heterochronous maturation of the CNS. Higher levels of neural organization and integration build upon or supersede more primitive mechanisms (which do not disappear or are not eliminated, for they reappear in cases of brain damage to higher, modulating structures) and behavioral reactions appear as these integrated levels mature. An example of this is the sudden appearance of fear responses to specific stimuli, as shown by Sackett (1966). Ontogenetic disturbances (i.e., environmental influences) would have more severe and permanent effects earlier in life when level I is organized, because subsequent development of levels II and III would be modified. Disturbances only at level III later in life would be less severe because levels I and II are now well formed and integrated. These observations are supported in Riesen's discussions (1958, 1961*a, b,* 1966), in that disturbances of one system early in life may have profound effects on the development of other systems and behavior patterns in later life. He also found that dark-raised cats can learn a visual-intensity discrimination as well as controls, but are inferior at pattern discrimination; thus the neurological level of development necessary for intensity discrimination was formed before isolation, whereas more complex visual functions require experience for integrative development of level III. These observations are supported by Morgan (1951), who reported that cats with neocortical lesions can make brightness (visual-intensity) discriminations but are unable to recognize or differentiate patterns.

One problem which arises in discussion of "sensitive" and "critical" periods is what brings the period to an end. It is known that if experience is denied until a certain age, after the end of a particular critical period, the capacity to respond is restricted or lessened. Possibly, therefore, subsequent development of "higher levels" of the CNS may inhibit or limit the capacity of response-organization at "lower levels" once the critical period in the development of these "lower levels" has passed. Thus a time-dependent process may be operating. Such a chronologically fixed ontogenetic patterning of development is evident in many organisms; the similarity between individuals of the same species implies that a common process is regulating development. What ends one critical or sensitive period may be the beginning of the next ontogenetically predetermined period; the onset of the next period may be modified, however, in terms of its time of onset and capacity to develop along normal lines, by the quantitative and qualitative experience (or stimulation) received during the preceding critical period.

Scott (1968) has formulated some useful principles in regard to these ontogenetic "organizational" processes. Organization of any kind tends to become stable and self-limiting. Thus, once development of a particular system is well advanced it is more resistant to modification; it is therefore more difficult to replace it and the organism is incapable of recapitulating the same process. This closely resembles Piaget's concept of centration, but Scott does not consider the phenomenon of decentration and the processes of accommodation and assimilation. Such ontogenetic processes provide the organism with some degree of plasticity and adaptability, allowing increments of new experience to be acquired and retained. Tinbergen (1968) and others have illustrated this plasticity and reaccommodation and assimilation, as in the development of motor abilities and constructive games in children, who elaborate a *Sollwerte* or central model as to how they should respond or perform. When their performance matches or is concordant with the model, they soon lose interest and elaborate a more complex model based on the earlier one; their performance and behavior repertoires attain higher levels of complexity through increments of experience. Both qualitative and quantitative increments of acquired and retained experiences are limited by the innate (genetic) capacity, age, or degree of cognitive, sensorimotor development and the earlier experience (or lack of experience) of the individual. Scott (1968) also emphasizes that different kinds of organizational processes proceed at different rates, as, for example, the different rates of development of visual and auditory perception in different breeds of dog: thus a developmental process may be accelerated or slowed down by genetic factors without appreciably affecting development in general. This notion is in close accord with Anokhin's theory of heterochronous systemogenesis. Scott also notes that because organization can be modified most drastically at the time when it is proceeding most rapidly, a critical period is clearly a period in which a given organizational process is proceeding most rapidly. Thus any period in life when a major new relationship is being formed is a critical one for determining the nature of that relationship (Scott 1968). Within a given system, such as the visual system, there may be several critical periods, or periods of integration, during which organizational processes are operating at genetically predetermined times. Thus in the visual system the neonate is, early in life, "cortically blind": perception improves as subcortical-cortical connections are established, and this organizational process is closely associated with the period of socialization. Other integrative periods may be recognized, as in the development of visual-motor and visual-proprioceptive coordination, visual-auditory, visual-olfactory, and visual-tactile associations (intermodality effects and transfer phenomena). These ontogenetically determined integrative processes may be severely disrupted if, before they become operative, integration with one component system is impaired, inhibited, or delayed. For example, Spigelman and Bryden (1967) have shown that blinding rats early in life severely impairs auditory spatial learning; blinding later in life, when some audiovisual integration has occurred as a result of association of experiences, produces less marked learning deficits. It is of interest that those blinded earlier in life did, however, perform better on a nonspatial auditory learning task. Earlier experiences (or lack of experience) therefore generally have a more profound (or generalized) and persistent effect on an organism than do similar experiences later in life. Clearly there are innumerable periods of integration within and between various systems, the onset of integration (or in Scott's terminology, organizational process) being temporally determined genetically, but also subject to earlier experiences' influencing ontogenetically more precocious integrative processes. The environmental or experiential influences operative during integration represent the "critical period" influences which affect the underlying integrative or organizational process in question. There may be a clearly defined hierarchy of these developmental sequences, leading to increasing integration of neural structures and gradual modification, refinement, and elaboration of behavior.

There has been considerable confusion in the use of certain terms in developmental psychobiology which pertain to rather specific developmental phenomena. Also, the investigator may actually miss or distort the full significance of some developmental process by rigidly adhering to one conceptual approach or developmental model. In attempting to partition some ontogenetic phenomena into sensitive periods, for example, the intrinsic complexity of different but interrelated developmental processes or stages may be overlooked. And the ecological fitness or phylo-ontogenetically programmed, adaptive maturation of sensorimotor abilities might not be revealed.

It may be valuable to divide development into stages; but to look for stages per se without investigating the ecological or social significance of such stages and the interrelationships between stages is to overemphasize the reductionistic analysis of ontogeny. Ideally, the molecular components should be reconstructed where possible, not only to show where further research is needed but also to put the new information within the framework of time and place—the framework of evolution and ontogeny in relation to the ecology or socioenvironmental milieu. This holistic reconstruction of ontogeny from available information is essential if we are to proceed further in the comparative analysis of the dynamic intrinsic complexity of evolution and development in different species under different environmental rearing conditions.

The developing organismic system is a link in the intrinsic complexity of interrelated systems, extending in two dimensions. In time, between ancestors and future generations, and in space or place—the organismic system within a complex of ecological and social systems. The investigator may qualitatively catalog and quantify—dissecting development at one of two levels—the process itself and the interrelationships between processes or systems.

Ontogeny might be advantageously divided into stages which represent particular levels of organization or clusters of behaviors (and often structures) related to a particular life-style (the larval, pupal, and imago phases of Lepidoptera is one example of the latter). Thus, in nonprecocial mammals neonatal, transitional, socialization, juvenile, and adult stages have been arbitrarily defined. Freud and Piaget, for example, have studied human development in terms of psychosexual and of cognitive stages.

Some behavior patterns are confined to one stage (e.g., sucking during the neonatal and transitional stages in the dog) and disappear or "mature out" of the animal's repertoire as it moves into a subsequent developmental stage. As an example, one major pitfall of dividing ontogeny into stages is that certain behavior patterns present at one stage may indeed persist, but in a different *context,* in subsequent stages. Ethologists refer to this as emancipation. There are several examples of neonatal behavior patterns in canids, such as rooting, head movements, alternate forelimb pawing and the inguinal response, which persist into maturity as behaviors associated with greeting and social investigation (Fox 1971*b*). These behaviors have been termed "derived" activities, originating from a different context at an earlier stage of development.

During development of a particular system, some degree of self-stabilization emerges; or, in other words, organization inhibits reorganization. This built-in resistance to change brings about developmental stability, essentially shielding the organism from environmental influences. The capacity to acquire or to be affected by such influences may be genetic. This developmental flexibility may be manifest at particular times during development, and may represent sensitive or critical periods.

One fundamental question is how dependent or independent a given system is upon external influences, and what quality, quantity, and duration of such stimulation is necessary at a particular time or dependent period. It has been proposed by Waddington (1961) and others that the canalizing factor that might guide development in a particular direction was originally environmental. By selection over successive generations, developmental canalization may be subsequently preset—part of the genetic program, as proposed by Anokhin (1964).

A distinction will now be made between critical and sensitive periods. Critical periods may be regarded as those definable times during development when the organism is dependent upon environmental influences for its development to continue normally. Such experiential dependence at one critical period may represent an epigenetic crisis, the onset and duration of the period being species-characteristic and therefore genetically programmed. There may also be interdependence between critical periods, where one critical period has an induction effect on a later period; later behavior is activated and influenced by experiences during the critical period earlier in life. An example is the development of song in certain birds.

Similarly, manipulations during certain sensitive periods may have a delayed effect and influence the time of onset of some later appearing behavior or hormonal process: thus handling stress in neonate rodents accelerates the onset of sexual activity.

These sensitive periods differ from critical periods in that the organism is not dependent upon stimulation during these periods for development to proceed along the genetically determined, environmentally adapted route. But at particular periods in development, environmental influences (or experimental hormone manipulations) may have a profound effect on subsequent development. It is during such sensitive periods that integration is occurring between component parts of a particular system, for example, adrenal or gonadal-hypophyseal axis. Experimental manipulations during such sensitive periods may therefore influence the integration of component parts of a particular system, and subsequently, indirectly affect the rate of development and associations between later-developing systems.

In summary, the interrelated factors which might be advantageously correlated in developmental psychobiology include such issues as experiential dependence or independence at different ages, stages or levels of organization; developmental stability and flexibility; critical and sensitive periods and underlying structurofunctional integration; latent or delayed consequences of previous experience; and canalization, heterochronous systemogenesis, and environmental fitness or adaptability.

Further analysis of these phenomena not only will provide us with pertinent information on development, plasticity, and adaptability of the brain and behavior, susceptibility of the genotype, and modifiability of the phenotype, but may also lead to the recognition of our own genetic and phenotypic potentials and limitations. From this point, education, in its broadest sense (in the context of environmental manipulation, or as defined by Teilhard de Chardin—education as biological accumulation), may be more appropriately structured and instigated in accordance with the optimal capacities and critical or sensitive periods of the developing human organism.

Summary

Various structural and functional aspects of the developing brain of the dog, development of behavior patterns and learning abilities, and effects of early experience are summarized from preceding chapters. Interdisciplinary correlations provide a holistic picture of ontogeny, in which the interactions of genetic and environmental/experiential variables are considered. A number of developmental concepts are discussed and compared, and on the basis of such concepts and more recent factual evidence, the hypothesis of integration is forwarded. This hypothesis of successive integrative processes, which are ontogenetically regulated but also subject to genetic and environmental influences, provides the basis for a more rigorous interdisciplinary approach to problems of brain and behavior development.

Epilogue

During the preparation of this book, there has been a very rapid growth of this multidisciplinary field. An international society and its journal *Developmental Psychobiology,* together with several new books and symposia, are evidence of this increased interest (Isaacson 1968; Ambrose 1969; Joffe 1969; Tobach 1969, 1970; Himwich 1970).

My own research has since been focused upon the comparative ontogeny of behavior in canids—wolves, coyotes, jackals, and their hybrids, and various fox species, including red, gray, and Arctic foxes. It is through the comparative ethological approach that some insights into the phylogeny or evolution of behavior might be gained from studying related species differing in degrees of sociability, ranging from the "solitary" red fox to the gregarious wolf. These studies also reveal differences in socioecological adaptation (Fox 1971*a*). One of the basic questions in developmental psychobiology is to what extent a given behavior pattern is dependent upon experience for its full development and integration into the animal's existing repertoire. In a sense this is a rephrasing of the nature versus nurture question. The other side of the coin is to what degree that behavior pattern is under genetic control. Studies of prey-killing behavior in canids and their hybrids, for example, are giving valuable results. In some species, no experience is necessary for prey catching and killing, whereas in others experience is essential. The concept of "instinct-training interlocking" is relevant here, and also the truism that the ability to learn or to modify existing behavior is "innate" or genetically endowed (Fox 1969*b*).

It is becoming increasingly evident to me that an objective behavioral or etho-

295

logical analysis of development, essentially a descriptive and to some extent quantitative account, gives a valuable profile of the animal. This will serve as a "template" for further studies on specific problems; the value of such preliminary work cannot be underestimated. Merely to investigate a specific developmental problem, without background information on the subjects' general development as it relates to the animal's ecology, is to put the cart before the horse. The investigator's perspective and approach may be too narrow, so that the value of his work may be questioned. Such premature reductionism is to be avoided when dealing with the complexities of pre- and postnatal development. A narrow or biased approach may overemphasize one ontogenetic phenomenon, such as "stages" of development or sensitive and critical periods. And if that phenomenon alone is studied without regard or knowledge of the integrative patterning of development, where the organization of behavior and of the behavioral phenotype is a consequence of both genetic and environmental (experiential) interactions, a very inadequate and possibly incorrect interpretation of ontogeny may be drawn.

Developmental psychobiology is a potentially rich field for research, and many questions pertaining to the ontogeny and phylogeny of behavior remain to be answered. Environmental influences and the optimization of development especially for the human being, where the life history may be "programmed" in terms of pre- and postnatal stimulation and experiential enrichment, have not yet been extensively evaluated. It is perhaps through this interdisciplinary approach that we may increase our knowledge and awareness of the phenomenon of life, and in particular, enhance the development of our own species where potentials have been neither explored nor fully developed. Comparative (animal) studies are essential, for without such basic research no findings on human development could be safely put into an evolutionary perspective. Also, developmental phenomena first revealed in animals may subsequently be identified in the human infant, which, because of the great influence of culture, is a difficult organism to study. Culture is a phenomenon almost unique to the higher primates and most highly evolved in man. Animal studies will reveal precultural or basic biological developmental phenomena which might then be looked for and dissected from interacting cultural influences in man. These cultural influences (e.g., methods of child rearing) may be classed as "socially inherited influences." Human development is therefore extremely complex, where genetic and "precultural" environmental influences (e.g., prenatal maternal anxiety) and socially inherited influences shape the developing behavioral phenotype and the subject's personality, linguistic and conceptual abilities, and social behavior and "silent language" or nonverbal repertoire. Crosscultural studies, analogous to interspecies comparative studies in animals and at present almost the exclusive domain of the social anthropologist, should also be investigated from the developmental point of view by psychobiologists. These cultural differences, acting like biological or ethological barriers between sub- or "pseudospecies," are a major cause of racial and international communication problems. Recognition of cultural differences and improvement of the cultural influences to which a child is exposed and by which it is molded, may greatly improve the quality of life and the actualization of human potential. The repercussions of this will help stabilize remedial programs which are now of top priority to restrain the quantity of life; namely population control and ecological conservation of the biosphere.

References

Ader, R. 1965. Effects of early experience and differential housing on behavior and susceptibility to gastric erosion in the rat. *J. Comp. Physiol. Psychol.* 60:233–38.

Ader, R., and Friedman, S. B. 1965. Differential early experience and susceptibility to transplanted tumor in the rat. *J. Comp. Physiol. Psychol.* 59:361–64.

Ader, R.; Friedman, S. B.; Grota, L. J.; and Schaefer, A. 1968. Attenuation of the plasma corticosterone response to handling and electric shock stimulation in the infant rat. *Physiol. Behav.* 3:327–31.

Adrianov, O. S., and Mering, T. A. 1964. *Atlas of the canine brain.* Translated by E. F. Domino. Ann Arbor, Michigan: Edwards Bros.

Agrawal, H. C., and Fox, M. W. 1967. Effects of cold exposure on CNS of pups. Unpublished data, Galesburg State Research Hospital.

Agrawal, H. C., Fox, M. W., and Himwich, W. A. 1967. Neurochemical and behavioral effects of isolation rearing in the dog. *Life Sci.* 6:71–78.

Almquist, J. O., and Hale, E. B. 1956. An approach to the measurement of sexual behavior and semen production of dairy bulls. In *Proc. III Int. Cong. Anim. Reprod.*, pp. 50–59. London: Brown, Knight, and Truscott.

Altman, J. 1966a. *Organic foundations of animal behavior.* New York: Holt, Rinehart & Winston.

———. 1966b. Proliferation and migration of undifferentiated precursor cells in the rat during postnatal gliogenesis. *Exp. Neurol.* 16:263.

———. 1967. Autoradiographic and histological studies of postnatal neurogenesis. II. *J. Comp. Neurol.* 128:431–74.

Altman, J., and Das, G. D. 1965. Postnatal origin of microneurones in the rat brain. *Nature* 207:953–56.

———. 1966. Autoradiographic and histological studies of postnatal neurogenesis. I. A longitudinal investigation of the kinetics, migration and transformation of cells incorporating tritiated thymidine in neonate rats, with special reference to postnatal neurogenesis in some brain regions. *J. Comp. Neurol.* 126:337.

Ambrose, J. A. ed. 1969. *Stimulation in early infancy.* New York: Academic Press.

Ambrose, J. A. 1961. The development of the smiling response in early infancy. In *Determinants of infant behavior,* ed. B. M. Foss, pp. 179–95. London: Methuen and Co.

297

Ambrose, J. A. 1963. The concept of a critical period for the development of social responsiveness. In *Determinants of infant behavior,* ed. B. M. Foss, pp. 201–26. London: Methuen and Co.

——. 1966. Ritualization in the human infant-mother bond. *Phil. Trans. Roy. Soc., Ser. B.* 251:359–62.

Ames, L. B., and Ilg, F. L. 1964. The developmental point of view with special reference to the principle of reciprocal neuromotor interweaving. *J. Genet. Psychol.* 105:195–209.

Andrew, R. J. 1963. The effect of testosterone on the behavior of the domestic chick. *J. Comp. Physiol. Psychol.* 56:933–40.

——. 1966. Precocious adult behavior in the young chicken. *Anim. Behav.* 14: 485–500.

Angermeier, E., and James, W. T. 1961. The influence of early sensory-social deprivation on the social operant in dogs. *J. Genet. Psychol.* 99:153–58.

Anokhin, P. K. 1964. Systemogenesis as a general regulator of brain development. In *Progress in brain research,* vol. 9, *The developing brain,* ed. W. A. Himwich and H. E. Himwich, pp. 55–86. Amsterdam: Elsevier.

Appel, S. H.; Davis, W.; and Scott, S. 1967. Brain polysomes: Response to environmental stimulation. *Science* 157:836–38.

Arshavsky, I. A. 1968. Physiological mechanisms of disorders of growth and development due to stress effects in early age periods. In *Postnatal development of phenotype,* ed. S. Kazda and V. H. Denenberg. London: Butterworth.

Astrom, K. E. 1967. On the early development of the isocortex in fetal sheep. In *Progress in brain research,* vol. 26, *Developmental neurology,* ed. C. G. Bernhard and J. P. Schadé. New York: Elsevier.

Ata-Muradova, F. 1960. The development of the activating functions of the reticular formation in the postnatal period. In *Evolution des fonctions physiologiques,* pp. 122–28. Leningrad: University Publications.

Ausubel, D. P. 1966. A critique of Piaget's theory of the ontogenesis of motor behavior. *J. Genet. Psychol.* 109:119–22.

Bacon, W. E., and Stanley, W. C. 1963. Effect of deprivation level in puppies on performance maintained by a passive person reinforcer. *J. Comp. Physiol. Psychol.* 56:783–85.

Bacon, W. E., and Stanley, W. C. 1970. Reversal learning in neonatal dogs. *J. Comp. Physiol. Psychol.* 70:344–50.

Bahrs, A. M. 1927. Notes on the reflexes of puppies in the first six weeks after birth. *Amer. J. Physiol.* 82:51–55.

Barcroft, J., and Barron, D. H. 1939. Movement of the mammalian foetus. *Ergeb. Physiol.* 42:107–52.

Bard, P. 1933. Studies on the cerebral cortex. 1. Localized control of placing and hopping reactions in the cat and their normal management by small cortical remnants. *Arch. Neurol. Psychiat.* 30:40–74.

Barfield, R. J., and Sachs, B. D. 1968. Sexual behavior: Stimulation by painful electrical shock to skin in male rats. *Science* 161:392–95.

Barnes, R. H. 1965. Malnutrition in early life and mental development. *N.Y. State J. Med.* 65:2816–17.

Barnett, S. A. 1958. Exploratory behaviour. *Brit. J. Psychol.* 49:289–310.

Barnett, S. A., and Burns, J. 1967. Early stimulation and maternal behaviour. *Nature* 213:150.

Baron, A.; Kish, G. B.; and Antonitis, J. J. 1962. Effects of early and late social isolation on aggregative behavior in the domestic chicken. *J. Genet. Psychol.* 100:355–60.

Bateson, P. P. G. 1966. The characteristics and context of imprinting. *Biol. Rev.* 41:177–220.

Baxter, B. L. 1966. Effect of visual deprivation during postnatal maturation on the electroencephalogram of the cat. *Exp. Neurol.* 14:224–35.

Beach, F. A., and Jaynes, J. 1954. Effects of early experience upon the behavior of animals. *Psychol. Bull.* 51:239–63.

Bell, F. R. 1960. The electroencephalogram of goats and ruminants. *Anim. Behav.* 8:39–42.

Bell, R. W.; Hendry, G. H.; and Miller, C. E. 1967. Prenatal maternal conditioned fear and subsequent ulcer-proneness in the rat. *Psychonom. Sci.* 9:269–70.

Benjamin, J. D. 1961. The innate and the experiential in child development. In *Lectures on experimental psychiatry,* ed. H. S. Brosin, pp. 19–42. Pittsburg: University of Pittsburgh Press.

Bennett, E. L.; Diamond, M. C.; Rosenzweig, M. R.; and Krech, D. 1964. Chemical and anatomical plasticity of brain. *Science* 146:610–19.

Berg, I. A. 1944. Development of behavior: The micturition pattern in the dog. *J. Exp. Psychol.* 34:343–68.

Berger, H. 1900. Expermentell-anatomische studien über die durch den Mangel, optischer Reize veranlassten entwicklung schemmungen in Occipitallapen des Hundes und der Katze. *Arch. Psychiat. Nervenkrankh.* 33:521–67.

Berkson, G. 1962. Food motivation and delayed response. *J. Comp. Physiol. Psychol.* 55:1040–43.

Berkson, G., and Mason, W. A. 1964. Stereotyped behaviors of chimpanzees: Relation to general arousal and alternative activities. *Percept. Motor Skills* 19:635–52.

Berl, S., and Purpura, D. P. 1963. Postnatal changes in amino acid content of kitten cerebral cortex. *J. Neurochem.* 10:237–40.

Berlyne, D. E. 1950. Novelty and curiosity as determinants of exploratory behaviour. *Brit. J. Psychol.* 41:68–80.

———. 1960. *Conflict, arousal and curiosity.* London: McGraw-Hill.

———. 1966. Curiosity and exploration. *Science* 153:25–55.

Bernhard, C. G.; Kaiser, I. H.; and Kolmodin, G. M. 1959. On the development of cortical activity in foetal sheep. *Acta Physiol. Scand.* 47:333–49.

Bernhard, C. G.; Kolmodin, G. M.; and Meyerson, B. A. 1967. On the prenatal development of function and structure in the somesthetic cortex of sheep. In *Progress in brain research,* vol. 26, *Developmental neurology,* ed. C. G. Bernhard and J. P. Schadé, pp. 60–77. New York: Elsevier.

Bernstein, L. 1957. The effects of variations in handling upon learning and retention. *J. Comp. Physiol. Psychol.* 50:162–67.

Berry, M., and Rogers, A. W. 1965. The migration of neuroblasts in the developing cerebral cortex. *J. Anat.* 99:691.

Bertler, A.; Carlsson, A.; and Rosengren, E. 1958. A method for the fluorimetric determination of adrenaline and noradrenaline in tissues. *Acta Physiol. Scand.* 44:273–92.

Beyer, C., and Sawyer, C. H. 1964. Effects of vigilance and other factors on non-specific acoustic responses in the rabbit. *Exp. Neurol.* 10:156–69.

Bleicher, N. 1962. Behavior of the bitch during parturition. *J.A.V.M.A.* 140:1076–82.

Bodian, D. 1968. Development of fine structure of spinal cord in monkeys. II. Pre-reflex period to period of long intersegmental reflexes. *J. Comp. Neurol.* 133: 113–66.

Bolwig, N. 1964. Facial expression in primates with remarks on a parallel development in certain carnivores. *Behaviour* 22:167–92.

Bonin, G. von. 1948. The frontal lobe of primates: Cytoarchitectural studies. *Res. Publ. Nerv. Ment. Dis.* 27:67–83.

Bonvallet, M., and Allen, M. B., Jr. 1963. Prolonged spontaneous and evoked reticular activation following discrete bulbar lesions. *Electroenceph. Clin. Neurophysiol.* 15:969–88.

Bovard, E. W. 1954. A theory to account for the effects of early handling on viability of the albino rat. *Science* 120:187.

Bowlby, J. L. 1951. *Maternal care of mental health.* World Health Organization Monograph no. 2.

———. 1952. Critical phases in the development of social responses in man and other animals. In *Prospects in psychiatric research,* ed. J. M. Tanner. Oxford: Blackwell.

———. 1958. The nature of the child's tie to his mother. *Int. J. Psychoanal.* 39:1–24.

Boyd, H. S., Jr. 1964. Early social experience and later trainability in the border collie. *Diss. Abstr.* 25:620–21.

Bradley, W.; Kaiser, I.; Morrell, F.; and Nelson, E. 1960. Maturation of electrical activity in the central nervous system. In *Mental retardation,* ed. P. W. Bowman and H. V. Mautner, pp. 98–111. New York: Grune and Stratton.

Bradley, W. E. and Wright, F. S. 1966. Visceral reflex activity: Development in the postnatal rabbit. *Science* 152:216–17.

Britton, S. W., and Kline, R. F. 1943. The pseudoaffective state and decerebrate rigidity in the sloth. *J. Neurophysiol.* 6:65–69.

Brizze, K. R., and Jacobs, L. A. 1959. Postnatal changes in volumetric and density relationships of neurons in cerebral cortex of cat. *Acta Anat.* 38:292–303.

Broadhurst, P. L. 1961. Analysis of maternal effects in the inheritance of behaviour. *Anim. Behav.* 9:129–41.

Brodbeck, A. J. 1954. An exploratory study on the acquisition of dependency behavior in puppies. *Bull. Ecol. Soc. Amer.* 35:73.

Bronson, G. 1965. The hierarchical organization of the central nervous system: Implications for learning processes and critical periods in early development. *Behav. Sci.* 10:7–25.

Brown, L. T. 1964. A critical period in the learning of motionless stimulus properties in chicks. *Anim. Behav.* 12:353–61.

Brutkowski, S. 1965. Functions of the prefrontal cortex in animals. *Physiol. Rev.* 45:721–46.

Buller, A. J.; Eccles, J. C.; and Eccles, R. M. 1960. Differentiation of fast and slow muscles in the cat hind limb. *J. Physiol.* 150:399–416.

Burdina, V. N.; Krasuskii, V. K.; and Chebykin, D. A. 1960. On the bearing of early rearing conditions on the development of higher nervous activity in dogs. *Zh. Vyssh. Nervn. Deiat.* 10:421–34.

Burgers, J. M. 1966. Curiosity and play: Basic factors in the development of life. *Science* 154:1680–81.

Burghardt, G. M., and Hess, E. H. 1966. Food imprinting in the snapping turtle, *Chelydra serpentina. Science* 151:108–9.

Burns, M., and Fraser, M. N. 1966. *Genetics of the dog.* London: Oliver and Boyd.

Butler, R. A. 1953. Discrimination learning by rhesus monkeys to visual exploration motivation. *J. Comp. Physiol. Psychol.* 46:95–98.

———. 1954. Incentive conditions which influence visual exploration. *J. Exp. Psychol.* 48:19–23.

———. 1957a. Discrimination learning by rhesus monkeys to auditory incentives. *J. Comp. Physiol. Psychol.* 50:239–41.

———. 1957b. The effect of deprivation of visual exploration motivation in monkeys. *J. Comp. Physiol. Psychol.* 50:177–79.

Buxton, D. F., and Goodman, D. C. 1967. Motor function and the corticospinal tracts in the dog and raccoon. *J. Comp. Neurol.* 129:341.

Cairns, R. B. 1966. Attachment behavior of mammals. *Psychol. Rev.* 73:409.

Cairns, R. B., and Johnson, D. L. 1965. The development of interspecies social attachments. *Psychonom. Sci.* 2:337–38.

Cairns, R. B., and Werboff, J. 1967. Behavior development in the dog: An interspecific analysis. *Science* 158:1070–72.

Caldwell, D. F., and Churchill, J. A. 1967. Learning ability in the progeny of rats administered a protein-deficient diet during the second half of gestation. *Neurology* 17:95–99.

Caley, D. W., and Maxwell, D. S. 1968a. An electron microscopic study of neurons during postnatal development of the rat cerebral cortex. *J. Comp. Neurol.* 133:17–44.

———. 1968b. An electron microscopic study of the neuroglia during postnatal development of the rat cerebrum. *J. Comp. Neurol.* 133:45–70.

Campbell, B. A. 1967. Development studies in learning and motivation in infraprimate mammals. In *Early behavior: Comparative and developmental approaches,* ed. H. W. Stevenson, E. H. Hess, and H. L. Rheingold, pp. 43–71. New York: Wiley.

Candland, D. K., and Campbell, B. A. 1962. Development of fear in the rat as measured by behavior in the open field. *J. Comp. Physiol. Psychol.* 55:593–96.

Candland, D. K., and Milne, D. 1966. Species differences in approach-behavior as a function of developmental environment. *Anim. Behav.* 14:539–45.

Carlsson, A., and Lindquist, M. 1962. *In vivo* decarboxylation of α methyl DOPA and α methyl metatyrosine. *Acta Physiol. Scand.* 54:87–94.

Carlsson, A., and Waldeck, B. 1958. A fluorimetric method for the determination of dopamine (3-hydroxytryptamine). *Acta Physiol. Scand.* 44:293–98.

Carmichael, L. 1927. A further study of development of behavior in vertebrates experimentally removed from the influence of external stimulation. *Psychol. Rev.* 34:34–47.

Casler, L. 1961. Maternal deprivation: A critical review of the literature. *Monogr. Soc. Res. Child Develop.* 26:1–64.

Caveness, W. F. 1961. The development of the EEG expression of sleep in the monkey. *Electroenceph. Clin. Neurophysiol.* 13:493–94.

———. 1962. *Atlas of electroencephalography: Macaca mulatta.* London: Addison-Wesley Publishing Co.

Chance, M. R. A. 1962. An interpretation of some agonistic postures: The role of "cut off" acts and postures. *Sym. Zool. Soc. Lond.* 8:71–89.

Charles, M. S., and Fuller, J. L. 1956. Developmental study of the electroencephalogram of the dog. *EEG Clin. Neurophysiol.* 8:645–52.

Cherkin, A. 1966. Toward a quantitative view of the engram. *Proc. Nat. Acad. Sci.* 55:88–91.

Chesler, A., and Himwich, H. E. 1943. The glycogen content of various parts of the central nervous system of dogs and cats at different ages. *Arch. Biochem.* 2:175–81.

Clark, R. G. 1963. Myelinization of the central nervous system of the Guineapig. *Anat. Rec.* 145:313.

———. 1966. Myelinization of the central nervous system of the New Zealand (albino) rabbit and the Syrian hamster. Doctoral diss., George Washington University, Washington, D.C.

Clarke, R. S.; Heron, W.; Fetherstonbaugh, M. L.; Forgays, D. G.; and Hebb, D. O. 1951. Individual differences in dogs: Preliminary report on the effects of early experience. *Canad. J. Psychol.* 5:150–56.

Coghill, G. E. 1929. *Anatomy and the problem of behavior.* New York: Cambridge University Press.

Cohen, C., and Fuller, J. L. 1953. The inheritance of blood types in the dog. *J. Hered.* 44:225–28.

Coleman, P. D., and Riesen, A. H. 1968. Environmental effects on cortical dendritic fields. I. Rearing in the dark. *J. Anat.* 102:363–74.

Collias, N. E. 1951. Social life and the individual among vertebrates. *Ann. N.Y. Acad. Sci.* 51:1074–92.

Conel, J. L. 1939. *The postnatal development of human cerebral cortex,* vol. 1, *The cortex of the newborn.* Cambridge: Harvard University Press.

———. 1941. *The postnatal development of human cerebral cortex,* vol. 2, *The cortex of the one-month infant.* Cambridge: Harvard University Press.

———. 1947. *The postnatal development of human cerebral cortex,* vol. 3, *The cortex of the three-month infant.* Cambridge: Harvard University Press.

———. 1951. *The postnatal development of human cerebral cortex,* vol. 4, *The cortex of the six-month infant.* Cambridge: Harvard University Press.

———. 1952. Histologic development of the cerebral cortex. *Biol. Ment. Health Dis.* 27:1–8.

———. 1955. *The postnatal development of human cerebral cortex,* vol. 5, *The cortex of the fifteen-month infant.* Cambridge: Harvard University Press.

———. 1959. *The postnatal development of human cerebral cortex,* vol. 6, *The cortex of the twenty-four month infant.* Cambridge: Harvard University Press.

Cooper, R. M., and Zubek, J. P. 1959. Effects of enriched and restricted environments on the learning ability of bright and dull rats. *Canad. J. Psychol.* 12:159–64.

Corder, R. L., and Latimer, H. B. 1949. The prenatal growth of the brain and of its parts and of the spinal cord in the dog. *J. Comp. Neurol.* 90:193–212.

Corner, M. A. 1964. Rhythmicity in the early swimming of anuran larvae. *J. Embryol. Exp. Morph.* 12:665–71.

Corner, M. A., and Bot, A. P. C. 1967. Developmental patterns in the central nervous system of birds. In *Progress in brain research,* vol. 26, *Developmental neurology,* ed. C. G. Bernhard and J. P. Schadé, pp. 214–36. New York: Elsevier.

Cornwell, A. C., and Fuller, J. L. 1961. Conditioned responses in young puppies. *J. Comp. Physiol. Psychol.* 54:13–15.

Coulombre, A. J. 1950. Age and strain differences in response to electroconvulsive stimulation (ECS) in the mouse. *Anat. Rec.* 108:60–61 (abstr.).

Cowley, J. J., and Griesel, R. D. 1966. The effect on growth and behavior of rehabilitating first and second generation low protein rats. *Anim. Behav.* 14:506–17.

Cragg, B. G. 1967. Changes in visual cortex on first exposure of rats to light. *Nature* 215:251–53.

Crain, S. M. 1952. Development of electrical activity in the cerebral cortex of the albino rat. *Proc. Soc. Exp. Biol. (N.Y.)* 81:49–51.

Crain, S. M., and Bornstein, M. B. 1964. Bioelectric activity of neonatal mouse cerebral cortex during growth and differentiation in tissue culture. *Exp. Neurol.* 10:425–50.

Crain, S. M.; Bornstein, M. B.; and Peterson, E. R. 1968. Development of functional organization in cultured fetal CNS tissues during chronic exposure to bioelectric blocking agents. In *Symposium Neuroontogeneticum, XIIth Scientific Conference, Prague,* pp. 19–25. Chapel Hill: University of North Carolina Press.

Crain, S. M., and Peterson, E. R. 1965. Onset and development of functional relations within and between explants of mammalian spinal cord ganglia during differentiation *in vitro. Anat. Rec.* 151:340.

Crisler, L. 1956. Observations of wolves hunting caribou. *J. Mamm.* 37:337–46.

Cruze, W. W. 1935. Maturation and learning in chicks. *J. Comp. Psychol.* 19:371–409.

Curry, J. J., III, and Heim, L. M. 1966. Brain myelination after neonatal administration of oestradiol. *Nature* 209:915.

Daanje, A. 1964. On locomotory movements in birds and the intention movements derived from them. In *Comparative psychology,* ed. S. C. Ratner and M. R. Denny, pp. 52–74. Homewood, Ill.: Dorsey Press.

Darwin, C. 1915. *The descent of man.* 2d ed. Chicago: Rand McNally.

———. 1920. *The expression of emotions in man and animals.* New York: Appleton Co.

Davison, A. N.; Cuzner, M. L.; Banik, N. L.; and Oxberry, J. 1966. Myelinogenesis in the rat brain. *Nature* 212:1373–74.

Davison, A. N., and Dobbing, J. 1966. Myelination as a vulnerable period in brain development. *Brit. Med. Bull.* 22:40–44.

Decker, J. D., and Hamburger, V. 1967. The influence of different brain regions on periodic motility of the chick embryo. *J. Exp. Zool.* 165:371–84.

DeFries, J. C.; Thomas, E. A.; Hegmann, J. P.; and Weir, M. W. 1967. Open-field behavior in mice: Analysis of maternal effects by means of ovarian transplantation. *Psychonom. Sci.* 8:207–8.

DeFries, J. C.; Weir, M. W.; and Hegmann, J. P. 1967. Differential effects of prenatal maternal stress on offspring behavior in mice as a function of genotype and stress. *J. Comp. Physiol. Psychol.* 63:332.

Degerbol, M. 1927. Uber prähistorische dänische Hunde. *Vidensk. Meddel. Dansk Naturhist. Kobenhavn* 84:17–72.

Dekeban, A. 1959. *Neurology of infancy.* Baltimore: Williams and Wilkins Co.

Delius, J. D. 1967. Displacement activities and arousal. *Nature* 214:1259–60.

Dement, W. 1958. The occurrence of low voltage, fast, electroencephalogram patterns during behavioural sleep in the cat. *Electroenceph. Clin. Neurophysiol.* 10:291–96.

DeMyer, W. 1967. Ontogenesis of the rat corticospinal tract. *Arch. Neurol.* 16:203–12.

Denenberg, V. H. 1962*a*. Critical periods in the rat. *J. Comp. Physiol. Psychol.* 55:813–15.

———. 1962*b*. The effects of early experience. In *The behaviour of domestic animals,* ed. E. S. E. Hafez, pp. 109–38. London: Braillère, Tindall and Cox.

———. 1963. Behavior of adult rats is modified by the experiences their mothers had as infants. *Science* 142:1192–93.

———. 1964. Critical periods, stimulation input and emotional reactivity: A theory of infantile stimulation. *Psychol. Rev.* 71:335–51.

———. 1967. Stimulation in infancy, emotional reactivity, and exploratory behavior. In *Biology and behavior: Neurophysiology and emotion,* ed. D. H. Glass. New York: Russell Sage Foundation and Rockefeller University Press.

———. 1968. A consideration of the usefulness of the critical period hypothesis as applied to the stimulation of rodents in infancy. In *Early Experience and Behavior,* ed. G. Newton and S. Levine. Springfield, Ill.: C. C. Thomas.

Denenberg, V. H., and Bell, R. W. 1960. Critical periods for the effects of infantile experience on adult learning. *Science* 131:227–28.

Denenberg, V. H.; Hudgens, G. A.; and Zarrow, M. X. 1964. Mice reared with rats: Modification of behavior by early experience with another species. *Science* 143:380–81.

———. 1966. Mice reared with rats: Effects of mother on adult behavior patterns. *Psychol. Rep.* 18:451–56.

Denenberg, V. H., and Kline, J. N. 1964. Stimulus intensity versus critical periods: A test of two hypotheses concerning infantile stimulation. *Canad. J. Psychol.* 18:1–5.

Denenberg, V. H., and Rosenberg, K. M. 1967. Nongenetic transmission of information. *Nature* 216:549.

Denny-Brown, D. 1960. Motor mechanisms—Introduction: the general principles of motor integration. In *Handbook of neurophysiology,* ed. J. Field, H. W. Magoun, and V. E. Hall, 2:208–18. Baltimore: Williams and Wilkins Co.

DeRobertis, E.; Gerschenfeld, H.; and Wald, F. 1958. Cellular mechanism of myelination in the central nervous system. *J. Biophys. Biochem. Cytol.* 4:651–58.

Dethier, V. G., and Stellar, E. 1964. *Animal behavior.* Englewood Cliffs, N.J.: Prentice-Hall.

De Vore, I. 1965. Male dominance and mating behavior in baboons. In *Sex and behavior,* ed. F. A. Beach, pp. 266–89. New York: John Wiley and Sons.

Deza, L., and Eidelberg, E. 1967. Development of cortical electrical activity in the rat. *Exp. Neurol.* 7:425–38.

Diamond, M. C.; Law, F.; Rhodes, H.; Lindner, B.; Rosenzweig, M. R.; Krech, D.; and Bennett, E. L. 1966. Increases in cortical depth and glia numbers in rats subjected to enriched environment. *J. Comp. Neurol.* 128:117.

Diamond, M. C.; Lindner, B.; and Raymond, A. 1967. Extensive cortical depth measurements and neuron size increases in the cortex of environmentally enriched rats. *J. Comp. Neurol.* 131:357–64.

Dickerson, J. W. T.; Dobbing, J.; and McCance, R. A. 1967. The effect of under-nutrition on the postnatal development of the brain and cord in pigs. *Proc. Roy. Soc., Ser. B.* 166:396–407.

DiPerri, R.; Himwich, W. A.; and Peterson, J. 1964. The evolution of the EEG in the developing brain of the dog. In *Progress in brain research,* vol. 9, *The developing brain,* ed. W. A. Himwich and H. E. Himwich, pp. 89–92. Amsterdam: Elsevier.

Dmitriyeva, N. I.; Kalinina, E. I.; Klyavina, M. P.; and Obraztosova, G. A. 1966. On the structural and functional development of the auditory analyser in ontogenesis in dogs. *J. Higher Nerv. Activ. I. P. Pavlov.* 16:839–46.

Dobbing, J. 1964. The influence of early nutrition on the development of myelination of the brain. *Proc. Roy. Soc. Biol.* 159:503.

———. 1966. The effect of undernutrition on myelination in the central nervous system. *Biol. Neonat.* 9:132.

Dodgson, M. C. H. 1962. *The growing brain.* Bristol, England: J. Wright and Sons.

Donovan, C. A. 1967. Some clinical observations on sexual attraction and deterrence in dogs and cattle. *Vet. Med.,* November, 1047–48.

Drachman, D. B., and Coulombre, A. J. 1962. Experimental clubfoot and arthrogryposis multiplex congenita. *Lancet,* September: 523–26.

Dravid, A. R.; Himwich, W. A.; and Davis, J. M. 1965. Some free amino acids in dog brain during development. *J. Neurochem.* 12:901–6.

Dreyfus-Brisac, C., and Blanc, C. 1956. Electroencéphalogramme et maturation cérébrale. *Encéphale* 45:205–41.

Drujan, B. D.; Diaz Borges, J. M.; and Alvarez, N. 1965. Relationship between the contents of adrenaline, noradrenaline and dopamine in the retina and its adaptational state. *Life Sci.* 4:473–77.

Duckett, S., and Pearse, A. G. E. 1968. The cells of Cajal-Retzius in the developing human brain. *J. Anat.* 102:183–87.

Dusser de Barenne, J. G. 1934. Some aspects of the problem of corticalization of function and of functional localization in the cerebral cortex. *Assoc. Res. Nerv. Ment. Dis.* 13:85–106.

Dustman, R. E., and Beck, E. C. 1966. Visually evoked potentials: Amplitude changes with age. *Science* 151:1013–14.

Dykman, R. A.; Murphree, O. D.; and Ackerman, P. T. 1966. Litter patterns in the offspring of nervous and stable dogs. II. Autonomic and motor conditioning. *J. Nerv. Ment. Dis.* 141:419–31.

Eayrs, J. T. 1961. Age as a factor determining the severity and reversibility of the effects of thyroid deprivation in the rat. *J. Endocrin.* 22:409–19.

Eayrs, J. T., and Goodhead, B. 1959. Postnatal development of the cerebral cortex in the rat. *J. Anat.* 93:385–402.

Eccles, J. C. 1964. *The physiology of synapses.* New York: Academic Press.

Eccles, J. C.; Eccles, R. M.; Iggo, A.; and Ito, M. 1961. Distribution of recurrent inhibition among motor neurons. *J. Physiol.* 159:479–99.

Eibl-Eibesfeldt, I. 1956. Angeborenes und Erworbenes in der Technik des Beutëtotens (Versuche am Iltis, *Putorius putorius* L.), *A. Säugetierkunde* 21:135–37.

Eibl-Eibesfeldt, I. 1963. Angeborenes und Erworbenes im Verhalten einiger Säuger. *Zeits. Tierpsychol.* 20:705–54.

Elens, A. A.; Mouravieff, A. N.; and Heuts, M. J. 1966. The age of reproduction as a factor of transmissible divergences in learning ability in the mouse. *Experientia* 22:186.

Ellingson, R. J. 1964. Studies of the electrical activity of the developing human brain. In *Progress in brain research,* vol. 9, *The developing brain,* ed. W. A. Himwich and H. E. Himwich, pp. 26–53. Amsterdam: Elsevier.

Ellingson, R. J., and Wilcott, R. C. 1960. Development of evoked responses in visual and auditory cortices of kittens. *J. Neurophysiol.* 23:363–75.

Elliot, O., and King, J. A. 1960. Effect of early food deprivation upon later behavior in puppies. *Psychol. Rep.* 6:391–400.

Elliot, O., and Scott, J. P. 1961. The development of emotional distress reactions to separation in puppies. *J. Genet. Psychol.* 99:3–22.

Ellis, P., and Pearce, A. P. 1962. Innate and learned behaviour patterns that lead to group formation in locust hoppers. *Anim. Behav.* 10:305–18.

Emlen, J. T., Jr. 1963. Determinants of cliff edge and escape responses in herring gull chicks in nature. *Behaviour* 22:1–15.

Engen, T.; Lipsitt, H. L. P.; and Kaye, H. 1963. Olfactory responses and adaptation in the human neonate. *J. Comp. Physiol. Psychol.* 56:73–77.

Fantz, R. L. 1965. Ontogeny of perception. In *Behavior of non-human primates,* ed. A. M. Schrier, H. F. Harlow, and F. Stollnitz, pp. 365–403. New York: Academic Press.

Ferreira, A. J. 1965. Emotional factors in prenatal environment. *J. Nerv. Ment. Dis.* 141:108–18.

Fikova, E. 1964. Development of spreading depression during ontogenesis in the rat. *Physiol. Bohemoslov.* 13:263–67.

Filiminoff, I. N. 1923. Über die Varianten der Hirnfurchen des Hundes. *J. Psychol. Neurol.* 36:22–43.

Fisher, A. E. 1955. The effects of differential early treatment on the social and exploratory behavior of puppies. Doctoral diss., Pennsylvania State University.

———. 1958. Effects of stimulus variation in sexual satiation in the male rat. *Amer. Psychol.* 13:382 (abstr.).

Fleschig, P. 1894. Gehirn und Seele. *Neurol. Centralbl.* Cited by Ramon y Cajal, S.,

1909–11, *Histologie du système nerveux de l'homme et des vertébrés*, 2:862–67. Paris: Maloine.

Fletcher, T. F. 1966. The lumbar, sacral and coccygeal tactile dermatomes of the dog. *J. Comp. Neurol.* 128:171.

Fletcher, T. F., and Kitchell, R. L. 1966. Anatomical studies on the spinal cord segments of the dog. *Amer. J. Vet. Res.* 27:1759.

Flexner, L. B.; Tyler, D. B.; and Gallant, L. J. 1950. Onset of electrical activity in developing cerebral cortex of fetal guinea pig. *J. Neurophysiol.* 13:427–30.

Folch-Pi, J. 1955. *Biochemistry of the developing nervous system.* New York: Academic Press.

Foley, J. P. 1934. First year development of a rhesus monkey (*Macaca mulatta*) reared in isolation. *J. Genet. Psychol.* 45:39–105.

Forgays, D. G., and Read, J. M. 1962. Crucial periods for free-environmental experience in the rat. *J. Comp. Physiol. Psychol.* 55:816–18.

Forgus, R. H. 1955. Early visual and motor experience as determiners of complex maze learning ability under rich and reduced stimulation. *J. Comp. Physiol. Psychol.* 48:215–20.

————. 1956. Advantage of early over late perceptual experiences in improving form discrimination. *Canad. J. Psychol.* 10:147–55.

Fowler, H. 1965. *Curiosity and exploratory behavior.* New York: Macmillan Co.

Fox, C. 1961. Neural correlates of psychophysiological developments in the young organism. In *Recent advances in biological psychiatry*, ed. J. Wortis, 4:313–28.

Fox, M. W. 1962. Observations on paw raising and sympathy lameness in the dog. *Vet. Rec.* 74:895–96.

————. 1963*a*. Development and clinical significance of superficial reflexes in the dog. *Vet. Rec.* 75:378–83.

————. 1963*b*. Gross structure and development of the canine brain. *Amer. J. Vet. Res.* 24:1240–47.

————. 1963*c*. Reflexes and innate behavioural mechanisms in the neonate dog. *J. Small Anim. Pract.* 4:85–99.

————. 1964*a*. Development of breed variables in the dog. *J. Hered.* 55:174–76.

————. 1964*b*. Effects of pentobarbital on the EEG of maturing dogs and a review of the literature. *Vet. Rec.* 76:768–70.

————. 1964*c*. The otocephalic syndrome in the dog. *Cornell Vet.* 54:250–59.

————. 1964*d*. A phylogenetic analysis of behavioral neuro-ontogeny in precocial and non-precocial mammals. *Canad. J. Comp. Med. Vet. Sci.* 28:196–202.

————. 1964*e*. The postnatal growth of the canine brain and correlated anatomical and behavioral changes during neuro-ontogenesis. *Growth* 28:135–41.

————. 1965*a*. *Canine behavior.* Springfield, Ill.: C. C. Thomas.

————. 1965*b*. The development of reflexes and neuro-ontogeny of the mouse. *Anim. Behav.* 13:234–41.

————. 1965*c*. Environmental factors influencing stereotyped and allelomimetic behavior in animals. *Lab. Anim. Care* 15:363–70.

————. 1965*d*. The neuro-ontogeny of some neuromuscular mutant mice. *J. Hered.* 56:55–60.

————. 1965*e*. The pathophysiology of neonatal mortality in the dog. *J. Small Anim. Pract.* 6:243–54.

Fox, M. W. 1965*f*. The visual cliff test for the study of visual depth perception in the mouse. *Anim. Behav.* 13:232–33.

———. 1966*a*. Age differences in the cellular response to cerebral lesions in the dog and mouse. *Experientia* 22:54.

———. 1966*b*. Behavioural and physiological aspects of cardiac development in the dog. *J. Small Anim. Pract.* 7:321–26.

———. 1966*c*. Brain to body relationships in ontogeny of canine brain. *Experientia* 22:111–12.

———. 1966*d*. *Canine pediatrics.* Springfield, Ill.: C. C. Thomas.

———. 1966*e*. The clinical significance of age differences in the effects of decerebration and spinal cord transection in the dog. *J. Small Anim. Pract.* 7:91–98.

———. 1966*f*. Further observations on age differences in the effects of formalin on the canine brain *in vitro. Experientia* 22:447–48.

———. 1966*g*. Neuro-behavioral ontogeny: A synthesis of ethological and neurophysiological concepts. *Brain Res.* 2:3–20.

———. 1966*h*. A syndrome in the dog resembling human infantile autism. *J.A.V.M.A.* 148:1387–90.

———. 1967*a*. Influence of domestication upon behavior of animals. *Vet. Rec.* 80:696–702.

———. 1967*b*. Postnatal development of the EEG of the dog: Parts I, II, and III. *J. Small Anim. Pract.* 8:71–111.

———. 1968. Socialization, environmental factors and abnormal behavioral development. In *Abnormal behavior in animals,* ed. M. W. Fox, pp. 332–55. Philadelphia: W. B. Saunders.

———. 1969*a*. The anatomy of aggression and its ritualization in Canidae. *Behaviour* 35:242–58.

———. 1969*b*. Ontogeny of prey-killing behavior in Canidae. *Behaviour* 35:259–72.

———. 1970*a*. Neurobehavioral development and the genotype-environment interaction. *Quart. Rev. Biol.* 45:131–47.

———. 1970*b*. Reflex development and behavioral organization. In *Developmental neurobiology,* ed. W. A. Himwich, pp. 553–80. Springfield, Ill.: C. C. Thomas.

———. 1971*a*. *The behaviour of wolves, dogs and related canids.* London: Jonathan Cape.

———. 1971*b*. Socio-infantile and socio-sexual signals in canids: A comparative and developmental study. *Z. Tierpsychol.* 28:185–210.

Fox, M. W., and Appelbaum, J. 1969. Ontogeny of the orienting-jump response of the rabbit. *Behaviour* 35:77–83.

Fox, M. W., and Inman, O. 1966. Persistence of Retzius-Cajal cells in developing dog brain. *Brain Res.* 3:192–94.

Fox, M. W.; Inman, O.; and Himwich, W. A. 1966. The postnatal development of neocortical neurons in the dog. *J. Comp. Neurol.* 127:199–206.

Fox, M. W., and Spencer, J. W. 1967. Development of the delayed response in the dog. *Anim. Behav.* 15:162–68.

Fox, M. W., and Weisman, R. 1970. Development of responsiveness to a social releaser in the dog: Effects of age and hunger. *Develop. Psychobiol.* 2:277–80.

Fraenkel, G. S., and Gunn, D. D. 1961. *The orientation of animals.* New York: Dover.

Frankova, S. 1966. Development of spontaneous motor activity in the early stages of ontogeny of the rat. *Activ. Nerv. Sup.* 8:248–57.

Fredericson, E. 1952. Perceptual homeostasis and distress vocalization in puppies. *J. Personality* 20:472–77.

Fredericson, E.; Gurney, M.; and Dubuis, E. 1956. Relationship between environmental temperature and behavior of puppies. *J. Comp. Physiol. Psychol.* 49:273.

Freedman, D. G. 1958. Constitutional and environmental interactions in the rearing of four breeds of dogs. *Science* 127:585–86.

Freedman, D. G.; King, J. A.; and Elliot, O. 1961. Critical period in the social development of dogs. *Science* 133:1016–17.

Freeman, L. W. 1952. Return of function after complete transection of the spinal cord of the rat, cat and dog. *Ann. Surg.* 136:193–205.

Friede, R. L., and Hu, K. H. 1967. Proximo-distal differences in myelin development in human optic fibers. *Z. Zellforsch.* 79:259–64.

Frisch, K. von. 1956. "Language" and orientation of bees. *Proc. Amer. Phil. Soc.* 100:515–19.

Fromme, A. 1941. An experimental study of factors of maturation and practice in the behavioural development of the embryo of the frog *Rana pipiens. Genet. Psychol. Monogr.,* 24:219–56.

Fuller, J. L. 1964. Effects of experiential deprivation upon behaviour in animals. *Proc. Third World Cong. Psychiat.* 3:223–27. Toronto: University of Toronto Press.

———. 1966. Transitory effects of experiential deprivation upon reversal learning in dogs. *Psychonom. Sci.* 4:273–74.

———. 1967. Experiential deprivation and later behavior: Emergence stress is postulated as the basis for behavioral deficits seen in dogs following isolation. *Science* 158:1645–52.

Fuller, J. L., and Clark, L. D. 1966*a*. Effects of rearing with specific stimuli upon postulation behavior in dogs. *J. Comp. Physiol. Psychol.* 61:258–63.

———. 1966*b*. Genetic and treatment factors modifying the postulation syndrome in dogs. *J. Comp. Physiol. Psychol.* 61:251–57.

———. 1968. Genotype and behavioral vulnerability to isolation in dogs. *J. Comp. Physiol. Psychol.* 66:151–56.

Fuller, J. L.; Clark, L. D.; and Waller, M. B. 1960. Effects of chlorpromazine upon psychological development in the puppy. *Psychopharmacologia* 1:393–407.

Fuller, J. L., and DuBuis, E. M. 1962. The behaviour of dogs. In *The behavior of domesticated animals,* ed. E. S. E. Hafez, pp. 415–52. London: Baillière, Tindall and Cox.

Fuller, J. L.; Easler, C.; and Banks, E. 1950. Formation of conditioned avoidance responses in young puppies. *Amer. J. Physiol.* 160:462–66.

Fuller, J. L., and Fox, M. W. 1968. The behavior of dogs. In *The behavior of domesticated animals,* ed. E. S. E. Hafez, pp. 438–81. London: Baillière, Tindall and Cox.

Fuller, J. L., and Gillum, E. 1950. A study of factors influencing performance of dogs on a delayed response test. *J. Genet. Psychol.* 76:241–51.

Gard, C.; Hard, E.; Larsson, K.; and Pattersson, V. A. 1967. The relationship between sensory stimulation and gross motor behavior during the postnatal development in the rat. *Anim. Behav.* 15:563–67.

Garstang, W. 1922. The theory of recapitulation: A critical restatement of the biogenetic law. *J. Linnean Soc. Lond.* 35:81.

Geber, W. F. 1966. Developmental effects of chronic maternal audiovisual stress on the rat fetus. *J. Embryol. Exp. Morph.* 16:1–16.

Geller, A. E.; Yuwiler, A.; and Zolman, J. F. 1965. Effects of environmental complexity on constituents of brain and liver. *J. Neurochem.* 12:949–55.

Gellhorn, E. 1967. The tuning of the nervous system: Physiological foundations and implications for behavior. *Perspect. Biol. Med.* 10:591–99.

Gerebtzoff, M. A. 1955. Development of cholinesterase activity in the nervous system. In *Biochemistry of the developing nervous system,* ed. H. Waelsch. Proc. First Internat. Neurochem. Symposium. New York: Academic Press.

Geren, B. B. 1954. Formation of the Schwann cell surface of myelin in the peripheral nerves of chick embryos. *Exper. Cell Res.* 7:156–62.

Gesell, A. 1945. *The embryology of behavior.* New York: Harper.

———. 1954. The ontogenesis of infant behavior. In *Manual of child psychiatry,* ed. L. Carmichael, pp. 335–73. New York: John Wiley and Sons.

Gibbs, F. A., and Gibbs, E. L. 1950. *Atlas of electroencephalography,* vol. 1. Reading, Mass.: Addison-Wesley Publishing Co.

Gibson, E., and Walk, R. D. 1956. The effect of prolonged exposure to visually presented patterns on learning to discriminate them. *J. Comp. Physiol. Psychol.* 49: 239–42.

Gibson, J. J., and Gibson, E. J. 1955. Perceptual learning: Differentiation or enrichment? *Psychol. Rev.* 62:32–41, 447–50.

Ginsburg, B. E., and Hovda, R. B. 1947. On the physiology of gene controlled audiogenetic seizures in mice. *Anat. Rec.* 99:621–22 (abstr.).

Glanzer, M. 1961. Changes and interrelations in exploratory behavior. *J. Comp. Physiol. Psychol.* 54:433–38.

Glass, H. G.; Snyder, F. F.; and Webster, E. 1944. The rate of decline in resistance to anoxia of rabbits, dogs and guinea pigs from the onset of viability to adult life. *Amer. J. Physiol.* 140:609–15.

Glickman, S. E., and Schiff, B. B. 1967. A biological theory of reinforcement. *Psychol. Rev.* 74:81–109.

Glickman, S. E., and Van Laer, E. K. 1964. The development of curiosity within the genus *Panthera. Zoologica* 49:109–14.

Globus, A., and Scheibel, A. B. 1966. Loss of dendrite spines as an index of presynaptic terminal patterns. *Nature* 212:436–65.

———. 1967*a*. The effect of visual deprivation on cortical neurons: A Golgi study. *Exper. Neurol.* 19:331–45.

———. 1967*b*. Synaptic loci on parietal cortical neurons: Terminations of corpus callosum fibers. *Science* 156:1127–29.

———. 1967*c*. Synaptic loci on visual cortical neurons of the rabbit: The specific afferent radiation. *Exp. Neurol.* 18:116–31.

Glücksman, A. 1951. Cell deaths in normal vertebrate ontogeny. *Biol. Rev.* 26: 59–86.

Gokhblit, I. I. 1958. Electroencephalographic characteristics during sleep and while awake in dogs of different age. *Biull. Eksp. Biol. Med.* 47:790–94.

————. 1964. On the nature of cerebrocortical polarization and its relation to the degree of impedance and demarcation in dogs of various ages. *Tr. Inst. Norm. Pat. Fiziol.* (*Moskova*) 7:35–36.

Gokhblit, I. I., and Kornienko, I. A. 1963. The analysis of the characteristics of electrical activity of the cortex cerebri in the conditions of transections of the brain stem in dogs at various ages. *Biull. Eksp. Biol. Med.* 28:14–19.

Golani, I. 1966. Observations on the behavior of the jackal *Canis aureus* L. in captivity. *Israel J. Zool.* 15:27–32.

Goldie, L., and Van Velzer, C. 1965. Innate sleep rhythms. *Brain* 88:1043–56.

Golubova, E. L. 1958. Physiology and pathology of the nervous system in animals and man in the early stages of development. *Pavlov J. Higher Nerv. Act.* 8:5.

Goodrick, C. 1966. Activity and exploration as a function of age and deprivation. *J. Genet. Psychol.* 108:239–52.

————. 1967. Exploration of nondeprived male Sprague Dawley rats as a function of age. *Psych. Rep.* 20:159–63.

Gottlieb, G. 1965. Imprinting in relation to parental and species identification by avian neonates. *J. Comp. Physiol. Psychol.* 59:345–56.

Gottlieb, G., and Kuo, Z. Y. 1965. Development of behavior in the duck embryo. *J. Comp. Physiol. Psychol.* 59:183–88.

Grafstein, B. 1963. Postnatal development of the transcallosal evoked responses in the cerebral cortex of the cat. *J. Neurophysiol.* 26:79–99.

Gray, E. G. 1959. Axo-somatic and axo-dendritic synapses of the cerebral cortex: An electron microscope study. *J. Anat.* 93:420–42.

Gray, P. H. 1958. Theory and evidence of imprinting in human infants. *J. Psychol.* 46:155–66.

Green P., and Gordon, M. 1964. Maternal deprivation: Its influence on visual exploration in infant monkeys. *Science* 145:292–94.

Green, P. C. 1967. Effects of early versus late lesions on cognitive-affective behavior in rats. *Psychonom. Sci.* 7:11–12.

Gregory, K. 1967. A note on strain differences in exploratory activity (rearing). *Life Sci.* 6:1253.

Grier, J. B.; Counter, S. A.; and Shearer, W. M. 1967. Prenatal auditory imprinting in chickens. *Science* 155:1692–93.

Griffiths, W. J., Jr. 1961. Effect of isolation on treadmill running in the albino rat. *Psychol. Rep.* 8:243–50.

Grohmann, J. 1938. Modifikation oder Funktionsregung? Ein Beitrag zur Klärung der wechselseitigen Beziehungen zwischen Instinkthanhlung und Erfahrung *Z. Tierpsychol.* 2:132–44.

Grossman, C. 1955. Electro-ontogenesis of cerebral activity. *Arch. Neurol. Psychiat.* (*Chic.*) 74:186–202.

Guiton, P. 1966. Early experience and sexual object-choice in the brown leghorn. *Anim. Behav.* 14:534–38.

Gyllenstein, L.; Malmfors, T.; and Norrlin-Grettve, M. L. 1966a. Development and functional alterations in the fiber composition of the optic nerve in visually deprived mice. *J. Comp. Neurol.* 128:413–18.

Gyllenstein, L.; Malmfors, T.; and Norrlin-Grettve, M. L. 1966*b*. Growth alteration in the auditory cortex of visually deprived mice. *J. Comp. Neurol.* 126:463–70.

———. 1967. Visual and non-visual factors in the centripetal stimulation of postnatal growth of the visual centers in mice. *J. Comp. Neurol.* 131:549–58.

Haddara, M. A. 1956. A quantitative study of the postnatal changes in the packing density of the neurons in the visual cortex of the mouse. *J. Anat.* 90:494–501.

Haddara, M. A., and Nooreddin, M. A. 1966. A quantitative study on the postnatal development of the cerebellar vermis of mouse. *J. Comp. Neurol.* 128:245.

Hague, E. B. 1964. Photo-neuroendocrine effects in circadian systems with particular reference to the eye. *Ann. N.Y. Acad. Sci.* 117:1–645.

Hailman, J. P. 1969. How an instinct is learned. *Sci. Amer.* 221:58–106.

Halliday, M. S. 1966. Some effects of early experience on exploratory behavior in the rat. *Anim. Behav.* 14:583.

Haltmeyer, G. C.; Denenberg, V. H.; Thatcher, J.; and Zarrow, M. X. 1966. Response of the adrenal cortex of the neonatal rat after subjection to stress. *Nature* 212:1371–73.

Hamburger, V. 1963. Some aspects of the embryology of behavior. *Quart. Rev. Biol.* 38:342–65.

Hamburger, V.; Balaban, M.; Oppenheim, R.; and Wenger, E. 1965. Periodic motility of normal and spinal chick embryo between 8 and 17 days of incubation. *J. Exp. Zool.* 159:1–14.

Hamburger, V., and Oppenheim, R. 1967. Prehatching motility and hatching behavior in the chick. *J. Exp. Zool.* 166:171–204.

Hamburger, V.; Wenger, E.; and Oppenheim, R. 1966. Motility in the chick embryo in the absence of sensory input. *J. Exp. Zool.* 162:133–60.

Hamilton, E. L. 1929. The effect of delayed incentive on the hunger drive in the white rat. *Genet. Psychol. Monogr.* 5:137–66.

Hansen, E. W. 1966. Squab-induced crop growth in Ring Dove foster parents. *J. Comp. Physiol. Psychol.* 62:120.

Harlow, H. F. 1949. The formation of learning sets. *Psychol. Rev.* 56:51–65.

———. 1959. The development of learning in the rhesus monkey. *Amer. Scientist* 47:459–79.

———. 1962. Development of affection in primates. In *Roots of behavior,* ed. E. L. Bliss. New York: Harper.

———. 1965*a*. Sexual behavior in the rhesus monkey. In *Sex and behavior,* ed. F. A. Beach, pp. 234–65. New York: John Wiley and Sons.

———. 1965*b*. Total social isolation: Effects on Macaque monkey behavior. *Science* 148:666.

Harlow, H. F.; Dodsworth, R. O.; and Harlow, M. K. 1965. Total social isolation in monkeys. *Proc. Nat. Acad. Sci.* 54:90–97.

Harlow, H. F., and Harlow, M. K. 1962. Social deprivation in monkeys. *Sci. Amer.* 207:137–46.

Harlow, H. F.; Harlow, M. K.; Dodsworth, R. O.; and Arling, G. L.1966. Maternal behavior of rhesus monkeys deprived of mothering and peer associations in infancy. *Proc. Amer. Phil. Soc.* 110:58–66.

Harlow, H. F.; Harlow, M. K.; and Hansen, E. W. 1963. The maternal affectional system of rhesus monkeys. In *Maternal behavior in mammals,* ed. H. O. Rheingold, chap. 8. New York: John Wiley and Sons.

Harlow, H. F.; Harlow, M. K.; and Meyer, D. R. 1950. Learning motivated by a manipulative drive. *J. Exp. Psychol.* 40:228–34.

Harlow, H. F., and Hicks, L. H. 1957. Discrimination learning theory: Uniprocess versus duoprocess. *Psych. Rev.* 64:104–90.

Harman, P. J. 1963. Cited personal communication in J. P. Scott's The process of primary socialization in canine and human infants. *Monogr. Soc. Res. Child Develop. no. 85* (28), p. 1.

Harris, G. W., and Levine, S. 1965. Sexual differentiation of the brain and its experimental control. *J. Physiol.* 181:379–400.

Haslerud, G. M. 1938. The effect of movement of stimulus objects upon avoidance reactions in chimpanzees. *J. Comp. Psychol.* 25:507–28.

Hatch, A.; Balazs, T.; Wiberg, G. S.; and Grice, H. C. 1963. Long-term isolation stress in rats. *Science* 142:507.

Havelka, J. 1956. Problem seeking behavior in rats. *Canad. J. Psychol.* 10:91–97.

Hebb, D. O. 1947. The effects of early experience on problem-solving at maturity. *Amer. Psychol.* 2:306–7.

———. 1949. *Organization of behavior.* New York: John Wiley and Sons.

———. 1955. Drives and the CNS (conceptual nervous system). *Psychol. Rev.* 62:243–54.

Hediger, H. 1950. *Wild animals in captivity.* London: Butterworth.

Heim, L. M. 1967. Brain maturation in the neonatal rat after varied light cycles. *Proc. Soc. Exper. Biol. Med.* 124: 223.

Hein, A., and Held, R. 1967. Dissociation of the visual placing response into elicited and guided components. *Science* 158:390–92.

Held, R., and Bauer, J. A., Jr. 1967. Visually guided reaching in infant monkeys after restricted rearing. *Science* 155:718–20.

Held, R., and Hein, A. 1963. Movement produced stimulation in the development of visually guided behavior. *J. Comp. Physiol. Psychol.* 56:872–76.

Henderson, N. D. 1964. Behavioral effects of manipulation during different stages in the development of mice. *J. Comp. Physiol. Psychol.* 57:284–89.

———. 1966. Inheritance of reactivity to experimental manipulation in mice. *Science* 153:650.

Hernández-Péon, R.; Scherrer, H.; and Jouvet, M. 1956. Modification of electrical activity in cochlear nucleus during "attention" in unanesthetized cats. *Science* 123:331–32.

Herre, W., and Stephan, H. 1955. Zur postnatalen morphogenese verschiedener Haushundrassen. *Gegenbaurs Morph. Jahrbuch* 96: 210–64.

Hess, E. H. 1959. Imprinting. *Science* 130:133–41.

———. 1964. Imprinting in birds. *Science* 146:1128–39.

Hibbard, E. 1959. Central integration of developing nerve tracts from supernumerary grafted eyes and brain in the frog. *J. Exp. Zool.* 141:323–52.

———. 1965. Orientation and direction of growth of Mauther's cell axons from duplicated vestibular nerve roots. *Exp. Neurol.* 13:289–301.

Hicks, S. P., and D'Amato, C. J. 1966. Effects of ionizing radiations on mammalian development. In *Advances in teratology,* ed. D. H. M. Woollmann, pp. 196–249. London: Logos Press.

Himwich, H. E., and Fazekas, J. F. 1941. Comparative studies of the metabolism of the brain of infant and adult dogs. *Amer. J. Physiol.* 132:454–59.

Himwich, W. A., ed. 1970. *Developmental neurobiology.* Springfield, Ill.: C. C. Thomas.

Himwich, W. A.; Davis, J. M.; and Agrawal, H. C. 1967. Biochemical substrate for the development of the matured evoked potential. In *Recent advances in biological psychiatry,* 9:271–79. New York: Plenum Press.

Hinde, R. A. 1954. Factors governing the changes in strength of a partially inborn response, as shown by the mobbing behaviour of the Chaffinch (*Fringilla coelebs*). I and II. *Proc. Roy. Soc., Ser. B.* 142:306–31, 358.

————. 1966. Animal behavior: *A synthesis of ethology and comparative psychology.* New York: McGraw-Hill.

Hines, M. 1942. The development and regression of reflexes and progression in the young Macaque. *Contr. Embryol. Carnegie Inst., Washington* 30: 153–209.

Hirsch, J. 1963. Behavior genetics and individuality understood. *Science* 142:1436–42.

Holloway, R. L. 1966. Dendritic branching: Some preliminary results of training and complexity in rat visual cortex. *Brain Res.* 2:393–96.

Hooker, D. 1952. *The prenatal origin of behavior.* Lawrence, Kansas: University of Kansas Press.

Horrocks, L. A. 1968. Composition of mouse brain myelin during development. *J. Neurochem.* 15:483–88.

Hosokawa, H., and Mannen, H. 1963. In *Morphology of neuroglia,* ed. J. Nakai, pp. 1–52. Springfield, Ill.: C. C. Thomas.

Howells, T. H., and Vine, D. C. 1940. The innate differential in social learning. *J. Abnorm. Soc. Psychol.* 35:537–48.

Hubel, D. H., and Wiesel, T. N. 1963. Receptive fields of cells in striate cortex of very young, visually inexperienced kittens. *J. Neurophysiol.* 26:994–1002.

Hudgens, G. A.; Denenberg, V. H.; and Zarrow, M. X. 1967. Mice reared with rats: Relations between mother's activity level and offspring's behavior. *J. Comp. Physiol. Psychol.* 63:304.

Humphrey, T. 1964. Some correlations between the appearance of human fetal reflexes and the development of the nervous system. In *Progress in brain research,* vol. 4, *Growth and maturation of the brain,* ed. D. P. Purpura and J. P. Schadé, pp. 93–133. Amsterdam: Elsevier.

Humphries, D. A., and Driver, P. M. 1967. Erratic display as a device against predators. *Science* 156:1767–68.

Hunt, W. E., and Goldring, S. 1961. Maturation of evoked response of the visual cortex in the postnatal rabbit. *Electroenceph. Clin. Neurophysiol.* 3:465–71.

Hunter, W. S. 1913. The delayed reaction in animals and children. *Behav. Monogr.,* vol. 2, no. 1.

Hutt, C., and Hutt, S. J. 1965. Effects of environmental complexity on stereotyped behaviors of children. *Anim. Behav.* 12:1–4.

Hutt, S. J.; Hutt, C.; Lee, D.; and Ounsted, C. 1965. A behavioural and electroencephalographic study of autistic children. *J. Psychiat. Res.* 3:181–97.

Huttenlocher, P. R. 1967. Development of cortical neuronal activity in the neonatal cat. *Exper. Neurol.* 17:247–62.

Hymovitch, B. 1952. The effects of experimental variations on problem solving in the rat. *J. Comp. Physiol. Psychol.* 45:313–21.

Illingworth, R. S. 1962. *An introduction to developmental assessment in the first year.* London: National Spastics Society.

Ingel, G. J., and Calvin, A. D. 1960. The development of affectional responses in infant dogs. *J. Comp. Physiol. Psychol.* 53:302–5.

Ingram, T. T. S. 1959. Muscle tone and posture in infancy. *Cereb. Palsy Bull.* 5: 6–10.

———. 1962. The clinical significance of infantile feeding reflexes. *Develop. Med. Child. Neurol.* 4:159.

Isaacson, R. L., ed. 1968. *The neuropsychology of development.* New York: John Wiley and Sons.

Jacobson, A. 1964. Learning in planarians: Current status in learning and associated phenomena in invertebrates. In *Animal Behavior Supplement,* ed. W. H. Thorpe and D. Davenport, 1:76–82.

Jacobson, M. 1968a. Cessation of DNA synthesis in retinal ganglion cells correlated with the time of specification of their central connections. *Develop. Biol.* 17:219–32.

———. 1968b. Development of neuronal specificity in retinal ganglion cells of Xenopus. *Develop. Biol.* 17:202–17.

———. 1969. Development of specific neuronal connections. *Science* 163:543–47.

Jacobson, S. 1963. Sequence of myelinization of the brain of the albino rat. A. Cerebral cortex, thalamus, and related structures. *J. Comp. Neur.* 121:5–29.

James, H., and Binks, C. 1963. Escape and avoidance learning in newly hatched domestic chicks. *Science* 139:1293–94.

James, W. T. 1949. Dominant and submissive behavior in puppies as indicated by food intake. *J. Genet. Psychol.* 75:33–43.

———. 1951. Social organization among dogs of different temperaments, terriers and beagles, reared together. *J. Comp. Physiol. Psychol.* 44:71–77.

———. 1952a. Observations on the behavior of newborn puppies. I. Method of measurement and types of behavior involved. *J. Comp. Physiol. Psychol.* 45: 329–35.

———. 1952b. Observations on the behavior of newborn puppies. II. Summary of movements involved in group orientation. *J. Comp. Physiol. Psychol.* 45: 329–35.

———. 1955. Behaviors involved in expression of dominance among puppies. *Psychol. Rep.* 1:299–301.

———. 1956. The geotropic reaction of newborn puppies. *J. Genet. Psychol.* 89: 127–30.

———. 1957. The effect of satiation on the sucking response in puppies. *J. Comp. Physiol. Psychol.* 50:375–78.

———. 1960a. The development of social facilitation of eating in puppies. *J. Genet. Psychol.* 96:123–27.

———. 1960b. Observations of the regurgitant feeding reflex in the dog. *Psychol. Rep.* 6:142.

James, W. T. 1961*a*. Preliminary observations on play behaviour in puppies. *J. Genet. Psychol.* 98:273–77.

————. 1961*b*. Relationship between dominance and food intake in individual and social eating in puppies. *Psychol. Rep.* 8:478.

James, W. T., and Cannon, D. 1952. Conditioned avoiding responses in puppies. *Amer. J. Physiol.* 168:251–53.

Jasper, H. H.; Bridgeman, C. S.; and Carmichael, L. 1937. An ontogenetic study of cerebral electrical potentials in the guinea pig. *J. Exp. Psychol.* 21:63–71.

Jensen, C., and Ederstorm, H. E. 1955. Development of temperature regulation in the dog. *Amer. J. Physiol.* 183:340–43.

Jensen, G. D., and Tolman, C. W. 1962. Mother-infant relationship in the monkey, *Macaca nemestrina:* The effect of brief separation and mother-infant specificity. *J. Comp. Physiol. Psychol.* 55:131–36.

Jewett, R. B., and Norton, S. 1966. Effect of tranquilizing drugs on postnatal behavior. *Exp. Neurol.* 14:33.

Jilek, L., and Fox, M. W. 1965. Effects of frontal lobectomy and age on conditioned responses following drug treatment. Unpublished data, Galesburg State Research Hospital, Galesburg, Ill.

Jilek, L., and Trojan, S. 1966. Development of the resistance to general stagnant anoxia (Ischemia) in dogs. *Physiol. Bohemoslov.* 15:62.

Joffe, J. M. 1965*a*. Effect of foster-mother's strain and pre-natal experience on adult behaviour in rats. *Nature* 208:815–16.

————. 1965*b*. Genotype and prenatal and premating stress interact to affect adult behavior in rats. *Science* 150:1844.

————. 1969. *Prenatal determinants of behavior.* New York: Pergamon Press.

John, E. R.; Herrington, R. N.; and Sutton, S. 1967. Effects of visual form on the evoked response. *Science* 155:1439–42.

Johnsgard, P. A. 1965. *Handbook of waterfowl behavior.* Ithaca, New York: Comstock Publishing Associates.

Jouvet, D.; Vimont, P.; Delmore, F.; and Jouvet, M. 1964. Etude de la privation sélective de la phase paradoxicale de sommeil chez le chat. *C.R. Soc. Biol.* 158:756–59.

Jouvet, M. 1962. Recherches sur les structures nerveuses et les mécanismes responsables des différents phases du sommeil physiologique. *Arch. Ital. Biol.* 100:125–206.

————. 1967. The states of sleep. *Sci. Amer.* 216:62–72.

Kagan, J. 1967. The need for relativism. *Amer. Psychol.* 22:131–42.

Kagan, J., and Beach, F. H. 1953. Effects of early experience on mating behavior in male rats. *J. Comp. Physiol. Psychol.* 46:204–8.

Kahn, M. W. 1961. The effect of socially learned aggression or submission on the mating behavior of C57 mice. *J. Genet. Psychol.* 98:211–17.

Kamarin, B. B. 1967. The effects of the immune tolerant state on early behaviour of domestic fowl. *Anim. Behav.* 15:217–22.

Kantrowitz, Z., and Shamaun. M. 1963. Paraplegic dogs: Urinary bladder evacuation with direct electric stimulation. *Science* 139:115–16.

Kaufman, I. C., and Rosenblum, L. A. 1967. Depression in infant monkeys separated from their mothers. *Science* 155:1030.

Keeley, K. 1962. Prenatal influence on behavior of offspring of crowded mice. *Science* 135:44–45.

Keller, A. D. 1945. Generalized atonia and profound dysreflexia following transection of the brain stem through the cephalic pons. *J. Neurophysiol.* 8:273–85.

Kennard, M. A. 1940. Relation of age to motor impairment in man and in subhuman primates. *Arch. Neurol. Psych.* 44:377–97.

Kessen, W.; Leutzendorff, A. M.; and Stoutsenberger, K. 1967. Age, food deprivation, non-nutritive sucking and movement in the human newborn. *J. Comp. Physiol. Psychol.* 63:82–86.

King, D. L. 1966. A review and interpretation of some aspects of the infant-mother relationship in mammals and birds. *Psychol. Bull.* 65:143–55.

King, J. A. 1958. Parameters relevant to determining the effect of early experience upon the adult behavior of animals. *Psychol. Bull.* 55:46–58.

King, J. A. 1968. Species specificity and early experience. In *Early experience and behavior,* ed. G. Newton and S. Levine, chap. 11. Springfield, Ill.: C. C. Thomas.

King, J. A., and Eleftheriou, B. 1959. Effects of early handling upon adult behavior in two sub-species of deermice, *Peromyscus maniculates. J. Comp. Physiol. Psychol.* 52:82–88.

King, J. S. 1966. A comparative investigation of neuroglia in representative vertebrates: A silver carbonate study. *J. Morphol.* 119:435–66.

Kiyota, K. 1959. Soluble protein fraction of the brain in relation to maturation of the brain. *Folia Psych. Neurol. Jap.* 13:15–22.

Kleiman, D. 1966. Scent marking in the Canidae. *Symp. Zool. Soc. Lond.* 18:167–77.

———. 1967. Some aspects of social behavior in the Canidae. *Amer. Zool.* 7:365–72.

Kliavina, M. P., and Obrastsova, G. A. 1966. Primary responses of the auditory area of the cortex in rabbits as dependent on the intensity of stimulation during ontogeny. *Proc. Acad. Sci. USSR* 169:1471.

Kling, A. 1966. Ontogenetic and phylogenetic studies on the amygdaloid nuclei. *Psychosom. Med.* 28:155–61.

Kling, A., and Coustan, D. 1964. Electrical stimulation of the amygdala and hypothalamus in the kitten. *Exp. Neurol.* 10:81–89.

Kling, A.; Finer, S.; and Nair, V. 1965. Effects of early handling and light stimulation on the acetylcholinesterase activity of the developing rat brain. *Int. J. Neuropharmacol.* 4:353–57.

Kling, A., and Green, P. C. 1967. Effects of neonatal amygdalectomy in the maternally reared and maternally deprived macaque. *Nature* 213:742.

Klinghammer, E. 1967. Factors influencing choice of mate in altricial birds. In *Early behavior,* ed. H. W. Stevenson, E. H. Hess, and H. L. Rheingold, chap. 2. New York: John Wiley and Sons.

Klopfer, P. H., and Hailman, J. P. 1965. Habitat selection in birds. In *Advances in the study of behavior,* ed. D. S. Lehrman, R. A. Hinde, and E. Shaw, pp. 279–303. New York: Academic Press.

———. 1967. *An introduction to animal behavior: Ethology's first century.* Englewood Cliffs, N.J.: Prentice-Hall.

Klosovskii, B. N. 1963. *The development of the brain and its disturbance by harmful factors.* New York: Macmillan Co.

Kobayashi, T. 1963. Brain to body ratios and time of maturation of the mouse brain. *Amer. J. Physiol.* 204:343–46.

Kobayashi, T.; Inman, O.; Buno, W.; and Himwich, H. E. 1963. A multidisciplinary study of changes in mouse brain with age. In *Recent advances in biological psychiatry,* 5:293–308. New York: Plenum Press.

Kolmodin, G. M., and Meyerson, B. A. 1966. Ontogenesis of paroxysmal cortical activity in foetal sheep. *Electroenceph. Clin. Neurophysiol.* 21:589.

Konishi, M. 1963. The role of auditory feedback in the vocal behavior of the domestic fowl. *Z. Tierpsychol.* 20:349–67.

———. 1965. Effects of deafening on song development in American robins and black-headed grosbeaks. *Z. Tierpsychol.* 22:584–99.

———. 1966. The attributes of instinct. *Behaviour* 27:316–28.

Konorski, J., and Lawicka, W. 1959. Physiological mechanism of delayed reactions. I. The analysis and classification of delayed reactions. *Acta Biol. Exp. Warsaw* 19:175–97.

Kortlandt, A. 1940. Ein Übersicht der angeborenen Verhaltungsweisen des Mittel-Europäischen Kormorans (Phalacrocorax carbo sinensis), ihre Funktion, ontogenetische Entwicklung und phylogenetische Herkunft. *Arch. Néerl. Zool.* 4:401–2.

Kovach, J. K., and Hess, E. H. 1963. Imprinting: Effects of painful stimulation upon the following response. *J. Comp. Physiol. Psychol.* 56:461–64.

Kovach, J. K., and Kling, A. 1967. Mechanisms of neonate sucking behaviour in the kitten. *Anim. Behav.* 15: 91–101.

Kozlova, L. N. 1964. Effects of age on the excitability of the cerebral cortex and on the equilibration of nervous processes in dogs. *Z. Vyssh. Nerv. Deiat.* 14:678–86.

Krech, D.; Rosenzweig, M. R.; and Bennett, E. L. 1966. Environmental impoverishment, social isolation and changes in brain chemistry and anatomy. *Physiol. Behav.* 1:99–104.

Kreiner, J. 1966. Myeloarchitectonics of the occipital cortex in dog and general remarks on the myeloarchitectonics of the dog. *J. Comp. Neurol.* 127:531.

Krnjevic, K., and Silver, A. 1966. Acetylcholinesterase in the developing forebrain. *J. Anat.* 100:63.

Kruijt, J. P. 1964. *Ontogeny of social behavior in Burmese red jungle-fowl.* Leiden: Brill.

Krushinskii, I. V. 1962. *Animal behavior.* New York: Consultant Bureau.

Kuffler, S. W.; Nicholls, J. G.; and Orkland, R. K. 1966. Physiological properties of glial cells in the central nervous system of amphibia. *J. Neurophysiol.* 29:768–87.

Kuffler, S. W., and Potter, D. D. 1964. Glia in the leech central nervous system; Physiological properties and neuron-glia relationship. *J. Neurophysiol.* 27:290–320.

Kuhme, W. 1965. Communal food distribution and division of labour in African hunting dogs. *Nature* 205:443–44.

Kulin, H. E.; Grunbach, M. M.; and Kaplan, S. L. 1969. Changing sensitivity of the pubertal gonadal hypothalamic feedback mechanism in man. *Science* 166:1012–13.

Kunkel, P., and Kunkel, I. 1964. Beiträge zur Ethologie des Hausmerschweinchen (Cavia aperea f. poecellus [L.]) : A contribution to the ethological analysis of the guinea pig (Cavia aperea f. poecellus [L.]). *Z. Tierpsychol.* 21:602–41.

Kuo, Z. Y. 1930. The genesis of the rats' response to the rat. *J. Comp. Psychol.* 11: 1–30.

―――. 1960. Studies on the basic factors in animal fighting. VII. Interspecies co-existence in mammals. *J. Genet. Psychol.* 97:211–25.

―――. 1963. Total patterns, local reflexes or gradients in response? *Proc. 16th Int. Congr. Zool.* 4:371–74.

Kurtsin, I. T. 1968. Physiological mechanisms of behaviour disturbances and cortico-visceral interrelations in animals. In *Abnormal behavior in animals,* ed. M. W. Fox, chap. 7. Philadelphia: W. B. Saunders and Co.

Kuypers, H. G. J. M. 1962. Corticospinal connections. Postnatal development in the rhesus monkey. *Science* 138:678–79.

Lagerspetz, K. 1962. The postnatal development of homoiothermy and cold resistance in mice. *Experientia* 18:282–84.

Laget, P., and Delhaye, N. 1962. Etude du développement néo-natal de diverses activités électriques corticales chez le lapin. *Actualités Neurophysiol.* 4:259–84.

Landauer, T. K., and Whiting, J. W. 1964. Infantile stimulation and adult stature of human males. *Amer. Anthropol.* 66:1007–28.

Langworthy, O. R. 1927. Histological development of cerebral motor areas in young kittens correlated with their physiological reaction to electrical stimulation. *Contrib. Embryol. Carnegie Inst. Wash.* 19:177–207.

―――. 1928. The behavior of the pouch-young opossums correlated with myelinization of tracts in the nervous system. *J. Comp. Neurol.* 46:201–48.

―――. 1929. A correlated study of the development of reflex action in fetal and young kittens and the myelinization of tracts in the nervous system. *Contrib. Embryol. Carnegie Inst. Wash.* 20:127–71.

―――. 1930. Medullated tracts in the brain stem of a seven month human fetus. *Contrib. Embryol. Carnegie Inst. Wash.* 21:37–52.

―――. 1933. Development of behavior and myelinization of the nervous system in the human fetus and infant. *Contrib. Embryol. Carnegie Inst. Wash.* 24:1–57.

Latimer, H. B. 1942. The weights of the brain and of its parts and the weight and length of the spinal cord in the dog. *Growth* 6:39–47.

―――. 1965. Changes in the relative organ weights in the fetal dog. *Anat. Rec.* 153:421–28.

Lehrman, D. S. 1958. Induction of broodiness by participation in courtship and nest-building in the ring dove (*Streptopelia risoria*). *J. Comp. Physiol. Psychol.* 51:32–37.

―――. 1963. On the initiation of incubation behavior in doves. *Anim. Behav.* 11: 433–38.

Lessac, M. S. 1966. The effects of early isolation and restriction on the later behavior of beagle puppies. *Diss. Abstr.* 26:(9) 5560.

Levi-Montalcini, R. 1964. Events in the developing nervous system. In *Progress in brain research,* vol. 4, *Growth and maturation of the brain,* ed. D. P. Purpura and J. P. Schadé, pp. 1–29. Amsterdam: Elsevier.

Levine, S. 1957. Infantile experience and resistance to physiological stress. *Science* 126:405.

———. 1962*a*. Plasma-free corticosteroid response to electric shock in rats stimulated in infancy. *Science* 135:795.

———. 1962*b*. The psychophysiological effects of early stimulation. In *Roots of behavior,* ed. E. Bliss, pp. 246–53. New York: Harper.

———. 1967. Maternal and environmental influences on the adrenocortical response to stress in weanling rats. *Science* 156:258–60.

Levine, S., and Alpert, M. 1959. Differential maturation of the CNS as a function of early experience. *AMA Arch. Gen. Psychiat.* 1:403–5.

Levine, S., and Broadhurst, P. L. 1963. Genetic and ontogenetic determinants of adult behavior in rats. *J. Comp. Physiol. Psychol.* 56:423–28.

Levine, S., and Mullins, R. F. 1966. Hormonal influences on brain organization in infant rats. *Science* 152:1585–92.

Levy, D. M. 1934. Experiments on the sucking reflex and social behavior of dogs. *Amer. J. Orthopsychiat.* 4:203–24.

———. 1944. On the problem of movement restraint, tics, stereotyped movements, hyperactivity. *Amer. J. Orthopsychiat.* 14:644–71.

Lewis, M. M. 1963. *Language, thought and personality.* London: Harrap.

Leyhausen, P. 1965. Cited by Scott, J. P. 1967. Comparative psychology and ethology. *Ann. Rev. Psychol.* 18:65–86.

Lindsley, D. B. 1960. Attention, consciousness, sleep and wakefulness. In *Handbook of physiology,* ed. J. Field. Oxford: Pergamon Press.

Lindsley, D. B.; Wendt, R. H.; Lindsley, D. F.; Fox, S. S.; Howell, J.; and Aday, W. R. 1964. Diurnal activity, behavior and EEG responses in visually deprived monkeys. *Ann. N.Y. Acad. Sci.* 117:564–87.

Lipsitt, L. P., and Serunian, S. A. 1963. Oddity-problem learning in young children. *Child Develop.* 34:201–6.

Loizos, C. 1967. Play in mammals. *Symp. Zool. Soc. Lond.* 18:1–9.

Lorenz, K. 1935. Der Kumpan in der Umwelt des Vogels. *J. Ornithol.* 83:137–213, 289–413.

———. 1941. Vergleichende Bewegungsstudien an Anatiden. *J. Ornithol.* 89:194–293.

———. 1950. The comparative method in studying innate behaviour patterns. *Symp. Soc. Exp. Biol.* 4:221–69.

———. 1952. *King Solomon's ring.* New York: Crowell.

———. 1954. *Man meets dog.* London: Methuen.

———. 1958. The evolution of behavior. *Sci. Amer.* 199:67–78.

———. 1965. *Evolution and modification of behavior.* Chicago: University of Chicago Press.

———. 1966. *On aggression.* New York: Harcourt, Brace and World.

Lorenz, K., and Tinbergen, N. 1951. Taxis and instinctive action in the egg-retrieving behavior of the graylag goose. In *Instinctive behavior,* ed. C. H. Schiller, pp. 176–208. New York: International Universities Press.

Lott, D.; Scholz, S. D.; and Lehrman, D. S. 1967. Exteroceptive stimulation of the reproductive system of the female ring dove (*Streptopelia risoria*) by the mate and by the colony milieu. *Anim. Behav.* 15:433–37.

Lovatt, E. C. 1956. *Starling's human physiology.* Philadelphia: Lea and Febiger.

Luria, A. R. 1961. *Speech and the regulation of behavior.* Oxford: Pergamon Press.

Luse, S. A. 1956. Formation of myelin in the central nervous system of mice and rats as studied by the electron microscope. *J. Biophys. Biochem. Cytol.* 3:725–83.

Lynn, R. 1966. *Attention arousal and the orientation reaction.* New York: Pergamon Press.

McCance, R. A., and Widdowson, W. M. B. 1951. The German background studies of undernutrition, Wuppertal, 1946–49. *Med. Res. Counc. Spec. Rep. (Lond.)* 275:1–20.

McClearn, G. E. 1959. The genetics of mouse behavior in novel situations. *J. Comp. Physiol. Psychol.* 52:62–67.

McClearn, G. E., and Meredith, W. 1966. Behavioral genetics. *Ann. Rev. Psychol.* 17:515–50.

McClure, R. C. 1964. The spinal cord and meninges. In *Anatomy of the dog,* ed. M. E. Miller, G. C. Christensen, and H. E. Evans, pp. 533–43. Philadelphia: W. B. Saunders Co.

McCouch, G. P.; Deering, I. D.; and Ling, T. H. 1951. Location of receptors for tonic neck reflexes. *J. Neurophysiol.* 14:191–95.

McCulloch, T. L., and Nissen, H. W. 1937. Equated and non-equated stimulus situations in discrimination learning by chimpanzees. *J. Comp. Psychol.* 23:377–81.

McDowell, A. A., and Brown, W. L. 1958. A comparison of normal and irradiated monkeys on an oddity-reversal problem. *S.A.F. Sch. Aviat. Med. Rep.* pp. 58–73.

McGinty, D. J., and Sterman, M. B. 1968. Sleep suppression after basal forebrain lesions in the cat. *Science* 160:1253–55.

McGraw, M. B. 1939. Later development of children specially trained during infancy. *Child Develop.* 10:1–19.

———. 1943. *The neuro-muscular maturation in the human infant.* New York: Columbia University Press.

———. 1946. In *Manual of child psychology,* ed. L. C. Carmichael, pp. 332–69. New York: Wiley and Sons.

MacKeith, R. C. 1961. Anencephaly and somatic stability. Cited in discussion, p. 288, Ciba Symposium, *Somatic stability of the newly born.* Boston: Little, Brown and Co.

MacKintosh, N. J. 1965. Selective attention in animal discrimination learning. *Psych. Bull.* 64:124–51.

Magni, F.; Moruzzi, G.; Rossig, F.; and Zanchetti, A. 1959. EEG arousal following inactivation of the lower brain stem by selective injection of barbiturate into the vertebral circulation. *Arch. Ital. Biol.* 97:33–46.

Magnus, R. 1925. Animal posture. Croonian lecture. *Proc. Roy. Soc., Ser. B.* 98:339–53.

Magoun, H. W., and Rhines, R. 1946. An inhibitory mechanism in the bulbar reticular formation. *J. Neurophysiol.* 9:165–71.

Mahut, H. 1958. Breed differences in the dog's emotional behavior. *Canad. J. Psychol.* 12:35–44.

Maier, N. R. F., and Schneirla, T. C. 1935. *Principles of animal psychology.* New York: McGraw-Hill.

Mainardi, D.; Marsan, M.; and Pasquali, A. 1965. Causation of sexual preferences of the house mouse: The behaviour of mice reared by parents whose odour was artificially altered. *Soc. Ital. Sci. Nat. Milan* 104:325–38.

Maletta, G. J.; Vernadakis, A.; Timiras, P. S. 1966. Pre- and postnatal development of the spinal cord: Increased acetylcholinesterase activity. *Proc. Soc. Exp. Biol. Med.* 121:1210.

Maling, H. M., and Acheson, G. H. 1946. Righting and other postural activity in low decerebrate and in spinal cats after d-amphetamine. *J. Neurophysiol.* 9:379–86.

Mandel, P.; Rein, H.; Harth-Edel, S.; and Mandel, B. 1962. Distribution and metabolism of ribonucleic acid in the vertebrate CNS. In *Comparative neurochemistry,* ed. D. Richter, pp. 149–63. New York: Pergamon Press.

Manning, A. 1967a. *An introduction to animal behaviour.* London: Edward Arnold.

———. 1967b. "Pre-imaginal conditioning" in Drosophila. *Nature* 216:338–40.

Marin-Padilla, M. 1967. Number and distribution of the apical dendritic spines of layer V pyramidal cells in man. *J. Comp. Neurol.* 131:475–90.

Marler, P. 1961. The filtering of external stimuli during instinctive behaviour. In *Current problems in animal behaviour,* ed. W. H. Thorpe and C. L. Zangwill, pp. 150–66. Cambridge: At the University Press.

Marler, P., and Hamilton, W. J., III. 1966. *Mechanisms of animal behavior.* New York: John Wiley and Sons.

Marler, P., and Tamura, M. 1964. Culturally transmitted patterns of vocal behavior in sparrows. *Science* 146:1483–86.

Marley, E., and Key, B. J. 1963. Maturation of the electrocorticogram and behavior in the kitten and guinea pig and the effect of some sympathomimetic amines. *Electroenceph. Clin. Neurophysiol.* 15:620–36.

Marr, J. N. 1964. Varying stimulation and imprinting in dogs. *J. Genet. Psychol.* 104:351–64.

Marr, J. N., and Gardner, L. E., Jr. 1965. Early olfactory experience and later social behavior in the rat: Preference, sexual responsiveness, and care of young. *J. Genet. Psychol.* 107:167–74.

Martins, T. 1949. Disgorging of food to the puppies by the lactating dog. *Physiol. Zool.* 22:169–72.

Marty, R. 1962. Développement post-natal des réponses sensorielles du cortex cérébral chez le chat et le lapin. Thèse de Séances. Paris: Masson.

———. 1967. Maturation post-natale du système auditif. In *Regional development of the brain in early life,* ed. A. Minkowski. London: Blackwell.

Marty, R., and Scherrer, J. 1964. Critères de maturation des systèmes afferents corticaux. In *Progress in brain research,* vol. 4, *Growth and maturation of the brain,* ed. D. P. Purpura and J. P. Schadé, pp. 226–36. Amsterdam: Elsevier.

Mason, W. A. 1967. Motivational aspects of social responsiveness in young chimpanzees. In *Early behavior,* ed. H. W. Stevenson, E. H. Hess, and H. L. Rheingold. New York: John Wiley and Sons.

Mason, W. A., and Green, P. C. 1962. The effects of social restriction on the behavior of rhesus monkeys. IV. Responses to a novel environment and to an alien species. *J. Comp. Physiol. Psychol.* 55:363–68.

Matthew, W. D. 1930. The phylogeny of dogs. *J. Mammol.* 11:117–38.

Mayr, E. 1963. *Animal species and evolution*. Cambridge: Harvard University Press.

Meier, G. W. 1961. Infantile handling and development in Siamese kittens. *J. Comp. Physiol. Psychol.* 54:284–86.

———. 1964. Behavior of infant monkeys: Differences attributable to mode of birth. *Science* 143:968–70.

Meier, G. W., and Berger, R. J. 1965. Development of sleep and wakefulness patterns in the infant rhesus monkey. *Exp. Neurol.* 12:257–77.

Meier, G. W., and Garcia-Rodriguez, C. 1966. Continuing behavioral differences in infant monkeys as related to mode of delivery. *Psychol. Rep.* 19:1219–25.

Melzack, R. 1952. Irrational fears in the dog. *Canad. J. Psychol.* 6:141–47.

———. 1962. Effects of early perceptual restriction on simple visual discrimination. *Science* 137:978–79.

Melzack, R., and Burns, S. K. 1963. Neuropsychological effects of early sensory restriction. *Bol. Inst. Estud. Med. Biol. (Mex.)* 21:407–24.

———. 1965. Neurophysiological effects of early sensory restriction. *Exper. Neurol.* 13:163–75.

Melzack, R., and Scott, T. H. 1957. The effects of early experience on the response to pain. *J. Comp. Physiol. Psychol.* 50:155–61.

Menzel, E. W. 1963. The effects of cumulative experience on responses to novel objects in young, isolation-reared chimpanzees. *Behaviour* 21:1–12.

Menzel, E. W.; Davenport, R. K.; and Rogers, C. M. 1963. The effects of environmental restriction upon chimpanzee's responsiveness to objects. *J. Comp. Physiol. Psychol.* 56:78–85.

Menzel, R., and Menzel, R. 1953. Some factors influencing nursing behavior of the mother bitch. *Behaviour* 5:289–304.

Meyer, A.; Pampiglione, G.; Platt, B. S.; and Stewart, R. J. C. 1961. Neurological EEG and neuropathological changes in dogs with experimental malnutrition. *VII Int. Cong. Neurol. Rome*. Excerpta med. Int. Congr. Series, no. 39, p. 15.

Meyer-Holzapfel, M. 1968. Abnormal behavior in zoo animals. In *Abnormal behavior in animals,* ed. M. W. Fox, pp. 476–503. Philadelphia: W. B. Saunders.

Meyerson, B. A. 1967. In *Regional development of the brain in early life,* ed. A. Minkowski, in discussion, p. 402. London: Blackwell.

———. 1968. Electrophysiological signs of interhemispheric functions during development. In *Symp. Neuroontogeneticum, XIIth Scientific Conference, Prague,* pp. 85–96. Chapel Hill: University of North Carolina Press.

Michael, R. P. 1966. The affinity of the neonatal rat brain for gonadal hormone. *Anim. Behav.* 14:584 (abstr.).

Miles, R. C. 1959. Discrimination in the squirrel as a function of deprivation and problem difficulty. *J. Exp. Psychol.* 57:15–19.

Miller, G. A.; Galanter, E.; and Pribram, K. H. 1960. *Plans and the structure of behavior*. New York: Holt, Rinehart and Winston.

Miller, N. E. 1961. Liberalization of basic S-R concepts: Extensions of conflict behavior, motivation and social learning. In *Psychology,* ed. S. Koch, 2:196–292. New York: McGraw-Hill.

Mishkin, M., and Pribram, K. H. 1956. Analysis of the effect of frontal lesions in monkeys. II. Variations of delayed response. *J. Comp. Physiol. Psychol.* 49: 36–40.

Mitchell, G. D. 1968. Persistent behavior pathology in rhesus monkeys following early social isolation. *Folia Primat.* 8:132–47.

Mitchell, G. D.; Raymond, E. J.; Ruppenthal, G. C.; and Harlow, H. F. 1966. Long-term effects of social isolation upon behavior of rhesus monkeys. *Psychol. Rep.* 18:567–80.

Molliver, M. E. 1967. An ontogenetic study of evoked somesthetic cortical responses in the sheep. In *Progress in brain research,* vol. 26, *Developmental neurology,* ed. C. G. Bernhard and J. P. Schadé, pp. 78–81. New York: Elsevier.

Moltz, H., and Stettner, L. J. 1961. The influence of patterned-light deprivation on the critical period for imprinting. *J. Comp. Physiol. Psychol.* 54:279–83.

Montgomery, K. C. 1953. The effect of activity deprivation upon exploratory behavior. *J. Comp. Physiol. Psychol.* 46:438–41.

———. 1955. Fear induced by novel stimulation and exploratory behavior. *J. Comp. Physiol. Psychol.* 48:254–60.

Montgomery, K. C., and Segall, M. 1955. Discrimination learning based upon the exploratory drive. *J. Comp. Physiol. Psychol.* 48:225–28.

Morag, M. 1967. Influence of diet on the behaviour pattern of sheep. *Nature* 213: 110.

Morgan, C. T. 1951. The psychophysiology of learning. In *Handbook of experimental psychology,* ed. S. S. Stevens, New York: Wiley.

Morris, D. 1958. The reproductive behavior of the ten-spined stickleback (*Pygosteus pungitius* L.). *Behaviour Suppl.* 6:1–154.

———. 1966. Abnormal rituals in stress situations: The rigidification of behaviour. *Phil. Trans. Roy. Soc., Ser. B.* 251:327–30.

Morrison, R. S., and Dempsey, E. W. 1943. Mechanism of thalamo-cortical augmentation and repetition. *Amer. J. Physiol.* 138:279–303.

Morton, J. R. 1968. Effects of early experience on behaviour. In *Abnormal behavior in animals,* ed. M. W. Fox, pp. 261–92. Philadelphia: W. B. Saunders.

Morton, J. R.; Denenberg, V. H.; and Zarrow, M. X. 1963. Modification of sexual development through stimulation in infancy. *Endocrinology* 72:439–42.

Moruzzi, G., and Magoun, H. W. 1949. Brain-stem reticular formation and activation of the EEG. *Electroenceph. Clin. Neurophysiol.* 1:455–73.

Mosley, D. 1925. The accuracy of the pecking response in chickens. *J. Comp. Psychol.* 5:75–97.

Mourek, J.; Himwich, W. A.; Myslivecek, J.; and Callison, D. A. 1967. The role of nutrition in the development of evoked cortical responses in rat. *Brain Res.* 6:241–51.

Moyer, K. E., and Korn, J. H. 1965. Behavioral effects of isolation in the rat. *Psychonom. Sci.* 3:503–4.

Murie, A. 1940. *Ecology of the coyote in the Yellowstone.* U.S.D.I. fauna series no. 4. Washington: Government Printing Office.

Murphree, O. D., and Dykman, R. A. 1966. Litter patterns in the offspring of nervous and stable dogs. I. Behavioral tests. *J. Nerv. Ment. Dis.* 141:321–32.

Murphree, O. D.; Peters, J. E.; and Dykman, R. A. 1969. Behavioral comparisons of nervous, stable and crossbred pointers at ages 2, 3, 6, 9 and 12 months. *Cond. Reflex* 4:20–23.

Myslivecek, J. 1965. Electrophysiological activity during maturation. *Activ. Nerv. Sup.* 7:105.

———. 1968. The development of the response to light flash in the visual cortex of the dog. *Brain Res.* 10:418–30.

Myslivecek, J.; Fox, M. W.; and Zahlava, J. 1966. Maturation retardée de l'activité bioélectrique corticale provoquée par malnutrition. *J. Physiol. (Paris)* 58:572–73.

———. 1967. Functional and morphological development of the cortical projections related to the nutrition (in Russian). Marienbad Symposium (Oct. 1966) on Brain-Body Relationships. *Activ. Nerv. Sup.* 9:305–6.

Nakai, J., ed., 1963. *Morphology of neuroglia.* Springfield, Ill.: C. C. Thomas.

Narayanan, C. H.; Fox, M. W.; and Hamburger, V. H. 1971. Prenatal development of behavior in the rat. *Behaviour,* in press.

Nauta, W. J. H. 1958. Hippocampal projections and related neural pathways to the mid-brain in the cat. *Brain* 81:319–40.

Nelson, K. 1964. The temporal patterning of courtship behavior in the glandulo-caudine fishes (Ostariophysi, Characidae). *Behaviour* 24:90–146.

Newell, T. G. 1967. Effect of maternal deprivation on later behavior in two inbred strains of mice. *Psychonom. Sci.* 9:119–20.

Nice, M. M. 1943. Studies in the life-history of the song sparrow. *Trans. Linn. Soc. N.Y.* 6:1–328.

Nicolai, J. 1964. Der Brutparasitismus der Viduinae als ethologisches Problem. *Z. Tierpsychol.* 21:129–204.

———. 1966. Cited by Lorenz, K. The psychobiological approach: Methods and results. *Phil. Trans. Roy. Soc., Ser. B.* 251:273–84.

Nissen, H. W. 1930. A study of exploratory behavior in the white rat by means of the obstruction method. *J. Genet. Psychol.* 37:361–76.

Nissen, H. W.; Chow, K. L.; and Semmes, J. 1951. Effects of restricted opportunity for tactual, kinesthetic and manipulative experience on the behavior of chimpanzees. *Amer. J. Psychol.* 64:485–507.

Noback, C. R., and Purpura, D. P. 1961. Postnatal ontogenesis of neurons in cat neocortex. *J. Comp. Neurol.* 117:291–307.

Nottebohm, F. 1970. Ontogeny of bird song. *Science* 164:950–56.

Novakova, V. 1966. The effect of starvation and thirst in early ontogeny on higher nervous activity in adult rats. *Activ. Nerv. Sup.* 8:36–38.

Nyman, A. J. 1967. Problem solving in rats as a function of experience at different ages. *J. Genet. Psychol.* 110:31–39.

Ochs, S. 1965. Cortical potentials and pyramidal cells: A theoretical discussion. *Perspect. Biol. Med.* 9:126.

O'Neill, J. J., and Duffy, T. E. 1966. Alternate metabolic pathways in newborn brain. *Life Sci.* 5:1849.

Oppenheim, R. 1966. Amniotic contraction and embryonic motility in the chick embryo. *Science* 152:528–29.

Ora, A. I. 1958. Rapid stain for myelin sheaths using formalin-fixed paraffin sections. *Amer. J. Clin. Path.* 29:510.

Otis, L. S., and Scholler, J. 1967. Effects of stress during infancy on tumor development and tumor growth. *Psychol. Rep.* 20:167–73.

Ottinger, D. R.; Denenberg, V. H.; and Stephens, M. H. 1963. Maternal emotionality, multiple mothering and emotionality in maturity. *J. Comp. Physiol. Psychol.* 56:313–17.

Ounsted, M., and Ounsted, C. 1966. Maternal regulation of intra-uterine growth. *Nature* 212:995–97.

Ourth, L., and Brown, K. B. 1961. Inadequate mothering and disturbance in the neonatal period. *Child Develop.* 32:287–95.

Pacella, B. L., and Barrera, S. E. 1940. Postural reflexes and grasp phenomena in infants. *J. Neurophysiol.* 3:213–18.

Padilla, S. G. 1935. Further studies on the delayed pecking of chicks. *J. Comp. Psychol.* 20:413–33.

Pampiglione, G. 1961. Alertness and sleep in young pigs. *Electroenceph. Clin. Neurophysiol.* 13:827.

———. 1963. *Development of cerebral function in the dog.* London: Butterworth.

Papez, J. W. 1929. *Comparative neurology.* New York: Hafner.

Pappas, G. D., and Purpura, D. P. 1961. Fine structure of dendrites in the superficial neocortical neuropil. *Exp. Neurol.* 4:507–30.

Parmelee, A. H.; Wenner, W. H.; Akiyama, Y.; Stern, E.; and Flescher, J. 1967. Electroencephalography and brain maturation. In *Regional development of the brain in early life,* ed. A. Minkowski, pp. 459–76. London: Blackwell.

Parry, H. B. 1953. Structure and development of the retina of the normal dog. *Brit. J. Ophthal.* 38:295.

Pastore, N. 1954. Discrimination learning in the canary. *J. Comp. Physiol. Psychol.* 47:389–90.

Paulson, G. W. 1965. Maturation of evoked responses in the duckling. *Exp. Neurol.* 11:324–33.

Paulson, G. W., and Gottlieb, G. 1968. Developmental reflexes: The reappearance of foetal and neonatal reflexes in aged patients. *Brain* 91:37–52.

Pavlov, I. P. 1927. *Conditioned reflexes.* Translated by G. V. Anrep. London: Oxford University Press.

Pawlowski, A. A., and Scott, J. P. 1956. Hereditary differences in the development of dominance in litters of puppies. *J. Comp. Physiol. Psychol.* 49:353–58.

Peeler, D. F. 1963. Development in kittens as a function of handling and pharmacological treatment. *Diss. Abstr.* 24:2140.

Perkins, L. C. 1961. The early postnatal development of the cerebellar cortex in the dog and the effect of early spinocerebellar tractotomy. Ph.D. diss., Duke University. *Diss. Abstr.* 22:706.

Peters, J. E., and Murphree, C. D. 1966. Emotional trauma in rats: Age as a factor in recovery. *Cond. Reflex* 1:51–56.

Peters, J.; Vonderahe, A.; and Schmid, D. 1965. Onset of cerebral electrical activity associated with behavioral sleep and attention in the developing chick. *J. Exp. Zool.* 160:255–62.

Petersen, J. C.; DiPerri, R.; and Himwich, W. A. 1964. The comparative development of the EEG in the rabbit, cat and dog. *Electroenceph. Clin. Neurophysiol.* 17:557–63.

Petersen, J. C., and Himwich, W. A. 1959. Development of the EEG in the dog. *Physiologist* 2:93.

Petre-Quadens, O. 1966. On the different phases of the sleep of the newborn with special reference to the activated phase, or phase d. *J. Neurol. Sci.* 3:151–61.

Pfaff, D. W. 1966. Morphological changes in the brains of adult male rats after neonatal castration. *J. Endocrinol.* 36:415.

Pfaffenberger, C. F., and Scott, J. P. 1959. The relationship between delayed socialization and trainability in guide dogs. *J. Genet. Psychol.* 95:145–55.

Phemister, R. D., and Young, S. 1968. The postnatal development of the canine cerebellar cortex. *J. Comp. Neurol.* 134:243–53.

Piaget, J. 1952. *The origins of intelligence in children.* New York: International Universities Press.

Pigareva, Z. D. 1964. Enzyme activity in different areas of the cerebral cortex of rabbits and dogs during growth. In *Problems of the biochemistry of the nervous system,* ed. A. V. Palladin, pp. 169–78. New York: Macmillan Co.

Pinneo, L. R. 1966. On noise in the nervous system. *Psychol. Rev.* 73:242–47.

Ploog, D. W. 1966. Biological bases for instinct and behavior: Studies on the development of social behavior in squirrel monkeys. In *Recent advances in biological psychiatry,* ed. J. Wortis, 8:199–224. New York: Plenum Press.

Plutchik, R., and Stelzner, D. 1966. Individual and breed differences in timidity and approach in dogs. *Proc. 74th Ann. Conv. APA,* pp. 149–50.

Pollock, L. J., and Davis, L. 1927. The influence of the cerebellum upon the reflex activities of the decerebrate animal. *Brain* 50:277–312.

Pompeian, O., and Morrison, A. R. 1966. Vestibular origin of the rapid eye movements during desynchronized sleep. *Experientia* 22:60.

Pratt, C. L., and Sackett, G. P. 1967. Selection of social partners as a function of peer contact during rearing. *Science* 155:1133–34.

Prechtl, H. F. R. 1965. Problems of behavioural studies in the newborn infants. In *Advances in the study of behavior,* ed. D. S. Lehrman, R. A. Hinde, and E. Shaw. New York: Academic Press.

Purpura, D. P. 1959. Nature of electrocortical potentials. *Int. Rev. Neurobiol.* 1:47–163.

Purpura, D. P.; Carmichael, M. W.; and Housepian, E. M. 1960. Physiological and anatomical studies of development of superficial axodendritic synaptic pathways in neocortex. *Exp. Neurol.* 2:324–47.

Purpura, D. P., and Housepian, E. M. 1961. Morphological and physiological properties of chronically isolated immature neocortex. *Exp. Neurol.* 4:377–401.

Purpura, D. P.; Shofer, R. J.; Housepian, E. M.; and Noback, C. R. 1964. Comparative ontogenesis of structure-function relations in cerebral and cerebellar cortex. In *Progress in brain research,* vol. 4, *Growth and maturation of the brain,* ed. D. P. Purpura and J. P. Schadé, pp. 187–221. Amsterdam: Elsevier.

Rajalakshmi, R., and Jeeves, M. A. 1965. The relative difficulty of reversal learning (reversal index) as a basis of behavioural comparisons. *Anim. Behav.* 13:203.

Ramirez de Arellano, M. I. R. 1961. Maturational changes in the electroencephalogram of normal monkeys. *Exp. Neurol.* 3:209–24.

Ramon-Moliner, E. 1958. A study of neuroglia: The problem of transitional forms. *J. Comp. Neurol.* 110:157–72.

Ramon-Moliner, E. 1961. The histology of the postcruciate gyrus in the cat. *J. Comp. Neurol.* 117:63–76.

Ramon y Cajal, S. 1952. *Histologie du système nerveux de l'homme et des vertèbres.* Madrid: Consejo Superior de Investigaciones Cientificas (reprinted).

———. 1959. *Studies on vertebrate neurogenesis.* Translated by L. Guth. Springfield, Ill.: C. C. Thomas.

Ratner, S. C. 1965. Comparisons between behaviour development of normal and isolated domestic fowl. *Anim. Behav.* 13:497–503.

Reading, A. J. 1966. Effect of maternal environment on the behavior of inbred mice. *J. Comp. Physiol. Psychol.* 62:437–40.

Redding, R. W.; Prynn, B.; and Colwell, R. K. 1964. The phenomenon of alternate sleep and wakefulness in the young dog. *J.A.V.M.A.* 144:605–6.

Reed, C. A. 1959. Animal domestication in the prehistoric near east. *Science* 130: 1629–39.

Reinis, S. 1965. Some histochemical properties of myelin in the course of ontogenesis. *Activ. Nerv. Sup.* 7:2.

Ressler, R. H. 1963. Genotype-correlated parental influences in two strains of mice. *J. Comp. Physiol. Psychol.* 56:882–86.

———. 1966. Inherited environmental influences on the operant behavior of mice. *J. Comp. Physiol. Psychol.* 61:264–67.

Rheingold, H. L. 1963. *Maternal behavior in mammals,* pp. 169–202. New York: Wiley and Sons.

Rheingold, H. L.; Gewirtz, J. L.; and Ross, H. W. 1959. Social conditioning of vocalizations in the infant. *J. Comp. Physiol. Psychol.* 52:68–73.

Riesen, A. H. 1947. The development of visual perception in man and chimpanzee. *Science* 106:107–8.

———. 1958. Plasticity of behavior: Psychological aspects. In *Biological and biochemical bases of behavior,* ed. H. F. Harlow and C. N. Woolsey. Madison: University of Wisconsin Press.

———. 1961a. Excessive arousal effects of stimulation after early sensory deprivation. In *Sensory deprivation,* ed. P. Solomon. Harvard University Press.

———. 1961b. Stimulation as a requirement for growth and function in behavioral development. In *Functions of varied experience,* ed. D. W. Fiske and S. R. Maddi. Homewood, Ill.: Dorsey Press.

———. 1966. Sensory deprivation. In *Progress in physiological psychology,* ed. E. Stellar and J. M. Sprague, 1:117–47. New York: Academic Press.

Riesen, A. H., and Kinder, E. F. 1952. *Postural development of infant chimpanzee.* New Haven: Yale University Press.

Rijnberk, G. van, and Ten Cate, J. 1939. Quelques reflexes chez la chien. *Arch. Neerl. Physiol.* 24:83.

Roffwarg, H. P.; Muzio, J. N.; and Dement, W. C. 1966. Ontogenetic development of the human sleep-dream cycle. *Science* 152:604–19.

Romanes, G. J. 1947. Prenatal medullation of sheeps' nervous system. *J. Anat. Lond.* 81:64.

Rose, G. H. 1965. The development of visually evoked responses in the kitten. *Diss. Abstr.* 26:509.

———. 1968a. The comparative ontogenesis of primary and secondary electrocortical responses to light flash in rat and cat. In *Symp. Neuroontogeneticum, XIIth Scientific Conference, Prague,* 1968, pp. 347–58. Chapel Hill: University of North Carolina Press.

———. 1968*b*. Immature secondary electrocortical responses to photic stimulation in kittens. *Brain Res.* 7:465–68.

Rose, G. H., and Lindsley, D. B. 1965. Visually evoked electrocortical responses in kittens: Development of specific and nonspecific systems. *Science* 148:1244–46.

———. 1968. Development of visually evoked potentials in kittens: Specific and nonspecific responses. *J. Neurophysiol.* 31:607–23.

Rose, J. E.; Adrian, H.; and Santibanez, G. 1957. Electrical signs of maturation in the auditory system of the kitten. *Acta Neurol. Lat-Amer.* 3:133–43.

Rosen, J., and Hart, F. M. 1963. Effects of early social isolation upon adult timidity and dominance in Peromyscus. *Psychol. Rep.* 13:47–50.

Rosenblatt, J. S., and Aronson, L. R. 1958. The decline of sexual behavior in male cats after castration with special reference to the role of prior sexual experience. *Behaviour* 12:285–338.

Rosenblatt, J. S., and Schneirla, T. C. 1962. The behavior of cats. In *The behavior of domesticated animals,* ed. E. S. E. Hafez. London: Baillière, Tindall and Cox.

Rosenblatt, J. S.; Turkewitz, G.; and Schneirla, T. C. 1959. Early socialization in the domestic cat as based on feeding and other relationships between female and young. In *Determinants of infant behavior,* ed. B. M. Foss, pp. 51–74. New York: Wiley.

Rosenblum, L. A., and Harlow, H. F. 1963. Approach/avoidance conflict in the mother-surrogate situation. *Psychol. Rep.* 12:83–85.

Rosenzweig, M. R.; Krech, D.; Bennett, E. L.; and Diamond, M. C. 1962. Effects of environmental complexity and training on brain chemistry and anatomy: A replication and extension. *J. Comp. Physiol. Psychol.* 55:429–37.

Rosenzweig, M. R.; Krech, D.; Bennett, K. L.; and Zolman, J. F. 1962. Variation in environmental complexity and brain measures. *J. Comp. Physiol. Psychol.* 55:1092–95.

Ross, S. 1950. Some observations on the lair dwelling behavior of dogs. *Behaviour* 2:144–62.

Ross, S.; Fisher, A. E.; and King, O. 1957. Sucking behavior: A review of the literature. *J. Genet. Psychol.* 91:63–81.

Ross, S., and Ross, J. G. 1949. Social facilitation of feeding behavior in dogs. I. Group and solitary feeding. *J. Genet. Psychol.* 74:97–108.

Ross, S.; Scott, J. P.; Cherner, M.; and Denenberg, V. H. 1960. Effects of restraint and isolation on yelping in puppies. *Anim. Behav.* 6:1–5.

Routtenberg, A. 1966. Neural mechanisms of sleep: Changing view of reticular formation function. *Psychol. Rev.* 73:481–99.

Ruckebusch, V. 1964. Sommeil et rêves chez les animaux. In *Psychiatrie animale,* ed. A. Brion and H. Ey, pp. 139–48. Paris: Desclee de Brouwer.

Rutter, R. J., and Pimlott, D. H. 1968. *The world of the wolf.* Philadelphia: J. B. Lippincott.

Sackett, G. P. 1963. A neural mechanism underlying unlearned, critical period and developmental aspects of visually controlled behavior. *Psychol. Rev.* 70:40–50.

Sackett, G. P. 1965. Effects of rearing conditions upon the behavior of rhesus monkeys (*Macaca mulatta*). *Child Develop.* 36:855–68.

———. 1966*a*. Development of preference for differentially complex patterns by infant monkeys. *Psychon. Sci.* 6:441–42.

———. 1966*b*. Monkeys reared in isolation with pictures as visual input: Evidence for an innate releasing mechanism. *Science* 154:1468–73.

Sackett, G. P.; Griffin, G. A.; Joslyn, C.; Danforth, W.; and Ruppenthal, G. 1967. Mother-infant and adult female choice behavior in rhesus monkeys after various rearing experiences. *J. Comp. Physiol. Psychol.* 63:376.

Sackett, G. P.; Porter, M.; and Holmes, H. 1965. Choice behavior in rhesus monkeys: Effect of stimulation during the first month of life. *Science* 147:304–6.

Saltmann, O. 1876. Experimentelle Studien über die Funktionem des Grosshirns der Neugeborenen. *Jahrb. Kinderh.* 9:106–48.

Salzen, E. A. 1967. Imprinting in birds and primates. *Behaviour* 28:232–54.

Salzen, E. A., and Cornell, J. M. 1968. Self-perception and species recognition in birds. *Behaviour* 30:44–65.

Sarkisov, S. A. 1966. *The structure and functions of the brain.* Bloomington: Indiana University Press.

Sarkissow, S. 1929. Über die postnatale Entwicklung einzelner cytoarchitektonischer Felder beim Hunde. *J. Psychol. Neurol.* 39:486–505.

Schadé, J. P. 1960. Origin of the spontaneous electrical activity of the cerebral cortex. In *Recent advances in biological psychiatry,* ed. J. Wortis, 2:23–42. New York: Grune and Stratton.

Schaefer, T., Jr. 1963. Early "experience" and its effects on later behavioral processes in rats. II. A critical factor in the early handling phenomenon. *Trans. N.Y. Acad. Sci.* 24:871–89.

———. 1967. The search for a critical factor in early handling: Some methodological implications. In *Early experience and behavior,* ed. G. Newton and S. Levine. Springfield, Ill.: C. C. Thomas.

Schaffer, H. R. 1958. Objective observations of personality development in early infancy. *Brit. J. Med. Psychol.* 31:174–83.

———. 1966. The onset of fear of strangers and the incongruity hypothesis. *J. Child Psychol. Psychiat.* 7:95–106.

Schapiro, S., and Norman, R. J. 1967. Thyroxine: Effects of neonatal administration on maturation, development and behavior. *Science* 155:1279–81.

Schapiro, S., and Vukovich, K. R. 1970. Early experience effects upon cortical dendrites: A proposed model for development. *Science* 167:292–94.

Scheibel, A. B. 1962. Neural correlates of psychophysiological developments in the young organism. In *Recent advances in biological psychiatry,* ed. J. Wortis, 4: 313–27. New York: Plenum Press.

Scheibel, M. E., and Scheibel, A. B. 1958. Neurons and neuroglia cells as seen with the light microscope. In *Biology of neuroglia,* ed. W. F. Windle, pp. 5–23. Springfield, Ill.: C. C. Thomas.

Schenkel, R. 1947. Ausdrucks-studien an Wölfen. *Behaviour* 1:81–129.

———. 1967. Submission: Its features and functions in the wolf and dog. *Amer. Zool.* 7:319–30.

Scherrer, J., and Fourment, A. 1964. Electrocortical effects of sensory deprivation during development. In *Progress in 'brain research.* vol. 9, *The developing brain,* ed. W. A. Himwich and H. E. Himwich, pp. 103–12. Amsterdam: Elsevier.

Scherrer, J., and Oeconomos, D. 1954. Cortical somesthetic responses of newborn mammals compared with adult. *Etudes Neo-Natales* 3:199.

Schiller, P. A. 1957. Innate motor action as a basis of learning. In *Instinctive behavior,* ed. C. H. Schiller, pp. 264–87. New York: International Universities Press.

Schmidt, R. S. 1955. The evolution of nest building behavior in *Apicotermes. Evolution* 9:157–81.

Schneirla, T. C. 1965. Aspects of stimulation and organization in approach/withdrawal processes underlying vertebrate behavioral development. In *Advances in the study of animal behavior,* ed. D. S. Lehrman, R. A. Hinde, and E. Shaw, vol. 1, chap. 1. New York: Academic Press.

———. 1966. Behavioral development and comparative psychology. *Quart. Rev. Biol.* 41:283–302.

Schneirla, T. C., and Rosenblatt, J. S. 1961. Critical periods in the development of behavior. *Science* 139:1110–15.

Schutz, F. 1965. Sexuelle Prägung bei Anatiden. *Z. Tierpsychol.* 22:50–103.

Scott, J. P. 1950. The social behavior of dogs and wolves: An illustration of sociobiological systematics. *Ann. N.Y. Acad. Sci.* 51:1009–21.

———. 1954. The effects of selection of domestication upon the behavior of the dog. *J. Nat. Cancer Inst.* 15:739–58.

———. 1958*a. Aggression.* Chicago: University of Chicago Press.

———. 1958*b.* Critical periods in the development of social behavior in puppies. *Psychosom. Med.* 20:42–54.

———. 1962. Critical periods in behavioral development. *Science* 138:949–58.

———. 1963. The process of primary socialization in canine and human infants. *Monogr. Soc. Res. Child Develop.* 28:1–47.

———. 1964. Genetics and the development of social behavior in dogs. *Amer. Zool.* 4:161–68.

———. 1967. Comparative psychology and ethology. *Ann. Rev. Psychol.* 18:65.

———. 1968. *Early experience and the organization of behavior.* Belmont, Calif.: Brooks-Cole.

Scott, J. P., and Bronson, F. H. 1964. Experimental exploration of the et-epimeletic or care-soliciting behavioral system. In *Psychobiological approaches to social behavior,* ed. P. H. Leiderman and D. Shapiro, pp. 174–93. Stanford, Calif.: Stanford University Press.

Scott, J. P., and Fuller, J. L. 1965. *Genetics and social behavior of the dog.* Chicago: University of Chicago Press.

Scott, J. P., and Marston, M. V. 1948. The development of dominance in litters of puppies. *Anat. Rec.* 101:696.

———. 1950. Critical periods affecting the development of normal and maladjustive social behavior in puppies. *J. Genet. Psychol.* 77:25–60.

Sears, R. R.; Maccoby, E. E.; and Levin, H. 1957. *Patterns of child rearing.* New York: Row, Peterson and Co.

Sears, R. R., and Wise, G. W. 1950. Relation of cup feeding in infancy to thumbsucking and the oral drive. *Amer. J. Orthopsychiat.* 20:123–38.

Seay, B.; Hansen, E. W.; and Harlow, H. F. 1962. Mother-infant separation in monkeys. *J. Child Psychol. Psychiat.* 3:123–32.

Sedlacek, J.; Svehlova, M.; Sedlackova, M.; Marsala, J.; and Kapras, J. 1961. New results in the ontogenesis of reflex activity. In *Functional and metabolic development of the central nervous system,* ed. P. Sobotka, p. 167. Pilsen Symposium, suppl. 3. Charles University Press.

Seitz, P. F. D. 1954. The effects of infantile experiences upon adult behavior in animal subjects. I. Effects of litter size during infancy upon adult behavior in the rat. *Amer. J. Psychiat.* 110:916–27.

Shagass, C., and Trusty, D. M. 1966. Somatosensory and visual cerebral evoked response changes during sleep. In *Recent advances in biological psychiatry,* ed. J. Wortis, 8:321–34. New York: Plenum Press.

Sheriff, G. A. 1953. Cell counts in the primate cerebral cortex. *J. Comp. Neurol.* 98:381–400.

Shaw, E. 1962. Environmental conditions and the appearance of sexual behavior in the platy-fish. In *Roots of behavior,* ed. E. L. Bliss, pp. 123–41. New York: Harper and Row.

Sherrington, C. S. 1910. Flexion-reflex of the limb, crossed-extension-reflex and reflex stepping and standing. *J. Physiol.* 40:28–121.

———. 1947. *Integrative action of the nervous system.* Rev. ed. Cambridge: Cambridge University Press.

Sholl, D. A. 1953. Dendritic organization in the neurons of the visual and motor cortices of the cat. *J. Anat.* 87:387–407.

Shurrager, P. S. 1956. Walking in spinal kittens and puppies. In *Regeneration in the central nervous system,* ed. W. F. Windle, pp. 208–18. Springfield, Ill.: C. C. Thomas.

Siegel, P. B., and Siegel, H. S. 1964. Rearing methods and subsequent sexual behaviour of male chickens. *Anim. Behav.* 12:270–83.

Siegel, S. 1956. *Nonparametric statistics for the behavioral sciences.* New York: McGraw-Hill.

Singer, M. 1962. *The brain of the dog in section.* Philadelphia: W. B. Saunders.

Singh, D.; Johnston, R. J.; and Klosterman, H. J. 1967. Effect on brain enzyme and behavior in the rat of visual pattern restriction in early life. *Nature* 216:1337–38.

Sisson, S., and Grossman, J. D. 1960. *The anatomy of domestic animals.* Philadelphia: W. B. Saunders Co.

Skinner, B. F. 1966. The phylogeny and ontogeny of behavior. *Science* 153:1205–13.

Skoglund, S. 1960a. The activity of muscle receptors in the kitten. *Acta Physiol. Scand.* 50:203–21.

———. 1960b. On the postnatal development of postural mechanisms as revealed by electromyography and myography in decerebrate cats. *Acta Physiol. Scand.* 49:299–317.

Slonaker, J. R. 1907. The normal activity of the white rat at different ages. *J. Comp. Neurol. Psychol.* 17:342–59.

Sluckin, W. 1965. *Imprinting and early learning.* Chicago: Aldine Publishing Co.

Smith, C. J. 1959. Mass action and early environment in the rat. *J. Comp. Physiol. Psychol.* 52:154–56.

Snyder, F. 1966. Toward an evolutionary theory of dreaming. *Amer. J. Psychiat.* 123:121–36.

Sokolov, E. N. 1960. Neuronal models and the orienting reflex. In *CNS and behavior,* ed. M. A. B. Brazier, 3:187–276. New York: Josiah Macy Jr. Found.

Solomon, R. L., and Wynne, L. C. 1954. Traumatic avoidance learning. *Psychol. Rev.* 61:353–85.

Spalding, D. 1873. Instinct: With original observations on young animals. *Macmillan's Mag.* 27:282–93. (Reprinted in *Brit. J. Anim. Behav.* 2:1–11, 1954.)

Sperry, R. W. 1958. Physiological plasticity and brain circuit theory. In *Biological and biochemical bases of behavior,* ed. H. F. Harlow and C. N. Woolsey. Madison: University of Wisconsin Press.

———. 1963. Chemoaffinity in the orderly growth of nerve fibre patterns and connections. *Proc. Nat. Acad. Sci.* 50:703–10.

Spigel, I. M. 1966. Variability in maze-path selection by the turtle. *J. Gen. Psychol.* 75:21–27.

Spigelman, M. N., and Bryden, M. P. 1967. Effects of early and late blindness on auditory spatial learning in the rat. *Neuropsychologia* 5:267–74.

Spitz, R. A., and Wolf, K. M. 1946. The smiling response: A contribution to the ontogenesis of social relations. *Genet. Psychol. Monogr.* 34:57–125.

Sprague, J. M. 1966. Interaction of cortex and superior colliculus in mediation of visually guided behavior in the cat. *Science* 153:1544–47.

Sprague, J. M., and Chambers, W. W. 1953. Regulation of posture in intact and decerebrate cat. I. Cerebellum, reticular formation, vestibular nuclei. *J. Neurophysiol.* 16:451–63.

Stanley, W. C. 1965a. The passive person as a reinforcer in isolated beagle puppies. *Psychonom. Sci.* 2:21–22.

———. 1965b. Personal communication, cited by Scott, J. P., and Fuller, J. L., in *Genetics and social behavior of the dog.* Chicago: University of Chicago Press.

Stanley, W. C., and Bacon, W. E. 1963. Suppression of sucking behavior in nondeprived puppies. *Psychol. Rep.* 13:175–78.

Stanley, W. C.; Cornwell, A. C.; Poggiani, C.; and Trattner, A. 1963. Conditioning in the neonate puppy. *J. Comp. Physiol. Psychol.* 56:211–14.

Stanley, W. C., and Elliot, O. 1962. Differential human handling as reinforcing events and as treatments influencing later social behavior in basenji puppies. *Psychol. Rep.* 10:775–88.

Stanley, W. C.; Morris, D. D.; and Trattner, A. 1965. Conditioning with a passive person reinforcer and extinction in Shetland sheepdog puppies. *Psychonom. Sci.* 2:19–20.

Stelmak'h, L. N. 1959. Ontogenetic development of external inhibition in the dog. *Pavlov J. Higher Nerv. Act.* 8:216.

Steriade, M. 1968. The flash evoked afterdischarge. *Brain Res.* 9:169–212.

Still, G. 1931. *The history of pediatrics.* London: Oxford University Press.

Stockard, C. R. 1941. *The genetic and endocrine basis for differences in form and behavior.* Philadelphia: Wistar Institute Press.

Strobel, M. G.; Clark, G. M.; and MacDonald, G. E. 1968. Ontogeny of the approach response: A radiosensitive period during embryological development of domestic chicks. *J. Comp. Physiol. Psychol.* 65:314–19.

Struhsaker, T. T. 1967. Behavior of vervet monkeys and other cercopithecines. *Science* 156:1197–1203.

Sutton, S.; Tueting, P.; Zubin, J.; and John, E. R. 1967. Information delivery and the sensory evoked potential. *Science* 155:1436–39.

Swanson, H. H. 1966. Sex differences in behavior of hamsters in open field and emergence tests: Effects of pre- and post-pubertal gonadectomy. *Anim. Behav.* 14:522–29.

———. 1967. Alteration of sex-typical behaviour of hamsters in open field and emergence tests by neo-natal administration of androgen or oestrogen. *Anim. Behav.* 15:209–16.

Talwar, G. P.; Chopra, S. P.; Goel, B. K.; and D'Monte, B. 1966. Correlation of the functional activity of the brain with metabolic parameters. III. Protein metabolism of the occipital cortex in relation to light stimulus. *J. Neurochem.* 13:109–16.

Tammimie, H. S., and Fox, M. W. 1967. The effects of continuous and intermittent light exposure on the embryonic development of chicken egg. *Comp. Biochem. and Physiol.* 20:793–800.

Tapp, J. T., and Markowitz, H. 1963. Infant handling: Effects on avoidance learning, brain weight and cholinesterase activity. *Science* 140:486–87.

Teitelbaum, P.; Chang, M.-F.; and Rozin, P. 1969. Stages of recovery and development of lateral hypothalamic control of food and water intake. *Ann. N.Y. Acad. Sci.* 157:849–58.

Tembrock, G. 1957. Zur Ethologie des Rotfuches (*Vulpes vulpes* L.), unter besondere Berücksichtigung der Fortpflanzung. *Zool. Garten* 23:289–532.

Ten Cate, J. 1952. Exteroceptive abdominal reflexes in dogs. *J. Neurophysiol.* 15:291–97.

Thiessen, D. D. 1965. Sensory regulation of open-field activity in mice: Visual stimulation and discontinuous development. *Psychonom. Sci.* 2:317–18.

Thistlethwaite, D. 1951. A critical review of latent learning and related experiments. *Psychol. Bull.* 48:97–129.

Thomas, A. 1940. *Equilibre et équilibration.* Paris: Masson.

Thomas, A.; Chesni. Y.; and Dargassies, S. 1961. *The neurological examination of the infant.* Little Club Dev. Med. no. 1.

Thompson, W. D., Jr., and Sontag, L. W. 1956. Behavioral effects in the offspring of rats subjected to audiogenic seizures during the gestation period. *J. Comp. Physiol. Psychol.* 49:454–56.

Thompson, W. R. 1953a. Exploratory behavior as a function of hunger in bright and dull rats. *J. Comp. Physiol. Psychol.* 46:323–26.

———. 1953b. The inheritance of behavior: Behavioral differences of 15 mouse strains. *Canad. J. Psychol.* 7:145–55.

———. 1954. The effects of restricting early experience on the problem-solving capacity of dogs. *Canad. J. Psychol.* 8:17–31.

———. 1957. Influence of prenatal maternal anxiety on emotionality in young rats. *Science* 125:698–99.

Thompson, W. R., and Heron, W. 1954. Exploratory behavior in normal and restricted dogs. *J. Comp. Physiol. Psychol.* 47:77–82.

Thompson, W. R., and McElroy, L. R. 1962. The effect of maternal presence on open-field behavior in young rats. *J. Comp. Physiol. Psychol.* 55:827–30.

Thompson, W. R.; Melzack, R.; and Scott, T. H. 1956. "Whirling behavior" in dogs as related to early experience. *Science* 123:939.

Thompson, W. R., and Olian, S. 1961. Some effects on offspring behavior of maternal adrenalin injection during pregnancy in three inbred mouse strains. *Psychol. Rep.* 8:87–90.

Thompson, W. R., and Schaefer, J. 1961. Early environmental stimulation. In *Functions of varied experience,* ed. D. W. Fiske and S. R. Maddi, pp. 81–105. Homewood, Ill.: Dorsey Press.

Thompson, W. R.; Watson, J.; and Charlesworth, W. R. 1962. The effects of prenatal stress on offspring behavior in rats. *Psychol. Monogr.* 557:1–26.

Thorpe, W. H. 1961*a*. *Bird-song*. Cambridge: Cambridge University Press.

———. 1961*b*. Sensitive periods in the learning of animals and men. In *Current problems in animal behaviour,* ed. W. H. Thorpe and O. L. Zangwill. Cambridge: Cambridge University Press.

———. 1964. *Learning and instinct in animals*. London: Methuen.

———. 1965*a*. Macromolecular coding in nerve cell and embryo. *Anim. Behav. Supp.* 1:183.

———. 1965*b*. The ontogeny of behavior. In *Ideas in modern biology,* ed. J. A. Moore, pp. 483–518. Garden City, N.Y.: Natural History Press.

———. 1966. Ritualization in ontogeny. I. Animal play. *Phil. Trans. Roy. Soc., Ser. B.* 251:311–19.

Tilney, F. 1933. Behaviour in its relation to development of brain: Correlation between development of brain and behaviour in albino rat from embryonic state to maturity. *Bull. Neurol. Inst. N.Y.* 3:252–358.

Tilney, F., and Casamajor, L. 1924. Myelinogeny as applied to the study of behavior. *Arch. Neurol. Psychol.* 12:1–66.

Tilney, F., and Kubie, L. S. 1931. Behavior in its relation to development of the brain. *Bull. Neurol. Inst. N.Y.* 1:231.

Tinbergen, N. 1951. *The study of instinct*. Oxford: Clarendon Press.

———. 1968. On war and peace in animals and man. *Science* 160:1411–18.

Tobach, E., ed. 1969. Experimental approaches to the study of emotional behavior. *Ann. N.Y. Acad. Sci.* 159:1–112.

———. 1970. *The biopsychology of development*. New York: Academic Press. In press.

Troshikhin, V. A., and Kozlova, L. N. 1961. The origin and development of mobility and inertia of nervous processes in the course of ontogenesis (in Russian). *Zh. Vyssh. Nerv. deiat.* 2:878–83.

Tsang, Y. C. 1936. Visual centers in blinded rats. *J. Comp. Neurol.* 66:211–61.

Tucker, T. J., and Kling, A. 1967. Differential effects of early and late lesions of frontal granular cortex in the monkey. *Brain Res.* 5:377–89.

Tuge, H. 1961. Comparative study of ontogenetic development of unconditioned and conditioned reflexes. In *Functional and metabolic development of the central nervous system,* ed. P. Sobotka. Pilsen Symposium, suppl. 3. Charles University Press.

Uexkull, J. von. 1909. *Umwelt und Innenwelt der Tiere*. Berlin: Springer Verlag.

Uyeno, E. T., and White, M. 1967. Social isolation and dominance behavior. *J. Comp. Physiol. Psychol.* 63:157–59.

Uzman, L. L., and Rumley, K. M. 1958. Changes in the composition of the developing mouse brain during early myelinization. *J. Neurochem.* 3:171–85.

Valatx, J. L.; Jouvet, D.; and Jouvet, M. 1964. Evolution électroencéphalographique des différents états de sommeil chez le chaton. *Electroenceph. Clin. Neurophysiol.* 17:218–33.

Valverde, F. 1967. Apical dendritic spines of the visual cortex and light deprivation in the mouse. *Exp. Brain Res.* 3:337–52.

———. 1968. Structural changes in the area striata of the mouse after enucleation. *Exp. Brain Res.* 5:274–92.

Vandenbergh, J. G. 1969. Male odor accelerates female sexual development in mice. *Endocrinology* 84:658–60.

Van der Loos, H. 1965. The "improperly" oriented pyramidal cell in the cerebral cortex and its possible bearing on problems of neuronal growth and cell orientation. *Bull. Johns Hopkins Hosp.* 117:228.

Vaulk, G. 1953. Modification of the behavior of dogs towards their prey in the course of domestication (in German). *Zool. Anz., Suppl.* 17:180–84.

Vavilova, N. M. 1968. Effects of electrical stimulation of the hippocampus and amygdala in dogs in ontogenesis. In *Symp. Neuroontogeneticum, XIIth Scientific Conference, Prague*, pp. 335–41. Chapel Hill: University of North Carolina Press.

Venturoli, M. 1962. L'elettroencefalogramma normale del cane. *Clin. Vet. (Bologna)* 85:525–44.

Verley, R., and Mourek, J. 1962. Evolution postnatale de l'amplitude de l'activité électrocorticale. *J. Physiol. (Paris)* 52:427–28.

Vernadakis, A.; Valcana, T.; Curry, J. J.; and Maletta, G. J. 1967. Alterations in growth of brain and other organs after electroshock in rats. *Exp. Neurol.* 17:403–19.

Verplank, W. S. 1957. A glossary of some terms used in the objective science of behavior. *Psychol. Rev.,* vol. 64, Suppl. no. 6.

Vince, M. A. 1961. Developmental changes in learning capacity. In *Current problems in animal behaviour,* ed. W. H. Thorpe and O. L. Zangwill. Cambridge: Cambridge University Press.

———. 1964. Social facilitation of hatching in the bobwhite quail. *Anim. Behav.* 12:531–34.

———. 1966a. Artificial acceleration of hatching in quail chicks. *Anim. Behav.* 14:389–94.

———. 1966b. Potential stimulation produced by avian eggs. *Anim. Behav.* 14:17.

Volokhov, A. A. 1959a. Comparative-physiological investigation of conditioned and unconditioned reflexes during ontogeny. *Pavlov J. Higher Nerv. Act.* 9:49–60.

———. 1959b. Development of unconditioned and conditioned reflexes in ontogenesis. *Eleventh International Congress of Physiological Sciences, Section of Physiology and Pharmacology, Buenos Aires, Argentina.*

———. 1961. On the significance of various levels of the central nervous system in the formation and development of motor reaction in embryogenesis. In *Functional and metabolic development of the central nervous system,* ed. P. Sobotka. Pilsen Symposium, suppl. 3, p. 141. Charles University Press.

————. 1968. Correlation of cortical and subcortical parts of the brain in the functional development in early ontogenesis in the rabbit. In *Symp. Neuroontogeneticum, XIIth Scientific Conference, Prague,* pp. 367–76. Chapel Hill: University of North Carolina Press.

Waddington, C. H. 1956. *Principles of embryology,* New York: Macmillan Co.

————. 1961. Genetic assimilation. In *Advances in genetics,* ed. E. W. Caspari and J. M. Thoday, 10:257–93. New York: Academic Press.

————. 1966. Fields and gradients. In *Major problems in developmental biology,* ed. Michael Locke, p. 105. Twenty-fifth Symposium of the Society for Developmental Biology.

Walk, R. D., and Gibson, E. J. 1961. A comparative and analytical study of visual depth discrimination. *Psychol. Monogr.* 75:519.

Waller, P. F., and Waller, M. B. 1963. Some relations between early experience and later social behavior in ducklings. *Behaviour* 20:343–63.

Walsh, E. G. 1956. *Physiology of the nervous system.* New York: Longmans, Green.

Walter, W. G. 1953. Electroencephalographic development of children. In U.N.W.H.O. study group on psychobiological development of the child. *W.H.O. Proc. First Meet., Geneva,* pp. 139–70.

————. 1956. In *Child development,* ed. J. M. Tanner and B. Inhelder. London: Tavistock Press.

Walton, A. C. 1915. The influence of diverting stimuli during delayed reaction in dogs. *J. Anim. Behav.* 5:259–63.

Warriner, C. C.; Lemmon, W. B.; and Ray, T. S. 1963. Early experience as a variable in mate selection. *Anim. Behav.* 11:221–24.

Watson, J. B. 1903. Animal education: An experimental study on the physical development of the white rat, correlated with the growth of its nervous system. *Contrib. Phil.* 4:5–122.

Wecker, S. C. 1963. The role of early experience in habitat selection by the prairie deer mouse. *Ecol. Monogr.* 33:307–25.

Weir, M. W., and DeFries, J. C. 1964. Prenatal maternal influence on behavior of mice: Evidence of a genetic basis. *J. Comp. Physiol. Psychol.* 58:412–17.

Weiss, P. 1939. *Principles of development.* New York: Henry Holt.

————. 1941. Does sensory control play a constructive role in the development of motor coordination? *Schweiz. Med. Wochenschr.* 71:591–95.

————. 1950. Experimental analysis of coordination by the disarrangement of central-peripheral relations. *Symp. Soc. Exp. Biol.* 4:92–111.

Welker, W. I. 1956. Effects of age and experience on play and exploration of young chimpanzees. *J. Comp. Physiol. Psychol.* 49:223–26.

————. 1959*a.* Factors influencing aggregation of neonatal puppies. *J. Comp. Physiol. Psychol.* 52:376–80.

————. 1959*b.* Genesis of exploratory and play behavior in infant raccoons. *Psychol. Rep.* 5:764.

————. 1961. The genesis of exploratory and play behavior. In *Functions of varied experience,* ed. D. Fiske and S. R. Maddi. Homewood, Ill.: Dorsey Press.

————. 1964. Analysis of sniffing in the albino rat. *Behaviour* 22:223–44.

Wells, M. J. 1958. Factors affecting reactions to *Mysis* by newly hatched *Sepia. Behaviour* 13:96–111.

Werboff, J. 1966. Tranquilizers in pregnancy and behavioural effects on the offspring. *Nature* 209:110.

Werboff, J.; Anderson, A.; and Hagge, B. N. 1968. Handling pregnant mice: Gestational and postnatal behavior effects. *Physiol. Behav.* 3:35–39.

Werner, J. 1961. Concerning the ontogenesis of brain potentials in the spontaneous EEG's of newborn dogs. *Electroenceph. Clin. Neurophysiol.* 12:256.

Wetzel, A.; Thompson, V. E.; Horel, J. A.; and Meyer, P. M. 1965. Some consequences of perinatal lesions of the visual cortex in the cat. *Psychonom. Sci.* 3: 381–82.

White, B. H., and Castle, P. W. 1964. Visual exploratory behavior following postnatal handling of human infants. *Percept. Motor Skills* 18:497–502.

Wickler, W. 1965a. The evolution of morphological and behavioral patterns. *Naturwissenschaft* 52:335–41.

———. 1965b. Mimicry and the evolution of animal communication. *Nature* 208: 519–21.

———. 1966. Origin and biological meaning of the presentation of the genitals in male primates (in German). *Z. Tierpsychol.* 23:422–37.

Wiesel, T. N., and Hubel, D. H. 1963a. Effects of visual deprivation on morphology and physiology of cells in the cat's lateral geniculate body. *J. Neurophysiol.* 26: 978–93.

———. 1963b. Single-cell responses in striate cortex of kittens deprived of vision in one eye. *J. Neurophysiol.* 26:1002–17.

———. 1965. Extent of recovery from the effect of visual deprivation in kittens. *J. Neurophysiol.* 28:1060–72.

Wilcock, J., and Broadhurst, P. L. 1967. Strain differences in emotionality: Openfield and conditioned avoidance behavior in the rat. *J. Comp. Physiol. Psychol.* 63:335.

Williams, C. D. 1966. Maze exploration in young rats of four ages. *J. Genet. Psychol.* 109:241–47.

Williams, E., and Scott, J. P. 1953. The development of social behavior patterns in the mouse in relation to natural periods. *Behaviour* 6:35–64.

Wilson, M.; Warren, J. M.; and Abbott, L. 1965. Infantile stimulation, activity, and learning by cats. *Child Develop.* 36:843–53.

Wilson, P. D., and Riesen, A. H. 1966. Visual development in rhesus monkeys neonatally deprived of patterned light. *J. Comp. Physiol. Psychol.* 61:87–95.

Windle, W. F. 1950. Reflexes of mammalian embryos and fetuses. In *A genetic neurology,* ed. P. Weiss, p. 214. Chicago: University of Chicago Press.

Windle, W. F.; Fish, M. F.; and O'Donnell, J. E. 1934. Myelinogeny of the cat as related to development of fiber tracts and prenatal behavior patterns. *J. Comp. Neurol.* 59:139–65.

Windle, W. F., and Orr, D. W. 1934. The development of behavior in chick embryos: Spinal cord structure correlated with early somatic motility. *J. Comp. Neurol.* 60:287–307.

Winer, B. J. 1962. *Statistical principles in experimental design.* New York: McGraw-Hill.

Woolpy, J. H., and Ginsburg, B. E. 1967. Wolf socialization: A study of temperament in a wild social species. *Amer. Zool.* 7:357–64.

Yakovlev, P. I., and Lecours, R. A. 1967. Myelogenetic cycles of regional maturation of the nervous system. In *International conference on regional maturation of the nervous system,* ed. A. Minkowski, chap. 1. London: Blackwell.

Young, S. P., and Goldman, E. A. 1944. *The wolves of North America.* Washington: American Wild Life Institute.

Young, S. P., and Jackson, H. H. T. 1951. *The clever coyote.* Washington: Wildlife Management Institute.

Young, W. C.; Goy, R. W.; and Phonenix, C. H. 1964. Hormones and sexual behavior. *Science* 143:212–17.

Yoshii, N., and Tsukiyama, K. 1951. Normal EEG and its development in the white rat. *Jap. J. Physiol.* 2:34–38.

Zahlava, J.; Chaloupka, Z.; and Myslivecek, J. 1966. The development of primary cortical auditory responses at various stimulation frequencies in dogs. *Activ. Nerv. Sup.* 8:175.

Zamenhof, S.; Marthens, E. van; and Margolis, F. L. 1968. DNA (cell number) and protein in neonatal brain: Alteration by maternal dietary protein restriction. *Science* 160:322–23.

Zamenhof, S.; Mosley, J.; and Schuller, E. 1966. Stimulation of the proliferation of cortical neurons by prenatal treatment with growth hormone. *Science* 152:1396.

Zeuner, F. E. 1963. *The history of domesticated animals.* London: Hutchinson.

Zeval'd, R. G. 1966. On the development of conditioned inhibition in ontogenesis in dogs. *Zh. Vyssh. Nerv. Deiat. Pavlov* 16:822–29.

Author Index

341

Subject Index

347